SOURCES OF EUROPEAN ECONOMIC INFORMATION

SECOND EDITION

SOURCES OF EUROPEAN ECONOMIC INFORMATION

SECOND EDITION

COMPILED BY

Cambridge Information and Research Services Ltd

Gower Press

Published by
GOWER PRESS, Teakfield Limited,
Farnborough, Hampshire, England

CAMBRIDGE INFORMATION AND RESEARCH SERVICES LTD

Sources of European Economic Information has been compiled by CIRS Ltd, an independent business information unit undertaking research on European and other overseas countries on a regular basis. The company provides work to client specification, acts as an editorial house and publishes its own research in the specialist field of the international energy markets.

Cambridge Information and Research Services Ltd,
8, Market Passage, Cambridge CB2 3PF. Tel. 0223 60087

Director: Andrew Buckley BA

The editorial house and publishers have used their best efforts in collecting and preparing material for inclusion in *Sources of European Economic Information.* They do not assume, and hereby disclaim, any liability to any party for any loss or damage caused by errors or omissions in *Sources of European Economic Information,* whether such errors or omissions result from negligence, accident or any other cause.

ISBN 0 566 02007 6

Printed in Great Britain by Biddles Ltd., Guildford, Surrey.

CONTENTS

FOREWORD

Economic information has to be up to date if it is to be of value for other than academic purposes. The market researcher and the business economist will be concerned very much more with what is happening *now* (or indeed likely future trends) in a particular geographical area or sector of industry than with the events of the more distant past. This new edition of *Sources of European Economic Information* will therefore be welcomed by both those whose business it is to observe these trends and the librarians and information officers who are called upon to supply the raw material.

In the first edition the publishers showed that they were aware of the size of the task they had set themselves and expressed their 'firm intention to eradicate any shortcomings in subsequent editions'. Examination of the present volume will demonstrate that much has been done in this direction. A larger number of countries is covered, and the arrangement within each is more helpful to the purposive searcher. At least for English-speaking users the mono-lingual approach will be an advantage, resulting as it does in a more compact presentation. The indexing of a guide of this kind is particularly important and special care has been applied to this.

So the process of discovering *what* is available has been much simplified. Of greater complexity is the locating of copies of many of the items listed, since few organisations have the resources to purchase every publication for which they may have only a short-term use. Some of the finest collections of economic and statistical materials have either to restrict entry to certain categories of users (as at the British Library of Political and Economic Science) or charge a subscription. The Statistical Information Service at Warwick University Library is possibly the most comprehensive example of a fee-charging service of this kind, and Midlands businessmen may find it worth investigation. Some national newspapers and market research agencies have also opened up their information resources on a similar basis.

However, there are those who would argue that the bulk of sources such as are listed here should be available for consultation without charge. In the United Kingdom the public library service has a proud record in this respect and users in the vicinity of large centres of population may find their needs well served, at least as far as British materials are concerned. The quality of business information provision is uneven, though, and very few public libraries will carry large stocks of overseas economic publications referred to. There is no national business library, but the Department of Trade's Statistics and Market Intelligence Library in Ludgate Hill, London, is undoubtedly the best source for statistical and market research materials from abroad.

Elsewhere in Europe the situation will vary considerably from country to country. In some the local chambers of commerce have significant libraries; elsewhere there may be major national resources, such as the Dutch Ministry of Economic Affairs library at The Hague. The apparent inadequacy of business information facilities in one great European financial centre was brought home recently to my own library when we were telexed from that country for data from *Who Owns Whom - Continental edition*. Perhaps it is unfortunate that business houses, who contribute on a large scale to national and local government funds, do not generally make known their needs and expectations in this respect.

The relevance of the foregoing in a welcome to the present volume may not be immediately apparent, but it is likely to become so as users of *Sources of European Economic Information* set out to obtain many of the publications listed here. The compilers are to be congratulated on assisting so ably in the winning of at least half the battle - knowing *what* to look for even if they cannot be expected to locate a copy of every item close at hand to every reader.

Malcolm Campbell, *Head Librarian, the City Business Library, London.*

INTRODUCTION AND HOW TO USE THE DIRECTORY

This second edition of 'Sources' provides an expanded coverage of basic references to European economic information. The number of entries has been more than doubled compared with the previous edition and now approaches two thousand. The number of countries has also been slightly increased with the addition of Iceland. But perhaps the most important expansion is in terms of the types of source materials included. In addition to the statistical bulletins, yearbooks, and more general publications and directories, we have this time included details of special supplements and reports which often provide a range of useful background information.

The objectives of the volume however remain the same: to signal the availability of statistical and economic data and to furnish the reader with the necessary direction to obtain the material. It provides not the information itself but a full synopsis of it, together with details of the issuing body.

In Part One, the directory of source publications, each entry contains wherever possible the following information:
- the full title of the source publication/material in the language of origin
- the name of the issuing body
- the language of publication
- the date of publication and approximate page extent
- the countries mainly covered by the source (indicated by motor code abbreviation). The international section at the beginning of Part One covers those sources relating to more than two countries.
- a summary in English of the contents of the material included in the source.

For source publications covering the United Kingdom and those classified as International the purchase price is also given in most cases. These we understand to be correct at the time of manuscript completion but intending purchasers would be wise to check in advance with the issuing organisation concerned. We hope to expand the pricing coverage in future editions and would welcome details from the publishing bodies for inclusion next time.

Part Two presents the full name, address and telephone/telex number of the issuing organisations, set out alphabetically by country. A unique source code number is allocated to each organisation. Those that issue international information appear in a special section at the beginning of Part Two.

The directory concludes with two indexes. The first lists all the sources alphabetically irrespective of country of coverage. The second provides a subject breakdown. This breakdown represents a considerable improvement on the first edition. There are now eight classifications and Category V (Industrial and Services Sectors) is further analysed into seventeen sub-categories. Within these classifications the source titles appear alphabetically by country.

The inclusion of this subject index allows the following procedure to be adopted for searching the information base. Firstly the reader should select the subject classification he is interested in and by using Index 2 identify any sources covering the country/ies under study. This will indicate the title and unique source code which can then be located in Part One. The entry here will provide an appreciation of the type of material the source contains and the name of the issuing organisation. Should he wish to obtain a copy of the source he can obtain the address of the organisation from Part Two.

(continued overleaf)

Throughout the publication we have ordered the countries by their internationally recognised motor codes. These are:

A	Austria	IRL	Republic of Ireland
B	Belgium	IS	Iceland
CH	Switzerland	L	Luxembourg
D	Germany	N	Norway
DK	Denmark	NL	Netherlands
E	Spain	P	Portugal
F	France	S	Sweden
GB	Great Britain	SF	Finland
I	Italy		

We would like to acknowledge here the kind assistance rendered by many parties including the libraries and research departments of overseas embassies and banks, regrettably too numerous to identify individually. We also wish to record our grateful thanks to the export intelligence section of the Department of Industry and the staff of the City of London Business Library. Staff from the Library provided invaluable guidance not only to the sources themselves but also to the type and coverage of the information and how users typically wish to access it.

PART ONE

SOURCE PUBLICATIONS

INT-INTERNATIONAL

001 ACCOUNTING IN EUROPE
Woodhead Faulkner (Publishers) Ltd., Cambridge

INT—English 1975 425pp £6.95

Country by country survey to accounting systems, laws,
financial reporting, auditing standards etc in the EEC.
Also includes chapters on the harmonisation of company
law and the role of international accounting firms.

002 ACCOUNTING SYSTEMS AND PRACTICE IN EUROPE
Gower Press, Farnborough

INT—English 1975 225pp £7.50

An eleven-country guide to accounting practice in the EEC
plus Sweden and Switzerland. Each country is analysed to
show: type of business unit; business records; the accounting
profession; statutory requirements; auditing and accounting
standards; extra-statutory requirement trends.

**003 ACQUISITION OF ASSETS, COMPANIES AND REAL
ESTATE IN BELGIUM, FRANCE, GERMANY, THE
NETHERLANDS AND THE UK**
The Financial Times Ltd., London

INT—English 1973 157pp £25.25

An analysis of company law, tax rules and fiscal restrictions
in Belgium, France, Germany, the Netherlands and the UK.

**004 ACQUISITIONS AND MERGERS—GOVERNMENT
POLICY IN EUROPE**
The Financial Times Ltd., London

INT—English 1976 104pp £50.48

An Economists Advisory Group study examining the ways
in which merger policies have affected business in the past and
are likely to in the future.

005 AGRA EUROPE
Agra Europe (London) Ltd., London

INT—English weekly c40pp £2.50 per issue—subscription
rate on request

Review of production, consumption and prices of agricultural
products and chemicals in Europe.

**006 AGRICULTURAL COMMODITIES—PROJECTIONS FOR
1975 AND 1985**
Food and Agricultural Organization of the United Nations,
Roma

INT—English 1967 3 vols

Projections for 1975 and 1985 for agricultural products in
three volumes:
Vol. 1: Summary and conclusion.
Vol. 2: General outlook for demand, production and trade.
Vol. 3: Gives projections by commodity groups.

007 AGRICULTURAL COMMODITY PROJECTIONS 1970-80
Food and Agricultural Organization of the United Nations,
Roma

INT—English 1971 2 vols

Agricultural commodity projections for 1970-80 in two
volumes:
Vol. 1: General outlook and projection by commodities.
Vol. 2: General methodology and detailed statistical index.

008 AGRICULTURAL STATISTICS 1955-68
Organisation for Economic Co-operation and Development,
Paris

INT—English/Français 1969 216pp £1.60

Data on: crop and livestock productions; foreign trade; food
consumption; prices; land utilisation; employment.

**009 AGRICULTURAL TRADE IN EUROPE: RECENT
DEVELOPMENTS—THE EUROPEAN MARKET FOR
FRUIT AND VEGETABLES**
Economic Commission for Europe, Genève

INT—English 1972

Study of recent developments in agricultural trade as a
whole, and a detailed examination of the European fruit
and vegetable market.

**010 AGRICULTURAL TRADE IN EUROPE: RECENT
DEVELOPMENTS—THE EUROPEAN MARKET FOR
VITICULTURAL PRODUCTS, WINE AND TABLE GRAPES**
Economic Commission for Europe, Genève

INT—English 1969

Study in two parts. 1: Recent developments in agricultural
trade as a whole. 2: Review of the European market for viticultural products.

011 AIRPORT TRAFFIC
International Civil Aviation Organization, Montreal

INT—English/Español/Français annual c380pp £4.00

Digest of air transport statistics classified by passenger type, freight and mail and presented by month for each airport.

012 ANNUAIRE DE STATISTIQUE INTERNATIONALE DES GRANDES VILLES
Institut International de Statistique, Den Haag

INT—English/Français annual

International statistical yearbook of large towns.

013 ANNUAL BULLETIN OF GENERAL ENERGY STATISTICS FOR EUROPE
United Nations, Genève

INT—English/Français annual c160pp $7.00

Detailed energy statistics including production, consumption and trade information for different types of fuel, presented by country.

014 ANNUAL BULLETIN OF HOUSING AND BUILDING STATISTICS FOR EUROPE
United Nations, Genève

INT—English/Français annual 86pp $5.00

Construction statistics including information on dwelling construction; labour; price indices; building materials.

015 ANNUAL BULLETIN OF STATISTICS
International Tea Committee, London

INT—English annual c60pp £5.00

Annual statistics on tea production, imports and exports, consumption, stocks and prices.

016 ANNUAL COFFEE STATISTICS
Pan American Coffee Bureau, New York

INT—English annual $5.00

Annual information on trade, production and consumption of coffee plus world-wide coffee prices.

017 ANNUAL REPORT OF THE EUROPEAN FREE TRADE ASSOCIATION
European Free Trade Association, Genève

INT—English annual c40pp free

Annual report presenting a survey for the year and details of international developments in EFTA and its external relations.

018 ANNUAL REVIEW OF OILSEEDS, OILS, OILCAKES AND OTHER COMMODITIES
Frank Fehr and Co. Ltd., London

INT—English annual c80pp

Annual review of oilseed, food oil, oilcakes and other commodities giving production, imports and exports and price data.

019 ANNUAL SUMMARY OF MERCHANT SHIPS LAUNCHED/ COMPLETED IN THE WORLD
Lloyd's Register of Shipping, London

INT—English annual free

Annual summary of recently launched merchant ships.

020 ASPECTS OF COMPETITION BETWEEN STEEL AND OTHER MATERIALS
Economic Commission for Europe, Genève

INT—English 1966 121pp £0.88

Study of the competition between steel and other materials, including plastics, timber, paper and paper products.

021 DER AUTOMOBILMARKT (THE MARKET FOR MOTOR-CARS)
Axel Springer Verlag AG, Hamburg

INT/D—Deutsch 1973 3 vols

Band 1: Automobile-Gesamtmarkt. (Motor cars-overall market): Personen-und Kombinationskraftwagen (Passenger and dual-purpose vehicles)
Band 2: Die Autofahrer (Motorist)
Band 3: Firmen-Information (Company information)
Gives a brief survey of the European motor vehicle industry, and a detailed analysis of the West German industry. Also surveys car ownership patterns, and costs of running a car in West Germany.

022 BALANCE OF PAYMENTS YEARBOOK
International Monetary Fund, Washington

INT—English annual c190pp $7.50

Analysis and commentary of balance of payments data.

023 BANKERS ALMANAC AND YEAR BOOK 1976-77
Thomas Skinner Directories, Haywards Heath

INT—English 1977 £22.50

Standard authoritative directory of the world's banks.

024 BANKING SYSTEMS AND MONETARY POLICY IN THE EEC
The Financial Times Ltd., London

INT—English 1974 178pp £30.25

An Economists Advisory Group study giving individual and comparative analyses of banking systems and monetary policies in the EEC: considering their roles in the various economies and relevance to Community policy.

025 DER BIER-MARKT (THE MARKET FOR BEER): MARKTE INFORMATIONEN FÜR DIE WERBEPLANUNG
Axel Springer Verlag, Hamburg

INT/D—Deutsch 1973

A survey on the West German brewing industry. Gives statistics of production, import and export prices, consumption and company information. There is a brief section on the European brewing industry.

O26 **BOAT INDUSTRY WESTERN EUROPE**
IPC Business Press Ltd., London

INT—English 1975 64pp £7.50

Survey of the boat industry in Western Europe providing a
comparative analysis of the industry and its markets in
various European countries.

O27 **BP STATISTICAL REVIEW OF THE WORLD OIL**
INDUSTRY
The British Petroleum Co. Ltd., London

INT—English annual c30pp free

Annual statistical review of the world oil industry, energy
consumption and supply.

O28 **THE BREWING INDUSTRY IN EUROPE**
D.A.F.S.A., Paris

INT—English 1972 c78pp

A general survey of the European brewing industry. Includes
information on production, prices and costs, consumption,
foreign trade, companies and structure of the industry.
Statistics cover various periods up to 1970.

O29 **BRITAIN IN THE COMMON MARKET**
Guildstream Research Services, Financial Times, London

GB/INT—English 1973 4 vols

Vol. 1: The Economic Consequences of Britain's First Year in
the Common Market. 61pp
Vol. 2: The Major European Economies. 20pp
Vol. 3: The Major European Industries. Contains information
on structure and background of European industries, with an
assessment of short and long-term prospects. 582pp
Vol. 4: The Major European Companies. 172pp

O3O **BUILDING PRODUCTS AND THE EUROPEAN**
COMMUNITY
National Building Agency, London

INT—English 1972 74pp £5.00

Provides a market analysis for building products in the nine
EEC countries plus Norway. Summarises the economic performance and size of the construction market in each
country plus a detailed analysis of demand for certain
specified building products.

O31 **BULLETIN OF THE EUROPEAN COMMUNITIES**
European Communities, Luxembourg

INT—English eleven issues per year, plus index £6.25

Covers events, activities, documentations of the Communities
with studies and supplements on particular topics.

O32 **BULLETIN OF STATISTICS ON WORLD TRADE IN**
ENGINEERING PRODUCTS
Economic Commission for Europe, Genève

INT—English/Français annual

Annual bulletin with details of exports of engineering
products by country of destination and by trading area presented for each exporting country.

O33 **BUSINESS ATLAS OF WESTERN EUROPE**
Gower Press, Farnborough

INT—English 1975 144pp £8.50

Business atlas presenting data on the main markets, consumer
trends and national economies of Western Europe.

O34 **CHEMICAL INDUSTRY DIRECTORY**
Benn Brothers Ltd., Tonbridge

INT—English 1976 £15.00

Comprehensive listing of international chemical and allied
industries, giving details of names, addresses, telephone and
telex numbers. Also includes a UK industry section, who's
who, buyers' guides to chemicals, chemical plant and equipment, laboratory apparatus and scientific instruments.

O35 **THE CHEMICAL INDUSTRY OF WESTERN EUROPE**
IPC Business Press Ltd., London

INT—English annual £35.00

Contains national surveys of the chemical industry in sixteen
Western European countries giving statistics of trade and production. Lists producers of organic and inorganic chemicals,
fertilizers, rubbers, resins, fibres, etc; European trade associations, technical and learned societies and chemical companies
by country.

O36 **COFFEE**
Barclays Bank, London

INT—English irregular

Review of coffee cultivation, production, processing,
marketing and prices.

O37 **THE COM MARKET IN THE UK AND THE CONTINENT**
OF EUROPE
G. G. Baker and Associates, Guildford

INT—English 1975 47pp

The second annual survey of its kind. Based on question-
naires sent out in May 1975, and an interview programme
conducted in June. Surveys the Computer Microfilm market
in the UK and Europe giving the number of installations,
the number of commercial bureaux providing COM services,
sales of recorders, replacement market and consumption of film.

O38 **COMMERCIAL MOTOR TABLES OF OPERATING**
COSTS
IPC Business Press Ltd., London

INT—English annual £0.65

Annual publication on costings for hire and reward operators
or own account operators for goods and passenger vehicles
and as a basis for individual costing systems.

O39 **COMPANY LAW IN WESTERN EUROPE**
Gower Press, Farnborough

INT—English 1975 300pp £15.00

Loose leaf survey covering existing company law in Western
Europe, with regular updates on new developments. Includes
a quick reference check list of the principal legal requirements
and a separate section for each country covering data on:
company formation; limited liability; share transfer; employee
legislation.

040   COMPANY POLICY FOR THE EEC
The Financial Times Ltd., London

INT—English 1976 113pp £20.50

Study aimed at companies entering or developing trading
with Europe. Contents: trends in direct investment; methods
of entry; host-country attitudes; labour; accounting practices;
taxation; EEC; control of foreign investment.

041   COMPENDIO STATISTICO
Associazione Nazionale dell'Industria Chimica, Milano

INT—Italiano annual

Annual survey of the international chemicals market, with
information on industrial trends, production, trade and consumption.

042   COMPENDIUM OF HOUSING STATISTICS 1971
United Nations, Genève

INT—English 1974 256pp £6.38

International coverage of housing statistics at the national and
urban/rural levels. Gives an overview of world housing conditions, including size of dwellings, density of population, etc.

043   THE COMPETITION LAW OF THE EEC
Kogan Page Ltd., London

INT—English 1974 316pp £8.00

Practical guide for the businessman trading within the EEC.
Outlines the objectives of the EEC Rules of Competition laid
down in Articles 85 and 86 of the Treaty of Rome, including
15 appendices of translations of the relevant articles and a
table of cases.

044   THE COMPETITION LAW OF THE EEC: SUPPLEMENT
Kogan Page Ltd., London

INT—English 1975 416pp £8.50

Supplement to "The Competition Law of the EEC" (No.
043) which brings the book up to date to July 1975 and includes detailed appendices, a table of important cases and a
full index.

045   CONSUMER EUROPE
Euromonitor Publications Ltd., London

INT—English annual c280pp

First edition 1976, of an annual survey based on research
conducted into the European market for 150 major consumer
products, complemented by general data on the structure of
households in 12 countries.

046   CONSUMER PRICE INDICES
Org. for Economic Co-operation and Development, Paris

INT—English/Français monthly

Monthly bulletin covering consumer price indices.

047   CONTAINERS, PALLETS OR LASH?
THE ECONOMICS OF GENERAL CARGO SHIPPING
Economist Intelligence Unit, London

INT—English 1973 £10.00

E.I.U. special report no. 13; analyses the economics of general

cargo shipping, including: container services versus conventional services; comparative costs of competing vessel types; cost
minimisation; berth throughputs and handling costs.

048   COTTON—WORLD STATISTICS
International Cotton Advisory Committee, Washington

INT—English quarterly

Quarterly information and statistics on the production, consumption, supply, distribution, trade and prices of cotton.

049   CURRENT EUROPEAN DIRECTORIES
CBD Research Ltd., Beckenham

INT—English 1977 430pp

Source book to directories and reference books published in
all countries of Europe, excluding Great Britain and Ireland.
Includes official yearbooks and almanacs, industrial
directories etc.

**050   DEMAND FOR, AND APPLICATIONS OF, EXTRA LARGE
ELECTRONIC DATA PROCESSING SYSTEMS IN THE
EUROPEAN COMMUNITY AND THE UNITED KINGDOM
IN THE SEVENTIES**
European Communities, Luxembourg

INT—English/Français/Deutsch/Italiano 1971 62pp £0.82

Summary of a detailed survey covering current and future
demand to 1980 for extra large data processing systems.

**051   DEMAND INTERRELATIONSHIPS BETWEEN MAJOR
FRUITS**
Food and Agriculture Organization of the United Nations,
Roma

INT—English 1969

Study examining the interrelationships between the demand
for dessert apples, oranges and bananas in the major consum-
ing countries of the world.

052   DEMOGRAPHIC YEARBOOK
United Nations, Genève

INT—English annual c700pp £14.00

Statistics for 250 countries covering: area, population, births,
deaths, expectation of life, marriage and divorce. Also gives
census data on: age, sex, occupation, status, and employment.

053   DIRECTION OF TRADE
International Monetary Fund, Washington

INT—English annual £4.17

Eleven issues a year plus an annual summary, giving values
of exports and imports and tables by countries and world
areas and regions.

054   DIRECTOR'S GUIDE TO EUROPE
Gower Press, Farnborough

INT—English 1975 782pp £7.50

Country by country business guide to Europe providing
information on the economy, trade, local practices and
customs, city guides, travel, eating and leisure advice and
details of local business organisations.

O55   **DIRECTORY OF FINANCIAL DIRECTORIES: A WORLD GUIDE**
Francis Hodgson, Guernsey

INT—English 1976 333pp £23.00

First edition of a new reference guide to over 1500 sources of financial information. Three types of material are included a) sources of financial activities - banking, insurance, accounting; b) sources which include financial details on companies and organisations; c) reference works indicating possible sources of financial information - libraries, research centres.

O56   **DIRECTORY OF INTERNATIONAL STATISTICS**
United Nations, Genève

INT—English 1975 296pp £6.50

Guide book of international statistics, including international statistical services, international statistical series, international statistical standards, computerized international statistics.

O57   **DIRECTORY OF TRADE UNIONS IN THE EUROPEAN ECONOMIC COMMUNITY**
Graham & Trotman Ltd., London

INT—English 1974 £2.45

Basic reference book to the leading trade union organisations and leaders in the Common Market.

O58   **ECONOMIC BULLETIN FOR EUROPE**
Economic Commission for Europe, Genève

INT—English twice a year c80pp £2.60

Bulletin covering recent changes in European trade.

O59   **ECONOMIC OUTLOOK**
Org. for Economic Co-operation and Development, Paris

INT—English twice a year 120pp £3.40 p.a.

General survey of the economic situation, with information on the trends of current balances.

O6O   **AN ECONOMIC REVIEW FOR THE FURNITURE INDUSTRY**
Furniture Industry Research Association, London

INT—English annual 87pp £6.00

Review of the domestic furniture industry, future prospects and articles on specific subjects of current interest.

O61   **ECONOMIC SITUATION IN THE EUROPEAN COMMUNITY**
European Communities, Luxembourg

INT—English quarterly £7.70 p.a.

Reviews the economic outlook and trends for the Community, giving data on: industrial production, consumer prices, unemployment, trade balances.

O62   **ECONOMIC SURVEY OF EUROPE**
Economic Commission for Europe, Genève

INT—English annual c180pp £3.50

Annual statistical data covering economic development and labour conditions in Europe.

O63   **ECONOMIC SURVEYS OF MEMBER COUNTRIES**
Org. for Economic Co-operation and Development, Paris

INT—English 19-21 issues per year £9.00 p.a.

Individual surveys for each member country, published as data becomes available, on: finance, money, the economic situation and policy. Also gives an analysis showing the developments in demand, production, wages and prices, balance of payments.
(See individual countries for specific entries)

O64   **EEC: YOUR QUESTIONS ANSWERED**
Department of Trade & Industry, London.

INT—English 1976 128pp free

Sets out to answer a wide variety of questions on trading in Europe. Includes, charts, tables, maps, reading list, useful addresses.

O65   **EFTA TRADE**
European Free Trade Association, Genève

INT—English annual c170pp

Annual summary of the pattern and trends of foreign trade in EFTA countries.

O66   **EIU WORLD COMMODITY OUTLOOK 1975-76: INDUSTRIAL RAW MATERIALS**
Economist Intelligence Unit, London

INT—English 1975 £15.00

Examines the prospects to mid-1976 for 25 industrial raw materials. Individual reports with statistical data assess likely trends in supply, demand and prices.

O67   **EIU WORLD COMMODITY OUTLOOK 1976: FOOD, FEEDSTUFFS AND BEVERAGES**
Economist Intelligence Unit, London

INT—English 1976 £15.00

Examines the prospects to mid-1976 for 23 commodities. Also includes individual reports, with statistics, which assess likely trends in supply, demand and prices.

O68   **EIU WORLD OUTLOOK**
Economist Intelligence Unit, London

INT—English annual £10.00

Provides separate detailed forecasts of expected trends in the economies of over 140 countries.

O69   **ELECTRICAL POWER IN EUROPE: THE PLANT SUPPLIERS AND THEIR CUSTOMERS**
National Economic Development Office, London

INT—English 1972 £3.15

Report on the heavy electrical plant industry in EEC and EFTA; surveys the present and future market structure and potential development.

O7O   **EMPLOYEE BENEFITS IN EUROPE**
Callund Company, London

INT—English 1976 261pp £25.00

Collection of surveys on the availability and requirement of

Social Security and private plans in each country, dealing
with: pensions, disability benefits, survivors benefits, accident
benefits, health insurance, unemployment benefits, taxation.

O71   EMPLOYMENT CONDITIONS IN EUROPE
Gower Press, Farnborough

INT—English 1976 250pp £10.50

Review of working procedures and standards within the EEC.
Emphasis is placed on inter-regional variations and key statistics are given on: wage rates, manpower resources, labour
procedures, unemployment rates, taxation, cost of living.

O72   THE EUROBOND MARKET
The Financial Times Ltd., London

INT—English 1975 188pp £50.50

A comprehensive and detailed analysis of the Eurobond
market and the techniques of its operation.

O73   EURO-COOPERAZIONE: STUDI ECONOMICI EUROPEI
Banco di Roma, Roma

I/INT—Italiano quarterly

Quarterly survey with statistics, on the European economy.

O74   EUROPA YEARBOOK: VOLUME 1—EUROPE
Europa, London

INT—English annual 1457pp £27.00

This yearbook gives basic reference information for each
country of Europe, listing government officials, political,
religious and media details, trade organisations, transport,
banking, insurance and other relevant bodies. (Volume II
covers Africa, Americas, Asia and Australasia.)

O75   EUROPE AND ENERGY
European Communities, Luxembourg

INT—English 1967

Survey of the energy supply and demand in the EEC and
consideration of the future energy situation.

O76   EUROPE: FINANCIAL TIMES SURVEY
The Financial Times, London

INT—English 6 Dec. 1976 20pp

Survey in the Financial Times newspaper, covering: West
European foreign policy; defence; direct elections; East-West
relations; migrant workers; agricultural and fisheries policies;
also includes a brief review of 18 European countries.

O77   EUROPE TODAY: A SURVEY OF EUROPEAN OPINION
LEADERS
The Times, London

INT—English 1971 14pp

Survey carried out among a sample of European politicians in
the EEC and EFTA countries and Spain, on various environmental problems facing Europe and the legislation needed to
combat them. It covered 33 daily and weekly publications
in Western Europe and the USA.

O78   EUROPEAN 5000 1977'
Dun & Bradstreet, London/AS Økonomisk Literatur, Oslo

INT—English 1977 436pp £25.00

Lists the top 5000 companies operating in 15 West European
countries giving key financial information on each organisation. Supplementary league tables show the leading companies
by industry sector.

O79   EUROPEAN ADVERTISING AND MARKETING
HANDBOOK
European Data and Research Ltd., London

INT—English 1975 235pp

Essential basic advertising and marketing data on 13
European countries.

O80   THE EUROPEAN AUTOMOTIVE INDUSTRY - WHERE
NOW?
Economist Intelligence Unit, London

INT—English 1976 £40.00

E.I.U. special report no. 34; Prospects for 1976, 1977 and
1980 including long-term effects of non-European manufacturers' activities.

O81   EUROPEAN BANKING TO 1985
Graham & Trotman Ltd., London

INT—English 1977 £45.00

Analysis and forecast of likely developments in banking
practices.

O82   EUROPEAN CHEMICAL BUYERS' GUIDE
IPC Business Press Ltd., London

INT—English/Français/Deutsch/Italiano/Español annual
c1000pp £20.00

Annual guide to suppliers of commercially available chemicals
in Europe.

O83   EUROPEAN CHEMICAL INDUSTRIES 1974-75
Gower Press, Farnborough

INT—English 1974 488pp £25.00

A survey of the chemical and plastics industries, covering ten
Western European countries. Analysis and comments on the
performance of these industries in the past and describes
trends in output, costs and related factors, including output
forecasts. Also containing a list of the top hundred organisations plus more detailed profiles of twenty selected organisations.

O84   EUROPEAN COMMUNITY DIRECTORY AND DIARY
Institute of Public Administration, Dublin

INT—English annual c235pp £12.00

Basic reference data on members of EEC and their institutions, government departments, European Parliament, its
committees, special interest groups, accredited press and
diplomatic representatives etc.

O85   EUROPEAN COMMUNITY - NEWSLETTER
European Communities Information Service, London

INT—English monthly free

Monthly magazine giving a concise view of current EEC affairs.

O86 EUROPEAN COMPANIES: A GUIDE TO SOURCES OF INFORMATION
CBD Research Ltd., Beckenham

English 1972 c240pp £10.00

Basic guide to the sources of information available on companies in 34 countries of Europe. Covers official records, publications and commercial services.

O87 EUROPEAN CONVENTION GUIDE 1976-77
AS Økonomisk Literatur, Oslo

INT—English 1976 411pp £8.50

Directory of hotels and centres offering conference and convention facilities in 16 Western European countries.

O88 EUROPEAN DIRECT MAIL DATABOOK
Gower Press, Farnborough

INT—English 1976 280pp £12.50

Concise data on the European mailing houses indicating what facilities each organisation offers and the size/cost characteristics of each specialised mailing list.

O89 EUROPEAN DIRECTORY OF ECONOMIC AND CORPORATE PLANNING 1975-76
Gower Press, Farnborough

INT—English 1975 442pp £12.50

Provides information on the organisations, units and individuals engaged in economic and corporate planning in Western Europe in private companies, national, regional and local authorities, research agencies, consultancies, banks and financial institutions.

O90 EUROPEAN DIRECTORY OF MARKET RESEARCH SURVEYS
Gower Press, Farnborough

INT—English 1975 400pp £25.00

Directory of 2000 limited circulation and multi-client market surveys available in Western Europe. Data is given for each entry on: name and address of issuing organisation, availability, price, frequency of publication, countries covered, data presented, methods, sources and sample sizes.

O91 EUROPEAN ENERGY MARKET TO 1980
Graham & Trotman Ltd., London

INT—English Vol. 1: 1975 £45.00
             Vol. 2: 1977 £30.00

Vol. 1 gives market forecasts to 1980 for Belgium, Denmark, France, West Germany, Ireland, Italy, the Netherlands, UK, Norway and Sweden.
Vol. 2 covers Switzerland, Portugal, Spain, Yugoslavia, Finland and Greece.

O92 EUROPEAN FINANCIAL ALMANAC 1974-75
Gower Press, Farnborough

INT—English 1974 755pp £21.00

Contents: 13 individual country surveys; directory of key organisations giving facts and figures of over 1200 financial institutions operating in Europe; Who's Who in European

finance, - c2500 biographical profiles of European financial personalities.

O93 EUROPEAN FOOD PROCESSING INDUSTRY
Noyes Data Corporation, Park Ridge (N.J.)

INT—English 1973 163pp S36.00

A market report on the food processing industry of Western Europe. Contains individual national surveys of 17 countries. Includes lists of major food processing companies.

O94 EUROPEAN INTELLIGENCE
European Intelligence Ltd., Tunbridge Wells

INT—English fortnightly £96.00 p.a.

Details on mergers, affiliations and other company activities in the Community. Also includes articles and news on general Community developments.

O95 EUROPEAN LEATHER GUIDE AND TANNERS OF THE WORLD
Benn Brothers Ltd., Tonbridge

INT—English 1976 £10.00

Details of over 4500 companies listed in sections—tanners and merchants; hide and skin suppliers; chemicals suppliers; machinery manufacturers. Also includes a five-language glossary and data section for tanners.

O96 EUROPEAN MARKETING DATA AND STATISTICS
Euromonitor Publications Ltd., London

INT—English annual c300pp £24.00

Marketing data and statistics giving information on: consumers, housing, employment, wages and related topics.

O97 EUROPEAN MARKETS FOR MINIATURE CHART RECORDERS
Sira Institute Ltd., Chislehurst

INT—English 1974 82pp £50.00

A survey of the development of the markets in Europe for miniature chart recorders and their future applications in the light of competitive technologies. The study covers the current market and forecasts demand up to 1978. Material for the study was gathered between October 1973 and March 1974. Includes a list of product specifications of major European suppliers.

O98 EUROPEAN OFFSHORE OIL AND GAS YEARBOOK 1976 77
Kogan Page Ltd., London

INT—English 1976 376pp £20.00

Covers offshore oil and gas exploration and production in the coastal waters around Europe, the North Sea, the Atlantic and the Mediterranean, with an individual review of progress in 15 countries.

O99 EUROPEAN PLASTICS BUYERS' GUIDE
IPC Business Press Ltd., London

INT—English/Français/Deutsch/Italiano/Español annual c850pp £15.00

Annual buyers' guide to materials, machinery, products and services available in 25 European countries. Contains over 3000 product headings and lists c13,000 companies.

100   EUROPEAN RETAIL TRADES 1975-76
Gower Press, Farnborough

INT—English 1975 378pp £25.00

Reviews market and company performances and prospects in
nine European countries. Charts historic trends in sales and
expenditure and provides a current appraisal of likely short
to medium term developments.

101   EUROPEAN SERIES
Political and Economic Planning/Royal Institute of
International Affairs, London

INT—English £0.80 — £1.75

Series of papers published between 1967-76 reviewing
problems and aspects of Britain's relationship with the EEC.

102   EUROPEAN TRENDS
Economist Intelligence Unit, London

INT—English quarterly c40pp £50.00 p.a.

Covers new EEC legislation and reviews developments in
European economic policies. Specially prepared statistical
tables show comparative trends in the main European economic
indicators.

103   EUROPEAN WOODWORKING MACHINERY DIRECTORY
Benn Brothers Ltd., Tonbridge

INT—English/Français/Deutsch/Italiano 1976 £8.00

Lists woodworking machinery available in Europe; includes
data from 750 manufacturers in four sections: manufacturing
companies index; companies by country; classified products;
agents.

104   EXCHANGE AND TRADE CONTROLS
Gower Press, Farnborough

INT—English 1975 352pp £13.50

Describes exchange controls and their relationships with
trade and other controls.

105   EXPORT DATA
Benn Brothers Ltd., Tonbridge

GB/INT—English annual c400pp £15.00

Monthly updating service giving details of changes in export
procedure throughout the world. Also includes data on the
EEC; Commonwealth preference regulations; ATA Carnet
scheme; VAT and exporters; containers and unit loads services
operating out of UK ports.

106   EXPORT MARKETING RESEARCH SURVEY: PHASE 1
Urwick Orr & Partners Ltd., London

GB/INT—English 1974 2 vols

Report prepared for the National Federation of Fruit and
Potato Trade and available from them. Comprises a survey
of export prospects in Europe for UK horticultural products
including potatoes. Includes information on consumption
levels for selected products, local production rates and
volumes, imports and exports by country, pricing patterns
and trends, and the trading infra-structure.

107   EXTEL EUROPEAN COMPANY SERVICE
Extel Statistical Services, London

INT—English prices on application

Basic financial information service covering 600 key
European companies quoted in Continental Exchanges.
Address and reference information, profit and loss, balance
sheet details etc. Historical series from five to twelve
years. Service, including weekly updates, available on
subscription.

**108   EXTERNAL RELATIONS OF THE EUROPEAN
COMMUNITY**
Political and Economic Planning/Royal Institute of Inter-
national Affairs, London

INT—English 1971 145pp £1.50

Report in the "European Series" examining the external
relations of the EEC.

109   FACTS ON EUROPE: EMPLOYMENT CONDITIONS
British Institute of Management/Metropolitan Pensions
Association Ltd., London

INT—English 1973 64pp free

Euro booklet No. 1; provides an initial guide to employment
conditions in 15 European countries giving details and
comparisons of the employment, remuneration and employers
obligations in each country.

110   FACTS ON EUROPE: LABOUR RELATIONS
British Institute of Management/Metropolitan Pensions
Association Ltd., London

INT—English 1973 72pp free

Euro booklet No. 2; provides an initial guide to employment
conditions in 15 European countries giving details and comparisons on: labour-management relations, contracts of
employment, collective agreements, disputes procedures.

111   FACTS ON EUROPE: PERSONAL TAXATION
British Institute of Management/Metropolitan Pensions
Association Ltd., London

INT—English 1973 63pp free

Euro booklet No. 4; provides an initial guide to employment
conditions in 15 European countries giving details and comparisons on: principal taxes, tax liability, tax rates, tax reliefs,
double taxation agreement.

112   FACTS ON EUROPE: SOCIAL SECURITY
British Institute of Management/Metropolitan Pensions
Association Ltd., London

INT—English 1973 67pp free

Euro booklet No. 3; provides an initial guide to employment
conditions in 15 European countries giving details and comparisons on: reciprocal arrangements for health services,
sickness, unemployment and maternity benefits, retirement
and widows pensions, family allowances, social security
contributions.

113   FACTUAL GUIDE TO THE COMMON MARKET
Midland Bank Ltd., London

INT—English 1971

Contents: information on the origins, institutions, current

situation, agricultural policy, economic and monetary
policy, UK agreement and transitional agreements, selected
statistics, foreign trade of the EEC.

114   FINANCIAL STATISTICS
       Org. for Economic Co-operation and Development, Paris

       INT—English annual £15.00

       Information on financial markets in 16 European countries,
       USA, Canada and Japan. Gives details of capital operations
       and financial transactions, balance sheets.

115   THE FINANCIAL TIMES WORLD HOTEL DIRECTORY
       The Financial Times Ltd., London

       INT—English 650pp £9.50

       Reference book covering the principal business hotels giving
       details on accommodation, price, etc. plus background
       material - climate, visa requirements etc. - on the countries.

116   THE FINANCIAL TIMES INTERNATIONAL BUSINESS
       YEAR BOOK
       The Financial Times Ltd., London

       INT—English annual c180pp £11.00

       Annual publication with data on the top 700 international
       financial, retailing, mining, transport and utility companies,
       including directors, shareholdings, output and financial
       status; statistical data of the main trading countries, table
       of international comparisons (trade, production,
       income); international economic groupings—EEC, OPEC,
       COMECON; operation and scope of the main commodity
       markets; also includes a French/German/English
       business vocabulary.

117   THE FINANCIAL TIMES WHO'S WHO IN WORLD
       BANKING 1975/76
       The Financial Times Ltd., London

       INT—English 1976 500pp £12.00

       Biographical and business information on leading figures in
       the world's principal commercial, clearing and merchant
       banks; also includes chief officers of the central banks in the
       majority of trading countries; separate index of executives
       listed by organisation.

118   THE FINANCIAL TIMES WORLD INSURANCE YEAR
       BOOK
       The Financial Times Ltd., London

       INT—English 1976 350pp £15.00

       The first edition of a year book giving key facts and figures
       on world insurance including five year analysis of over 600
       companies which conduct insurance business in more than 20
       leading markets - names, addresses, company structure,
       capitalisation and assets, controlling shareholders, investment
       performance; also includes data on: national insurance
       markets; international data and comparisons; sectional index
       of companies by main classes or combination of classes
       written - life, general non-life reinsurance, motor,
       marine/MAT'

119   THE FINANCIAL TIMES WORLD SHIPPING YEAR BOOK
       The Financial Times Ltd., London

       INT—English annual c650pp £14.00

Contents: data on the world's major shipowners, shipbuilders,
repairers, engine-builders, salvage/marine equipment, towage
companies, merchant fleet tonnages, shipbuilding capacity,
trade, principal ports of leading maritime countries. Also
includes details of marine insurers, giving: addresses,
executives, size of fleet, financial status; separate supplier's
directory and buyers guide.

120   FISHERY POLICIES AND ECONOMIES 1957-66
       Org. for Economic Co-operation and Development, Paris

       INT—English/Français 1970 513pp £3.45

       Commentary and statistics on policies, production, catches,
       consumption, trade in fish and fishing fleets.

121   FOOD CONSUMPTION STATISTICS 1955-71
       Org. for Economic Co-operation and Development, Paris

       INT—English 1973 320pp £2.66

       Review of production, stocks, foreign trade and consumption
       of each food product. Also gives global balance (calories,
       protein, fat) for each OECD member country.

122   FOOTWEAR, RAW HIDES, SKINS AND LEATHER
       INDUSTRY IN OECD COUNTRIES 1973-74
       STATISTICS
       Org. for Economic Co-operation and Development, Paris

       INT—English 1975 92pp £2.00

       Annual statistics on production, consumption and trade.

123   FROM FREE TRADE TO INTEGRATION IN WESTERN
       EUROPE?
       Political and Economic Planning/Royal Institute of
       International Affairs, London

       INT—English 1975 107pp £1.75

       Paper from the PEP European series which reviews the major
       trends in Europe's post-war trade, the development of
       international trade policies and the implications of the
       extension of the EEC.

124   FRUIT
       Commonwealth Secretariat, London

       INT—English 1972 278pp £3.00

       Review of production and trade relating to fresh,
       canned, frozen and dried fruit, fruit juices and wine, with
       an emphasis on Commonwealth data.

125   FRUIT INTELLIGENCE
       Commonwealth Secretariat, London

       INT—English monthly £20.00 p.a.

       Monthly bulletin giving data on production, trade and
       consumption of fresh and preserved fruit and vegetables
       with emphasis on Commonwealth data.

126   FUTURE WORLD TRENDS
       Cabinet Office/HMSO

       INT/GB—English 1976 26pp £0.60

       Review and commentary on world trends in: population,
       food, mineral resources, energy, pollution — and their
       implications for the UK.

**127 GENERAL REPORT ON THE ACTIVITIES OF THE
EUROPEAN COMMUNITIES**
European Communities, Luxembourg

INT—English annual c350pp £2.40

Annual report on the development of the European
Community, covering: community institutions and bodies,
community policies, external relations, community law.

128 GENERAL STATISTICAL BULLETIN
European Communities, Luxembourg

INT—English monthly c180pp £15.25

Short-term economic trends in the enlarged European
community including data on employment, industry,
construction, transport and foreign trade.

**129 GENERAL SURVEY OF THE FRESH FRUIT AND
VEGETABLE MARKETS IN SEVEN EUROPEAN
COUNTRIES**
International Trade Centre, UNCTAD - GATT,
Genève

INT—English 1968 2 vols

Survey of the fresh fruit and vegetable markets in 7
countries; in 2 volumes - vol. 1: the market for selected fresh
fruit; vol. 2: the market for vegetables.

**13O GESELLSCHAFT FÜR KONSUM-MARKT- UND
ABSATZFORSCHUNG E V (EUROPE BASIC MARKET
DATA)**
Verlag Moderne Industrie, Zürich

INT—English 1975 600pp £250.00

Contains seventeen national surveys of European marketing
data. Includes regional information on population and
purchasing power, households, ownership of certain
consumer durables, number of establishments in industry
and distributive trades with analysis by size and employment.

131 GRAIN BULLETIN
Commonwealth Secretariat, London

INT—English monthly £12.00 p.a.

Monthly bulletin with data on the production, trade,
utilisation and price of grain crops with special emphasis on
data from Commonwealth countries.

132 GRAIN CROPS
Commonwealth Secretariat, London

INT—English 1973 £2.25

Review of production, trade, consumption and prices
relating to wheat, flour, maize, barley, oats, rye and rice with
emphasis on Commonwealth data.

**133 GRAPHS AND NOTES ON THE ECONOMIC SITUATION
IN THE EUROPEAN COMMUNITY**
European Communities, Luxembourg

INT—English monthly £6.00 p.a.

Monthly bulletin with coloured graphs and commentaries
illustrating the monthly position of industrial production,
unemployment, prices, trade balances.

134 GUIDE TO EUROPEAN COMMUNITY LAW
Sweet and Maxwell Limited, London

INT—English 1975 £7.80

Community law; treaties establishing the Community;
institutions of the Communities; financial provisions;
acts of the Communities.

135 GUIDE TO WORLD COMMODITY MARKETS
Kogan Page Ltd., London

INT—English 1976 300pp £10.00

Directory of commodity markets with background
information on individual commodities.

136 HOUSING AND THE EUROPEAN COMMUNITY
National Building Agency, London

INT—English 1973 European Studies Part 2 in five volumes
Vol. 1: Netherlands, Belgium, Luxembourg 139pp £25.00
Vol. 2: Denmark, Republic of Ireland, Norway, United
         Kingdom 175pp £25.00
Vol. 3: France 61pp £25.00
Vol. 4: West Germany 51pp £25.00
Vol. 5: Italy 53pp £25.00

Provides a detailed analysis of the housing market in the
nine EEC countries plus Norway, in a series of national
surveys. Examines the size of the market, importance of the
public and private sectors, the type of dwelling, housing
standards and average prices, regional distribution of housing:
and surveys the structure of the building industry with
information on labour, number and size of firms, cost,
materials used etc.

137 INDUSTRIAL EXPANSION IN EUROPE
Gower Press, Farnborough

INT—English 1973 300pp £12.50

Background data and information on opportunities for
industrial expansion including details of financing,
communications and development prospects.

138 INDUSTRIAL FIBRES
Commonwealth Secretariat, London

INT—English 1973 £3.25

Review of production, trade and consumption of wool,
cotton, man-made fibres, silk, flax, jute, hard fibres
and other hemps, mohair and coir, with emphasis on
Commonwealth data.

**139 INDUSTRIAL MARKETING AND ADVERTISING IN
EUROPE**
Institute of Practitioners in Advertising, London

INT—English 1970 32pp £0.25

Contents: basic facts, geography and demography; the media
- press, outdoor, cinema, fairs, direct mail; advertising
agencies and services; research; taxes; laws and regulations;
advertising and related organisations.

14O INDUSTRIAL PROPERTY RIGHTS IN THE EEC
Gower Press, Farnborough

INT—English 1974 200pp £5.75

Examines the effect of the EEC rules of competition on
industrial property rights such as trademarks, patents,
copyright and technical information.

141 INDUSTRIAL STATISTICS
European Communities, Luxembourg

INT—English quarterly with annual yearbook £7.25 p.a.

Gives production data for selected manufactured goods and raw materials, together with industrial production indices.

142 L'INDUSTRIE DE LA MACHINE-OUTIL DANS LES PAYS DE LA CEE
Société Belge d'Economie et de Mathématique Appliqué SA, Bruxelles

INT— Français 1968

Survey of the machine tool industries in the EEC with comparative figures for the UK and the USA.

143 INSTITUTIONS OF THE EUROPEAN COMMUNITY
Political and Economic Planning/Royal Institute of International Affairs, London

INT—English 1968

Paper number 8 in the "European Series," covering the institutions of the EEC.

144 INTERNATIONAL ADVERTISING CONDITIONS
Institute of Practitioners in Advertising, London

INT—English 20pp

Series of individual booklets covering a number of countries. See individual country entries.

145 INTERNATIONAL CURRENCY PROSPECTS
Economist Intelligence Unit, London

INT—English 1976 £40.00

E.I.U. special report no 35; Study which provides an insight into recent trends in currency parities and indicates the outlook for particular currencies.

146 INTERNATIONAL DIRECTORY OF MARKET RESEARCH ORGANISATIONS
Market Research Society, London

INT—English

Basic reference data, including facilities and services offered, on market research organisations, arranged geographically.

147 INTERNATIONAL DIRECTORY OF PUBLISHED MARKET RESEARCH
British Overseas Trade Board in association with Research and Finance Management Ltd., London

INT—English 1976 £8.50

Available from BOTB, International Research Directory, Export House, 50 Ludgate Hill, London EC4.

148 INTERNATIONAL ECONOMIC INDICATORS
U.S. Department of Commerce, Washington

INT—English quarterly c50pp

Quarterly European economic summary covering: statistics on trade, exports and imports, indexes of industrial production, indicators on trade, prices, production and labour costs.

149 INTERNATIONAL FINANCIAL STATISTICS
International Monetary Fund, Washington

INT—English monthly £8.50 p.a.

Detailed financial analysis of the accounts of 100 countries including EEC members.

150 INTERNATIONAL LAW AND THE INDEPENDENT STATE
Gower Press, Farnborough

INT—English 1975 250pp £7.50

Examines international law, the meaning of independence and self-determination, restrictions on a State's power, immunity, rules on transit, pollution and human rights.

151 INTERNATIONAL MARKETING DATA AND STATISTICS
Euromonitor Publications Ltd., London

INT—English 1976 c280pp £25.00

First edition of a new annual directory giving data on 43 countries, covering: population; employment; production; trade; economy; standard of living; consumption; housing; health; education; culture; mass media; communications; tourism.

152 INTERNATIONAL SHIPPING AND SHIPBUILDING DIRECTORY
Benn Brothers Ltd., Tonbridge

INT—English 1976 £20.00

Contents: details of shipowners, sea-borne container companies, shipbuilders, ship-repairers, marine engine builders, towage, salvage and offshore services, ships index, shipbuilding marine compendium, buyers' guide to shipyard plant and marine equipment manufacturers, ships machinery and equipment.

153 INTERNATIONAL STEEL STATISTICS
British Steel Corporation, Croydon

INT—English

Production, consumption and trade data for steel, issued in a series of separate publications for most countries at irregular intervals. (Details of price and availability on demand).

154 INTERNATIONAL TOURISM DEVELOPMENT: FORECASTS TO 1985
Economist Intelligence Unit, London

INT—English 1976 £40.00

E.I.U. special report no. 33: Provides detailed and specific forecasts of expenditure on international tourism by tourist origin countries for 1980 and 1985.

155 INTERNATIONAL TOURISM AND TOURISM POLICY IN OECD MEMBER COUNTRIES
Org. for Economic Co-operation and Development, Paris

INT—English/Français 1972 160pp £4.40

Report on international tourism covering tourist traffic, transport, accommodation and government policy.

156 INTERNATIONAL TOURISM QUARTERLY
Economist Intelligence Unit, London

INT—English quarterly £50.00 p.a.

Quarterly data and comment and analysis of the world tourism industry. Includes in-depth reports at national and regional levels, with information on trends within the industry and current developments.

157   INTERNATIONAL TRAVEL STATISTICS
International Union of Official Travel Organizations, Genève

INT—English annual

Annual statistics of the number of visitors and tourists entering the member countries of the International Union of Official Travel Organizations.

158   INVESTMENT IN THE COMMUNITY COALMINING AND IRON AND STEEL INDUSTRIES
European Communities, Luxembourg

INT—English 1975 93pp £4.40

Report containing the results of the 1975 survey of past and future investment by coal and steel enterprises in the European Coal and Steel Community (ECSC) and the impact of investment on production potential. Covers: coalmining; coking and briquetting plant; iron ore mining; iron and steel industries; also includes a detailed statistical appendix.

159   IRON AND STEEL
European Communities, Luxembourg

INT—English/Deutsch/Français/Italiano/Nederlands c450pp £12.00

Yearbook of detailed iron and steel statistics covering: production; orders and deliveries; imports and exports; consumption.

160   IRON AND STEEL: BIMONTHLY STATISTICS
European Communities, Luxembourg

INT—English/Deutsch/Français/Italiano/Nederlands quarterly c170pp £21.45 p.a.

Regular bulletin of iron and steel statistics, with coverage as entry 159.

161   JANE'S MAJOR COMPANIES OF EUROPE
Jane's Yearbooks, London

INT—English annual 1244pp £30.00

Handbook of financial and trading information on the principal European companies. Lists directors, management, constitution, subsidiaries, activities etc. as well as extracts from the profit and loss account and balance sheet.

162   LABOUR FORCE STATISTICS 1958-1969
Org. for Economic Co-operation and Development, Paris

INT—English/Français 1971 413pp £3.00

Information on population, labour force, employment and unemployment, and wages.

163   LABOUR RELATIONS AND EMPLOYMENT CONDITIONS IN THE EUROPEAN ECONOMIC COMMUNITY
The Coventry and District Engineering Employers' Association, Coventry

INT—English 1972 148pp £2.50

Statistical survey of labour relations and employment conditions in the EEC covering collective bargaining, the unions, employment and earnings, free movement and training, social security systems and employee participation.

164   LNG:1974-90: MARINE OPERATIONS AND MARKET PROSPECTS FOR LIQUIFIED NATURAL GAS
Economist Intelligence Unit, London

INT—English 1974 £15.00

E.I.U. special report no. 17: Study which examines world trade in LNG, carrier capacity and financing in the context of the total LNG system.

165   MACKINTOSH YEARBOOK OF WEST EUROPEAN ELECTRONICS DATA
Mackintosh Consultants Company Ltd., Luton

INT—English 1976 annual c140pp £50.00

A survey of the West European electronics market reviewing the situation and prospects in each country. Includes data on production and consumption in particular types of electronics products.

166   MAIN ECONOMIC INDICATORS
Org. for Economic Co-operation and Development, Paris

INT—English monthly c160pp £17.00 p.a.

Monthly tables of national accounts, industrial production, labour, wages, prices, balance of payments, foreign trade.

167   MAIN ECONOMIC INDICATORS: HISTORICAL STATISTICS 1960-75
Org. for Economic Co-operation and Development, Paris

INT—English 1976 589pp £8.50

Historical data for most of the information published in the monthly issues. Includes basic data for economic analysis and model building.

168   MARCHES AGRICOLES (PRIX)
Direction Générale de l'Agriculture, Bruxelles

INT—Français/Deutsch/Italiano/Nederlands twice monthly c60pp

Prices of selected agricultural products, including meat.

169   MARITIME TRANSPORT
Org. for Economic Co-operation and Development, Paris

INT—English annual c160pp £3.30

Annual survey of international shipping developments with detailed statistics.

170   THE MARKET FOR WINDOWS IN THE ORIGINAL EEC COUNTRIES
Building Management and Marketing Consultants Ltd., London

INT—English 1973 5 vols

Major study on new house construction in the six countries of West Germany, Italy, the Netherlands, Belgium, Luxembourg and France. Separate volumes for each country with Belgium and Luxembourg treated together.

171 MARKET PROFILES FOR WESTERN EUROPE AND CANADA
U.S. Department of Commerce, Washington

INT—English 1975 25pp free

Overseas Business Report No. OBR 75-59.
Series of one-page summaries of basic economic data on the economies of 21 Western European countries and Canada.

172 MARKET TRENDS AND PROSPECTS FOR CHEMICAL PRODUCTS
Economic Commission for Europe, Genève

INT—English 1969 3 vols

Survey of market trends and prospects for chemical products, covering the chemical industry in Europe, chemical products and prospects for development of the chemical industries.

173 MARKETING IN EUROPE
Economist Intelligence Unit, London

INT—English monthly £95.00 p.a.

Monthly detailed studies of markets for specific consumer products in Europe; subscription covers quarterly issues of three product groups covering:
1: Food, drink and tobacco;
2: Clothing, furniture and leisure goods;
3: Chemists' goods, household goods and domestic appliances.

174 MARKETING IN EUROPE
Institute of Practitioners in Advertising, London

INT—English

A series of booklets on aspects of marketing in Europe.

175 MARKETING POTENTIALS OF EUROPE'S REGIONS
Europotentials & Planning Ltd., London

INT—English 1973 44pp £6.75

Shows how marketing potential in real terms is distributed throughout West Europe, and enables comparisons on a common basis through developing a common unit account.

176 DER MARKT DER OBERBEKLEIDUNG (THE MARKET FOR OUTERWEAR): MARKTE INFORMATIONEN FÜR DIE WERBEPLANUNG
Axel Springer Verlag, Hamburg

INT/D—Deutsch 1973 3 vols

Band 1: Damenoberbekleidung (Ladies' Outerwear)
Band 2: Herren- und Knabenoberbekleidung (Men's and Boys' Outerwear): Kinderoberbekleidung (Children's Outerwear); Freizeitkleidung, Strickwaren, Jeans (Leisure Wear, Knitwear, Jeans).
Band 3: Firmeninformation (Company Information)

A detailed survey of the West German outerwear industry, giving data for the period 1968-72. Includes a brief survey of the industry in Hong Kong, Italy, France, Great Britain and the United States.

177 MEAT
Commonwealth Secretariat, London

INT—English 1974 £2.50

Review of production, trade, consumption and prices of beef, live cattle, mutton and lamb, live sheep, bacon and hams, pork, live pigs, canned meat, offal and poultry meat with emphasis on Commonwealth data.

178 MEAT BALANCES IN OECD MEMBER COUNTRIES 1959-72
Org. for Economic Co-operation and Development, Paris

INT—English 1974 196pp £1.60

Annual statistics of meat balances in the OECD.

179 IL MERCATO EUROPEO DEI PRODOTTI ORTOFRUTTICOLI SURGELATI (THE EUROPEAN MARKET FOR DEEP-FROZEN FRUIT AND VEGETABLE PRODUCTS)
Istituto per la Ricerche e le Informazione di Mercato e la Valorizzazione della Produzione Agricola, Roma

INT—Italiano 1971 2 vols.

A study of the European deep-frozen food industry, giving information and statistics for various periods up to 1970. Covers production, distribution, structure of the industry, foreign trade, prices and consumption figures with forecasts to 1980. Contents list also in English but text only in Italian. Volume 2 is a statistical appendix.

180 METAL BULLETIN HANDBOOK
Metal Bulletin Ltd., London

INT—English annual £7.00

Annual survey of production, trade and prices in non-ferrous metals.

181 MILK AND MILK PRODUCTS BALANCES IN MEMBER COUNTRIES 1960-73
Org. for Economic Co-operation and Development, Paris

INT—English 1975 192pp £2.80

Annual statistics of milk and milk products balances in the OECD.

182 MONTHLY BULLETIN OF AGRICULTURAL ECONOMICS AND STATISTICS
Food and Agricultural Organization of the United Nations, Roma

INT—English/Français monthly £3.20 p.a.

Monthly bulletin giving latest statistics available on production, external trade and prices.

183 MONTHLY BULLETIN OF STATISTICS
United Nations, Genève

INT—English/Français monthly £21.00 p.a.

Monthly statistics on: population, manpower, forestry, industrial production, mining, manufacturing, construction, electricity and gas, imports and exports, transport, wages and prices, national accounts and finance.

184 MOTOR BUSINESS
Economist Intelligence Unit, London

INT—English quarterly £95.00 p.a.

Detailed coverage of trends and statistics in the international automotive industry. Examines both passenger and commercial vehicles with full coverage of domestic market size, import penetration, level of exports and production trends.

185 THE MOTOR VEHICLE INDUSTRY
United Nations, Genève

INT—English 1972 96pp £0.63

Review of the motor vehicle industry in developing
countries including forecasts of demand and production
to 1980.

186 MULTINATIONAL UNIONS
The Financial Times Ltd., London

INT—English 1974 141pp £10.25

Reports on the evolution, structure, aims, tactics and
strategies of the world's multinational union groupings.

187 NEWSPAPER PRESS DIRECTORY
IPC Business Press Ltd., London

INT—English 1976 900pp £20.00

Reference book of world publications covering newspapers,
periodicals and directories. Also gives data on UK regional
radio and television outlets.

188 THE NON-FERROUS METALS INDUSTRY
Org. for Economic Co-operation and Development, Paris

INT—English/Français annual

Details of production, consumption, trade and uses at first
processing stages of the principal non-ferrous metals.

189 NORTH SEA OIL INFORMATION SOURCES
Kogan Page Ltd., London

INT—English 1975 80pp £12.00

Guide to sources of information for companies working
in the offshore oil, gas and related industries. Lists over 70
distinct sources - government, professional and research
organisations, publishers, technical and commercial
services. Also includes a bibliography of recently published
articles and a section on media data.

**190 THE NORTH SEA OIL PROVINCE: AN ATTEMPT TO
SIMULATE ITS DEVELOPMENT AND EXPLOITATION,
1969-2029**
Kogan Page Ltd., London

INT—English 1975 74pp £20.00

Study which predicts that the ultimate, technically
recoverable reserves of the North Sea will be between
80 and 140 billion barrels - at least twice and up to four
times the conventional estimates.

191 OECD ECONOMIC OUTLOOK
Org. for Economic Co-operation and Development, Paris

INT—English/Français twice yearly £3.40 p.a.

General survey of the economic situation, covering domestic
and international prospects, monetary and financial
developments in major countries.

192 OIL AND GAS IN 1975
Shell Briefing Service, London

INT—English 1976 9pp free

Data on production, movement and use of oil.

193 OIL STATISTICS SUPPLY AND DISPOSAL
Org. for Economic Co-operation and Development, Paris

INT—English annual c180pp £3.50

Tables for all OECD member countries on supply,
disposal, processing, refinery output and consumption.

194 OIL WORLD SEMI-ANNUAL
Mielke & Company, Hamburg

INT—English twice yearly

Survey of the situation and prospects for food oils and fats.

195 OIL: WORLD STATISTICS
Institute of Petroleum, London

INT—English 1972 £0.10

Statistics of production, consumption, refining and trade for
oil and petroleum.

**196 OPTIMAL DEVELOPMENT OF THE NORTH SEA'S
OILFIELDS**
Kogan Page Ltd., London

INT—English 1976 150pp £30.00

A study of divergent government and company interests
and their reconciliation.

**197 ORGANISATION OF THE TOURIST INDUSTRY
IN COMMONWEALTH COUNTRIES**
Commonwealth Secretariat, London

INT—English 1971 225pp £2.00

Review of the organisation of the tourist industry in the
Commonwealth presented country by country.

**198 PAPER AND BOARD CONSUMPTION PATTERNS
AND DEVELOPMENT TRENDS IN THE OECD
COUNTRIES 1950-67**
Org. for Economic Co-operation and Development, Paris

INT—English/Français 1970

Study of paper and board consumption patterns and
development trends with an appendix containing specialist
demand projections.

199 PAPER AND PACKAGING BULLETIN
Economist Intelligence Unit, London

GB/INT—English quarterly £90.00 p.a.

Analysis of trends in packaging materials, both paper and
plastic, and of printing papers for consumers and producers.
Gives statistics for the UK and the EEC on production and
exports of pulp and paper by grades, imports, consumption
and stocks, plus a guide to UK paper prices.

200 PHILLIPS PAPER TRADE DIRECTORY
Benn Brothers Ltd., Tonbridge

INT—English 1976 £16.00

Contents: world pulp, paper and paperboard mills by country
and by company; products; European machinery; equipment;
materials; agents; watermarks; brand names; merchants; UK
processors and converters sections.

201 PLANT LOCATION IN EUROPE
The Financial Times Ltd., London

INT—English 1974 65pp £15.25

A report on the use of location and expansion
techniques with European case histories.

**202 POLLUTION CONTROL IN THE FOOD INDUSTRY
IN THE EUROPEAN COMMUNITY**
Graham & Trotman Ltd., London

INT—English 1977 £15.00

A description of means to control pollution in the food
industries of the EEC.

**203 POLLUTION CONTROL LAW AND PRACTICE IN THE
MEMBER STATES OF THE EUROPEAN COMMUNITIES**
Graham and Trotman Ltd., London

INT—English 9 books: £7.50 per book: £62.00 per set

Definitive coverage of anti-pollution laws and practices
in the 9 EEC member countries.

204 POPULATION AND VITAL STATISTICS REPORT
United Nations, Genève

INT—English quarterly $10.00

Data from latest census returns and demographic statistics
for all reporting countries.

205 PORTS OF THE WORLD
Benn Brothers Ltd., Tonbridge

INT—English 1976 £25.00

Detailed port information, giving data on: position, authority,
accommodation, all types of terminals and facilities, bunkers,
shiprepairers, charges, towage, pilotage, traffic, airports,
local holidays, working hours, officials.

206 THE POTENTIAL FOR NEW COMMODITY CARTELS
Economist Intelligence Unit, London

INT—English 1975 £20.00

E.I.U. special report no. 27: Study which examines: latest
developments on international commodity agreements and
cartel attempts; circumstances in which effective cartelisation
is possible; the suitability of individual commodities for
cartelisation.

207 PREISE LOHNE WIRTSCHAFTSRECHNUNGEN
Statistisches Bundesamt, Wiesbaden

D/INT—Deutsch annual

Cost-of-living comparison for 50 countries including data on
prices, wages and household budgets.

**208 PRICES OF AGRICULTURAL PRODUCTS AND
FERTILIZERS IN EUROPE**
Economic Commission for Europe, Genève

INT—English annual

Statistics on prices of agricultural products and fertilizers
including comparative data for recent years.

209 PRODUCTION YEARBOOK
Food and Agricultural Organization of the United Nations,
Roma

INT—English/Español/Français annual 198pp £4.00

Agricultural production yearbook giving data on: land,
population, prices, production, wages, crop production, livestock and associated products.

**210 PROFITABILITY AND PERFORMANCE OF THE WORLD'S
LARGEST INDUSTRIAL COMPANIES**
The Financial Times Ltd., London

INT—English 1975 165pp £30.50

An Economists Advisory Group study analysing the growth,
structure, size and profitability of the world's largest companies in the non-Communist world.

**211 PROSPECTS FOR UNMANUFACTURED TOBACCO TO
1984**
Economist Intelligence Unit, London

INT—English 1975 £15.00

E.I.U. special report no. 29: Provides a long-term perspective
for the world tobacco industry, presenting forecasts of
production, consumption, prices and the role of tobacco
supplements.

**212 PROVISIONAL INDICATIVE WORLD PLAN FOR
AGRICULTURAL DEVELOPMENT**
Food and Agricultural Organization of the United Nations,
Roma

INT—English 1970 2 vols £3.40

Study analysing the factors affecting agricultural production,
trade and growth in developing countries.

213 PUBLIC PROCUREMENT IN EFTA
European Free Trade Association, Genève

INT—English 1971

List of public agencies and enterprises responsible for
purchases of at least one million dollars (US) per year. Data
is presented by country giving each agency's address, type
of goods purchased and amounts in dollars for which
purchases were made for two selected years.

214 PULP AND PAPER INDUSTRY 1972-73
Org. for Economic Co-operation and Development, Paris

INT—English 1974 340pp £2.60

Details of pulp and paper markets in N. America, Europe,
Japan and Australia. Tables of production capacity from
1972-77 country by country and by categories of products.

215 PULP AND PAPER QUARTERLY STATISTICS
Org. for Economic Co-operation and Development, Paris

INT—English quarterly £3.60 p.a.

Quarterly statistics on stocks of paper, pulp and waste
paper, production, trade, shipments of market pulp.

**216   QUARTERLY BULLETIN OF COAL STATISTICS
FOR EUROPE**
United Nations, Genève

INT—English quarterly c50pp $3.00

Basic data on current developments in the field of solid
fuels in Europe and the USA.

**217   QUARTERLY BULLETIN OF STEEL STATISTICS FOR
EUROPE**
United Nations, Genève

INT—English quarterly c60pp $5.00

Statistics on production and trade for European countries,
Canada, USA and Japan.

218   QUARTERLY ECONOMIC REVIEW SERVICE
Economist Intelligence Unit, London

INT—English quarterly £25.00 p.a.

77 separate economic reviews, published quarterly giving
current economic and commercial information for about
150 countries.

219   RAILWAY DIRECTORY AND YEAR BOOK
IPC Business Press Ltd., London

INT/GB—English annual c700pp £8.00

Reference work with statistics and general data on the major
railways of the world. Includes over 100 maps showing the
main railway systems.

220   REGIONAL INTEGRATION
Org. for Economic Co-operation and Development, Paris

INT—English/Français 1969 125pp

Special annotated bibliography on regional economic integration, covering the EEC and EFTA documents published
between 1965 and 1969.

221   A REGIONAL POLICY FOR THE COMMUNITY
European Communities, Luxembourg

INT—English 260pp £1.25

Detailed consideration of regional problems, policies and
instruments in the EEC.

222   REGIONAL STATISTICS YEARBOOK
European Communities, Luxembourg

INT—English annual c250pp £2.10

Details of movements and density of population within
regions of the European community. Includes data on: rate
of female employment; agricultural land and employment;
transport and traffic through seaports and airports.

223   REPORT ON COMPETITION POLICY
European Communities, Luxembourg

INT—English annual £1.70

Official report on developments in Common Market
competition policy.

**224   REPORT ON THE LONG AND MEDIUM TERM DEVELOP-
MENT OF THE SHIPBUILDING MARKET**
European Communities, Luxembourg

INT—English 1972

Report on the development of the shipbuilding market, the
demand for new building and world shipbuilding supply, in
both the long and medium term.

225   REVIEW
Fearnley and Egers Chartering Co. Ltd., Oslo

INT—English annual

Statistical review of the major aspects of international
shipping.

226   REVIEW OF FISHERIES IN OECD MEMBER COUNTRIES
Org. for Economic Co-operation and Development, Paris

INT—English/Français annual c240pp £4.00

General survey of the fishing industry with individual
country reports including details of vessels, fish landings,
utilisation of catch and external trade.

**227   REVIEW OF THE AGRICULTURAL SITUATION IN
EUROPE AT THE END OF 1970**
Economic Commission for Europe, Genève

INT—English 1971 2 vols

Vol. 1: General survey and details of grain, livestock and
         meat   (164pp)
Vol. 2: Examines the situation for dairy products and eggs
         (161pp)

228   RICE BULLETIN
Commonwealth Secretariat, London

INT—English monthly £20.00 p.a.

Details of production, trade, utilisation and prices for rice
with emphasis on data from Commonwealth countries.

229   RUBBER TRENDS
Economist Intelligence Unit, London

INT—English quarterly £90.00 p.a.

Analysis and interpretation of international data relating to
rubber consumers and producers. Includes quarterly concise
summary of the current global position for natural and
synthetic rubber supplies. Country reports cover: production,
consumption and trade statistics set in the context of macro-
economic trends.

230   SAVINGS FLOWS IN EUROPE
The Financial Times Ltd., London

INT—English 1976 191pp £50.60

An Institute of European Finance research study, on personal
saving and borrowing in Europe.

231   SEASONALITY IN TOURISM
Economist Intelligence Unit, London

INT—English 1975 £20.00

A study which examines the principal methods of analysing
seasonality and trends, using a computer programme. The

examples presented relate to tourism, travel and accommodation but the methods are applicable to other industries and businesses.

232   SELECTED AGRICULTURAL FIGURES OF THE EEC
Ministry of Agriculture and Fisheries of the Netherlands,
Den Haag

INT—Nederlands/Deutsch/English/Français annual

Production consumption and price data on the main agricultural commodities and information on the size of holdings and production and consumption of fertilizers and farm equipment.

233   SELECTIVE MANAGEMENT BIBLIOGRAPHY
Bowker Publishing Co. Ltd., Epping

INT—English 1975 402pp £12.50

Classified guide to c7000 books and articles published in English, French and German, the majority since 1970, on management.
Classification of Business Studies, and comprehensive author and subject indexes are included. Also gives a list of names and addresses of book and journal publishers.

234   SELF SERVICE
Internationale Selbstbedienungs-Organisation, Köln

INT—Deutsch/English/Français annual

Annual survey of self-service and supermarkets in Europe including details of establishments and turnover.

235   SHIPPING IN THE SEVENTIES
United Nations, Conference on Trade and Development,
Genève

INT—English 1972

Survey of potential trends and problems for international shipping.

236   SHIPPING MARKS ON TIMBER
Benn Brothers Ltd., Tonbridge

INT—English 1976 £10.00

Comprehensive reference book to the marks used by shippers of timber, plywood and board from over 60 countries, with details of average annual production and shippers' agents.

237   SOLVING EUROPEAN BUSINESS PROBLEMS
Business International, Genève

INT—English 1968 100pp $40

Case studies of over 150 companies, reprinted from Business Europe, indicating business and marketing opportunities in Europe.

**238   SOURCES AND MANAGEMENT OF EXPORT
         FINANCE**
Gower Press, Farnborough

INT—English 157pp £4.50

Describes the nature of export trading, sources of assistance and how to establish control systems.

**239   SOURCES OF CORPORATE FINANCE IN WESTERN
         EUROPE**
Graham & Trotman Ltd., London

INT—English 1976 £45.00

Describes and compares sources of company finance in Europe. Chapters deal individually with countries giving notes on depreciation and other investment allowances, incentives and special sources of finance.

240   SPOTLIGHT ON OVERSEAS TRADE
Midland Bank Ltd., London

INT—English

Periodic booklets dealing with individual countries covering the economic situation, markets, exports.

241   THE STATE OF FOOD AND AGRICULTURE 1971
Food and Agricultural Organization of the United Nations,
Roma

INT—English 1971 c205pp £5.60

World review of food and agriculture, giving data on production, trade, prices, agricultural requisites, detailed review by geographical regions, water pollution data.

242   STATISTICAL BULLETIN
International Sugar Organization, London

INT—English monthly

Monthly bulletin giving data on: production, consumption, supply and foreign trade of sugar.

243   STATISTICAL HANDBOOK
British Steel Corporation, Croydon

INT—English irregular 2 vols

Provides trade and production statistics for steel and steel products, by country, over a five year period.

**244   STATISTICAL SUMMARY OF THE MINERAL INDUSTRY
         1966-70**
Institute of Geological Sciences HMSO

INT—English 1972

Presents statistics for the mineral industry for the period 1966-70 covering production, imports and exports and classified by country and type of mineral.

245   STATISTICAL YEARBOOK
United Nations, Genève

INT—English/Français annual c850pp £15.40

Contents: statistics on population, manpower, agriculture, forestry, fishing, industrial production, mining and quarrying, construction, manufacturing, energy, external and internal trade, transport and communications, balance of payments, wages and prices, national accounts, finance, international capital flow, education, housing, health, science and technology, culture.

246 **STATISTICAL YEARBOOK**
United Nations Educational, Scientific and Cultural
Organization, Paris

INT—English annual c800pp £18.90

Annual tables of reference on, population area of density,
illiteracy and educational attainment, based on censuses and
surveys. Statistics of levels of education, expenditure,
science and technology, culture and communication.

247 **STATISTICS - EUROPE**
CBD Research Ltd., Beckenham

INT—English 1976 480pp £15.00

Source book to economic statistics published both by
government and private organizations.

248 **STATISTICS OF ENERGY 1959-73**
Org. for Economic Co-operation and Development, Paris

INT—English/Français 1975 564pp £7.40

Basic statistics of production, trade and consumption of
energy in OECD countries.

249 **STATISTIQUE DE L'ENERGIE**
European Communities, Luxembourg

INT—Deutsch/English/Français quarterly and annual

Statistics on production, consumption, prices and foreign
trade in coal, gas, electricity and oil.

250 **STATISTIQUE HORTICOLE EUROPEENNE**
Internationaler Verband des Gewerbgartenbaues, Den Haag

INT—Deutsch/English/Français 1969

Data on production, trade, consumption, and related
information for horticultural products in Europe.

251 **SUGAR YEARBOOK**
International Sugar Organization, London

INT—English annual c370pp £2.50

Annual statistics of world production, imports and exports,
consumption, retail and wholesale prices of sugar in
individual member countries.

252 **A SURVEY OF EUROPE TODAY**
The Readers Digest Association Limited, London

INT—English 1970 212pp

Commentary and statistics on a range of socio-economic
aspects on Western Europe. Includes results of the
publishers' own enquiries.

253 **TAX HAVENS AND THEIR USES**
Economist Intelligence Unit, London

INT—English 1976 £10.00

E.I.U. special report no. 2I: Analyses the ways in which
individuals and companies are using tax havens.

254 **TAX POLICY AND INVESTMENT IN THE EUROPEAN
COMMUNITY**
European Communities, Luxembourg

INT—English 1975 £11.56

Part 1: Describes and analyses the various tax instruments
aimed at influencing private investment in the nine EEC
countries. Part 2: Attempts to discover how indications of
the relative efficiency of instruments of tax policy can be
given a basis in economic theory.

255 **TAX STATISTICS YEARBOOK 1974**
European Communities, Luxembourg

INT—English 1975 c130pp £3.40

Tax figures for the years 1968-73 for OECD member
countries.

256 **TAXATION IN WESTERN EUROPE**
Confederation of British Industry, London

INT/GB—English £7.50

Summary of the taxation structure of West European and
Scandinavian countries.

257 **TEXTILE INDUSTRY IN THE OECD COUNTRIES**
Org. for Economic Co-operation and Development, Paris

INT—English/Français annual c150pp £3.00

General trends in the textile industry, with data on
production, trade, consumption, competition, stocks, prices,
manpower.

258 **TEXTILE ORGANON**
Textile Economics Bureau Inc., New York

INT—English monthly

Monthly bulletin with information on man-made fibres and
wool.

259 **TIMBER BULLETIN FOR EUROPE**
Food and Agricultural Organization of the United Nations,
Roma

INT—English/Français twice a year

Bulletin giving information on production trade and prices
for timber and timber products.

260 **TRADE AND INDUSTRIAL RESOURCES OF THE
COMMON MARKET AND EFTA COUNTRIES**
Garnstone Press, London

INT—English 1970 158pp £15.75

Comparative statistical analysis of imports and exports and
industrial activities of EEC and EFTA countries.

261 **THE TRADE EFFECTS OF EFTA AND THE EEC**
European Free Trade Association, Genève

INT—English 1972

Study of the effects of the creation of EFTA and the EEC
as two separate trading groups on the economies of the
member countries of both groups.

262   TRADE UNIONS AND FREE LABOUR MOVEMENT IN THE EEC
Political and Economic Planning/Royal Institute of
International Affairs, London

INT—English 1969 50pp £0.80

Paper number 10 in the "European Series" covering trade
unions and the movement of labour in the EEC.

263   TRADE UNIONS IN EUROPE
Gower Press, Farnborough

INT—English 1975 240pp £9.50

Part 1: European trade unions organization; the institutions,
international organizations and major problems facing the
European unions. Part 2: Profiles on each country:
economic background, union structure and membership,
collective bargaining and industrial relations.

264   TRADE YEARBOOK
Food and Agricultural Organization of the United Nations,
Roma

INT—English/Español/Français c610pp £6.00

Agricultural trade yearbook giving statistics on a wide range
of agricultural commodities and requisites over the past five
years.

265   TRANSPORT POLICY OF THE EUROPEAN COMMUNITIES
The Political and Economic Planning/Royal Institute of
International Affairs, London

INT—English 1969 83pp £0.80

Paper number 12 in the "European Series", covering
policy of the EEC.

266   TRANSPORT STATISTICS - MONTHLY TABLES
European Communities, Luxembourg

INT—English monthly £7.25 p.a.

Basic guide to transport movements within the EEC.

267   TRENDS AND PROBLEMS IN THE WORLD GRAIN ECONOMY 1950-70
International Wheat Council, London

INT—English/Español/Français 1966

Summary of the main developments in the wheat and
coarse grain situation since 1950 and their significance for
future trends.

268   TRENDS IN GRAIN CONSUMPTION
International Wheat Council, London

INT—English/Español/Français 1970

Basic data on the consumption of wheat for both
humans and animals.

269   ULRICH'S INTERNATIONAL PERIODICALS DIRECTORY
Bowker Publishing Company Ltd., Epping

INT—English biennial c2700pp £30.00

Reference work for world periodical literature, giving data
on c60,000 periodicals covering 160 countries. Includes
titles and subject indexes.

270   URANIUM: RESOURCES, PRODUCTION AND DEMAND
Org. for Economic Co-operation and Development, Paris

INT—English/Français 1970

Review of uranium resources, demand and production,
presented by country.

271   USING EFTA
European Free Trade Association, Genève

INT—English 1968

Basic information on exporting to EFTA countries with
information on each country.

272   VEGETABLE OILS AND OILSEEDS
Commonwealth Secretariat, London

INT—English 1973 £3.50

Review of production, trade, utilisation and prices relating
to groundnuts, cottonseed, linseed, soya beans, coconut and
oil palm products, olive oil and other oilseeds and oils with
emphasis on Commonwealth data.

273   WALTER SKINNER'S MINING INTERNATIONAL YEAR BOOK
The Financial Times Ltd., London

INT—English annual c700pp £11.00

Annual data on the world's top international mining
companies, includes data on: properties, production, claims,
mineral deposits, ore reserves, capital structure, profits,
dividends, financial data including high/low share prices for
the past three years. Also includes suppliers directory and
buyers' guide with c3000 entries.

274   WALTER SKINNER'S NORTH SEA AND EUROPE OFFSHORE YEAR BOOK AND BUYERS' GUIDE
The Financial Times Ltd., London

INT—English annual c350pp £19.50

Annual guide giving information on: companies operating
in the offshore areas (executives, type of business);
exploration licensing conditions already legislated by
European coastal states; oil production legislation in
European countries; proven offshore oil and gas strikes, with
maps; maps showing exploration and production licence
concessions; onshore bases and platform construction yards;
operational rigs; equipment suppliers; materials and services
for offshore programmes.

275   WALTER SKINNER'S OIL AND GAS INTERNATIONAL YEAR BOOK
The Financial Times Ltd., London

INT—English annual c750pp £11.00

Contents: information on the world's major oil and gas
companies, giving data on: executives, subsidiaries, financial
status; North Sea section showing map and UK concession
holders; geographical index listing companies under country
of operation; cross-referenced index to all companies
mentioned in the text; production, refining, consumption
and tanker tables; suppliers directory and buyers' guide.

276 **WALTER SKINNER'S WHO'S WHO IN WORLD OIL AND
     GAS**
     The Financial Times Ltd., London

     INT—English annual c700pp £13.00

     Annual directory giving biographical details of senior
     executives, scientists, government representatives and
     consultants directly involved in the oil and gas industries;
     also includes a cross-reference index to the organizations
     and countries of the executives.

277 **WEST EUROPEAN LIVING COSTS**
     Confederation of British Industry, London

     INT—English annual £6.00

     Cost of living survey covering 13 countries with details on
     accommodation, clothing, food, etc.

278 **WEST EUROPEAN MARKETS FOR LABORATORY
     ANALYTICAL INSTRUMENTS:
     VOLUME 2: CONTINENTAL EUROPE**
     Sira Institute, Chislehurst

     INT—Deutsch/Français/Italiano/English 1975

     Volume 1 covers the United Kingdom. Vol. 2 covers ten West
     European countries giving data on production, imports
     and exports. Contains more detailed surveys of West
     Germany, France and Italy, with market size analysed by
     product group and by market sectors, with forecasts of
     growth to 1979. Includes sections of major suppliers plus a
     profile of the country concerned in economic and
     statistical terms.

279 **WILLINGS PRESS GUIDE**
     Thomas Skinner Directories, Haywards Heath

     INT—English annual £8.00

     Comprehensive index to British, European and United States
     newspapers, periodicals and journals.

280 **WORKER PARTICIPATION**
     Economist Intelligence Unit, London

     INT—English 1975 £15.00

     E.I.U. Special Report no. 20: Examines the main form that
     worker participation has taken or could take, and
     analyses worker participation in West Germany, Sweden,
     Yugoslavia and the U.K.

281 **WORLD AGRICULTURAL PRODUCTION**
     Econtel Research Ltd., London

     INT—English 1970 20pp £3.00

     Digest of agricultural production statistics for 70 countries.

282 **WORLD AIR TRANSPORT STATISTICS**
     International Air Transport Association, Montreal

     INT—English annual

     Annual statistics of the air transport industry.

283 **WORLD AUTOMOTIVE MARKET SURVEY**
     McGraw-Hill, New York

     INT—English

Market research of the automotive industry including
statistics of the 1966 world motor census.

284 **WORLD BANK ATLAS 1975**
     World Bank Group, Washington

     INT—English 1975 30pp

     International data on population, per capita product and
     growth rates, of 188 countries and territories.

285 **WORLD COFFEE SURVEY**
     **Food and Agricultural Organization of the United Nations,
     Roma**

     INT—English 1968

     Survey of coffee production giving data by country on
     aspects of production marketing and future trends.

286 **WORLD COMMUNICATIONS**
     **United Nations Educational, Scientific and Cultural
     Organization/Gower Press, Farnborough**

     INT—English 1975 750pp £8.50

     Reference data and commentary on the communications
     facilities in c200 countries. Covers the press, radio, television,
     film, news agencies.

287 **THE WORLD DAIRY ECONOMY IN FIGURES**
     **Food and Agricultural Organization of the United Nations,
     Roma**

     INT—English/Español/Français

     Statistics on milk and milk products by country with data
     on production, trade and consumption over a twenty year
     period.

288 **WORLD ECONOMIC SURVEY 1973**
     United Nations, Genève

     INT—English Part 1: 1974 210pp £3.96
                 Part 2: 1973 170pp £3.52

     Part 1: Mid term review and appraisal of progress in the
             implementation of the International Development
             Strategy.
     Part 2: Current economic developments.

     Comprehensive survey of the world economic conditions,
     international trade, payments and production. Part 1 is a
     study of a major economic subject of current interest;
     Part 2 shows current trends in the world economy.

289 **WORLD ENERGY SUPPLIES 1969-72**
     United Nations, Genève

     INT—English 1974 212pp £3.30

     Energy production, trade and consumption statistics
     classified by type of fuel and by country.

290 **WORLD INDUSTRIAL PRODUCTION**
     Econtel Research Ltd., London

     INT—English annual

     World-wide indices of industrial production.

291 WORLD INFLATION
Econtel Research Ltd., London

INT—English 1969

Statistics on the rate and magnitude of inflation in 80
countries over the period 1950-68.

**292 WORLD MARKET FOR ELECTRIC POWER EQUIPMENT
RATIONALISATION AND TECHNICAL CHANGE**
Science Policy Research Unit, University of Sussex, Brighton

INT—English 1972

The Survey is essentially concerned with the interaction of
technical change and rationalisation on structure of the
world market for electric power equipment. Includes a
review of the pattern of international trade and individual
surveys of the market in North America, Japan, Switzerland
and West Germany.

293 WORLD MOTOR VEHICLE DATA
Motor Vehicles Manufacturers Association, Detroit

INT—English 1974 annual

A survey of world motor vehicle production and registrations,
includes production totals by manufacturers as well as
country. Contains forecast information to 1985.

**294 WORLD MOTOR VEHICLE PRODUCTION AND
REGISTRATION**
US Bureau of International Commerce, Washington

INT—English annual

Annual survey of production and registration of world motor
vehicles.

295 WORLD OUTLOOK
Economist Intelligence Unit, London

INT—English annual c130pp £15.00

Guide to worldwide economic prospects, combining the
latest individual forecasts of likely trends in over 150
countries, published in the E.I.U.'s 77 Quarterly Economic
Reviews.

296 WORLD PETROCHEMICALS
The Financial Times Ltd., London

INT—English 1975 127pp £50.35

A collection of papers from a Financial Times conference on
the present situation of the world's petrochemicals industry,
which surveys the likely role that oil producing states will
assume in the development of their by-products.

**297 WORLD REPORT: THE MONTHLY BULLETIN OF
INTERNATIONAL EMPLOYMENT**
Employment Conditions Abroad Ltd., London

INT—English monthly £19.50 p.a.

Monthly bulletin giving current information on all aspects of
employment, both expatriate and local, throughout the
world.

298 WORLD TANKER FLEET REVIEW
John I. Jacobs & Co. Ltd., London

INT—English 1972

Review of aspects of the world tanker fleet industry.

**299 WORLD TRADE OUTLOOK FOR WESTERN EUROPE
AND CANADA**
US Department of Commerce, Washington

INT—English 1976 15pp

Overseas Business Report no. OBR 76-35.
Brief economic summary of Western Europe and Canada
focusing on market opportunities.

300 WORLD-WIDE ROBOT MARKETS AND OPPORTUNITIES
Theta Technology Corporation, Wethersfield (Conn).

INT—English 1972 102pp

Report on the nature, extent and scope of the market
opportunities for robots in the United States and international
industrial complexes. The study covers market size, market
factors, applications, considerations. It includes forecast
information to 1980.

**301 YEARBOOK OF CONSTRUCTION STATISTICS
1963-72**
United Nations, Genève

INT—English 1975 232pp £7.92

First in a series of annual statistical surveys on world construction. National data on major items of construction
activity for 106 countries or areas. National tables contain
details on: principal indicators of construction activity,
gross fixed capital formation, permits, and completed new
constructions.

**302 YEARBOOK OF INDUSTRIAL STATISTICS
(FORMERLY: THE GROWTH OF WORLD INDUSTRY)**
United Nations, Genève

INT—English/Français annual 2 vols c1350pp

Comprehensive statistical survey of world industry;
Vol. 1: general industrial statistics;
Vol. 2: commodity production data.

303 YEARBOOK OF NATIONAL ACCOUNTS STATISTICS
United Nations, Genève

INT—English 1975 1890pp £21.12

In three volumes not sold separately:
Vols 1 & 2: individual country tables—showing detailed
accounts and estimates for 120 countries and territories;
Vol. 3: International Tables—give data on per capita gross
domestic product, national income and national disposable
income for 138 countries.

A-AUSTRIA

400 ALMANACH DER ÖSTERREICHISCHEN AKTIENGESELLSCHAFTEN
Zentralverband Österreichischer Aktiengesellschaften

A— Deutsch annual 400pp

Yearbook of Austrian joint-stock companies containing: major companies, listed alphabetically, with details of address, directors, capital, balance sheet summary.

401 AUSTRIA FACTS AND FIGURES
Federal Press Service

A—English 1973 232pp

General introduction which includes: the country and its people; government and politics; Austrian economy; social services; sport and culture; education; science and research; the media.

402 AUSTRIA—FINANCIAL TIMES SURVEY
The Financial Times

A—English 28 Jan. 1975 p.11-14

Survey in the Financial Times newspaper covering: banking; exports; energy supplies; tourism; relations with Yugoslavia.

403 AUSTRIA TODAY
Austria Today Ltd.

A—English quarterly

A quarterly journal reviewing trends and developments in industry, commerce, politics, science and the arts.

404 THE AUSTRIAN CONCENSUS
The Financial Times

A—English 25 Sept. 1975 p.29-32

Survey in the Financial Times newspaper examining Austria's industrial relations policy and the development of the social partnership philosophy.

405 AUSTRIAN EXPORTS
The Financial Times

A—English 17 March 1976 p.24-25

Review in the Financial Times newspaper which analyses the importance of exports to the country's economy and examines the efforts being made to increase Austria's share of the world market.

406 AUSTRIAN INDUSTRIAL DEVELOPMENT
The Financial Times

A—English 29 Sept. 1975 p.9-11

Survey in the Financial Times newspaper examining how Austria is combating inflation and unemployment.

407 AUSTRIAN TRADE NEWS
Austrian Trade Delegation

A—English monthly

Monthly journal with regular news of Austrian trade.

408 AUSTRIA'S MONETARY DEVELOPMENT 1955-65
Creditanstalt-Bankverein

A—English 1965

Concise survey of basic trends in economic and monetary developments from 1955-65.

409 BASIC DATA ON THE ECONOMY OF AUSTRIA
U.S. Department of Commerce

A—English 1973 17pp

Overseas Business Report no. OBR 73-13.
General report on the Austrian economy covering: basic structure; industrial sectors; labour market; trade; finance; economic outlook.

410 BESTANDS-STATISTIK DER KRAFTFAHRZEUGE IN ÖSTERREICH NACH DEM STANDE VOM 31 DEZEMBER
Österreichisches Statistisches Zentralamt

A—Deutsch annual

Statistics of motor vehicles registered in Austria, giving numbers of different types of vehicles e.g. motor cars, trucks, motor bikes, by make, by province and subdivided by age of vehicle.

411 **BETRIEBSSTATISTIK: ERZEUGUNG UND VERBRAUCH ELEKTRISCHER ENERGIE IN ÖSTERREICH. TEIL 1, GESAMTERGEBNISSE**
Bundesministerium für Verkehr und Verstaatlichte Unternehmungen

A—Deutsch annual

Electricity production by state and private undertakings and consumption by different branches of industry.

412 **DIE BUCHFÜHRUNGSERGEBNISSE AUS DER ÖSTERREICHISCHEN LANDWIRTSCHAFT IM JAHR . . .**
Bundesministerium für Land-, Forstwirtschaft und die Präsidentenkonferenz der Landwirtschaftskammern

A—Deutsch 1968 138pp

Results of an enquiry into the Austrian agricultural economy. Detailed breakdown of expenditure in the agricultural sector, including expenditure on agricultural machinery, fertilizer and related goods.

413 **COMMENT IMPLANTER VOTRE ENTREPRISE EN AUTRICHE?**
Société Générale Alsacienne de Banque AG

A—Français 1973 56pp

Practical advice and information for those considering setting up a business in Austria. Concentrates on legal, fiscal and tax formalities.

414 **ECONOMIC LETTER - AUSTRIAN ECONOMY IN BRIEF**
Creditanstalt-Bankverein

A—English monthly

Brief monthly review of the Austrian economy.

415 **ECONOMIC REPORT - AUSTRIA**
Lloyds Bank Ltd.

A—English 1975 19pp

Reviews the current economic situation in Austria and the opportunities for exporters. Also provides brief summaries and statistics on: nationalised industries; agriculture and forestry; minerals; tourism; exports; balance of payments.

416 **ERGEBNISSE DER ERHEBUNG DES BESTANDES AN LANDWIRTSCHAFTLICHEN MASCHINEN UND GERÄTEN**
Österreichisches Statistisches Zentralamt

A—Deutsch five-yearly c150pp

Results of a survey into the amount of agricultural machinery and equipment in use.

417 **ERGEBNISSE DER LANDWIRTSCHAFTLICHEN STATISTIK**
Österreichisches Statistisches Zentralamt

A—Deutsch annual

Statistics on land under cultivation, average crop yields for each province and parish, number of cattle and related agricultural data.

418 **FINANZ-COMPASS ÖSTERREICH**
Compass-Verlag

A—Deutsch annual c1400p

Details of Austrian companies, broadly classified, and with details of: address; date established; directors; capital and other financial data; company activities; number of employees; alphabetical index by company name.

419 **FOREIGN TRADE REGULATIONS OF AUSTRIA**
US Department of Commerce

A—English 1972 11pp

Overseas Business Report no. OBR 71-031. Concise report with information covering the regulations governing trade; customs documentation; tariffs; import and export controls.

420 **DIE FREMDENVERKEHR IN ÖSTERREICH IM JAHR...**
Österreichisches Statistisches Zentralamt

A—Deutsch annual

Statistics of tourists by country of origin and specifying the part of Austria they visited. Also provides details on accommodation available with the number of hotels and beds.

421 **GOF ORTSVERZEICHNIS VON ÖSTERREICH FÜR WIRTSCHAFT UND VERKEHR**
GOF-Verlag Gustav O Friedl

A—Deutsch c280p

GOF Gazetteer of Austria for industry and commerce. Classified, A-Z by places, with data on: province, police district, local authority, postal code number, transport services.

422 **HANDBUCH DER ÖSTERREICHISCHEN WISSENSCHAFT**
Österreichischer Bundesverlag für Unterricht, Wissenschaft und Kunst

A—Deutsch c800p

Handbook of Austrian science containing information on: government departments, university and research institutes, museums, libraries and archive collections.

423 **HANDBUCH DES ÖFFENTLICHEN LEBENS IN ÖSTERREICH**
Verlag Heinreich

A—Deutsch annual 740p

Handbook of public affairs in Austria covering: government and parliamentary offices; local authorities; provincial governments; trade unions; social insurance; banks; chambers of commerce; transport; churches; political parties; major industrial companies; the media.

424 **HANDBUCH ÖSTERREICHISCHER BIBLIOTHEKEN**
Österreichische Nationalbibliotheken

A—Deutsch c360p

Handbook of Austrian libraries, classified by type of library, then by provinces and towns A-Z. Each entry has details of: address, telephone number, date established, special collections, holdings and facilities. Separate indexes: libraries A-Z; subject; geographical.

425 **HANDELS-COMPASS ÖSTERREICH**
Compass-Verlag

A—Deutsch annual c2300p

Lists trading companies, broadly classified, with data on:
address; date established; directors; capital; products handled;
employees. Separate sections for banks, insurance companies,
chambers of commerce.

426 **HANDELSREGISTER ÖSTERREICH**
Jupiter Verlag

A—Deutsch 1976 348pp

Commercial register of Austria, with alphabetical arrangement
by companies. Details on: address; directors; activities; products.

427 **HEROLD ADRESSBUCH VON ÖSTERREICH FÜR
INDUSTRIE, HANDEL, GEWERBE**
Herold Vereinigte Anzeigenges. GmbH

A—Deutsch 1976 3 vols

Herold directory of Austria for industry, trade and business.
Vol. 1: Index of towns; A-Z registered businesses
with details of address, directors, registration number.
Classified list of exporters; A-Z foreign firms with Austrian
agents. Vol. 2: Steiermark, Kärnten, Oberösterreich, Salzburg,
Tirol, Vorarlberg: A-Z towns in each Land with basic data,
official information, plus classified directory.
Vol. 3: Wien, Niederösterreich, Burgenland; arrangement as
in Vol. 2.

428 **HEROLD EXPORT-ADRESSBUCH VON ÖSTERREICH**
Herold Vereinigte Anzeigenges.GmbH

A—Deutsch/English/Français c500p

Austrian export directory containing: A-Z names and addresses
of manufacturers and exporters; also classified section with
data on: addresses, telephone, telex, date established, directors,
products. Separate product index.

429 **HINTS TO BUSINESS MEN—AUSTRIA**
British Overseas Trade Board

A—English 1975 48pp

Practical guide for travelling executives covering: general
information; travel; hotels; restaurants and tipping; postal
and telephone facilities; economic factors; import and exchange
control regulations; methods of doing business; government and
commercial organisations; reading list; map.

430 **INDEX DER VERBRAUCHERPREISE**
Österreichisches Statistisches Zentralamt

A—Deutsch 1967

Describes the compilation and production of the Austrian
consumer price index published in the "Statistische
Nachrichten", the monthly statistical report.

431 **INDUSTRIAL POLICY OF AUSTRIA**
Organisation for Economic Co-operation and Development

A—English 1971 168pp

Detailed report on Austrian industrial policy which describes:
evolution of Austrian industry; industrial policy objectives;
nationalised industries; competition policy, quality control
and export promotion; research and development; manpower;
prices and wages; environmental protection.

432 **INDUSTRIE-COMPASS ÖSTERREICH**
Compass Verlag

A—Deutsch annual c3000p

Industrial companies broadly classified, with data on:
address, telephone and telex, date established, directors,
capital, products, employees. Also contains a separate
products classification and an A-Z index of companies.

433 **INDUSTRIESTATISTIK**
Bundesministerium für Handel, Gewerbe und Industrie

A—Deutsch twice a year

Statistics for each industry group covering number of
undertakings by the number of their employees; total
labour force; numbers of workers and salaried personnel;
total man-hours worked; value of gross production by
month.

434 **INVESTING IN AUSTRIA; FACTS AND FIGURES**
Girozentrale und Bank der Österreichischen Sparkassen AG

A—English 1974 50pp

Introductory study for potential business investors with
information on: internal and external economy; money
and finance; promoted financing; special credits and
guarantees; legal aspects of establishing and operating a
company in Austria.

435 **KOOPERATIVE FORSCHUNG IN ÖSTERREICH**
Vereinigung der Kooperative Forschungsinstitute der
gewerblichen Wirtschaft

A—Deutsch c150p

Co-operative research in Austria containing details of industrial
research institutes with a description of their activities.

436 **LÄNDERBANK: STATISTICAL DATA ON AUSTRIA**
Österreichische Länderbank

A—English 1975 24pp

Booklet of concise statistics including: geography; population;
tax rates; balance of payments; bank deposits; national product;
prices and wages; labour market; industrial production; mining;
iron and steel; electric power; coal, oil, and gas; tourism; foreign
trade; exports and imports.

437 **LAND- UND FORSTWIRTSCHAFTLICHE BETRIEBZAHLUNG**
Österreichisches Statistisches Zentralamt

A—Deutsch 1960 11 vols

Census of agriculture and forestry.
Teil A: Agriculture
Teil B: Forestry
Remaining 9 vols on the nine provinces of Austria.

438 **MARKETING IN AUSTRIA**
US Department of Commerce

A—English 1976 30pp

Overseas Business Report no. OBR 76-08. Contents: foreign
trade outlook; industry trends; transportation; distribution;
advertising and research; credit; trade regulations; investment
in Austria.

439   MITTEILUNGEN DES DIREKTORIUMS DER ÖSTERREICHISCHEN NATIONALBANK
Verband Österreichischer Banken und Bankiers

A—Deutsch/English monthly

Articles on the Austrian economy and a regular statistical series of economic indicators. English supplement on Austria's monetary situation.

440   MONATSBERICHTE DES ÖSTERREICHISCHEN INSTITUTS FÜR WIRTSCHAFTSFORSCHUNG
Österreichisches Institut für Wirtschaftsforschung

A/INT—Deutsch monthly

Economic journal with a statistical supplement: "Statistische Übersichten" in each issue. Contains statistics covering: banking; capital markets; prices and incomes; fuel and power; industrial production; labour; retail trade. Also includes a section on international statistics.

441   OECD ECONOMIC SURVEYS: AUSTRIA
Organisation for Economic Co-operation and Development

A—English 1976 54pp

Analyses the following recent developments and short-term prospects: a) 1975 downturn in retrospect: foreign trade; prices and incomes; labour and productivity; b) stabilisation of fiscal, monetary and selective policies; c) short-term prospects for gross fixed investment; consumer demand; imports and employment.

442   ÖSTERREICHISCHE NATIONALBANK; ANNUAL REPORT
Österreichische Nationalbank

A—English annual

Reviews the Austrian economy for the year and gives detailed information on: money and credit; capital market and insurance; public finance; production and markets; balance of payments; price indices.

443   ÖSTERREICHISCHE TEXTILINDUSTRIE
Fachverband der Textilindustrie Österreichs

A—Deutsch annual 860pp

Austrian textile industry, includes a statistical section with figures on: foreign trade; production by fibre and end use; number of employees; imports by fibre; exports by commodity and country.

444   ÖSTERREICHISCHER AMTSKALENDER
Druck und Verlag der Österreichischen Staatsdruckerei

A—Deutsch annual c1000p

Official yearbook of Austria, covering government departments, national services and public offices including the names of officers.

445   ÖSTERREICHS INDUSTRIE
Österreichisches Statistisches Zentralamt

A—Deutsch annual c130pp

Statistics on Austrian industry, including the quantity and value of industrial production. Also gives the number of establishments in each industry by province and size.

446   PARTICIPATION IN AUSTRIAN BUSINESS
Creditanstalt-Bankverein

A—English

Introductory guide for potential Austrian business investors, covering: regulations governing trade and industry; partnerships and companies; foreign exchange law; labour and tax law.

447   PERSONEN—COMPASS
Compass-Verlag

A—Deutsch annual c900p

Details of directors, executives, managers of the major Austrian companies A-Z.

448   PRODUCTION OF FRUIT AND VEGETABLES IN OECD MEMBER COUNTRIES: GERMANY, AUSTRIA
Organisation for Economic Co-operation and Development

A/D—Deutsch/English/Français 1969

Survey of the fruit and vegetable industry analysing the current situation and presenting future prospects.

449   PRODUKTION UND VERBRAUCH AUSGEWÄHLTER GROSSGEWERBLICHER BETRIEBE
Österreichisches Statistisches Zentralamt

A—Deutsch annual c80pp

Statistics on quantity, value and consumption of raw materials by selected major business undertakings.

450   QUARTERLY ECONOMIC REVIEW — AUSTRIA
Economist Intelligence Unit

A—English quarterly with annual supplements

Analysis of current economic trends including: government; population; employment; currency; national accounts; agriculture; industry; fuel and power; transport and communications; tourism; finance; foreign trade payments and agreements.

451   REPORT OF TRADE MISSION TO SWITZERLAND AND AUSTRIA, 19-27 JANUARY 1971
British Hosiery and Knitwear Export Group

A/CH—English 1971 10pp

Details on the market for knitted goods in Switzerland and Austria.

452   SELLING IN AUSTRIA
US Department of Commerce

A—English 1972 19pp

Overseas Business Report no. OBR 72-029.
Concise information for firms wishing to sell to Austria, covering: commercial practices; import regulations and media information.

453   STATISTICAL DATA ON AUSTRIA
Österreichische Länderbank

A—English annual

Brief statistical tables and notes on the Austrian economy.

**454   STATISTISCHES HANDBUCH FÜR DIE REPUBLIK
ÖSTERREICH**
Österreichisches Statistisches Zentralamt

A—Deutsch annual

Annual statistical handbook of Austria, including data on:
population; geography and climate; agriculture; industrial
production; internal and foreign trade; tourism; transport;
wages; prices; employment; public finance; education; health;
arts; sport.

455   STATISTISCHE NACHRICHTEN
Österreichisches Statistisches Zentralamt

A—Deutsch monthly

Statistical news, containing reports on the current work of
the central statistical office and 44 pages of statistical data
on national product; finance; budget; prices and wages;
agriculture; industry; building; social security; tourism;
transport; external trade.

**456   STATISTISCHES JAHRBUCH ÖSTERREICHISCHER
STÄDTE**
Österreichisches Statistisches Zentralamt

A—Deutsch annual c70pp

Compiled jointly with Österreichischer Städtebund. Gives
local statistics for towns and parishes with populations over
10,000 and less detailed statistics for those with a
population over 5,000.

**457   STATISTIK DER AKTIENGESELLSCHAFTEN IN
ÖSTERREICH**
Österreichisches Statistisches Zentralamt

A—Deutsch annual

Statistics on Austrian companies including an abbreviated
balance sheet and profit and loss accounts for industry
groups.

458   STATISTIK DES AUSSENHANDELS ÖSTERREICHS
Österreichisches Statistisches Zentralamt

A—Deutsch

Statistics on Austrian imports and exports, classified by
country and commodity. Four series: 1A: Commodity by
country (quarterly); 1B: Country by commodity (half-yearly);
Commodities by SITC (half-yearly); Transit trade (half-
yearly).

**459   DER VERBRAUCH DER STÄDTISCHEN UND
BAUERLICHEN BEVÖLKERUNG ÖSTERREICHS:
ERGEBNISSE DER KONSUMERHEBUNG 1964**
Österreichisches Statistiches Zentralamt

A—Deutsch 1966

Consumption statistics of the urban and rural population of
Austria taken from a consumer survey in 1964.

**460   VERSUCHS- UND FORSCHUNGSANSTALTEN IN
ÖSTERREICH**
Wirtschaftsförderungsinstitute der Bundeshandelskammer

A—Deutsch c150p

Experimental and research establishments in Austria. Lists
government, university and other research establishments
with details of: address, research staff and subject of
research. Separate indexes: organizations A-Z; subject;
persons.

461   VIENNA — FINANCIAL TIMES SURVEY
The Financial Times

A—English 25 June 1976 p.29-32

Survey in the Financial Times newspaper which reports on
how Vienna is consolidating its position as an international
centre.

462   VOLKSZAHLUNGSERGEBNISSE 1961
Österreichisches Statistisches Zentralamt

A—Deutsch 1962-66

Census in 17 volumes: Vol. 1: Preliminary results. Vols 2-10:
Detailed results for eight provinces of Austria and Vienna.
Vol. 11: Austria. Vol. 12: Households. Vol. 13: Breakdown of
resident population according to demographic and cultural
characteristics. Vol. 14: Working population by occupation.
Vol. 15: Working population by economic classification.
Vol. 16: Employed persons by municipalities in which they
live and work. Vol. 17: Resident population by sources of
income and economic activity.

463   WHO'S WHO IN AUSTRIA
Intercontinental Book and Publishing Co.

A—English c900p

A-Z biographies of prominent Austrian people.

**464   WIENER BÖRSE KAMMER: BERICHT ÜBER DAS
GESCHÄFTSJAHR 1975**
Wiener Börse Kammer

A—Deutsch annual

Report and review of the Vienna Stock Exchange. Includes
detailed graphs of share index, prices and interest yields.

465   WIRTSCHAFTSSTATISTISCHES HANDBUCH
Kammer für Arbeiter und Angestellte in Wien

A—Deutsch annual c470pp

Handbook of economic statistics, including: population;
social affairs; labour market; finance; prices; wages; cost of
living; land and forestry; mining and industry; trade;
transport and tourism.

466   DIE WOHNBAUTÄTIGKEIT
Österreichisches Statistisches Zentralamt

A—Deutsch annual

Statistics on the construction of dwellings, but excluding
industrial or office buildings.

B-BELGIUM

500   ADVERTISING CONDITIONS IN BELGIUM
Institute of Practitioners in Advertising

B—English

Concise guide to the daily newspaper and periodical press
in Belgium.

**501   ANNUAIRE ADMINISTRATIF ET JUDICIAIRE DE
BELGIQUE ET DE LA CAPITALE DU ROYAUME**
Ets Emile Bruylant

B—Français/Nederlands annual c2300pp

Administrative and legal directory of Belgium, with data on:
central and local government departments; judiciary;
religious bodies; universities; national education; learned
societies. Also contains Brussels street directory.

**502   ANNUAIRE DU COMMERCE ET DE L'INDUSTRIE DE
BELGIQUE**
Edition Mertens and Rozez

B—Français(English index) annual

Directory of the commerce and industry of Belgium
including details of: government departments; societies and
institutions. Also includes classified, A-Z street directory
of Brussels.

**503   ANNUAIRE GENERAL DE LA BELGIQUE ET DU
MARCHE COMMUN**
Annuaire Général de la Belgique

B—Français(English index) annual c800pp

General directory of Belgium and the Common Market.
Classified listing of manufacturers and trade associations.

**504   ANNUAIRE LASSALLE DU COMMERCE ET DE
L'INDUSTRIE DE LA PROVINCE DE LIEGE**
Lasalle et Cie

B—Français annual

Lassalle's directory of the trade and industry of the province
of Liège. A-Z classified firms.

505   ANNUAIRE STATISTIQUE
**Fédération Professionnelle des Producteurs et Distributeurs
d'Electricité de Belgique**

B—Français annual

Statistical yearbook including data on: equipment;
production of electricity; sales of electricity to neighbouring
countries; consumption.

506   ANNUAIRE STATISTIQUE DE LA BELGIQUE
Institut National de Statistique

B—Français/Vlaams annual c700pp

Annual abstract of general statistics covering aspects of
economic and social life including: populations, climate and
geography; building and housing; legal system; industrial
production; agriculture and fishing; imports and exports;
communications; tourism; employment; wages; prices.

507   ANNUAIRE STATISTIQUE DE L'INDUSTRIE DU GAZ
Fédération de l'Industrie du Gaz

B/INT—Français/Nederlands annual

Statistical yearbook of the gas industry, including data on:
equipment and investments; sales; employment. Data covers
Belgium and also Western Europe.

508   ANNUAIRE STATISTIQUE DE POCHE
Institut National de Statistique

B—Français annual c230pp

Abridged pocket edition of "Annuaire Statistique de la
Belgique", the annual abstract of statistics.

509   APERÇU DE L'EVOLUTION ECONOMIQUE
Ministère des Affaires Economiques

B/INT—Français monthly

An account of economic development. Review of the
economic situation abroad and in Belgium, with annual,
quarterly and monthly statistics which include: employment;
industrial production; prices and wages; investment;
internal trade; foreign trade; public finance; money and
credit.

**510   ASSOCIATION BELGE DES NEGOCIANTS
         EXPORTATEURS ET IMPORTATEURS
         ABNEI**

B—Français/Nederlands(English index)

Belgian export and import merchants association directory.
A-Z members, including address, goods handled. Separate
classified index.

**511   BANQUE NATIONALE DE BELGIQUE - ANNUAL
         REPORT**
         Banque Nationale de Belgique

B/INT—Français/English/Nederlands annual

Reviews international economic and financial trends with
comparative data for other European communities. Detailed
survey of the Belgian economy including: banking and
financial statistics; manufacturing industries; building;
energy; agriculture and fishing; employment; wages; prices;
transactions of the B.L.E.U. with foreign countries.

512   BARCLAYS COUNTRY REPORTS - BELGIUM
         Barclays Bank

B—English 1976 2pp

Brief economic summary covering: payments; prices and
wages; external position; economic outlook.

513   THE BELGIAN CHEMICAL INDUSTRY
         Kredietbank

B—English

General survey of the chemical industry with statistics on:
employees; production; foreign trade. Figures cover both
organic and inorganic chemical products.

**514   BELGIAN INDUSTRY, PRODUCTION AND
         PROFESSIONAL ORGANISATIONS**
         Fédération des Industries Belges

B—English

Directory of leading trade associations.

515   BELGIAN PROPERTY
         The Financial Times

B—English 6 Dec. 1976 p.16-19

Survey in the Financial Times newspaper covering: escalating
costs of office developments; out of town shopping; private
house sales; industrial property.

516   BELGIAN TEXTILE INDUSTRY
         Kredietbank

B—English 1966-67

Part 1: Cotton, wool, flax, jute. Reports on size, capacity,
production and trade for all sections of these industries.
Part 2: Artificial fibres and sundries; carpet weaving;
furnishing and upholstery fabrics; blankets; knitwear; sundry
textile articles and finishing sector. Indicates structure,
production, trade and trends.

517   BELGIUM - ECONOMIC AND TECHNICAL
         Office Belge du Commerce Extérieur

B—Français/Nederlands/English/Español/Deutsch

Bulletin for the foreign press giving economic and technical
information.

518   BELGIUM - FINANCIAL TIMES SURVEY
         The Financial Times

B—English 20 July 1976 p.21-24

Survey in the Financial Times newspaper which discusses
how Belgium is trying to become a Federal State by
introducing some form of federal constitution.

519   BELGIUM, LAND OF INVESTMENT
         Banque de Bruxelles

B—English 1972 86pp

Background information for the prospective investor in
Belgium, covering: investment incentives; financing a business
in Belgium; mergers and acquisitions; industrial and
commercial law; exchange control regulations; taxation.

520   BELGIUM NEWS
         Ministère des Affaires Etrangères et du Commerce Extérieur

B—English

Series of booklets on various economic subjects.

521   BELGIUM - SPECIAL REPORT
         The Times

B—English 30 March 1976 p.11-13

Survey in the Times newspaper covering: economic revival;
banking; property; tourism; the port of Antwerp.

**522   BOURSE INDUSTRIELLE DE BELGIQUE: LISTE DES
         INDUSTRIELS PRODUCTEURS AYANT DES
         REPRESENTANTS ET AGENTS FREQUENTANT LES
         REUNIONS DE MERCREDI**
         Bourse Industrielle de Belgique

B—Français c450pp

Industrial exchange of Belgium: list of manufacturers with
representatives or agents. Separate indexes of: firms A-Z;
executives; products.

**523   BRITAIN IN THE COMMON MARKET:
         OPPORTUNITIES FOR BELGIUM**
         Banque de Bruxelles

B/INT—English/Français/Nederlands

Identifies potential new openings in the UK for Belgian
producers. Information and statistics on: external trade of
B.L.E.U. with the EEC and UK; sector analysis of trade
between the B.L.E.U. and the UK and breakdown of
manufactured goods by material - rubber, wood, paper,
yarn, iron and steel.

**524   BRITISH CHAMBER OF COMMERCE FOR BELGIUM
         AND LUXEMBOURG: YEAR BOOK**
         British Chamber of Commerce

B/L—English annual c200pp

Includes members A-Z, with details of: address, products and activities, agencies held. Separate classified index and list of trade associations.

525   BRUSSELS STOCK EXCHANGE
The Bourse

B—Français/English/Nederlands   1975   19pp

A survey of the current position of the Brussels Bourse, its organisation and methods and future development. Gives statistics on the market value of Belgian companies and details of the 25 most active companies in 1974.

526   BRUSSELS STOCK EXCHANGE IN A NUTSHELL
Stock Exchange Press Committee

B—English 1975

Small brochure with diagrammatic descriptions of the laying out of the markets, procedure for treating stock exchange orders and characteristics of different markets.

527   BULLETIN DE CONJONCTURE
Banque de Bruxelles

B/INT—Français monthly

Financial situation in Belgium and more briefly in seven other countries.

528   BULLETIN DE LA FIB
Fédération des Industries Belges

B—Français quarterly

Information on all matters affecting employers, including: taxation; labour legislation; social insurance; commercial law; transport; case law; tenders and exhibitions. The FIB also publishes occasional booklets on these topics.

529   BULLETIN DE LA SOCIETE GENERALE DE BANQUE
Société Générale de Banque

B/INT—Français monthly

Stock market reports from Brussels and the chief foreign exchanges. Includes articles on various financial and economic issues affecting Belgium and the international economy.

530   BULLETIN DE STATISTIQUE
Institut National de Statistique

B—Français monthly

Monthly digest of general statistics, including data on: transport; finance; employment; prices; imports and exports; agriculture and fishing; population; industrial production.

531   BULLETIN DES CONTRIBUTIONS
Administration Centrale des Contributions

B—Français monthly

Official journal giving new regulations, tax tables, Ministry circulars and Parliamentary answers.

532   BULLETIN D'INFORMATION ET DE DOCUMENTATION DE LA BANQUE NATIONALE DE BELGIQUE
Banque Nationale de Belgique

B—Français monthly

Financial statistics; economic bibliography; brief notes of recent legislation; articles and studies on economic and financial matters.

533   BULLETIN DU MINISTERE DES AFFAIRES ECONOMIQUES: ADMINISTRATION DES MINES
Ministère des Affaires Economiques, Administration des Mines

B—Français monthly

Monthly economic bulletin including statistics on: mines; quarries; fuel; steel and non-ferrous metals.

534   BULLETIN MENSUEL
Office National de l'Emploi

B—Français monthly

Monthly journal giving statistics and information on aspects of employment.

535   BULLETIN MENSUEL DU COMMERCE EXTERIEUR DE L'UNION ECONOMIQUE BELGO-LUXEMBOURG
Institut National de Statistique

B/L—Français/Vlaams monthly

Monthly bulletin of the foreign trade of the B.L.E.U. Includes: imports and exports arranged by commodity classification, subdivided by countries of origins and destination. Other tables give total imports and exports by broad commodity groups, by countries of origin and destination and transit trade.

536   BUSINESS ECONOMICS LIBRARY
Kredietbank

B—English

Occasional surveys of specific industries.

537   CAHIERS ECONOMIQUES DE BRUXELLES
Département d'Economie Appliquée de l'Université Libre de Bruxelles

B—Français quarterly

Quarterly bulletin and occasional papers on economic matters.

538   CHAMBRE DE COMMERCE DE BRUXELLES: ANNUAIRE OFFICIEL
Chambre de Commerce de Bruxelles

B—Français/Nederlands annual

Official directory of the Brussels chamber of commerce, listing members, individual and firms, A-Z; also lists members of affiliated groups. Separate classified index.

539   CHAMBRE D'INDUSTRIE D'ANVERS: ANNUAIRE
Chambre d'Industrie d'Anvers

B—Français/Nederlands annual

Yearbook of the Antwerp chamber of industry with details of: members A-Z plus address and business; members of specialist associations affiliated to the Chamber. Separate classified index.

540   COMMERCE 1900-61
Institut National de Statistique

B—Français

Economic survey of commerce, including, tourism, transport and communications.

541   LE COMMERCE EXTERIEUR DE L'UNION BELGO—
LUXEMBOURG
Office Belge du Commerce Extérieur

B/INT—Français annual

Analysis of foreign trade and detailed trade statistics with each major region of the world.

542   COMMON MARKET REPORTS - ISSUE 106 PART II
Commerce Clearing House Inc.

B—English

The Belgian value added tax code.

543   COMMUNIQUE HEBDOMADAIRE
Institut National de Statistique

B—Français/Nederlands weekly

Weekly report and digest of statistics on: industry; commerce; transport; finance and agriculture. Updates many of the tables in "Bulletin de Statistique" and is supplied free to existing subscribers.

544   LES COMPTES NATIONAUX DE LA BELGIQUE
Institut National de Statistique

B—Français 1975 69pp

National accounts of Belgium giving details on national production and national accounts. Based on 1966-73 statistics.

545   DEVELOPMENTS OF THE FLEMISH ECONOMY IN THE
INTERNATIONAL PERSPECTIVE
European Communities

B—English/Nederlands 1973 83pp

Summary of a detailed survey, completed in 1972, of the socio-economic development of the Flemish region and the options of policy.

546   LA DISTRIBUTION EN 1980
Office Belge pour l'Accroissement de la Productivité

B—Français/English/Nederlands

Review examining factors that will affect distribution and changes in consumption patterns.

547   ECONOMIC REPORT — BELGIUM AND LUXEMBOURG
Lloyds Bank Ltd.

B/L—English 1975 31pp

Current economic and financial survey on United Kingdom and foreign trade with the Belgo-Luxembourg Economic Union (B.L.E.U.). Information on: marketing; import regulations; purchasing power; recent economic trends; advice on establishing a business in Belgium or Luxembourg.

548   L'ECONOMIE BELGE
Ministère des Affaires Economiques

B—Français annual

Annual economic survey and statistics.

549   L'ECONOMIE BELGE ET INTERNATIONALE
TABLEAUX SYNOPTIQUES 1913-68
Université Libre de Bruxelles

B/INT—Français 1969

Belgian and international economy. Part 1: Survey of the Belgian economy, transport and industry. Part 2: Similar economic information for the principal countries around the world.

550   ESTIMATION DE LA PRODUCTION AGRICOLE
Institut National de Statistique

B—Français annual

Annual agricultural production statistics.

551   ETUDES D'ACTIONS
Société Générale de Banque

B—Français

Informative occasional papers on individual quoted companies.

552   ETUDES DU MARCHE AUTOMOBILES ET
MOTORCYCLES
Chambre Syndicale du Commerce Automobile de Belgique

B—Français annual

Annual study of the car and motorcycle markets.

553   FEDERATION DES INDUSTRIES CHIMIQUES DE
BELGIQUE
Fédération des Industries Chimiques de Belgique

B—Français annual

Annual report on the Belgian chemical industry containing reviews and statistics on: employment; research and development; imports and exports.

554   FEDERATION NATIONALE DES CHAMBRES DE
COMMERCE ET D'INDUSTRIE DE BELGIQUE:
ANNUAIRE
Fédération Nationale des Chambres de Commerce

B—Français/Nederlands annual c200pp

Yearbook of the National Federation of Belgian chambers of commerce and industry. Lists chambers affiliated to the Federation with details of: date established; address; officers and members.

555   THE 500 LARGEST COMPANIES IN BELGIUM
Etudes Financières et Economiques

B—English/Français/Nederlands 1975 102pp

Lists the top 500 companies with data on: ranking by sales;
capital; assets; invested capital; invested capital as a
percentage of assets; profit; sales per employee; exports.
Also contains special surveys on current and potential
economic trends.

**556   FOREIGN TRADE REGULATIONS OF BELGIUM-
LUXEMBOURG**
US Department of Commerce

B/L—English 1973 14pp

Overseas Business Report no. OBR 73-26.
Contents: trade policy; import tariff system; special customs
provisions; internal taxes; shipping documentation; non-tariff
and import controls; Belgium-Luxembourg export controls.

557   GUIDE DES MINISTERES
Revue de l'Administration Belge

B—Français/Nederlands annual c1140pp

Directory of ministries, arranged by ministries and giving
officers, departments and definitions of functions;
international organisations; provincial and city governments;
communes A-Z.

**558   HINTS TO BUSINESSMEN — BELGIUM AND
LUXEMBOURG**
British Overseas Trade Board

B/L—English 1976 72pp

Practical guide for travelling executives, covering: general
information; travel; hotels; restaurants and tipping; postal
and telephone facilities; economic factors; import and
exchange control regulations; methods of doing business;
government and commercial organisations; reading list; map.

559   INDICATEUR PUBLICITAIRE
Union Belge des Annonceurs

B—Français

Complete guide to the daily and periodical press and other
media in Belgium.

560   INDUSTRIE
Fédération des Industries Belges

B—Français monthly

General information on industrial topics.

**561   L'INDUSTRIE DU VETEMENT: L'INDUSTRIE DE
CONFECTION ET DU CUIR**
Kredietbank

B—Français

Statistics of the ready-to-wear clothing and leather industries.

562   INDUSTRIE: LA REVUE DE L'INDUSTRIE BELGE
Fédération des Industries Belges

B—Français monthly

Articles on economic, financial, technical and social aspects
of Belgian industry. Commercial and economic reports on
foreign countries. Production indices and statistics for major
industries. General economic statistics for Belgium.

**563   INFORMATION BULLETIN OF THE SOCIETE
GENERALE DE BELGIQUE**
Société Générale de Belgique

B—Français/English/Nederlands monthly

News of financial and industrial developments in various
companies.

**564   INVENTAIRE DES CENTRES BELGES DE RECHERCHE
DISPOSANT D'UNE BIBLIOTHEQUE OU D'UN SERVICE
DE DOCUMENTATION**
Centre National de Documentation Scientifique et
Technique

B—Français/Nederlands   2039750

Directory of Belgian research libraries and documentation
services, listing organisations A-Z under towns A-Z.
Includes details of: address, director or librarian, subject
specialisation, description of library. 3 separate indexes;
organisations A-Z; subjects; persons.

565   INVESTISSEMENTS ETRANGERS EN BELGIQUE
Ministère des Affaires Economiques

B—Français annual

Data on foreign investments in Belgian companies by area
and activity.

566   JOURNAL OF THE BELGIAN CHAMBER OF COMMERCE
Belgian Chamber of Commerce

B—English quarterly

Concentrates on trade enquiries and commercial information.

**567   KOMPASS: REPERTOIRE DE L'ECONOMIE DE LA
BELGIQUE ET DU LUXEMBOURG**
Kompass Belgium NV

B—Deutsch/English/Español/Français/Nederlands annual
c2400pp

Register of industry and commerce in Belgium and
Luxembourg, listing companies geographically under towns,
with details of: company address, products, directors, capital
employed, employees. Separate product charts and indexes
for companies A-Z and products.

568   LES LIGNES DE FORCE DU PLAN 1971-75
Ministère des Affaires Economiques

B—Français

Outline of the third economic expansion plan.

**569   LISTE DES SOCIETES SAVANTES ET LITTERAIRES
DE BELGIQUE**
Service Belge des Echanges Internationaux

B—Français/Nederlands c150pp

List of Belgian learned and literary societies, classified
geographically with details of: address, officers, date
established, scope, publications. Also separate A-Z
organisations index.

570   LOCALISATION DES INDUSTRIES
Office National de l'Emploi

B—Français

Atlas of 37 maps showing the location of industries in each
region and commune; also the geographic distribution of the
labour force in industry.

571   MANUEL DE LA TVA
Institut Belge d'Information et de Documentation

B—Français

Guide to value added tax.

572   MARKETING IN BELGIUM/LUXEMBOURG
US Department of Commerce

B/L—English 1976 35pp

Overseas Business Report no. OBR 76-32
Contents: market analysis for selected products; industry
trends; distribution and sales channels; government
procurement; transportation and ports; credit; import-export
regulations; investment in Belgium; employment; taxation.

573   MEDIA INFORMATION — BELGIUM
J. Walter Thompson Co. Ltd.

B—English

Media information on Belgium.

574   MEMO FROM BELGIUM
Ministère des Affaires Etrangères et du Commerce Extérieur

B—English

Series of booklets on various economic subjects.

575   NEWS LETTER
Belgian Chamber of Commerce

B—English

Information on trade and commerce.

576   NOTES MENSUELLES SUR LA SITUATION
ECONOMIQUE
Conseil Central de l'Economie

B/INT—Français monthly

Monthly review of the economic situation in Belgium and
other western countries.

577   OECD ECONOMIC SURVEYS — BELGIUM/LUXEMBOURG
Organisation for Economic Co-operation and Development

B/L—English/Français annual

Individual analyses of the Belgian and Luxembourg
economies, covering recent developments in demand, output,
employment, prices and incomes and the broad lines of
economic policies affecting fiscal, employment, industrial
restructuring and prices and incomes.

578   LA POLITIQUE ENERGETIQUE EN 1967-75
Direction Générale des Etudes et de la Documentation

B—Français/Vlaams

Discusses energy policy covering coal, natural gas, oil and
nuclear power.

579   LE PROBLEME DE L'ENERGIE EN BELGIQUE
Ministère des Affaires Economiques

B—Français/Vlaams 1957

Energy plans for 1955-75

580   PRODUCTION MENSUELLE NETTE D'ENERGIE
Administration de l'Energie

B—Français/Vlaams monthly

Monthly survey of electricity production statistics.

581   QUARTERLY ECONOMIC REVIEW — BELGIUM,
LUXEMBOURG
Economist Intelligence Unit

B/L—English quarterly with annual supplement

Analysis of current economic trends including: government;
population; employment; exchange rates; national accounts;
agriculture; mining; fuel and power; manufacturing
industries; transport and communications; finance.

582   RAPPORT ANNUEL
L'Association Nationale des Tisseurs de Lin

B—Français/Vlaams annual

Annual report for the linen industry, including statistics and
data on: production; stocks; internal and foreign trade.

583   RAPPORT ANNUEL DE LA FEDERATION DES
INDUSTRIES BELGES
Fédération des Industries Belges

B—Français

Annual report and detailed survey of Belgian industry.

584   RAPPORT SUR L'EXECUTION DE LA LOI DU 25 JUIN
1930 RELATIVE AU CONTROLE DES ENTREPRISES
D'ASSURANCE SUR LA VIE PENDANT L'ANNEE 1968
Ministère des Affaires Economiques

B—Français 1973

Report on the execution of the law relating to the control of
life insurance companies. Data on a number of enterprises,
profits, developments, financial accounts.

585   RECENSEMENT AGRICOLE ET HORTICOLE
Institut National de Statistique

B—Français annual

The results of the annual census of cultivated land, animals, crops, labour, for all Belgium, its provinces and regions.

586 RECENSEMENT ANNUEL DES CHOMEURS COMPLETS
Office National de l'Emploi

B—Français annual

Detailed annual statistics of the unemployed. Data on the wholly unemployed by: district; profession; education; length of unemployment.

587 RECENSEMENT DE L'INDUSTRIE ET DU COMMERCE AU 31 DECEMBRE 1961
Institut National de Statistique

B—Français 4 vols

Census of industry and commerce. Vol. 1: General results. Vol. 2: Detailed tables. Vol. 3: (2 parts). Principal tables by areas. Vol. 4: Tables by enterprise.

588 RECENSEMENT DES EMBLAVURES D'HIVER ET DU BETAIL
Institut National de Statistique

B—Français annual

Annual census of winter corn and cattle.

589 RECHERCHES ECONOMIQUES DE LOUVAIN
Centre de Recherches Economiques

B/INT—Français

Occasional papers on economic subjects covering the Belgian and international markets.

590 LE RECUEIL FINANCIER: ANNUAIRE DES VALEURS COTEES AUX BOURSES DE BELGIQUE
Ets Emile Bruylant

B—Français annual 4 vols c4000pp

The financial compendium: directory of securities quoted on the stock exchanges of Belgium. Lists principal Belgian companies with details on: address, date established, directors, extensive extracts from annual reports and financial statistics. Each volume contains an A-Z companies index and separate executives index.

591 RECUEIL OFFICIEL DES MARQUES DE FABRIQUE ET DE COMMERCE
Ministère des Affaires Economiques

B—Français/Nederlands monthly

Official register of trade marks and names in order of registration date; includes details of: manufacturer's name, address, class of goods.

592 REPERTOIRE HALLET D'EXPORTATION
Hallet Sprl

B—Deutsch/English/Español/Français/Nederlands

Hallet export directory in 14 parts, issued on a monthly renewal basis; Part 1: A-Z manufacturers including data on: address; date established; capital; number of employees; directors; branch details; trade names; Part 2: A-Z product index; Part 3-14; classified directories of principal industrial sectors.

593 REVUE DE LA TVA
Central Administration of the TVA

B—Français 5 issues a year

Official journal giving new regulations, Ministry circulars and rulings on value added tax.

594 REVUE DU TRAVAIL
Ministère de l'Emploi et du Travail

B—Français monthly

Official journal dealing with labour and employment.

595 STATISTICAL MARKETING GUIDE FOR BELGIUM
Netherlands Chamber of Commerce for Belgium and Luxembourg

B—Nederlands/Français/English 1971 157pp

Detailed statistics on: communication and transport; population; income and expenditure; energy; social services; industry; production; construction; retail and wholesale trade; finance; publicity; imports and exports.

596 STATISTIQUE ANNUELLE DU TRAFFIC INTERNATIONAL DES PORTS
Institut National de Statistique

B—Français/Vlaams annual 2 vols

Annual statistics of international traffic of the Belgian ports. Part 1: Antwerp. Part 2: Other Belgian ports.

597 STATISTIQUE DE LA NAVIGATION INTERIEURE
Institut National de Statistique

B—Français 1972

Statistics of internal shipping. Data is now included in "Bulletin de Statistique" and "Statistiques des Transports", but also issued as a separate extract.

598 STATISTIQUE DE LA NAVIGATION MARITIME
Ministère des Affaires Economiques

B—Français annual

Annual statistics of shipping by port used, by tonnage and by destination.

599 STATISTIQUE DE L'ELECTRICITE
Administration de l'Energie

B/INT—Français/Vlaams annual 2 vols

Electricity statistics — two volumes giving data on: electricity production; distribution; consumption and investment — covering Belgium and other countries.

600 STATISTIQUE ELECTRICITE
Administration de l'Energie

B—Français/Nederlands 1974 11pp

Electricity statistics, with data on the electric power stations
throughout Belgium at 1st January 1974.

**601 STATISTIQUE MENSUELLE DES VEHICULES NEUFS
IMMATRICULES EN BELGIQUE**
Fédération Belge des Industries de l'Automobile et du Cycle

B—Français monthly

Monthly statistics of new vehicles registered in Belgium.
Data on countries of manufacture and make of cars, coaches,
goods vehicles and tractors.

**602 STATISTIQUE MENSUELLE DU TRAFFIC
INTERNATIONAL DES PORTS**
Institut National de Statistique

B—Français monthly

Monthly statistics of international port traffic. 2 vols each
month: Vol. 1: Antwerp. Vol. 2: All other Belgian ports.
Data includes statistics of goods traffic by sea, river, canal
and rail.

**603 STATISTIQUE TRIMESTRIELLE DE LA NAVIGATION
MARITIME**
Institut National de Statistique

B—Français quarterly

Quarterly statistics of shipping, containing data on: sea-
going ships entering Belgian ports by nationality or flag;
tonnage; countries of origin and destination.

604 STATISTIQUES AGRICOLES
Institut National de Statistique

B—Français monthly

Agricultural statistics, including monthly and quarterly
figures on: climate; state of agriculture; milk industry; sea
fishing; abattoirs; price indices.

605 STATISTIQUES ANNUELLES DE LA PRODUCTION
Institut National de Statistique

B—Français annual

Annual statistics on production, includes data on: coal; coke;
oils; tobacco; textiles; clothing; wood and wood products;
rubber; cement; non-ferrous metals; electricity and gas; food;
beverages; dairying; leather and leather goods; paper;
petroleum refineries; pottery and earthenware; metal goods.

**606 STATISTIQUES DE LA CONSTRUCTION ET DU
LOGEMENT**
Institut National de Statistique

B—Français

Statistics of construction and housing, with data on: licences
to build; buildings commenced, under construction,
demolished; employment and wages; production and prices.
Issues are published irregularly, one or two a year.

607 STATISTIQUES DEMOGRAPHIQUES
Institut National de Statistique

B—Français

Population statistics.

608 STATISTIQUES DES BATIMENTS ET DES LOGEMENTS
Institut National de Statistique

B—Français annual

Annual statistics on building and accommodation and
general survey of construction statistics.

**609 STATISTIQUES DES VEHICULES A MOTEUR EN
CIRCULATION**
Institut National de Statistique

B—Français 1973 69pp

Statistics on registered motor vehicles, based on figures
available in 1972.

610 STATISTIQUES DU COMMERCE
Institut National de Statistique

B/INT—Français monthly

Statistics of trade, giving data on: retail trade; wholesale
trade; tourism; also foreign trade of B.L.E.U. arranged by
commodities.

611 STATISTIQUES DU TRANSPORT
Institut National de Statistique

B—Français monthly

Transport statistics, including data on: the activity at ports;
inland waterways; railway transport; air transport; motor
vehicles; road accidents; mode of transport or freight.

612 STATISTIQUES FINANCIERES
Institut National de Statistique

B—Français/Nederlands

Financial statistics, which are issued irregularly, about 2-3
times a year. Each issue deals with a specific financial topic.

**613 STATISTIQUES...HOUILLE-COKES-AGGLOMERES-
METALLURGIE-CARRIERES**
Ministère des Affaires Economique, Administration des Mines

B/INT—Français/Nederlands annual

Annual statistics on: coal; coke; aggregates; metals;
quarries. Also data on the sale of solid fuels; quarries; EEC
statistics.

614 STATISTIQUES INDUSTRIELLES
Institut National de Statistique

B—Français monthly

Industrial statistics - monthly indices of production statistics
of major industries, annual statistics and statistical surveys of
different industries, including: coal; food; tobacco; textiles;
hosiery; wood; paper; leather; chemicals; petroleum;
electricity and water.

615 STATISTIQUES INDUSTRIELLES 1900-61
Institut National de Statistique

B—Français

Historical statistics covering a wide range of industries.

616 STATISTIQUES SOCIALES
Institut National de Statistique

B—Français

Social statistics, including: employment; earnings; hours of work; strikes; industrial accidents.

617 WEEKLY BULLETIN OF THE KREDIETBANK
Kredietbank

B—Français/English/Nederlands weekly

Articles on specific industries and financial and economic case studies. Includes data on: gold; foreign exchange; commodity and stock markets.

618 WHERE TO BUY IN BELGIUM
Belgian Chamber of Commerce

B—English annual c120pp

Directory of member firms of the Belgian Chamber of Commerce. Classified listing with address and product details. Also lists UK agents for Belgian manufacturers.

619 WHO'S WHO IN BELGIUM AND GRAND DUCHY OF LUXEMBOURG
Intercontinental Book and Publishing Co. Ltd.

B/L—English c1350pp

A-Z biographies of prominent people in Belgium and Luxembourg.

620 ZEEBRUGGE - FAST EXPANDING PORT COMPLEX
The Financial Times

B—English 3 March 1976 p.20-21

Special study in the Financial Times newspaper which examines the growing importance of Zeebrugge for the shipment of container goods and petroleum products.

621 ZONINGS INDUSTRIELS EXISTANTS EN BELGIQUE
Office National de l'Emploi

B—Français

Maps of existing and planned industrial estates with lists of all firms established, nature of their business and numbers employed.

CH-SWITZERLAND

650 ADRESSBUCH DER SCHWEIZ FÜR INDUSTRIE, GEWERBE, HANDEL UND EXPORT
Mosse-Annoncen AG

CH–Deutsch annual 2 vols c3250pp

Directory of Switzerland for industry, business, commerce, and export. Vol. 1: A-Z registered businesses, with details of address, date established, business, capital, principals. Vol. 2: Businesses classified under towns A-Z, cantons A-Z. Separate indexes for: products and services; government and public offices, trade associations. Street maps and indexes.

651 ANNUAIRE STATISTIQUE DE LA SUISSE
Bureau Fédéral de Statistique

CH–Français/Deutsch annual c700pp

Statistical yearbook of Switzerland, including: population; geography and climate; agriculture and forestry; industrial production; internal and foreign trade; tourism; transport; money and credit; insurance; price indices; employment; company information; public finance; education; health; arts; sport; justice; elections; international statistics.

652 ARCHIVE, BIBLIOTHEKEN UND DOKUMENTATIONSSTELLEN DER SCHWEIZ
Schweiz. Vereiniging für Dokumentation

CH–Deutsch/Français/Italiano c150pp

Archives, libraries and documentation centres in Switzerland. A-Z libraries under towns A-Z. Details given on each library: address; date established, stock, subject specialisations. Separate indexes: A-Z libraries; subjects; persons.

653 THE BANKS IN A TIME OF CHALLENGE
Union de Banques Suisses

CH/INT–English 1975 19pp

Shareholders address delivered by the Chairman of the Board of the Union Bank of Switzerland, reviewing Swiss economic growth and bank expansion; Switzerland as an international centre of finance, compared to other financial centres; foreign exchange; short-term foreign investments.

654 BANQUE NATIONALE SUISSE - ANNUAL REPORT
Banque Nationale Suisse

CH–Français annual

Annual review on the organisation and activities of the Swiss National Bank, including information on: international economy; Swiss economy; financial statistics on credit, capital taxation, interest rates.

655 BASIC DATA ON THE ECONOMY OF SWITZERLAND
US Department of Commerce

CH–English 1969 14pp

Overseas Business Report no. OBR 69-3.
Contents: general information; structure of the economy; labour; finance; foreign trade.

656 THE BASLE STOCK EXCHANGE
Bourse de Bâle

CH–English/Deutsch/Français 1973 8pp

Fact sheet on the Basle Stock Exchange.

657 BERICHT ÜBER HANDEL UND INDUSTRIE DER SCHWEIZ
Schweizerischer Handels- und Industrie-Verein

CH–Deutsch/Français 1973 187pp

Report on the trade and industry of Switzerland, including: population; professions; retail trade; insurance; tourism; traffic; wages; strikes and lockouts; employment; price indices; state taxes for commerce; foreign trade; balance of payments; GNP.

658 BOURSE DE BALE: RAPPORT ANNUEL
Bourse de Bâle

CH–Français/Deutsch annual

Annual report of the Basle Stock Exchange.

659 BULLETIN MENSUEL
Banque Nationale Suisse

CH–Français/Deutsch monthly

Monthly bulletin of economic reviews with data and graphs on: gold; capital; shares; banks; public finance; prices; salaries; GNP; production; industry; commerce; transport.

660   BUSINESS FACTS AND FIGURES
Union de Banques Suisses

CH—English monthly

Brief summaries and statistics on: employment; savings;
prices; issues and interest rates; Swiss and foreign stock
markets; developments of share prices; gold, silver, platinum,
palladium.

661   CHARGE FISCALE EN SUISSE
Bureau Fédéral de Statistique

CH—Français/Deutsch annual

Survey on taxation giving details of revenue raised, compiled
by the Federal Administration for Taxation.

**662   DIRECTORY OF SWISS MANUFACTURERS AND
PRODUCERS**
Swiss Office for the Development of Trade

CH—English c1425pp

Contents: manufacturers A-Z with details of: address, date
formed, employees, products. Export and trading transit
firms A-Z with details of: address; date formed; goods
handled; markets; associates. Three separate indexes:
classified; trade marks and names; products.

663   THE DOCUMENTARY CREDIT
Union de Banques Suisses

CH/INT—English 1975 43pp

Brief guide to Uniform Customs and Practice for
Documentary Credits — UCPDC, including data on: varied
forms; practical execution; areas of application; glossary of
terms; list of references for more detailed study.

664   ECONOMIC PANORAMA
Union de Banques Suisses

CH—English quarterly

Quarterly economic bulletin including: current and future
economic outlook; industry; power; construction and civil
engineering; retail trade; finance.

**665   ECONOMIC REPORT — SWITZERLAND AND
LIECHTENSTEIN**
Lloyds Bank Ltd.

CH—English 1975 27pp

Reviews the current economic situation with details and
statistics on: export opportunities; imports; foreign
investment; agriculture; tourism; fuel and power;
manufacturing industries; prices, incomes and employment.

666   ECONOMIC SURVEY OF SWITZERLAND 1975
Union de Banques Suisses

CH—English/Deutsch/Français 1976 80pp

Reviews economic trends and developments including:
power production; transportation; tourism; banking and
insurance; commerce; machinery and metals; construction;
chemicals; textiles; food, drink and tobacco; newspapers;
graphic arts and advertising.

667   L'ECONOMIE SUISSE 1975
Union de Banques Suisses

CH—Français 1975 89pp

Survey of the Swiss economy with data on: energy;
transport; tourism; banks and insurance; commerce;
industrial chemistry; textiles; food, drink and tobacco;
newspapers; graphic arts; advertising.

**668   EFFECTIF DES VEHICULES A MOTEUR (SELON LES
MARQUES DE FABRIQUE) EN SUISSE**
Bureau Fédéral de Statistique

CH—Français/Deutsch 1975 79pp

Number of motor vehicles (according to make) in
Switzerland.

**669   EFFECTIF DES VEHICULES...PAR CANTONS, PAR
DISTRICTS ET PAR COMMUNES**
Bureau Fédéral de Statistique

CH—Français/Deutsch 1969

Numbers of motor vehicles in Switzerland, by cantons,
districts and municipalities.

670   ESTABLISHING A BUSINESS IN SWITZERLAND
US Department of Commerce

CH—English 1968 17pp

Overseas Business Report no. OBR 68-73.
Contents: investments; business organisation; legislation;
employment; taxation; availability of capital.

**671   LES FINANCES DE LA CONFEDERATION, DES
CANTONES ET DES COMMUNES, 1938-71**
Bureau Fédéral de Statistique

CH—Français/Deutsch 1974 121pp

Finances of the State, the cantons and municipalities.

672   FINANCIAL CENTRES OF THE WORLD — ZURICH
The Times

CH—English 6 June 1972

Survey in The Times newspaper which discusses why
Switzerland is the most important source of money for the
Eurobond market.

673   FOREIGN EXCHANGE QUOTATIONS
Union de Banques Suisses

CH/INT—English annual 43pp

Foreign exchange rates A-Z by country including data on:
currency and denomination; gold parity or central rate;
average rate; import and export of local currency bank notes
for travellers; exchange control regulations.

674   FOREIGN TRADE REGULATIONS OF SWITZERLAND
US Department of Commerce

CH—English 1969 7pp

Overseas Business Report no. OBR 69-22.
Contents: trade policy; import tariff systems; special customs provisions; internal taxes; shipping documentation; non-tariff and import controls.

675 FOUNDING A COMPANY IN SWITZERLAND
Union de Banques Suisses

CH—English 1976 39pp

Short presentation of the most important economic, legal and fiscal aspects of forming a corporation in Switzerland. This latest edition (8th), incorporates the latest developments in the corporate field.

676 FREE ENTERPRISE WILL SURVIVE
Union de Banques Suisses

CH—English 1976 11pp

Shareholders address delivered by Dr. A. Schaefer, Chairman of the Board of the Union Bank of Switzerland, which reviews the recent recession and comments on: limits of government activity; inflation; the state, the economy and the unions.

677 GOLD
Union de Banques Suisses

CH/INT—English 1974 29pp

Pamphlet aimed at prospective buyers of gold including: basic terminology; catalogue of selected gold coins from — Switzerland, Europe, Africa, North and South America, USA; statistics on gold bullion; introduction to the gold trade.

678 THE GROWTH OF THE SWISS ECONOMY
Schweizerischer Bankverein

CH—English

Booklet reviewing the growth of the Swiss economy.

679 HINTS TO BUSINESSMEN — SWITZERLAND AND
LICHTENSTEIN
British Overseas Trade Board

CH—English 1976 60pp

Practical guide for travelling executives covering: general information; travel; hotels; restaurants and tipping; postal and telephone facilities; economic factors; import and exchange control regulations; methods of doing business; government and commercial organisations; reading list; map.

680 KOMPASS: INFORMATIONWERK DER
SCHWEIZERISCHEN WIRTSCHAFT
Editions Kompass Suisse SA

CH—Deutsch/English/Français/Español/Italiano annual
    2 vols c2500pp

Register of Swiss industry and commerce containing: A-Z companies under towns A-Z; company data; address; directors; capital; employees; products and services. Systematic product charts. Separate product index.

681 MARKET FACTORS IN SWITZERLAND
US Department of Commerce

CH—English 1970 11pp

Overseas Business Report no. OBR 70-69. Contents: outlook; nature of the market; competition; market analysis by selected commodities.

682 MARKETING IN SWITZERLAND
US Department of Commerce

CH—English 1976 20pp

Overseas Business Report no. OBR 76-19. Contents: foreign trade outlook; industry trends; distribution and sales channels; transportation; credit; import-export regulations; investment in Switzerland.

683 MOUVEMENT DE LA POPULATION EN SUISSE
Bureau Fédéral de Statistique

CH—Français/Deutsch 1975 97pp

Vital statistics on movements in population.

684 LE MOUVEMENT HOTELIER EN SUISSE
Bureau Fédéral de Statistique

CH—Français/Deutsch 1972 73pp

Tourists in Switzerland, data on: arrivals and departures; nights spent in hotels; details of hotels; rooms and beds.

685 OECD ECONOMIC SURVEYS: SWITZERLAND
Organisation for Economic Co-operation and Development
CH—English/Français 1976 58pp

Examines the main features of the present recession; the stance of demand management policies; monetary, fiscal and economic outlook.

686 LES PRINCIPALES ENTREPRISES DE SUISSE EN 1975
Union de Banques Suisses

CH—Français/Deutsch 1976 25pp

League table of the top 90 Swiss companies, listed by performance in 1975 (1974 performance for comparison). Also lists top 20 companies by growth.

687 PRODUCTION OF FRUIT AND VEGETABLES IN OECD
MEMBER COUNTRIES: NETHERLANDS AND
SWITZERLAND
Organisation for Economic Co-operation and Development

CH/NL—English/Français 1966

Survey of the production of fruit and vegetables.

688 QUARANTE ANS D'IMPOTS
Bureau Fédéral de Statistique

CH—Français/Deutsch 1974 242pp

Forty years of taxation; detailed statistics on: general taxation; taxation of the cantons; fiscal legislation.

689 QUARTERLY ECONOMIC REVIEW OF SWITZERLAND
Economist Intelligence Unit

CH—English quarterly with annual supplement

Analysis of current economic trends including: government; population; employment; exchange rates; national accounts; agriculture; mining; fuel and power; manufacturing industries; transport and communications; finance.

690 RAPPORT SUR LE COMMERCE ET L'INDUSTRIE DE LA SUISSE, AINSI QUE COMMUNICATIONS SUR LES AFFAIRES TRAITEES PAR LE 'VORORT'
Union Suisse du Commerce et de l'Industrie

CH—Français 1973 187pp

Report on the commerce and industry of Switzerland, together with information on matters dealt with by the Union. Part 1 reviews the Swiss economy; Part 2 gives statistics on the development of the economy.

691 RECENSEMENT
Bureau Fédéral de Statistique

CH—Français/Deutsch 1970 34 vols

Census of population in 1970. The main volumes are: houses, apartments and households by towns; households by mode of heating and fuel, by communities; population by communities, 1950-1970 - 25 vols one per canton, various prices; 6 vols covering the whole of Switzerland with data on: sex of population; origin; place of birth; mother tongue; status; age and education; profession; housing; domicile and place of work of employed persons.

692 RECENSEMENT FEDERAL DE L'AGRICULTURE
Eidgenössisches Statistisches Amt

CH—Deutsch/Français 1969 3 vols

Census of agriculture — Vol. 1: Crops. Vol. 2: Agricultural cultivation. Vol. 3: Horticulture.

693 RECENSEMENT FEDERAL DES ENTERPRISES: INDUSTRIE, ARTS ET METIERS, COMMERCE ET SERVICES
Bureau Fédéral de Statistique

CH—Français/Deutsch 1965 7 vols

Federal census of enterprises: industry, arts and professions, commerce and services. Vols 1 & 2 contain principal results of the census for Switzerland as a whole in French and German (FrS 6.00 and 5.50). Vols 3 & 4 contain similar data by cantons and large and small towns (FrS 20.00 and 7.50). Vols 5 & 6 deal with special questions for Switzerland and the cantons and towns (FrS 9.50 and 16.00). Vol. 7 deals with employment (FrS 6.00).

694 RECENSEMENT SUISSE DE LA CIRCULATION ROUTIERE
Eidgenössisches Statistisches Amt

CH—Deutsch/Français 1970 65pp

Census of Swiss road traffic.

695 REPORT OF TRADE MISSION TO SWITZERLAND AND AUSTRIA, 19-27 JANUARY 1971
British Hosiery and Knitwear Export Group

CH/A—English 1971 10pp

Details on the market for knitted goods in Switzerland and Austria.

696 SCHWEIZER JAHRBUCH DES ÖFFENTLICHEN LEBENS
Verlag Schwabe and Co

CH—Deutsch/Français annual c600pp

Swiss yearbook of public affairs covering: federal government and ministeries; local government; diplomatic services; political parties; trade and professional associations; learned societies; churches; cultural and sporting organisations. Separate subject and persons indexes.

697 DIE SCHWEIZ IN ZAHLENBILD
Eidgenössisches Statistisches Amt

CH—Deutsch/Français 1968 82pp

Switzerland in figures - condensed version of the statistical yearbook of Switzerland. Published every 10 or more years.

698 SCHWEIZERISCHE BIBLIOGRAPHIE FÜR STATISTIK UND VOLKSWIRTSCHAFT
Eidgenössisches Statistisches Amt

CH—Deutsch annual

Swiss bibliography of statistics and political economy. Published annually, it includes both statistical and non-statistical material.

699 SCHWEIZERISCHE BUNDESBAHNEN — STATISTISCHES JAHRBUCH
Schweizerische Bundesbahnen

CH—Deutsch/Français 200pp

Annual statistics on the Swiss railways. Includes data on: fixed installations; rolling stock; personnel; passenger and goods traffic; lines; lubricants; accidents.

700 SCHWEIZERISCHE REGIONENBUCH ... VERZEICHNIS DER IM SCHWEIZERISCHEN HANDELSREGISTER EINGETRAGENEN
Orell Füssli Verlag

CH—Deutsch/Français/Italiano annual 3 vols c5500pp

Swiss firms register directory of firms entered in the Swiss commercial register. Vols 1 & 2: A-Z firms under towns A-Z, under cantons A-Z; data on each firm: address, business, capital, directors or partners. Index of towns. Vol. 3: Classified directory, subdivided by towns A-Z. Separate indexes; firms and persons; government departments, trade bodies.

701 SELLING IN SWITZERLAND
US Department of Commerce

CH—English 1972 13pp

Overseas Business Report no. OBR 72-028.
Contents: import requirements; commercial practices; marketing; government procurement; notes for business travellers.

702 STAATSKALENDER
Bundeskanzlei

CH—Deutsch/Français/Italiano annual c350pp

Federal yearbook covering: national assembly; government
departments — address, telephone, names of officers.
Separate indexes for: persons; commissions; councils and
delegations with details of president, members and
representatives.

703   THE STATE AS EMPLOYER
Union de Banques Suisses

CH—English 1974 31pp

This paper discusses such topics as: growing government
influence on the economy; justification of State companies;
pros and cons of government-run businesses; limits of
state intervention.

704   STATISTIQUE ANNUELLE DU COMMERCE EXTERIEUR
DE LA SUISSE
Direction Générale des Douanes

CH—Français/Deutsch annual 3 vols

Annual statistics of the foreign trade of Switzerland. 3
volumes of detailed foreign trade statistics covering: Europe,
Africa and Asia. Vol. 1: data on imports and exports of
commodities classified by Swiss customs tariff and subdivided by countries of origin and destination. Vol. 2: data
on imports and exports arranged by countries of origin and
subdivided by commodities according to BTN. Vol. 3: data
on direct and indirect transit trade, returned goods, summary
of customs revenue, rates of duty.

705   STATISTIQUE DU COMMERCE EXTERIEUR DE LA
SUISSE: COMMENTAIRES ANNUELS
Direction Générale des Douanes

CH—Français/Deutsch annual

Annual commentary on foreign trade statistics, by country.

706   STATISTIQUE FORESTIERE SUISSE
Bureau Fédéral de Statistique

CH—Français/Deutsch annual c60pp

Swiss forestry statistics, including: forests; forestry; foreign
trade in forestry products; consumption of forest products in
Switzerland.

707   STATISTIQUE MENSUELLE DU COMMERCE
EXTERIEUR DE LA SUISSE
Direction Générale des Douanes

CH—Français/Deutsch monthly

Monthly statistics of the foreign trade of Switzerland. Totals
of foreign trade by countries of origin and destination.

708   STATISTIQUE SUISSE DES TRANSPORTS
Office Fédéral de Transports

CH—Français annual

Transport statistics of Switzerland, giving data on: railways,
trams, buses, motor vehicles, inland shipping, oil and gas
distribution and air traffic.

709   STOCK AND BOND LIST
Union de Banques Suisses

CH/INT—English/Deutsch/Italiano monthly

General information on the major stock exchanges, including;
mutual funds; medium-term notes; savings accounts; Swiss
and European shares; Swiss and foreign bonds; convertible
bonds; gold; taxes at source.

710   SUBVENTIONS ET PARTS DES RECETTES FEDERALES
REVENANT AUX CANTONS
Bureau Fédéral de Statistique

CH—Français/Deutsch 1971 91pp

Federal subsidies and cantons' shares of federal revenue.
Main source of public finance statistics for Switzerland.

711   LA SUISSE EN GRAPHIQUES
Bureau Fédéral de Statistique

CH—Français annual c80pp

General statistics, similar in coverage to "Annuaire
Statistique de la Suisse", but in summary form.

712   SWISS ECONOMIC DATA 75
Crédit Suisse

CH—English 1975 6pp

Brochure giving details on: production and prices; money and
currency; capital market; foreign trade; balance of
payments; foreign assets; finance and taxation; geography
and population.

713   SWISS MARKET SURVEY
International Chamber of Commerce

CH—English 1970 202pp

Mainly 1968 data on: population; politics; the economy;
industry; salaries and wages; housing; insurance.

714   SWITZERLAND, AN ECONOMIC SURVEY
Union de Banques Suisses

CH—English annual c90pp

General economic survey with tables and statistics on:
foreign trade; index of industrial production; industrial
construction projects; index of consumer prices.

715   SWITZERLAND – BARCLAYS COUNTRY REPORTS
Barclays Bank

CH—English 1976 2pp

Brief economic summary covering: current economic
activity; government policy; prices and wages; exports;
future outlook.

716   SWITZERLAND – FINANCIAL TIMES SURVEY
Financial Times

CH—English 8 Nov. 1973 p.34-39

Survey in the Financial Times newspaper covering: stock
exchange; banking; tourism; foreign trade; machinery
exports; chemicals.

717   **SWITZERLAND IN FIGURES 1976**
       Union de Banques Suisses

       CH—English annual

       Small leaflet giving concise data on: cantons; population;
       finances and taxes; economy; national product and income;
       foreign trade; prices and earnings; banks; capital; industrial
       production.

718   **TAX AND TRADE GUIDE: SWITZERLAND**
       Arthur Andersen & Co

       CH—English 1965 184pp

       Information on: government regulations and control; types
       of business organisations; employment; banking and finance;
       direct and indirect taxation.

719   **TOURISME EN SUISSE**
       Bureau Fédéral de Statistique

       CH—Français/Deutsch monthly

       Tourism in Switzerland, containing monthly data on:
       numbers of visitors by regions; by nights; by categories;
       special issues are devoted to specific aspects of tourism.

720   **URANIUM AND NUCLEAR POWER**
       Union de Banques Suisses

       CH/INT—English 1976 39pp

       Basic introduction to the most important aspects of nuclear
       energy, including: uranium deposits; nuclear fuel cycle;
       uranium as a source of energy; nuclear power plants; current
       and future international uranium supplies; nuclear power in
       Switzerland; future developments.

721   **VEHICULES A MOTEUR IMPORTES, VEHICULES A**
       MOTEUR NEUFS MIS EN CIRCULATION
       Bureau Fédéral de Statistique

       CH—Français/Deutsch monthly

       Number of motor vehicles imported and number registered.
       Contains data on: imports and registrations of private cars,
       motor cycles and commercial vehicles, specifying makes of

imported vehicles and naming the cantons in which they
were registered.

722   **VERÖFFENTLICHUNGEN, 1860-1970**
       Eidgenössisches Statistisches Amt

       CH—Deutsch/Français every 2 years

       List of publications issued by the Federal Bureau of
       Statistics arranged in subject order.

723   **VERZEICHNIS DER VERWALTUNGSRATE DER**
       SCHWEIZERISCHEN AKTIENGESELLSCHAFTEN
       Mosse-Annoncen AG

       CH—Deutsch c1050pp

       Directory of directors of Swiss joint stock companies.

724   **LA VIE ECONOMIQUE: RAPPORTS ECONOMIQUES ET**
       DE STATISTIQUE SOCIALE
       Departement Fédéral de l'Economie Publique

       CH—Français monthly

       Economic life: economic reports and social statistics.
       Monthly review with quarterly supplements and abstracts,
       covering: population; salaries and wages; prices; exports;
       construction industry; agriculture; transport and commerce;
       public finance; insurance.

725   **WHO'S WHO IN SWITZERLAND, INCLUDING THE**
       PRINCIPALITY OF LIECHTENSTEIN
       Intercontinental Book and Publishing Co.

       CH—English 680pp

       A-Z biographies of prominent Swiss people.

726   **ZURICH STOCK EXCHANGE — ANNUAL REPORT**
       Bourse de Zurich

       CH—English/Deutsch annual

       Describes the organisation of the Zurich Stock Exchange
       and provides data on: new listings; statistics of membership
       and listed securities; turnover; price and index data.

D-GERMANY

---

750 ABC DER DEUTSCHEN WIRTSCHAFT: INDUSTRIELLE
INFORMATIONEN UND REFERENZEN
ABC der Deutschen Wirtschaft Verlagsges. GmbH

D—Deutsch biennial 4 vols

ABC of German industry: industrial information and
references. Information is arranged systematically in broad
industrial groups; in each section firms are listed A-Z under
towns A-Z. The following data is given for each firm:
address, giro number, date established, directors or owners,
number of employees, products, markets. Each volume
includes an A-Z index of firms.

751 ABC DER DEUTSCHEN WIRTSCHAFT: ORTSLEXIKON
FÜR WIRTSCHAFT UND VERKEHR
ABC der Deutschen Wirtschaft Verlagsges. GmbH

D—Deutsch annual c1200pp

ABC of German industry: gazetteer for industry and
transport. Lists cities and towns A-Z with details of
postcode, population, administrative district, local authorities.
Also includes separate indexes of provinces and districts.

752 ABC DER DEUTSCHEN WIRTSCHAFT: QUELLENWERK
FÜR EINKAUF-VERKAUF
ABC der Deutschen Wirtschaft Verlagsges. GmbH

D—Deutsch(English index) annual c3800pp

ABC of German industry: buyers' and sellers' guide. Lists
manufacturers classified by products. Also includes list of
import and export merchants and agents classified by
products handled and subdivided by towns A-Z.

753 ADVERTISING CONDITIONS IN GERMANY (FEDERAL
REPUBLIC)
Institute of Practitioners in Advertising

D—English 1976 23pp

Contents: basic facts—geographic, demographic, economic;
media—press, TV, radio, posters, transport advertising,
cinema, direct mail, advertising agencies and services; taxes,
laws and regulations, organisations in the advertising field.

754 AGRARSTATISTISCHE ARBEITSUNTERLAGEN
Statistisches Bundesamt

D—Deutsch annual

Annual survey based on the results of agricultural,
viticultural and horticultural holdings, rural settlements, land
re-distribution as well as on the agricultural training and
advisory service.

755 AMERICAN CHAMBER OF COMMERCE IN GERMANY:
DIRECTORY
Macnens Germany Verlag GmbH

D—English/Deutsch annual c130pp

A-Z list of members of the American Chamber of Commerce,
with details of: address, executives, products or activities.
Separate indexes of products and activities.

756 AMTLICHE NACHRICHTEN DER BUNDESANSTALT
FÜR ARBEITSVERMITTLUNG UND
ARBEITSLOSENVERSICHERUNG
Bundesanstalt für Arbeit

D—Deutsch monthly

Monthly review of the general labour situation.

757 AMTLICHES GEMEINDEVERZEICHNIS FÜR DIE
BUNDESREPUBLIK DEUTSCHLAND
Verlag W Kohlhammer GmbH

D—Deutsch c950pp

Official list of communities in the Federal Republic of
Germany; published after each census, contains places A-Z
with details of: area and population; number of dwellings
and households; status; statistical serial number; postcode;
registry office; industrial and administrative courts; chambers
of commerce. Also includes systematic lists by
administrative districts and Länder.

758 DAS ARBEITSGEBIET DER BUNDESSTATISTIK
Statistisches Bundesamt

D—Deutsch 1971

Survey of German Federal Statistics.

759 ARBEITS- UND SOZIALSTATISTISCHE MITTEILUNGEN
Bundesministerium für Arbeits- und Sozialordnung

D—Deutsch monthly

Monthly bulletin of labour and social statistics.

760 AUSSENHANDEL
Statistisches Bundesamt

D—Deutsch

Foreign trade; comprising seven different series.
Series 1: General summary (monthly and annual)
Series 2: Imports and exports classified by commodities and subdivided by countries (monthly).
Series 3: Imports and exports by countries subdivided by commodity groups (quarterly).
Series 4: Imports and exports of mineral oils.
Series 5: Special trade according to the Classification for Statistics and Tariffs (quarterly, in English).
Series 6: Transit trade.
Series 7: Special issues mainly: Germany's trade with EEC; OECD; Eastern Europe.
Series 8: Foreign trade of foreign countries.

761 DER AUTOMOBILMARKT
Axel Springer Verlag AG

D—Deutsch 1973 3 vols

The market for motorcars; survey of the European motor vehicle industry and a detailed analysis of the West German industry. Also surveys car ownership patterns and costs of running a car in West Germany. In three volumes. Vol. 1: motor cars—overall market; passenger and dual-purpose vehicles. Vol. 2: motorists. Vol. 3: company information.

762 BANKENSTATISTIK NACH BANKENGRUPPEN
Deutsche Bundesbank

D—Deutsch/English monthly

Statistical supplement to the monthly report of the Deutsche Bundesbank giving data on assets and liabilities of all types of banks by principal groupings and details of their business activities.

763 BASIC DATA ON THE ECONOMY OF THE SOVIET ZONE OF GERMANY
US Department of Commerce

D—English 1967 21pp

Overseas Business Report no. OBR 67-5.
Contains data on: population; structure of the economy; agriculture; mineral resources; construction; power; transportation and communication; labour; finance; foreign trade.

764 BAUWIRTSCHAFT, BAUTÄTIGKEIT, WOHNUNGEN
Statistisches Bundesamt

D—Deutsch

Construction, building activity, dwellings. Series of reports on the building and construction industry in the Federal Republic:
Series 1: Selected figures for the construction industry (monthly)
Series 2: Local units and enterprises of building industry—(annual, in 2 parts)

Series 3: Building activity (annual)
Series 4: Licences for officially sanctioned housing projects (quarterly)
Series 5: The housing supply (annual)
Series 6: Rents (twice a year)

765 BAUWIRTSCHAFT, BAUTÄTIGKEIT, WOHNUNGEN; 1% WOHNUNGSSTICHPROBE 1965
Statistisches Bundesamt

D—Deutsch 1970 3 parts

Construction, building activity, dwellings: 1% census of housing 1965. Issued in 3 parts. Part 1: Housing; residential buildings/residential areas, rents. Part 2: Size and type of household and accommodation. Part 3: Household income, rent and cost of dwellings.

766 BDI-DEUTSCHLAND LIEFERT: OFFIZIELLER EXPORT-BEZUGSQUELLENNACHWEIS DES BUNDESVERBANDES DER DEUTSCHEN INDUSTRIE
Gemeinschaftsverlag GmbH

D—Deutsch/English/Español/Français annual c2500pp

Official export register of the Federation of German Industries. Includes a list of manufacturers classified by products and a separate A-Z listing with data on manufacturers address, telephone and telex numbers and product groups. Also includes a separate product index.

767 DIE BEKLEIDUNGSINDUSTRIE IN DER BUNDESREPUBLIK DEUTSCHLAND
Bundesverband Bekleidungsindustrie eV

D—Deutsch annual c50pp

Clothing industry in the Federal Republic of Germany. Contains data on the structure of the clothing industry, including production, foreign trade, wholesale and retail prices, indexes of production and trade and wages in the clothing industry.

768 BERICHTE
Deutsches Institut für Wirtschaftsforschung

D—Deutsch monthly

Monthly report on studies on various aspects of the German economy.

769 BEVÖLKERUNGSSTRUKTUR UND WIRTSCHAFTSKRAFT DER BUNDESLÄNDER
Statistisches Bundesamt

D—Deutsch c235pp

Population structure and economic resources of the Federal provinces. Contains the major demographic and economic data available for each of the provinces.

770 DER BIER-MARKT
Axel Springer Verlag AG

D/INT—Deutsch 1973

The market for beer: survey of the West German brewing industry, with statistics of: production; import and export prices; consumption; company information. Brief section on the European brewing industry.

771 BRITISH GERMAN TRADE
The German Chamber of Industry and Commerce in the UK

D/GB—English monthly

Monthly journal giving details of the trade between Britain and the Federal Republic.

772 BULLETIN
The German Chamber of Industry and Commerce in the UK

D/GB—Deutsch/English monthly

Monthly review giving details of German-British trade enquiries.

773 BUNDES FIRMENREGISTER
Walter Dorn KG

D—Deutsch 2 vols c7000pp

Register of firms in the Federal Republic. List of firms A-Z under towns A-Z under Länder. Gives data on each firm on: address, telephone number, telex number, products. Also includes a separate classified index. In 2 vols. Vol. 1: North and West Germany. Vol. 2: South Germany.

774 DIE BUNDESREPUBLIK DEUTSCHLAND, VEREINIGT MIT HANDBUCH FÜR DIE BUNDESREPUBLIK DEUTSCHLAND
Carl Heymanns Verlag KG

D—Deutsch c3500pp

Contains details of Federal and Land governments; public authorities, offices and departments with names of officers; diplomatic representatives; societies and institutes; international and European organisations. Also includes subject and persons indexes.
(Incorporates the "Handbook for the Federal Republic of Germany.")

775 THE BUSINESS CYCLE IN WEST GERMANY 1950-69
Econtel Research Ltd.

D—English 1970

Business cycle series no. 3. Provides a guide to fluctuations in business during the period 1950-69 including fluctuations in industrial production, wages, prices and share prices.

776 DER CASH AND CARRY-GROSSHANDEL IN DER BUNDESREPUBLIK DEUTSCHLAND
Neuer Handels-Verlag GmbH

D—Deutsch 1973

The Cash and Carry wholesale trade in the Federal Republic of Germany, including data on sales and structure of the sector with statistics for various periods up to 1972.

777 LA CONSOMMATION D'ENERGIE DES MENAGES EN REPUBLIQUE FEDERALE D'ALLEMAGNE: EVOLUTION RETROSPECTIVE ET PREVISION JUSQU'EN 1975
European Communities

D—Français 1967

Household consumption of energy in the Federal Republic of Germany: past situation and prospects up to 1975.

778 CONSTRUCTION INDUSTRY EUROPE
House Information Services Ltd.

D/INT—English/Français 1976 c320pp £18.75

A comprehensive survey and directory of the construction industry in Germany and other European countries. Covers standards, controls, unions, research, markets, professional practices, organisations, bibliography etc.

779 DAS DEUTSCHE FIRMEN-ALPHABET, FRÜHER ALPHABETISCHES FIRMEN-REGISTER . . . 500,000 ADRESSEN A-Z
Deutscher Adressbuch-Verlag für Wirtschaft und Verkehr GmbH

D—Deutsch annual c2800pp

This publication, formerly "Alphabetical Firms Register". . . lists 500,000 addresses A-Z. Includes an A-Z list of firms and trade associations with details of address, telephone number and business. Also contains a separate list of trade names A-Z under products with details of manufacturer's name, address and telephone number.

780 DER DEUTSCHE MARKT FÜR KRANKEN-HAUSARTIKEL: LEITFADEN FÜR EXPORTEURE
Nederlands-Duitse Kamer van Koophandel

D—Deutsch 1972

The German market for hospital equipment: guide for exporters.

781 DER DEUTSCHE UND SEIN AUTO
Spiegel-Verlag

D—Deutsch 1971

The German and his car; a survey of car ownership patterns in West Germany including data on buying habits and preferences, use and maintenance.

782 DEUTSCHER VERBAND TECHNISCH-WISSENSCHAFTLICHER VEREINE: HANDBUCH
Deutscher Verband Technisch-Wissenschaftlicher Vereine

D—Deutsch c150pp

German association of technical and scientific societies handbook: A-Z listing of societies with details of address; date established; membership data; objects; publications.

783 DEUTSCHES BUNDES-ADRESSBUCH—BEZUGSQUELLENTEIL: EINKAUFS—1 X 1 DER DEUTSCHEN INDUSTRIE
Deutscher Adressbuch-Verlag für Wirtschaft und Verkehr GmbH

D—Deutsch annual c1800pp

German Federation directory-Buyers' guide, purchasing cross-reference to German industry. Manufacturers are classified in a single A-Z sequence of products and trade names. Also gives details of government authorities and trade associations.

784 DEUTSCHES BUNDES-ADRESSBUCH DER FIRMEN AUS INDUSTRIE, HANDEL UND VERKEHR; 500,000 ADRESSEN NACH ORTEN
Deutscher Adressbuch-Verlag für Wirtschaft und Verkehr GmbH

D—Deutsch annual 3 vols. c4000pp

German Federation directory of firms in industry, trade and commerce: 500,000 addresses arranged by places. Details of firms and trade associations A-Z under towns in each Land with address, telephone number and type of business. Also gives information on public authorities, local authorities and industries in each Land.

785 DIRECTORY OF AMERICAN BUSINESS IN GERMANY
Seibt Verlag Dr Artur Seibt

D—English/Deutsch biennial

In two sections: Part 1 lists German firms A-Z with details of their address, business partners in the USA and type of business relationship. Part 2 lists American firms A-Z with details of address, and business partners in Germany.

786 DOKUMENTATION GASTGEWERBE NW: BETRIEBSVERGLEICH 1972
Betriebsberatung Gastgewerbe GmbH

D—Deutsch 1974

Documentation on the hotel trade in Nordrhein Westfalen. Survey of the hotel and restaurant trades with data for the types of accommodation available, comparing demand, facilities and prices.

787 ECONOMIC BULLETIN: MONTHLY SELECTION FROM THE INSTITUTE'S "WOCHENBERICHT"
Deutsches Institut für Wirtschaftsforschung

D—English monthly

Monthly review containing English translation of articles on the German economy which appeared in the Wochenbericht.

788 THE ECONOMIC SITUATION IN THE FEDERAL REPUBLIC OF GERMANY
Bundesministerium für Wirtschaft

D—Deutsch/English quarterly

General economic review.

789 THE ECONOMIC STRUCTURE OF THE FEDERAL REPUBLIC OF GERMANY
Frankfurter Allgemeine Zeitung

D—English

Statistics on the economic situation; also includes distribution and readership figures for "Frankfurter Allgemeine".

790 DER EINZELHANDEL IN DER BUNDESREPUBLIK
Axel Springer Verlag AG

D—Deutsch 1971 4 vols.

The retail trade in the Federal Republic of West Germany. Four volume survey containing an overall assessment plus detailed analysis of individual sectors.

791 ELECTRONIC EQUIPMENT FOR HOME ENTERTAINMENT
Gruner und Jahr AG & Co.

D—English 1974

Surveys the West German market for television, radios, tape recorders and records. Includes data on: production; sales; foreign trade; manufacturers; ownership patterns; advertising expenditure. Statistics cover the period 1970-72.

792 ELEKTRIZITÄTSWIRTSCHAFT
Vereinigung Deutscher Elektrizitätswerke

D—Deutsch annual

Annual detailed review of the electricity supply industry including data on supply, public consumption, financial data, supply to industry and total electricity supplied in the Federal Republic.

793 THE ELEVEN BILLION MARK MARKET: A STUDY OF THE MARKET FOR LADIES OUTERWEAR IN WEST GERMANY
National Economic Development Office

D—English 1971

Survey prepared on behalf of the Economic Development Committee for the Clothing Industry. Provides detailed information on: the characteristics of the market; the demands made on manufacturers by retailers; type of competition; methods of selling and promoting goods in the market.

794 EMPLOYMENT PRACTICES IN EEC TEXTILE INDUSTRIES
National Economic Development Office

GB/F/D/I—English 1973 free

Report on the visit by members of the Wool Textile EDC Manpower Working Party to textile employers' organisations and trade unions in France, Germany and Italy.

795 EURO-DATA 75 BAND 1: VERBRAUCH UND VERBRAUCHER IN DER BRD
Marplan Forschungsgesellschaft für Markt und Verbrauch GmbH

D—Deutsch 1975

Consumption and consumers in the Federal Republic of Germany. The first of five volumes designed to provide data on European consumption and consumers. Includes data on general economy and demography with detailed information on consumption patterns.

796 FACTS ABOUT GERMANY
Press and Information Office of the Government of the Federal Republic of Germany

D—English 1975 476pp

General introduction to the Federal Republic of Germany, with information on: history; government; journalism; the economy; social life; education and science; culture.

797 FEDERAL REPUBLIC OF GERMANY—BARCLAYS COUNTRY REPORTS
Barclays Bank

D—English 1976 2pp

Brief economic summary, covering: current economic situation; aggregate demand; industry and labour; money supply; balance of payments.

798 **THE FEDERAL REPUBLIC OF GERMANY STATISTICS**
Dresdner Bank

D—English annual

Brief digest of statistics on: industry, wages and prices,
finance, capital market, foreign trade, balance of payments,
GNP.

799 **FINANZEN UND STEUERN**
Statistisches Bundesamt

D—Deutsch

Finance and taxes; nine series providing detailed statistics on
all aspects of finance in the Federal Republic:
Series 1: The economy of the Federal Republic, Länder
and local authorities (annual).
Series 2: Taxation in the Federal Republic, Länder and
local authorities (quarterly).
Series 3: Debts and assets of the Federal Republic, Länder
and local authorities (annual).
Series 4: Personnel in the Federal Republic, Länder and local
authorities (annual).
Series 5: Special contributions on financial statistics (annual)
Series 6: Income and property taxes (every 3 years).
Series 7: Turnover tax (every two years).
Series 8: Indirect taxes (annual).
Series 9: Taxes on commercial transactions (annual).

800 **FREIZEITEINRICHTUNGEN IN DER**
BUNDESREPUBLIK 1980: BEDARFSENTWICKLUNG
UND ANGEBOTSLÜCKEN IM ÖFFENTLICHEN UND
PRIVATEN BEREICH
Logon GmbH

D—Deutsch 1974 4 vols

Leisure facilities in the Federal Republic of Germany: trends
in demand and gaps in supply in the public and private
sector. Vol. 1: general survey. Vol. 2: open countryside.
Vol. 3: sports and games. Vol. 4: urban facilities, restaurants
and the hotel trade. Statistics cover various periods up to
1972, with forecasts to 1980.

801 **GARTENPFLEGE**
Gruner und Jahr AG & Co

D—Deutsch 1972

Survey of the West German market for garden tools. Data on:
production; sales; consumption; advertising expenditure.
Statistics cover various periods up to 1971, plus some forecast data for consumption to 1985.

802 **GERMAN/ENGLISH GLOSSARY OF TERMS USED IN**
FREIGHT FORWARDING
National Economic Development Office

D—English 1971

A short glossary based on the German freight forwarders'
standard terms and conditions.

803 **GERMAN FREIGHT FORWARDERS' STANDARD TERMS**
AND CONDITIONS
National Economic Development Office

D—English 1971

A translation of terms and conditions customarily used in the
German forwarding trade.

804 **THE GERMAN MARKET FOR AMERICAN PRODUCTS**
Gruner und Jahr AG & Co

D—English 1974

Report designed to indicate examples of sales and marketing
possibilities for American products in the West German
market. Part 1: Basic data on the population and economy
of the Federal Republic. Part 2: Data on selected market
areas: office and information processing equipment; banking
and savings accounts; photographic equipment; credit cards;
leasing; alcoholic beverages; aircraft industry.

805 **THE GERMAN MARKET FOR JAPANESE PRODUCTS**
Gruner und Jahr AG & Co

D—English/Deutsch 1974

Survey of the openings on the German market for Japanese
products. Part 1: Basic data on the German population and
economy. Part 2: Details of production, total imports and
imports from Japan in specific markets. Gives data on the
market for: cameras and cine cameras; office equipment;
cars and motor cycles; textiles and clothing; foodstuffs.

806 **GERMANY IN THE SEVENTIES: BUSINESS PROSPECTS**
IN EUROPE'S LEADING MARKET
Business International SA

D—English 1973

Examines the transformations in Germany's investment
climate, with the impact on future policy and international
business. Contains information on the economic and
political situation including finance, regional development,
labour and investment.

807 **GROSS- UND EINZELHANDEL, GASTGEWERBE,**
FREMDENVERKEHR
Statistisches Bundesamt

D—Deutsch

Wholesale and retail trade, hotel and catering industry,
tourism. Series of reports on the catering and distributive
trades, including: 1: Wholesale trade—in two parts: Part 1:
Sales and turnover (monthly and annual). Part 2: Purchase
of goods, stocks and gross profits (annual). 2: Retail trade, in
two parts: Part 1: Sales and turnover (monthly and annual).
Part 2: Purchase of goods, stocks and gross profits (annual).
3: Tourism, in two parts: Part 1: Tourist trade in places
offering accommodation (monthly, biannual, annual). Part 2:
Number of beds available in places making regular returns
(annual).

808 **DER GROSSE HARTMANN (FRÜHER REICHS-**
BRANCHEN-ADRESSBUCH)
Adressbuchverlag Georg Hartmann KG

D—Deutsch(English index) annual c3400pp

Classified directory of manufacturers, wholesalers, exporters
and importers (formerly "Classified Directory of the Reich").

809 **GUIDELINES ON EXPORTING TO THE FEDERAL**
REPUBLIC OF GERMANY
German Chamber of Industry and Commerce in the UK

D—English 10pp

Booklet for potential exporters to the Federal Republic
including advice on how to establish business relations with
German buyers.

810 HANDBOOK OF ECONOMIC STATISTICS: FEDERAL REPUBLIC OF GERMANY AND WESTERN SECTORS OF BERLIN
American Embassy, Bonn

D—English quarterly

An abstract of the general economic statistics of the Federal Republic giving details of GNP, industrial production, agriculture, foreign and domestic trade, finance, investment, labour, wages and prices. Also includes data on US economic aid and some similar information for West Berlin.

811 HANDBOOK OF STATISTICS FOR THE FEDERAL REPUBLIC OF GERMANY
Statistisches Bundesamt

D—English/Français/Español

An English version of "Statistisches Taschenbuch", issued three times a year, giving statistics of the main economic and social trends.

812 HANDBUCH DER DEUTSCHEN AKTIENGESELLSCHAFTEN
Verlag Hoppenstedt & Co

D—Deutsch annual 7 vols c7500pp

Handbook of German joint-stock companies. Gives details of quoted companies in no determined order. Data is given on: address, telephone numbers, date established, directors, capital, extensive financial data, products and activities. Each volume contains a complete A-Z companies index giving volume and page references to current and previous editions. Vol. 7: includes a supplement listing companies in the process of liquidation and companies in East Germany converted to public ownership.

813 HANDBUCH DER DEUTSCHEN WISSENSCHAFTLICHEN GESELLSCHAFTEN
Franz Steiner Verlag

D—Deutsch c750pp

Handbook of German scientific societies, includes c500 independent scientific societies, industrial and economic associations and research institutes broadly classified and including data on: address; officers; date established; status; objectives; activities; membership data; publications; participation in international organisations.

814 HANDBUCH DER DIREKTOREN UND AUFSICHTSRÄTE
Finanz- und Korrespondenz-Verlag Dr Gisela Mossner

D—Deutsch(English index) annual 2 vols c1700pp

Handbook of directors and executives. Vol. 1: A-Z directors with brief curriculum vitae and appointments. Vol. 2: A-Z companies, with details of: directors, address, telephone numbers, capital, products.

815 HANDBUCH DER GROSS-UNTERNEHMEN
Verlag Hoppenstedt & Co

D—Deutsch(English index) annual 3 vols c4000pp

Yearbook of large enterprises in Germany. Lists c15,000 substantial industrial companies A-Z under towns A-Z, with data on: address, telephone numbers, date established, capital, directors, turnover, number of employees, products. Also includes separate classified and firms A-Z indexes.

816 HANDBUCH DER ÖFFENTLICHEN BÜCHEREIEN
Deutscher Büchereiverband

D—Deutsch c260pp

Directory of public libraries: lists public libraries by towns A-Z with details of: address; telephone numbers; date established; stock; staff; director. Also includes a separate A-Z listing of members of Verein Deutscher Volksbibliothekare.

817 HINTS TO BUSINESSMEN—THE FEDERAL REPUBLIC OF GERMANY AND WEST BERLIN
British Overseas Trade Board

D—English 1976 70pp

Practical guide to travelling executives covering: general information; travel; hotels; restaurants and tipping; postal and telephone facilities; economic factors; import and exchange control regulations; methods of doing business; government and commercial organisations; reading list; map.

818 IFO SCHNELLDIENST
Ifo-Institut für Wirtschaftsforschung

D—Deutsch weekly

Weekly review containing text and tables relating to various aspects of the German economy.

819 DIE INDUSTRIE- UND HANDELSKAMMERN UND IHRE ZUSAMMENSCHLÜSSE IN DER BUNDESREPUBLIK DEUTSCHLAND UND WEST-BERLIN
Deutscher Industrie- und Handelstag

D—Deutsch c250pp

Chambers of industry and commerce in the Federal Republic of Germany and Berlin. Lists chambers by cities A-Z with details of: address; telephone numbers; bankers; areas served; names, addresses and telephone numbers of officers and details of branch offices. Also includes a personnel index.

820 INDUSTRIE UND HANDWERK
Statistisches Bundesamt

D—Deutsch

Industry and handicrafts: nine different series containing current figures for industry and handicrafts. Series 1: Industrial establishments and enterprises; in two parts— provides data on employment, turnover, fuel supply, consumption in industry, (monthly and annual). Series 2: Production of selected industrial commodities, index of industrial production of about 500 items (monthly). Series 3: Industrial production—gives quantity and value data for some 2,500 commodities on the basis of quarterly censuses; also yield and utilization of source of power (quarterly and annual). Series 4: Special contributions to industrial statistics—official results of industrial enquiries (annual). Series 5: Power and water supply—3 parts: Part 1: Gives number and capacity of boilers and prime movers for electricity generating; output and generating plant data. Part 2: Data on industrial water supply. Part 3: Data on domestic and public water supply. Series 6: Orders received in major branches of industry (monthly). Series 7: Handicrafts; (quarterly and annual). Series 8: Industry of foreign countries (irregular). Series 9: Specialised statistics—4 parts: Part 1: Iron and steel (monthly and quarterly). Part 2: Fertilizer industry (monthly and annual). Part 3: Wood and wood products (quarterly). Part 4: Leather (monthly).

821 JAHRBUCH DER DEUTSCHEN BIBLIOTHEKEN, HERAUSGEGEBEN VOM VEREIN DEUTSCHEN BIBLIOTHEKARE
Verlag O Harrasowitz

D—Deutsch c580pp

Yearbook of German libraries, compiled by the Association of German Librarians. Includes libraries by towns A-Z with details of: address, telephone numbers, stock, facilities, hours, officers, publications. Also includes a list of library schools and a separate A-Z listing of librarians with brief curriculum vitae.

822 KAUF, KONSUM- UND KOMMUNIKATIONS-VERHALTEN DER BUNDESBEVÖLKERUNG
Spiegel Verlag

D—Deutsch 1976 3 vols

Purchasing, consumption and communications behaviour among the German people. A detailed survey of consumption patterns in West Germany including data on purchases of cars, domestic appliances and consumer goods.

823 DER KOSMETIKMARKT IN DER BUNDESREPUBLIK
Axel Springer Verlag AG

D—Deutsch 1974

The market for cosmetics in the German Federal Republic. Includes data on: production; prices; imports and exports; company information.

824 KÜRSCHNERS DEUTSCHER GELEHRTEN-KALENDER
Walter de Gruyter & Co

D—Deutsch 2 vols c3000pp

A-Z biographies of prominent German scholars and academics. Also includes separate subject index.

825 LAND- UND FORSTWIRTSCHAFT, FISCHEREI
Statistisches Bundesamt

D—Deutsch annual

Agriculture, forestry and fisheries statistics, in 5 volumes: Vol. 1: Annual statistics on land utilisation and yields of field crops and grassland, plus reports on weather conditions and their influence on crops. Vol. 2: Horticulture and viticulture; annual survey of cultivation of fruit and vegetables including areas devoted to vines and ornamental plants and flowers. Vol. 3: Livestock farming; data on stocks of cattle, milk production, slaughtering, average deadweight, average meat yield and inspection of meat and cattle for slaughter. Vol. 4: Fisheries; annual data on catches and the main working methods used in sea and coastal fishing. Vol. 5: Data on holdings, labour force and technical equipment.

826 LATEST FROM GERMANY
Embassy of the Federal Republic of Germany

D—English weekly c10pp

Regular news bulletin and short features on the current economic and social situation in the Federal Republic.

827 LEITENDE MÄNNER DER WIRTSCHAFT
Verlag Hoppenstedt & Co

D—Deutsch annual c1400pp

Leading men of the economy. A-Z listing of c36,000 directors and executives, giving details of address and appointments.

828 MAJOR MARKETS FOR EDIBLE TREE NUTS AND DRIED FRUITS
International Trade Centre

D/GB—English 1973

Market study on nuts and dried fruit in the Federal Republic of Germany, Japan, UK and USA. Gives statistical data on: world supply and demand of the major producing, exporting and importing countries.

829 MÄNNER & MÄRKTE II: BESITZ, KONSUM- UND INFORMATIONSVERHALTEN DER MÄNNLICHEN BUNDESBEVÖLKERUNG
Spiegel Verlag

D—Deutsch 1973 3 vols

Attitudes to ownership, consumption and information shown by the male population of the Federal Republic of Germany. A survey of the buying habits and consumer attitudes of the West German male population, including data on: holidays; leisure; ownership of cars; consumer durables; clothing; toiletries.

830 THE MARKET FOR ROAD VEHICLES
Gruner & Jahr AG & Co

D—English 1974

Provides a general view of the West German market for passenger cars, commercial vehicles, motor cycles, trailers and bicycles. Gives statistics for various periods up to 1972.

831 THE MARKET FOR SPIRITS
Gruner & Jahr AG & Co

D—Deutsch 1974

The market for spirits. Report designed for foreign advertisers giving information on the market for spirits in West Germany including data on: production; sales; foreign trade; consumption; expenditure; prices. Surveys the most important producers and their products. Statistics are for the period 1970-72.

832 THE MARKET IN SOUTH GERMANY FOR SCIENTIFIC AND INDUSTRIAL INSTRUMENTS AND APPARATUS
British Overseas Trade Board

D—English 1972

Market survey with information on: market size and growth; analysis of key user requirements; the strength of the West German instrument industry; strength of foreign suppliers. Also discusses the opportunities for British instrument manufacturers.

833 MARKETING IN THE FEDERAL REPUBLIC OF GERMANY AND WEST BERLIN
US Department of Commerce

D—English 1975 40pp

Overseas Business Report no. OBR 75-52.
Contents: foreign trade outlook; market profile; industry trends; distribution and sales channels; government procurement; advertising and research; credit; trade representation; investments in Germany; guidance for businessmen abroad.

834 MARKETING MANUAL FOR THE FEDERAL REPUBLIC OF GERMANY
Gruner und Jahr AG & Co

D—English/Deutsch 1975 2 vols

Vol. 1: The German consumer: consumption, leisure and media exposure. Presents a detailed statistical portrait of the German consumer with data on: number; regional distribution; age; occupation; education; income; household expenditure; consumer habits. Vol. 2: Industry, commerce and advertising. Presents a broad analysis of the economic performance and structure of these sectors.

835 DER MARKT DER OBERBEKLEIDUNG
Axel Springer Verlag AG

D/INT—Deutsch 1973 3 vols

The market for outerwear. Vol. 1: Ladies' outerwear. Vol. 2: Men's and boys' outerwear; Children's outerwear; Leisure wear; knitwear; jeans. Vol. 3: Company information. Detailed survey of the West German outerwear industry giving data for the period 1968-72. Includes a brief survey of the industry in Hong Kong, Italy, France, Great Britain, USA.

836 DER MARKT DER UNTERHALTUNGSELEKTRONIK IN DER BUNDESREPUBLIK DEUTSCHLAND
Axel Springer Verlag AG

D—Deutsch 1974

The TV, radio and recording equipment market in the Federal Republic of Germany. A detailed survey of the West German market for televisions, radios, tape-recorders, record players and hi-fi equipment. Statistics cover various periods from 1967-73.

837 DER MARKT DER ZAHN- UND MUNDPFLEGEMITTEL
Axel Springer Verlag AG

D—Deutsch 1973

The market for oral hygiene and dental care products, in West Germany. Detailed surveys of the markets for: toothpaste; denture cleaning products; mouthwashes; toothbrushes. Also gives information on some of the major companies operating in this field.

838 DER MARKT FÜR BROT- UND BACKWAREN (OHNE DAUERBACKWAREN)
Deutscher Fachverlag GmbH

D—Deutsch 1974

The market for bread and pastry, except long-life products. Survey of the West German bread and pastry industry giving statistics on: production; sales; prices; imports and exports; consumption; company information. Data covers various periods from 1968-72.

839 MARKT- UND STRUKTURZAHLEN DER GROSSVERBRAUCHER
Deutscher Fachverlag GmbH

D—Deutsch 1974

The market for and structure of the restaurant trades. Survey of the restaurant business in West Germany covering various establishments including restaurants, cafés, bars, canteens and institutions. Compares the facilities offered. Statistics cover various periods up to 1972 with some forecast information.

840 MEET GERMANY
Atlantik-Brücke

D—English 1976 140pp

General introduction to Germany, including: German politics; economic and social policies; changing society in Germany; culture and mass media.

841 MILCH- UND MÖLKEREIPRODUKTE
Axel Springer Verlag AG

D—Deutsch 1973

Milk and milk products market survey in West Germany, covering the period 1967-71.

842 MITTEILUNGEN DES INSTITUTS FÜR HANDELSFORSCHUNG AN DER UNIVERSITÄT KÖLN
Universität zu Köln, Institut für Handelsforschung

D—Deutsch monthly

Report of the Institute's work including text and tables relating to the wholesale and retail trade in Germany.

843 MONTHLY REPORT OF THE DEUTSCHE BUNDESBANK
Deutsche Bundesbank

D—English monthly

Includes articles on various aspects of economic and monetary affairs in the Federal Republic. Gives financial statistics and other data relating to general economic conditions, foreign trade and balance of payments. Special subject supplements are published separately.

844 MÜLLERS GROSSES DEUTSCHES ORTSBUCH
Post- und Ortsbuchverlag

D—Deutsch c1300pp

Müller's German gazetteer. Includes places A-Z with details of: population; postcode; post town; local authority; registry office; nearest railway station; administrative districts.

845 OECD ECONOMIC SURVEY: GERMANY
Organisation for Economic Co-operation and Development

D—English/Français annual c70pp

Annual survey of economic trends and developments in the Federal Republic.

846 ÖFFENTLICHE VERSORGUNG
Verlag Hoppenstedt & Co

D—Deutsch c1300pp

Public supply services; includes localities A-Z listing
organisations responsible for local government services—
water, electricity, gas, canals, hospitals, schools, taxes.

**847   THE POTENTIAL FOR BRITISH PLASTICS IN WEST
      GERMANY**
British Plastics Federation

D/GB—English 1975

Includes a survey of the West German economy, industry and
business practices. Discusses export opportunities for the
British plastics industry and gives information on key
industrial markets, the consumer market and the German
plastics industry.

848   PREISE, LÖHNE, WIRTSCHAFTSRECHNUNGEN
Statistisches Bundesamt

D—Deutsch 18 vols

Prices, wages, family budget surveys - a series of 18 volumes:
Vol. 1: Prices and price indices for foreign goods (monthly
and annual). Vol. 2: Index and basic materials (monthly and
annual). Vol. 3: Prices and price indices of industrial
products (monthly and annual). Vol. 4: Prices and price
indices of agricultural products (monthly and annual). Vol. 5:
Prices and price indices for buildings and building land
(quarterly and annual). Vol. 6: Prices and cost of living
indices (monthly and annual). Vol. 7: Transport prices
(quarterly). Vol. 8: Wholesale prices (monthly and annual).
Vol. 9: Prices in foreign countries (monthly and annual).
Vol. 10: International comparison of consumer prices
(monthly and annual). Vol. 11: Agreed wages and salaries
(quarterly and half-yearly). Vol. 12: Earnings and wages in
foreign countries (annual). Vol. 13: Family budget survey
(monthly and annual). Vol. 14: Wages in agriculture (annual).
Vol. 15: Wages in industry and commerce (quarterly).
Vol. 16: Wages in crafts (half-yearly). Vol. 17: Survey of
wages and salary structure (irregular). Vol. 18: Sample
survey on income and expenditure (irregular).

849   PURCHASING POWER MAP OF GERMANY
GFK

D—English annual

Details of purchasing power in Germany.

**850   QUARTERLY ECONOMIC REVIEW—GERMANY
      (FEDERAL REPUBLIC)**
Economist Intelligence Unit

D—English quarterly with annual supplement c20pp

Analysis of current economic trends including: government;
population; employment; currency; national accounts;
agriculture; industry; fuel and power; transport and
communications; tourism; finance; foreign trade payments
and agreements.

**851   RADEMACHER HANDBUCH FÜR INDUSTRIE UND
      EXPORT**
K Rademacher & Co

D—Deutsch(English index) annual 2 vols c3000pp

Rademacher directory for industry and export. Classified
directory of manufacturers and wholesalers. Also includes
separate indexes covering: products; banks; forwarding
agents; export merchants.

852   DER REIFENMARKT
Axel Springer Verlag AG

D—Deutsch 1974

The market for tyres; survey of the West German tyre
industry with a detailed analysis of marketing factors,
including: production; prices; product information; imports
and exports; sales; distribution; consumption. Also includes
a section on company information.

853   REPORT ON CONSUMER RESEARCH IN GERMANY
Marplan Ltd.

D—English 1975 2 vols

A companion study to Market Datasearch's survey of the
wallcoverings market in West Germany, comprising a detailed
survey of German consumer demand.

854   SAISONBEREINIGTE WIRTSCHAFTSZAHLEN
Deutsche Bundesbank

D—Deutsch/English monthly

Seasonally adjusted economic data; statistical supplement to
the monthly report of the Deutsche Bundesbank giving
details of the origin of the GNP, employment indices,
industrial production, productivity and wage costs, prices and
wages, retail sales, value of imports and exports, balance of
payments details.

**855   SALING: AKTIENFÜHRER—DIE AKTIENWERTE DER
      DEUTSCHEN BÖRSEN**
Verlag Hoppenstedt & Co

D—Deutsch(English index) annual c1000pp

Saling's shares guide—the securities quoted on German stock
exchanges. Lists c800 companies, including some non-
German, with details of: address, date established, directors,
capital, shareholders, balance sheet, holdings, products and
activities.

**856   SEIBT EXPORT DIRECTORY . . . FORMERLY OFFICIAL
      HANDBOOK OF THE FEDERATION OF GERMAN
      INDUSTRIES**
Seibt Verlag Dr Artur Seibt

D—English biennial c1750pp

Directory of manufacturers classified in systematic product
groups, with details of address and telephone numbers. Also
includes three separate indexes: Firms A-Z; products
(c70,000); trade marks and names.

**857   SPOTLIGHT ON OVERSEAS TRADE—SELLING TO
      WESTERN GERMANY**
Midland Bank

D—English 1975 4pp

Contents: the economy; the country; market opportunities;
the approach to the market; regulations and documentary
requirements; company formation in Western Germany;
statistics of UK exports to Western Germany.

858   STARTING A BUSINESS IN GERMANY
German Chamber of Industry and Commerce in the UK

D—English 1975 40pp

Contents: permits and registrations; setting up a branch office; setting up a: GmbH; AG; oHG; KG; GmbH & Co KG; requirements of German company law; taxation in Germany; labour law; investment incentives; agency law.

859   STATISTICAL POCKETBOOK OF THE GERMAN DEMOCRATIC REPUBLIC
Staatliche Zentralverwaltung für Statistik

D—English c160pp

An English version of "Statistisches Taschenbuch".

860   STATISTIK DES HAMBURGISCHEN STAATES: . . . HANDEL UND SCHIFFAHRT DES HAFENS, HAMBURG
Statistisches Landesamt

D—Deutsch annual

Statistics of the Hamburg State: trade and shipping of the port of Hamburg; contains details of imports and exports through the port of Hamburg arranged by commodities and by countries. Also gives shipping movements to and from the port.

861   STATISTISCHE PRAXIS
Staatliche Zentralverwaltung für Statistik

D—Deutsch monthly

Statistical application: monthly review containing economic and statistical articles. A four-page supplement "Statistische Monatszahlen" contains data on: production; retail trade; building; agriculture; transport; investment.

862   STATISTISCHER WOCHENBERICHT
Statistisches Bundesamt

D—Deutsch weekly

Weekly statistical service; contains a selection of official statistics of immediate current interest.

863   STATISTISCHES HANDBUCH FÜR DEN MASCHINENBAU
Verein Deutscher Maschinenbau-Anstalten eV

D—Deutsch annual

Statistical handbook of the mechanical engineering industries; contains general population and economic data, statistics of production, imports and exports of engineering products, indexes of production and wholesale prices, labour force and international trade in engineering products.

864   STATISTISCHES JAHRBUCH FÜR DIE BUNDESREPUBLIK DEUTSCHLAND
Statistisches Bundesamt

D/INT—Deutsch annual

Statistical yearbook for the Federal Republic of Germany; main sections; geography; population; health; education; agriculture and forestry; labour; construction; internal trade; foreign trade; public finance; wages. Also includes statistical tablesconcerning East Germany and the Soviet sector of Berlin, plus international statistics.

865   STATISTISCHES JAHRBUCH ÜBER ERNÄHRUNG, LANDWIRTSCHAFT UND FORSTEN DER BUNDESREPUBLIK DEUTSCHLAND
Bundesministerium für Ernährung, Landwirtschaft und Forsten (Verlag Paul Parey)

D/INT—Deutsch annual c400pp

Statistical yearbook of food, agriculture and forestry in the Federal Republic of Germany; includes tables on the general economy and detailed statistics on agriculture, land use, labour, education, machinery, use of fertilizers and other products, crops, horticulture, viticulture, livestock, marketing, wood, forestry, prices and wages. Also includes a section on agriculture in the EEC.

866   STATISTISCHES TASCHENBUCH FÜR DIE BUNDESREPUBLIK DEUTSCHLAND
Statistisches Bundesamt·

D—Deutsch/Français/English/Español

Statistical pocketbook for the Federal Republic of Germany, an abridged version of the "Statistisches Jahrbuch".

867   STRUCTURE OF THE PUMP, VALVE AND FABRICATED PROCESS PLANT INDUSTRIES: FRANCE AND WEST GERMANY
National Economic Development Office

D/F—English 1973

A comparative analysis and assessment of industry structures in both countries: also identifies the major companies and individual product suppliers.

868   SURVEY OF THE WALLCOVERINGS MARKET IN WEST GERMANY
Market Datasearch Ltd.

D—English 1974

Detailed information on the market, supply and distribution of wallcoverings in West Germany. Includes a list of major manufacturers and distributors and details of a separate consumer survey conducted by Marplan.

869   TASCHENBUCH DES ÖFFENTLICHEN LEBENS
Festland Verlag GmbH

D—Deutsch c600pp

Pocket book of public affairs; gives details of Federal and Land government departments and other public offices. Also lists societies and institutes.

870   TASCHENBUCH DES TEXTILEINZELHANDELS
Verlag der "Textil-Wirtschaft" Deutscher Fachverlag GmbH

D—Deutsch annual

Textile retail trade pocket book.

871   TATSACHEN UND ZAHLEN AUS DER KRAFTVERKEHRSWIRTSCHAFT
Verband der Automobilindustrie eV

D/INT—Deutsch annual c400pp

Facts and figures of the motor transport industry. Detailed statistics of: production, shipments from works, imports and exports, stocks, sales and licences issued. Also give data on:

fuels, roads and transport in general. Includes a section of international information.

872   TEST OF STILTON CHEESE IN HAMBURG
RSL International

D—English 1975

Report prepared for the National Dairy Council, presents the findings of a survey towards Stilton cheese. Data on attitudes towards pricing, packaging and purchasing.

873   TEXTIL FAKTEN 1973-74: MARKT- UND STRUKTURDATEN DER TEXTIL- UND BEKLEIDUNGS-WIRTSCHAFT
Deutscher Fachverlag GmbH

D—Deutsch 1973

Textile facts 1973-74: Market data and structure of the textile and clothing industries in West Germany.

874   DIE TEXTILINDUSTRIE DER BUNDESREPUBLIK DEUTSCHLAND
Gesamtverband der Textilindustrie in der Bundesrepublik Deutschland

D/INT—Deutsch annual c120pp

The textile industry of the Federal Republic of Germany. A commentary on the state of the textile industry including data on: production; foreign trade; prices of different types of textiles. Also includes some international data.

875   THIS IS YOUR GERMAN MARKET
Axel Springer Verlag AG

D—English 1973

Gives figures on: population; industry; trade; finance; tourism; advertising; projections for the economy.

876   THE TOBACCO MARKET
Gruner und Jahr AG & Co

D—English 1974

General review of the West German market for tobacco and tobacco products, including data on: production; sales; foreign trade; consumption and expenditure. Also includes a survey of the structure of the industry and its distribution channels. Statistics are for various periods up to 1972.

877   THE UK AND WEST GERMAN MANUFACTURING INDUSTRY 1954-72
National Economic Development Office

D/GB—English 1976

Analyses and compares changes in the structure and performance of the UK and West German manufacturing industries, including analysis of individual industries' economic problems and performance, plus an assessment of future prospects under alternative growth circumstances.

878   UNTERNEHMEN UND ARBEITSSTÄTTEN
Statistisches Bundesamt

D—Deutsch annual 3 series

Three series giving detailed information on the structure of industries: Series 1: Cost structure in the economy; provides data on the structure of costs, in relation to productive value. This series is in 4 parts—Part 1: Industry and power. Part 2: Handicrafts. Part 3: Transport. Part 4: Professions. Series 2: Joint stock companies. Series 3: Public concerns; data on business concluded by public utilities and public transport undertakings.

879   VADEMECUM DEUTSCHER LEHR- UND FORSCHUNGSSTÄTTEN. . . HANDBUCH DES WISSENSCHAFTLICHEN LEBENS
Stifterverband für die Deutsche Wissenschaft

D—Deutsch c800pp

Guide to German educational and research establishment . . . handbook of the scientific world. Includes research institutes, university faculties and technical universities, classified by subjects and with details of: address; telephone numbers and professors. Also includes details of: learned societies and institutes; Federal, Land and industrial libraries; scientific museums, botanical and zoological gardens. Three separate indexes covering: persons, towns and subjects.

880   VERBÄNDE, BEHÖRDEN, ORGANISATIONEN DER WIRTSCHAFT
Verlag Hoppenstedt & Co

D—Deutsch annual c680pp

Associations, authorities and organisations of the economy. Classified listing of organisations with details of address, telephone numbers and officers. Also includes two separate indexes of subjects and persons.

881   VERKEHR
Statistisches Bundesamt

D—Deutsch 9 vols

Transport; nine volumes giving detailed transport statistics in the Federal Republic. Vol. 1: Inland transport (monthly and annual). Vol. 2: Seaborne shipping (monthly and annual). Vol. 3: Air transport (monthly and annual). Vol. 4: Rail transport (monthly and annual). Vol. 5: Road transport (monthly and annual). Vol. 6: Road accidents (monthly and annual). Vol. 7: Foreign and inter-zonal travel (monthly and annual). Vol. 8: News media (irregular). Vol. 9: Freight transport in the various sections (quarterly and annual).

882   VERÖFFENTLICHUNGSVERZEICHNIS DES STATISTISCHEN BUNDESAMTES
Statistisches Bundesamt

D—Deutsch every 2 years

List of publications of the Federal Statistics Office. For current information, the journal "Wirtschaft und Statistik" includes a monthly list of new publications of the Federal Statistical Office.

883   DER VERSANDHANDEL: ZAHLEN, DATEN, FAKTEN
Bundesverband des Deutschen Versandhandels

D—Deutsch 1974

Mail order trade figures, data, facts. Surveys the structure of the West German mail order business, analysing the market and giving sales figures for the major companies.

884 VERZEICHNIS DER SPEZIALBIBLIOTHEKEN,
     HERAUSGEGEBEN VON DER ARBEITSGEMEINSCHAFT
     DER SPEZIALBIBLIOTHEKEN
     Verlag J A Mayer

     D–Deutsch c230pp

     Directory of special libraries, compiled by the Special
     Libraries Working Group; Classified list of libraries with
     details of: address, telephone numbers, director, stock
     facilities. Also separate indexes of towns and personnel.

885 VERZEICHNIS VON SCHRIFTTUM-
     AUSKUNFTSSTELLEN
     Beuth-Vertrieb GmbH

     D–Deutsch c220pp

     Directory of documentation centres. Classified list of
     documentation centres with details of: address; telephone
     numbers; subjects; stock; documentation data. Three indexes
     for subjects; towns; organisations A-Z.

886 VIERTELJAHRESHEFT ZUR WIRTSCHAFTSFORSCHUNG
     Deutsches Institut für Wirtschaftsforschung

     D–Deutsch quarterly

     Analysis of market conditions; with articles and tables on
     special subjects affecting the economy of the Federal
     Republic.

887 VOLKS- UND BERUFSZÄHLUNG
     Statistisches Bundesamt

     D–Deutsch 1961 21 vols

     Population and occupation census taken in 1961, in 21
     volumes. Vol. 1: Basic methodology. Vol. 2: Selected
     population groups: Germans and foreigners. Vol. 3: Present
     and future position of the population. Vol. 4: Age and
     family status. Vol. 5: Population by religions. Vol. 6:
     Expellees and Germans from East Germany. Vol. 7:
     Foreigners. Vol. 8: Population by institutions. Vol. 9:
     Trends. Vol. 10: Working population. Vol. 11: Wage earners
     and dependants. Vol. 12: Wage earners in the high income
     bracket. Vol. 13: Wage earners in the professions. Vol. 14:
     Population gainfully employed in regular work. Vol. 15:
     Self-employed persons. Vol. 16: Demographic and economic
     structure of households and families (10% sample).
     Vol. 17: Occupational activities of women and mothers (10%
     sample). Vol. 18: Children and young people in families (10%
     sample). Vol. 19: Living conditions of older citizens (10%
     sample). Vol. 20: Religious beliefs in families (10% sample).
     Vol. 21: Examination of the method and accuracy of the
     census.

888 WARENVERZEICHNIS FÜR DIE
     AUSSENHANDELSSTATISTIK
     Statistisches Bundesamt

     D–Deutsch c600pp

     Commodity classification for foreign trade statistics. Guide
     to the classification used, arranged by subject groupings with
     an A-Z index of commodities.

889 WARENVERZEICHNIS FÜR DIE INDUSTRIESTATISTIK
     Statistisches Bundesamt

     D–Deutsch 2 vols

Commodity classification for industrial statistics. A guide to
the classifications used for German industrial statistics,
including the publications "Industrie und Handwerk". One
volume is arranged by subject grouping and the other A-Z
by subject.

890 WATER POLLUTION CONTROL IN WEST GERMANY
     AND THE NETHERLANDS: THE MARKETS FOR
     TREATMENT PLANT AND INSTRUMENTATION
     Sira Institute

     D/NL–English 1973 2 vols

     Report on instruments for measuring and controlling water
     pollution. Also gives market coverage for water and effluent
     treatment plant. Examines three main sectors: public sewage
     treatment and surface water control; drinking supply;
     effluent treatment in industry. Gives data on the structure
     and market size of each sector for the base years 1971-72
     with forecasts for 1977.

891 WER GEHÖRT ZU WEM–MUTTER UND
     TOCHTERGESELLSCHAFTEN VON A-Z
     Commerzbank AG

     D–Deutsch(English index) biennial c770pp

     Who belongs to whom–parent and subsidiary companies
     A-Z: Lists subsidiary companies A-Z with details of capital;
     principal shareholders; size of holdings. Also includes a
     separate A-Z listing of parent companies with details of their
     subsidiaries and associates. Index of non-German companies
     with holdings in German companies.

892 WERTPAPIERSTATISTIK
     Deutsche Bundesbank

     D–Deutsch monthly

     Securities statistics; statistical supplement to the monthly
     reports of the Deutsche Bundesbank, giving detailed
     information on sale, redemption, average prices, yields of
     domestic bonds, foreign bonds, stocks and shares, stock
     exchange transactions of investment companies.

893 DER WESTDEUTSCHE MARKT IN ZAHLEN
     DIVO Inmar Gesellschaft für Marktforschung, Marktplanung
     und Marketingberatung GmbH

     D–Deutsch

     The West German market in figures; Detailed statistics on
     population; employment; income; disposition of income;
     consumption habits; leisure; advertising.

894 THE WEST GERMAN CONSUMER: A STATISTICAL
     PROFILE
     Metra Consulting Group Ltd.

     D–English 1975

     Based on Der Westdeutsche Markt in Zahlen published every
     five years by Metra Divo, Frankfurt. Contains data on:
     population; housing; consumer durables; clothing; transport;
     expenditure; consumption; leisure activities; media advert-
     ising. Most of the figures are based on an interviewing
     programme carried out in 1974.

895 THE WEST GERMAN FURNITURE MARKET: MARKETS,
     MEDIA, ADVERTISING
     Gruner und Jahr AG & Co

     D–English/Deutsch 1973

Report aimed at assisting furniture manufacturers wishing to compete in the West German market. Gives data on: production; foreign trade; analysis of the retail trading structure; advertising expenditure; potential consumer market. Statistics cover periods up to 1972, plus some forecast information to 1980.

896   THE WEST GERMAN MARKET
Contimart Ltd.

D—English

Marketing data on West Germany.

897   WEST GERMANY, THE UNITED KINGDOM'S PARTNER IN COMMERCE AND TRADE
Gruner und Jahr AG & Co

D—English/Deutsch 1974

This report is in 3 sections: Part 1: population and economic data on the Federal Republic of Germany. Part 2: Data on specific markets. Part 3: Advertising media availability and costs.

898   WHO'S WHO IN GERMANY
Intercontinental Book & Publishing Co

D—English 2 vols

A-Z biographies of prominent German people. Also includes a classified list of organisations with names in English and German.

899   WIRTSCHAFT UND STATISTIK
Statistisches Bundesamt

D—Deutsch/English/Français monthly

Economics and statistics, in two parts: Part 1: Articles on basic methodological questions and comments on the results of new and current statistics. Cumulative subject index for the year to date and a list of new publications issued during the month. Part 2: Statistical tables on population, health, education, agriculture and fisheries, building construction and housing, internal and foreign trade, tourism, transport, public finance, prices and wages, national accounts.

900   DIE WIRTSCHAFTLICHE LAGE IN DER BUNDESREPUBLIK DEUTSCHLAND: VIERTELJAHRESBERICHT
Bundesministerium für Wirtschaft

D—Deutsch quarterly

The economic situation in the Federal Republic of Germany: quarterly review. Contains text and statistics on: industrial production; labour; wages; prices; foreign trade; the economic situation in West Berlin.

901   WIRTSCHAFTSENTWICKLUNG IN DER BUNDESREPUBLIK
IFO-Institut für Wirtschaftsforschung

D—Deutsch quarterly 45pp

Economic development in the Federal Republic. Diagrams and tables showing the most important figures for assessment of the economic situation. Updated by weekly IFO Flash Reports.

902   WIRTSCHAFTSKONJUNKTUR
IFO-Institut für Wirtschaftsforschung

D—Deutsch quarterly

Tables and graphs giving information on the general trend of economic development.

903   WOCHENBERICHT
Deutsches Institut für Wirtschaftsforschung

D—Deutsch weekly

Information on labour and the money market.

904   ZAHLUNGSBILANZSTATISTIK
Deutsche Bundesbank

D/INT—Deutsch/English monthly

Balance of payments statistics; statistical supplements to the monthly reports of the Deutsche Bundesbank. Gives detailed data on balance of payments and balance of trade between the Federal Republic and other countries.

DK-DENMARK

950 ARBEJDLØSHEDEN
Danmarks Statistik

DK—Dansk/English 1974 75pp

Summary of unemployment data for the last 10 years. Also the rate of employment by age for the year under review (1973).

951 BARCLAYS COUNTRY REPORTS — DENMARK
Barclays Bank

DK—English 1976 2pp

Brief economic summary covering: payments; prices and wages; external position; economic outlook.

952 BASIC DATA ON THE ECONOMY OF DENMARK
US Department of Commerce

DK—English 1968 18pp

Overseas Business Report no. OBR 68-84. Concise economic report covering: the industrial sectors; labour force; finance; foreign trade.

953 BEFOLKNINGENS BEVAEGELSER
Danmarks Statistik

DK—Dansk/English 1973 l33pp

Vital statistics on births, marriages, deaths, divorces, migration and estimated age distribution. Based on 1971 figures.

954 BRITISH TRADE DRIVE IN DENMARK 1972: MARKET SURVEY ON AGRICULTURAL EQUIPMENT (EXCLUDING TRACTORS)
BNEC Export Council for Europe

DK—English 1971 32pp

Contents: survey of findings and recommendations. Danish agriculture and the prospect for mechanisation; EEC farm mechanisation practices; livestock management; farm machinery manufacture in Denmark and Britain; farm machinery marketing in Denmark.

955 BRITISH TRADE DRIVE IN DENMARK 1972: MARKET SURVEY ON FOOD PACKAGING MACHINERY
BNEC Export Council for Europe

DK—English 1971 30pp

Details on: distribution of food in Denmark; Danish food packaging industry by product group; promotion and reputation of British food packaging machinery in Denmark.

956 BRITISH TRADE DRIVE IN DENMARK 1972: MARKET SURVEY ON METALWORKING MACHINE TOOLS
BNEC Export Council for Europe

DK—English 1971 68pp

Provides details on: the market background for metalworking machine tools in Denmark; Danish and foreign competition; distributors; estimates of the future market 1971-75; exploiting the Danish market.

957 BRITISH TRADE DRIVE IN DENMARK 1972: MARKET SURVEY ON SCIENTIFIC AND INDUSTRIAL INSTRUMENTS INCLUDING MEDICAL EQUIPMENT
BNEC Export Council for Europe

DK—English 1971 44pp

Details on the markets for medical, electrical, analytical, navigational and process measuring and control instruments. Also includes technical and commercial requirements for selling instruments in Denmark.

958 DANISH ECONOMY IN BRIEF
København Handelsbank

DK—English twice a year

Leaflet containing statistics on: foreign trade; production; prices; banking; securities; geography and population.

959 THE DANISH MARKET
Contimart

DK—English 1963

Report on the Danish market with data on: population; the economy; external trade; economic and social policies; consumer earnings and expenditure; distribution and advertising.

960 DANMARKS NATIONALBANK MONETARY REVIEW
Danmarks Nationalbank

DK—English quarterly

Quarterly economic review with data on: assets and liabilities of the Nationalbank; Denmark's internal liquidity; prices and wages; government financial lending and borrowing; commercial banks: liquidity; insurance and pension funds; bonds.

961 DANMARKS NATIONALBANK: REPORT AND ACCOUNTS
Danmarks Nationalbank

DK—Dansk/English annual

Annual report and accounts including: foreign exchange; finance; credit; bond market. Information provided in tabular, diagrammatic and statistical format.

962 DANMARKS SKIBE OG SKIBSFART
Danmarks Statistik

DK—Dansk(English headings) 1972 130pp

Danish ships and shipping with data based on 1970.

963 DANMARKS VAREINDFØRSEL OG -UDFØRSEL
Danmarks Statistik

DK—Dansk 1974 2 vols

Foreign trade of Denmark. Vol. 1: statistics of foreign trade giving tables of imports and exports arranged by commodity classification, based on BTN. Vol. 2: statistics of foreign trade giving tables of imports and exports arranged by SITC, subdivided by countries of origin and destination. Data based on 1972 figures.

964 DANSK ELVAERKSSTATISTIK
Dansk Elvaerkers Forening

DK—Dansk annual

Statistics of electricity and a general survey of electricity supply industry with data on: number of undertakings; plant and power stations; output; sales of electrical energy; revenues and expenditure.

965 DANSK IMPORTAGENTERS FORENING
Danske Importagenters Forening

DK—Dansk c200pp

Import agents in Denmark, listed by trade group and classified by goods handled.

966 DENMARK
Financial Times

DK—English 9 Feb. 1971 p. 21-25

Survey in the Financial Times newspaper covering: banking; exports; shipbuilding; agriculture; engineering and chemical industries.

967 DENMARK FARMS ON: DANISH FARM PRODUCTS TODAY
Danish Agricultural Producers

DK—English 1970 127pp

Contents: Danish farming, past and present; Danish farm products; quality control; co-operation and research; Danish agricultural organisations.

968 DENMARK — INVESTORS CHRONICLE SURVEY
Investors Chronicle

DK—English 21 Feb. 1975 9pp

Survey in the Investors Chronicle journal covering: the political scene; new banking rules; Danish trade; farming.

969 DENMARK — QUARTERLY REVIEW
København Handelsbank

DK—English quarterly

Articles on economic development plus economic indicators for: manufacturing industries; agriculture; shipping; employment and wages; banks; balance of payments.

970 DENMARK — SPECIAL REPORT
The Times

DK—English 29 April 1976 4pp

Survey in The Times newspaper covering: the Welfare State; political scene; farming; fishing; industrial taxation; oil prospecting.

971 DETAILPRISER
Danmarks Statistik

DK—Dansk quarterly

Retail prices — detailed statistics of food prices from a cross-section of municipalities with urban areas.

972 ECONOMIC REPORT — DENMARK
Lloyds Bank Ltd.

DK—English 1975 266pp

Reviews the current economic situation in Denmark with information and statistics on: export opportunities; imports; foreign investment; agriculture; tourism; fuel and power; manufacturing industries; incomes; prices and employment.

973 THE ECONOMIC SITUATION IN DENMARK
Den Danske Landmandsbank

DK—English quarterly

Quarterly statistics and economic information on: currency; share and bond transactions; the Danish economy.

974 ECONOMIC SURVEY OF DENMARK
Royal Danish Ministry of Foreign Affairs

DK—English annual

Survey of the Danish economy for the year with forecasts for the coming year. Includes statistical supplement.

975 ESTABLISHING A BUSINESS IN DENMARK
US Department of Commerce

DK—English 1970 15pp

Overseas Business Report no. OBR 70-11. Concise information on setting up a business in Denmark, including:

factors affecting investment; organisation of businesses; employment; taxation.

976   EXPORT DIRECTORY OF DENMARK
Krak

DK—English/Dansk/Deutsch/Espanol/Français annual c950pp

A-Z manufacturers plus details of address, date established, products. Separate product index and trade marks section. (Distributed free through Danish diplomatic offices.)

977   FISKERIBERETNING
Fiskeriministeriet

DK—Dansk(English summaries) 1973 104pp

Statistical data by the Ministry of Fisheries including: number of fishermen; equipment (vessels, nets); catches; canned and cured fish; fish exports.

978   FOLKEMAENGDEN 27 SEPTEMBER 1965 OG
DANMARKS ADMINISTRATIVE INDDELING
Danmarks Statistik

DK—Dansk/English 1968

Detailed population statistics in capital and provincial towns and urban localities, by: size; rural population; number of households; persons per households; density of population; changes in administrative units.

979   FOREIGN TRADE REGULATIONS OF DENMARK
US Department of Commerce

DK—English 1971 9pp

Overseas Business Report no. OBR 71-051. Concise report on regulations governing foreign trade in Denmark, covering: tariffs; customs regulations; internal taxes; documentation.

980   GREEN'S DANSKE FONDS OG AKTIER
Børsen's Forlag

DK—Dansk annual 2 vols. 1100pp

Green's Danish stocks and shares. Vol. 1: State and other loans, banks, insurance, transport, property. Vol. 2: Industrial, commercial and other companies — details of address, date established, capital, directors. Separate A-Z companies index.

981   HINTS TO BUSINESSMEN — DENMARK
British Overseas Trade Board

DK—English 1976 48pp

Practical guide for travelling executives, covering: general information; travel; hotels; restaurant and tipping; postal and telephone facilities; economic factors; import and exchange control regulations; methods of doing business; government and commercial organisations; reading list; map.

982   INDKOMST- OG FORMUER VED SLUTLIGNINGEN
Danmarks Statistik

DK—Dansk(English headings) 1974 97pp

Income and property assessments, including data on: number of principal taxpayers and married women with own incomes,

divided by counties; number of taxpayers by municipalities and size of assessed income; amount paid by taxpayers.

983   INDUSTRIAL PRODUKTIONSSTATISTIK
Danmarks Statistik

DK—Dansk annual

Detailed statistics of manufactured industrial products classified by BTN and SITC. Data on: production; materials consumed; index of production and hours worked in specific industries; number of establishments; employees; wages; working hours.

984   INDUSTRISTATISTIK
Danmarks Statistik

DK—Dansk(English notes) 1972 351pp

Industrial statistics, including: employment; economic statistics of industrial establishments; investment; volume and production indexes; profit and loss.

985   INDUSTRY IN DENMARK
Financial Times

DK—English 2 May 1973 p.19-30

Survey in the Financial Times newspaper covering: political climate; exports; foreign investment; banking; shipbuilding; engineering exports; pharmaceuticals; hospital equipment. electronics; textiles; food machinery.

986   INFORMATION GUIDE FOR DOING BUSINESS IN
DENMARK
Price, Waterhouse and Co.

DK—English 1967

Guide to business in Denmark covering: formation and conduct of business enterprises; accounting practices; company taxation; labour and social welfare regulations; patents; trademarks; copyright; individual taxation; inheritance and gift taxes.

987   KOMPAS-DANMARK: INDEKS OVER DANMARKS
INDUSTRI OG NOERINGSLIV
A/S Forlaget Kompas-Danmark

DK—English/Dansk/Deutsch/Español/Français annual
c1900pp

Register of Danish industry and commerce listing companies geographically, with details of: address; products; directors; capital employed; employees. Systematic product charts and separate product index.

988   KONGELIG DANSK HOF- OG STATSKALENDER:
STÅTHANDBOG FOR KONGERIGET DANMARK
A/S J H Schultz

DK—Dansk

Royal Danish court and official handbook. Information on: Royal household; titled people; public offices and government departments; institutes; societies; organisations. Separate indexes: A-Z organisations; A-Z persons.

989 **KONGERIGET DANMARKS HANDELSKALENDER**
Kongeriget Danmarks Handelskalender A/S

DK—Dansk c2600pp

Trade directory of the Kingdom of Denmark; classified
directory for all Denmark listing provincial towns A-Z, with
general information, maps and classified directories. A-Z
businesses in Copenhagen, also lists businesses in the rest of
Denmark A-Z. Separate indexes; towns; Copenhagen streets.

990 **KONJUNKTUROVERSIGT**
Danmarks Statistik

DK—Dansk quarterly

Economic trends — quarterly supplement to Statistiske
Efterretninger.

991 **KRAKS VEJVISER**
Krak

DK—Dansk annual 3 vols c6400pp

General commercial directory for Denmark, containing:
Vol. 1: Classified manufacturers and traders; products and
services index; A-Z companies and firms with data on:
registration, legal form, directors, capital, products;
directories of Faroe Islands and Greenland. Vol. 2:
80,000 classified businesses; organisations, societies and
institutes; A-Z local authorities; street maps. Vol. 3:
Copenhagen street directory with maps.

992 **KVARTALSSTATISTIK FOR INDUSTRIEN**
Danmarks Statistik

DK—Dansk(English notes) quarterly

Quarterly statistics of industry, including data on sales of
manufacturing industries products arranged by BTN.

993 **KVARTDSSTATISTIK OVER UDENRIGSHANDELEN**
Danmarks Statistik

DK—Dansk quarterly

Quarterly bulletin of foreign trade statistics arranged by BTN
and SITC. Imports and exports listed by countries of origin
and consumption.

994 **LANDBRUGSSTATISTIK, HERUNDER GARTNERI OG
SKOVBRUG**
Danmarks Statistik

DK—Dansk/English 1974 351pp

Statistics of agriculture, horticulture and forestry. Includes
data on: number of farms; agricultural areas; crop yield;
livestock; feeding stuffs; animal products; vegetable sales;
labour; machinery; wages. Based on 1972 figures.

995 **MAIN FEATURES OF THE DANISH ECONOMY,
DECEMBER 1975**
Den Danske Landmandsbank

DK—English 1975 6pp

Brief summary, with diagrams, of the current economic
climate with details of the new monetary policy.

996 **MÅNEDSSTATISTIK OVER UDENRIGSHANDELEN**
Danmarks Statistik

DK—Dansk(English notes) monthly

Monthly bulletin of foreign trade with monthly and
cumulative figures arranged by BTN and SITC. Imports and
exports by countries of origin and consumption.

997 **LE MARCHE DU MATERIEL DE CAMPING ET DE
CARAVANING AU DANEMARK**
Centre Français du Commerce Extérieur

DK—Français 1974

The market for camping and caravaning equipment in
Denmark. A detailed market survey with data on: national
production; imports; exports; consumption and the
distributive structure of the industry. Includes a selective
list of Danish manufacturers and importers in this field.

998 **NORDISK HANDELS KALENDER**
Scan Report A/S

DK/N/S/SF—English/Dansk/Deutsch annual c2000pp

Scandinavian trade directory with separate classified section
for each country.

999 **OECD ECONOMIC SURVEYS — DENMARK**
Organisation for Economic Co-operation and Development

DK—English/Français July 1975 70pp

Details on: supply and use of resources; economic indicators;
manufacturing unit labour costs; private income and
expenditure; consumer prices; import and export trends;
balance of payments.

1000 **QUARTERLY ECONOMIC REVIEW — DENMARK,
ICELAND**
Economist Intelligence Unit

DK/IS—English quarterly with annual supplement

Analysis of current economic trends including: government;
population; employment; exchange rates; national accounts;
agriculture; mining; fuel and power; manufacturing
industries; transport and communications; finance.

1001 **THE SCANDINAVIAN MARKET**
København Handelsbank

DK/N/S/SF—Dansk/English

Business survey of the four Scandinavian countries, published
every second autumn.

1002 **SCANDINAVIAN RESEARCH GUIDE: DIRECTORY OF
RESEARCH INSTITUTIONS WITHIN TECHNOLOGY
AND PHYSICAL SCIENCES**
Scandinavian Council for Applied Research

DK/N/S/SF—English c450pp

Survey of research organisations in each country. Includes
central research organisations, academies, research councils,
universities, colleges, institutes of technology, research units,
classified broadly by subjects. Separate indexes: subjects;
organisations; personnel.

1003 SETTING UP IN DENMARK
København Handelsbank

DK—English 1974 32pp

Introduction for the potential business investor in Denmark,
giving details on the economic, legal and financial aspects of
foreign investment.

1004 SKOVE OG PLANTAGER
Danmarks Statistik

DK—Dansk annual

Census of forestry with statistics on the number of forests,
size, composition and yield.

1005 STATISTIK ÁRBOG
Danmarks Statistik

DK—Dansk 1974 664pp

Statistics on: area and population; property; agriculture;
manufacturing, construction and commerce; foreign trade;
transport and communications; prices; insurance; wages and
labour; education; public finance; taxes; Faroe Islands;
Greenland.

1006 STATISTIK TIÁRS-OVERSIGT
Danmarks Statistik

DK—Dansk annual c100pp

Ten-year statistical survey of economic and social
developments. Covers similar subjects to Statistisk Árbog,
but in less detail.

1007 STATISTISKE EFTERRETNINGER
Danmarks Statistik

DK—Dansk 80 issues a year

Statistical news, with index numbers and articles and
summaries of enquiries published in other Danmarks
Statistik publications, "Statistik Tabelvaerk" and
"Statistike Meddelelser".

**1008 STATISTISKE UNDERSOGELSER NO. 27:
BEFOLKNINGSPROGNOSER 1970**
Danmarks Statistik

DK—Dansk 111pp

Statistical enquiries, number 27: population progressions.
Gives population forecasts from 1970-2000.

1009 SUPERMARKEDER
Per Press

DK—Dansk/English 1974 200pp

Supermarkets: tables on number and geographic
distribution; size of sales areas; number of cash registers.

1010 SURVEY OF DENMARK
The Economist

DK—English 13 Mar. 1971 30pp

A special supplement on Denmark issued with the Economist
journal. Includes information on: Danish exports and
imports; the political scene; industrial expansion; foreign
trade.

1011 THE THOUSAND LARGEST COMPANIES IN DENMARK
Teknisk Forlag A/S

DK—English/Dansk 1975 158pp

Lists the top 1000 companies with data on: ranking by sales;
capital; assets; invested capital; invested capital as a
percentage of assets; profits; sales per employee; exports.
Also contains special surveys on current and potential
economic trends.

1012 UDENRIGS HANDELSKALENDEREN FOR DANMARK
Udenrigs Handels Informationsbureau

DK—Dansk c1900pp

Foreign trade directory of Denmark.

1013 VARESTATISTIK
Danmarks Statistik

DK—Dansk/English quarterly(annual subscription)

Sales of commodities. Industrial statistics and sales arranged
by BTN; turnover of manufacturing industries; shipyard
statistics.

**1014 VIDENSKABELIGE OG FAGLIGE BIBLIOTEKER I
KØBENHAVN**
Rigsbibliotekarembedet

DK—Dansk c50pp

Scientific and technical libraries in Copenhagen, classified
with details of stock, subject collections. Separate indexes:
subjects; A-Z.

E-SPAIN

1050 ANUARIO ESTADISTICO DE ESPAÑA (EDICION MANUAL)
Instituto Nacional de Estadística

E—Español annual c300pp

Statistical yearbook of Spain, pocket edition; an abridged version of the statistical yearbook, Anuario Estadístico de España.

1051 ANUARIO ESTADISTICO DE ESPAÑA (EDICION NORMAL)
Instituto Nacional de Estadística

E/INT—Español annual c800pp

Statistical yearbook of Spain covering: geography and climate; demography; agriculture; forestry; cattle; fisheries; industry; transport and communications; finance; prices and wages; employment; social security; health; education; tourism; justice; foreign trade; African provinces. Also includes some international statistics.

1052 ANUARIO ESTADISTICO DE LA PRODUCCION AGRICOLA
Instituto Nacional de Estadística

E—Español annual

Statistical yearbook of agriculture production, giving data on: crops; fruit; wine; tobacco. Includes data for the whole of Spain and the provinces.

1053 BANCO DE BILBAO: ANNUAL REPORT AND ACCOUNTS
Banco de Bilbao

E—Español annual c110pp

Annual report including commentary and statistics on the economy.

1054 BANCO DE ESPAÑA: INFORME ANUAL
Banco de España

E—Español annual c400pp

Annual report including commentary and detailed statistics on the Spanish economy.

1055 BARCLAYS COUNTRY REPORT — SPAIN
Bàrclays Bank

E—English

Brief summary covering: payments; prices and wages; external positions; economic outlook.

1056 BASIC DATA ON THE ECONOMY OF SPAIN
US Department of Commerce

E—English 1968 19pp

Overseas Business Report no. OBR 68-110. General report on the Spanish economy covering: basic structure; industrial sectors; labour market; trade; finance; economic outlook.

1057 BOLETIN INFORMATIVO
Banco Central

E—Español monthly

Monthly bank bulletin giving current information on the financial and trade situation and the stock market.

1058 BOLETIN MENSUAL DE ESTADISTICA
Instituto Nacional de Estadística

E—Español monthly

Monthly bulletin of statistics, including data on: population; tourism; production; consumption; transport and communications; finance; labour; prices; the media; foreign trade.

1059 BUSINESS IN SPAIN
Lloyds Bank International

E—English 1974 7 parts 40pp

Part 1: Foreign investment and industrial property. Part 2: Foreign exchange and trade. Part 3: Forms of business organisation. Part 4: Taxation. Part 5: Development incentives. Part 6: Labour legislation. Part 7: Banking and credit.

1060 CATALOGO DESCRIPTIVO DE PUBLICACIONES ESTADISTICAS
Instituto Nacional de Estadística

E—Español c400pp

Complete listing of statistical publications giving full
descriptions of contents.

1061 CATALONIA
The Financial Times

E—English 18 April 1975 p.19-26

Survey in the Financial Times newspaper covering: the
economy; politics; trade; banking and finance; labour
relations; industrial development; tourism.

1062 CENSO AGRARIO DE ESPAÑA
Instituto Nacional de Estadística

E—Español 1962

Census of agriculture, covering employment, combines,
services to the agricultural community. Includes national
survey, provincial tables and some provisional results.

1063 CENSO DE LA POBLACION Y DE LAS VIVIENDAS DE
ESPAÑA
Instituto Nacional de Estadística

E—Español 4 vols

Census of the population of Spain. Vol. 1: General volume.
Vol. 2: Housing. Vols 3 & 4: Provincial tables.

1064 CENSO DE MAQUINARIA AGRICOLA
Instituto Nacional de Estadística

E—Español c50pp free

Census of agricultural machinery; data on: agricultural
machinery in existence by province; increases in machinery
usage; graphs and maps.

1065 CONTABILIDAD NACIONAL DE ESPAÑA
Instituto Nacional de Estadística

E—Español annual c100pp

National accounts of Spain; giving data on: general economic
situation; GNP; national accounts.

1066 ECONOMIC REPORT: THE SPANISH ECONOMY
Banco de Bilbao

E—English/Français/Deutsch annual c80pp

Abridged version of the Bank of Bilbao's annual report
presenting a commentary and statistics on the Spanish
economy and indicating future trends in the development
of the economy.

1067 ENCUESTA NACIONAL DE COMERCIO INTERIOR
Instituto Nacional de Estadística

E—Español 1968

Survey of internal trade, classified by type of business. Data
on: volume of business; establishments by type of service; by
numbers and status of personnel; by ownership. Each
section is devoted to a province of Spain.

1068 ESTADISTICA DE PESCA
Ministerio de Comercio

E—Español annual c300pp

Fishing statistics; data on: fish and shell fish caught and
landed by type and region.

1069 ESTADISTICA DE TRANSPORTE
Instituto Nacional de Estadística

E—Español annual

Annual transport statistics issued by the Spanish National
Institute of Statistics.

1070 ESTADISTICA DEL COMERCIO EXTERIOR DE
ESPAÑA
Dirección General de Aduabas

E—Español quarterly

Statistics of the foreign trade of Spain with tables showing
imports and exports arranged by commodities and subdivided
by countries of origin and destination. Also includes tables
of transit trade, and imports and exports by countries of
origin and destination subdivided by commodities.

1071 ESTADISTICA DEL COMERCIO EXTERIOR DE ESPAÑA:
COMERCIO POR ADUANAS Y TRAFICO DE
PERFECCIONAMIENTO EN NDB
Dirección General de Aduanas

E—Español annual c450pp

Statistics of the foreign trade of Spain including imports for
improvement and re-exports.

1072 ESTADISTICA DEL COMERCIO EXTERIOR DE ESPAÑA:
COMERCIO POR PRODUCTOS POR PAISES EN NDB
Dirección General de Aduanas

E—Español annual c1000pp

Statistics of the foreign trade of Spain; trade by commodities
(BTN) subdivided by countries.

1073 ESTADISTICA DEL COMERCIO EXTERIOR DE ESPAÑA:
COMERCIO POR PRODUCTOS Y POR PAISES EN SITC
(CUCI)
Dirección General de Aduanas

E—Español annual c1100pp

Statistics of the foreign trade of Spain; trade by commodities
(SITC) subdivided by countries.

1074 ESTADISTICA DEL COMERCIO EXTERIOR DE ESPAÑA:
COMERCIO POR ZONAS, ADMISIONES, DEPOSITOS Y
TRANSITOS
Dirección General de Aduanas

E—Español annual c430pp

Statistics of the foreign trade of Spain: trade between Spain
and its colonies; temporary imports, free deposits and transit
trade.

1075 ESTADISTICAS DE LA POBLACION DE ESPAÑA
DEDUCIDAS DE PADRON MUNICIPAL DE
HABITANTES DEL 1965
Instituto Nacional de Estadística

E—Español 1965 229pp

Estimates of the population of towns of more than 10,000
inhabitants.

1076 ESTADISTICAS DE PRODUCCION INDUSTRIAL
Servicio Sindical de Estadística

E—Español annual 2 vols

Statistics of industrial production. Vol. 1: Data on:
production of fruit and vegetables; sugar; food; mineral
waters; fish; leather; textiles; timber; paper; printing;
chemicals; construction; glass; pottery; metals; water; gas;
electricity. Vol. 2: Mainly textual analysis of the results
contained in Volume 1.

1077 ESTADISTICAS DE PRODUCCION INDUSTRIAL:
INFORMACION MENSUAL
Servicio Sindical de Estadística

E—Español monthly

Monthly bulletin on industrial production statistics with
similar coverage to the annual volume.

1078 LA EVOLUCION MONETARIA: NOVEMBRE 1976
Banco de España

E—Español 1976 4pp

Reviews the changing monetary climate in Spain.

1079 HINTS TO BUSINESSMEN — SPAIN (INCLUDING THE
CANARY ISLANDS)
British Overseas Trade Board

E—English 1976 56pp

Practical guide to travelling executives covering: general
information; travel; hotels; restaurants and tipping; postal
and telephone facilities; economic factors; imports and
exchange control regulations; methods of doing business;
government and commercial organisations; reading list; map.

1080 HOW TO INVEST IN SPAIN
Banco de Bilbao

E—English

Information for potential business investors in Spain.

1081 HOW TO LOOK AFTER YOUR INTERESTS IN SPAIN
WITHOUT ACTUALLY BEING THERE
Banco de Bilbao

E—English 1973 10pp

Details of the Bank of Bilbao's Spanish services for businessmen and investors.

1082 INDICADORES ECONOMICOS
Instituto Nacional de Estadística

E—Español monthly

Economic indicators; monthly publication of indices of:
industrial production; employment; hours worked; hourly
wages; wholesale prices; cost of living; foreign trade; tourism;
transport; housing.

1083 INDUSTRIAL PROSPECTS IN SPAIN: THE POLITICAL
CLIMATE
Focus Research Ltd.

E—English 1976 55pp

Contents: the new Government; the democratic opposition
in Spain; Spain and the EEC; the economy; industrialisation
and foreign investment.

1084 INFORME ANUAL SOBRE EL COMERCIO EXTERIOR
Dirección General de Aduanas

E—Español annual c150pp

Annual report on foreign trade, subdivided by broad
economic groups.

1085 INFORME MENSUAL SOBRE EL COMERCIO EXTERIOR
Dirección General de Aduanas

E—Español monthly

Monthly report on foreign trade, giving tables of imports and
exports.

1086 INFORME SOBRE LA DISTRIBUCION DE LAS RENTAS
Instituto Nacional de Estadística

E—Español annual c130pp

Report on the distribution of income; individual statistics of
national income; personal incomes; employment; wages; cost
of living.

1087 LAST WEEK IN SPAIN
Banco Español en Londres

E—English weekly

Weekly news-sheet giving data on the stock exchange, industry
and the general economic situation.

1088 MOVIMIENTO NATURAL DE LA POBLACION
Instituto Nacional de Estadística

E—Español annual

Annual statistics on demography and population movements.

1089 OECD ECONOMIC SURVEYS — SPAIN
Organisation for Economic Co-operation and Development

E—English/Français 1976 54pp

Individual analysis of the Spanish economy, covering recent
developments in demand, output, employment, prices and
incomes and the broad lines of economic policies affecting
fiscal, employment, industrial restructuring and prices and
incomes.

1090 QUARTERLY ECONOMIC REVIEW — SPAIN
Economist Intelligence Unit

E—English quarterly with annual supplement

Analysis of current economic trends including: government;
population; employment; exchange rates; national accounts;
agriculture; mining; fuel and power; manufacturing industries;
transport and communications; finance.

1091 RENTA NACIONAL DE ESPAÑA: Y SU DISTRIBUCION
PROVINCIAL
Banco de España

E—Español annual c220pp

Commentary and details of the revenue and accounts of the Spanish provinces.

1092 RESEÑAS ESTADISTICAS PROVINCIALES
Instituto Nacional de Estadística

E—Español

Review of provincial statistics; subject coverage similar to Anuario Estadístico de España, and there are separate volumes for each of the Spanish provinces.

1093 REVISTA SINDICAL DE ESTADISTICA
Servicio Sindical de Estadística

E—Español quarterly

Review of the Servicio Sindical de Estadística; containing articles on economic subjects — agriculture, transport, services. Includes statistical tables.

1094 SALARIOS
Instituto Nacional de Estadística

E—Español quarterly

National Institute of Statistics quarterly data on wages.

1095 SPAIN
The Financial Times

E—English 29 June 1976 p.17-24

Special survey in the Financial Times newspaper covering: slow-down in economic growth; banking; chemical industry; nuclear energy; tourism.

1096 SPAIN: EUROPE'S NEW INDUSTRIAL FRONTIER
Business International SA

E—English 1974 144pp

Contents: industrial progress and prospects; foreign investment; obtaining investment approvals; taxes; regional investment; incentives; financing Spanish operations; labour; selling to the Spanish market; Spain as an export base.

1097 SPAIN: SPECIAL REPORT
The Times

E—English 20 June 1975 p.21-25

Special report in the Times newspaper covering: the economy; shipbuilding; wine industry; tourism.

1098 SPANISH BANKING
The Times

E—English 3 Oct. 1974 p.25-27

Survey in the Times newspaper of the Spanish banking system.

1099 SPANISH INDUSTRY
The Financial Times

E—English 20 Nov. 1974 p.19-26

Survey in the Financial Times newspaper covering: banking; foreign investment; labour problems; shipbuilding; energy crisis; chemical industry; car production; steel-making.

1100 SPANISH ISLANDS: SPECIAL REPORT
The Times

E—English 15 March 1975 6pp

Special report in the Times newspaper which shows the importance of tourism to the economy of the Canary Islands.

1101 SPANISH SHIPBUILDING
The Times

E—English 22 July 1974 p.22-23

Review in the Times newspaper of the shipbuilding industry in Spain.

1102 SPOTLIGHT ON OVERSEAS TRADE — SELLING TO SPAIN
Midland Bank International

E—English 1973 4pp

Contents: economic situations; market opportunities; regulations and documentary requirements; company formation in Spain; UK exports to Spain.

1103 STUDY OF SPANISH ECONOMIC AND SOCIAL DEVELOPMENT
Banco de Bilbao

E—English

Review and commentary of the social and economic development of Spain.

F-FRANCE

1150 ADVERTISING CONDITIONS IN FRANCE
Institute of Practitioners in Advertising

F—English 1974 20pp

Contents: basic facts — geography and demography; the media — press, outdoor, cinema, fairs, direct mail; advertising agencies and services; research; taxes, laws and regulations; advertising and related organisations.

1151 L'ANNEE ECONOMIQUE ET FINANCIERE EN FRANCE EN 1975
Crédit Commercial de France

F—Français 1976 67pp

Commentary and statistics on the French economy including a detailed report on the French Stock Exchange.

1152 ANNUAIRE DE STATISTIQUE INDUSTRIELLE
Service Central de la Statistique et des Informations Industrielles

F—Français annual c300pp

Yearbook of industrial statistics; data on: electricity; gas; fuels; petroleum and petroleum products; minerals; foundry industry; mechanical and electrical industry; glass; ceramics; chemicals and pharmaceuticals; rubber; agriculture; food; textiles; wood; paper. Also includes a general index of industrial production statistics.

1153 ANNUAIRE STATISTIQUE DE LA FRANCE
Institut National de la Statistique et des Etudes Economiques

F—Français annual c700pp

Statistical yearbook of France. Main sections: geography and climate; population; economic resources; agriculture, forestry, fishery; transport and communications; internal trade; prices, incomes; consumption; finance; international data.

1154 ANNUAIRE STATISTIQUE DE L'INDUSTRIE FRANCAISE DU JUTE
Syndicat Général de l'Industrie du Jute

F—Français annual

Annual statistics of the French jute industry. Gives data on: production; wages; prices; imports and exports of jute and jute products.

1155 ANNUAIRE STATISTIQUE DES TRANSPORTS
Ministère de l'Aménagement du Territoire, de l'Equipement, du Logement et du Tourisme, Service des Affaires Economiques et Internationales (Institut National de la Statistique et des Etudes Economiques)

F—Français annual

Annual digest of transport statistics.

1156 ANTIFER - A NEW OIL TERMINAL
French Embassy, London

F—English 1974

Facts, Figures France: no. A/101/74. Description of the new oil terminal at Antifer.

1157 AREA DEVELOPMENT AND REGIONAL PLANNING IN FRANCE - THE DATAR
French Embassy, London

F—English 1974

Facts, Figures France: no A/102/9/74. Objectives and policy of DATAR - Délégation à l'Aménagement du Territoire et à l'Action Régionale — The French regional development body.

1158 AUVERGNE
French Embassy, London

F—English 1973

Facts, Figures France: no. B/72/5/73. Description and facilities of the Auvergne.

1159 BALANCE DES PAIEMENTS
Ministère de l'Economie et des Finances, Direction du Trésor

F—Français annual

Supplement to "Statistiques et Etudes Financières", giving statistics on the balance of payments.

1160 BANQUE DE FRANCE: COMPTE RENDU
Banque de France

F—Français annual c140pp

Contains statistical charts and economic commentary.

1161 BANQUE POPULAIRE: BULLETIN D'INFORMATION
Banque Populaire

F—Français monthly

Monthly summary of general economic and financial
information.

1162 BARCLAYS COUNTRY REPORT — FRANCE
Barclays Bank

F—English

Brief summary covering: balance of payments; prices and
wages; external positions; economic outlook.

1163 BRITTANY: A REGIONAL STUDY
French Embassy, London

F—English 1970 10pp

Facts, Figures France: no. B/51/2/9 Commentary and plans
for the regional development of Brittany.

1164 BULLETIN MENSUEL DE STATISTIQUE
Institut National de la Statistique et des Etudes Economiques

F—Français monthly

Monthly bulletin of statistics; gives weekly and monthly
statistics on the French economy.

1165 BULLETIN MENSUEL DE STATISTIQUE DU TOURISME
Commissariat Général du Tourisme

F—Français monthly

Monthly bulletin of statistics on tourism.

1166 BULLETIN MENSUEL DE STATISTIQUE INDUSTRIELLE
Service Central de la Statistique et des Informations
Industrielles, Ministère du Développement Industriel et
Scientifique

F—Français monthly

Monthly bulletin of industrial statistics; updates much of
the information in Annuaire de Statistique Industrielle
(no. 1152)

**1167 BULLETIN MENSUEL D'INFORMATIONS FINANCIERES
ET BOURSIERES**
Société Générale, Siège Social

F—Français/English monthly

Monthly economic review of the French and overseas stock
markets.

1168 BUSINESS IN FRANCE
Lloyds Bank International

F—English 1973 7 parts

A series of 7 booklets, covering: 1: Foreign exchange,
investment and trade. 2: Forms of business organisation.
3: Taxation. 4: Regional development policy. 5: Labour
legislation. 6: Protection of industrial property and leasing.
7: Banking and credit.

1169 BUSINESS NEWSLETTER
French Commercial Counsellor

F—English fortnightly

Regular bulletin giving details of French exports to the UK,
trade exhibitions, business opportunities and technical news
from France.

**1170 THE CENTRE NATIONALE DE LA RECHERCHE
SCIENTIFIQUE**
French Embassy, London

F—English 1970

Facts, Figures France: no. B/58/5/70. Description of the
Centre's organisation and objectives.

**1171 CHARLES DE GAULLE AIRPORT AT ROISSY-EN-
FRANCE**
French Embassy, London

F—English· 1974

Facts, Figures France: no. A/93/1/74. Description of the
new airport.

1172 LES COLLECTIONS DE L'INSEE
Institut National de la Statistique et des Etudes
Economiques

F—Français irregular

Complete list of the results of the studies conducted by the
INSEE.

**1173 LE COMMERCE EXTERIEUR DES REGIONS PROVENCE,
COTE-D'AZUR ET CORSE EN 1975**
Chambre de Commerce et d'Industrie de Marseille

F/INT—Français 1976 105pp

Commentary and statistics on foreign trade of Provence,
Côte d'Azur and Corsica with East Europe, West Europe and
the USA.

1174 LES COMPTES DE LA NATION
Institut National de la Statistique et des Etudes Economiques

F—Français annual 3 vols

National accounts. Vol. 1: The Reports. Vol. 2: Tables and
comment. Vol. 3: Aggregate accounts — wide coverage,
including international statistics; population; employment;
production; consumption; investment; prices; wages; social
services.

1175 CONJONCTURE
Société Générale, Service Conjoncture

F—Français monthly

Monthly economic summary and special articles on current
developments.

1176 LA CONSTRUCTION ELECTRIQUE
Syndicat Générale de la Construction Electrique

F—Français monthly

Electrical construction; statistical tables on: production;
employment. Subscription also includes the annual "Rapport
statistique", giving data on: structure of the industry;
production; wages; investment; productivity;
foreign trade.

1177 CONSUMER PROTECTION IN FRANCE
French Embassy, London

F—English

Facts, Figures France: no. B/52/3/9. Summary of legislation
protecting the consumer in France.

1178 THE DATA PROCESSING INDUSTRY IN FRANCE
French Embassy, London

F—English 1976 16pp

Facts, Figures France: no. A/114/9/76. Government policy
on computers; large computer industry; mini-computer
industry; peri-informatics industry.

1179 ECONOMIE ET STATISTIQUE
Institut National de la Statistique et des Etudes
Economiques

F—Français monthly

A monthly review of the work of INSEE of general economic
interest and including statistical data.

1180 ENERGY IN FRANCE
French Embassy, London

F—English 1974 12pp

Facts, Figures France: no. A/94/1/74. Contents: energy
consumption; production estimates for 1972-2000; oil; gas;
coal; nuclear energy.

**1181 L'ESPACE ECONOMIQUE FRANCAIS FASCICULE II:
POPULATION ACTIVE**
Institut National de la Statistique et des Etudes Economiques

F—Français

Special number of "Etude et Conjoncture" giving an
economic and statistical study of France's working
population.

**1182 ESTABLISHMENT OF FOREIGN BUSINESSES IN
FRANCE**
Crédit Lyonnais

F—English

Information on setting up a business in France, including:
taxation; social security; legal formalities.

**1183 LES ETABLISSEMENTS INDUSTRIELS ET
COMMERCIAUX EN FRANCE EN 1966**
Institut National de la Statistique et des Etudes
Economiques

F—Français 3 vols

Industrial and commercial establishments in France; each
volume gives statistical data on the number and type
of establishments and the number of employees. Vol. 1:
Data on individual local areas. Vol. 2: Data on the
Departments of France. Vol. 3: Data on the country as a whole.

1184 FACTS AND FIGURES: PORT OF MARSEILLE
Port of Marseille Authority

F—English 1974 59pp

Contents: Marseille region and port area: the Port of Marseille
Authority; harbour areas; port and industrial development
area of Fos; inland communications; shipping services.

1185 FRANCE: A DIVIDED NATION
The Economist

F—English 23 Feb. 1974 42pp

A survey in The Economist examining the political and
economic situation in France.

**1186 FRANCE: A NEW INVESTMENT CLIMATE
DATAR**

F—English 1975 62pp

Practical advice and information for the company
considering establishing a manufacturing unit in France.

1187 FRANCE AND BRITAIN
The Times

F—English 22 June 1976 6pp

Special report in The Times newspaper, covering: France/UK
trade; Concorde; tourism.

1188 FRANCE AND THE UNITED NATIONS
French Embassy, London

F/INT—English 1970

Facts, Figures France: no. B/60/11/70

1189 FRANCE: FINANCIAL TIMES SURVEY
The Financial Times

F—English 22 June 1976 p.15-26

Survey in the Financial Times newspaper covering: French
economy; chemicals; oil; shipbuilding; nuclear energy;
aerospace industry.

1190 FRANCE IN FIGURES
French Embassy Press and Information Service

F—English 1976 8pp

Booklet giving brief statistical data on: population;
manpower; GNP; national accounts; taxation; the Budget;
energy; industrial production; agriculture; transport; foreign
trade; balance of payments; education; health; social security.

1191 FRANCE: INVESTORS CHRONICLE SURVEY
Investors Chronicle

F—English 21 June 1974 22pp

Survey in the Investors Chronicle journal covering: property
market; tourism; the Bourse; regional development; retailing.

1192 FRANCE: SPECIAL REPORT
Commerce International

F—English 1973 10pp

A special report by Commerce International covering:
UK/France trade; investment in France; setting up a company
in France; Paris as a financial centre.

1193 FRANCE: SPECIAL REPORT
The Times

F—English 25 Nov. 1975 10pp

Report in the Times newspaper covering: French foreign
policy; exports; State participation in industry; motor
industry; electronics; Concorde; tourism.

1194 THE FRENCH BANKING SYSTEM
French Embassy, London

F—English 1976 22pp

Facts, Figures France: no. A/112/2/76. Contents:
Government reforms; banking structures; foreign banks;
credit and savings banks.

1195 THE FRENCH CLOTHING INDUSTRY
French Embassy, London

F—English 1970

Facts, Figures France: no. A/69/5/9. Commentary and
statistics on the French clothing industry.

1196 THE FRENCH MARKET FOR WALLCOVERINGS:
MARKET DESCRIPTION STUDY
Confremca

F—English 1975

A survey of the French market giving information on market
size, structure, advertising expenditures, and an analysis of
future trends, including a detailed study of distributive
structure of industry. A consumer survey was conducted
separately by Marplan. Includes a list of wholesalers.

1197 FRENCH MARKETS REVIEW 1975-76 A GUIDE TO
BUSINESS PROSPECTS AND PROCEDURES
Gower Press

F—English 1975

Begins with a general survey of French economy, and
individual industrial sectors. Includes practical information
on doing business in France and establishing a company.
Contains a list of top 100 industrial companies, and a
directory of principal financial institutions.

1198 FRENCH NATIONAL DEFENCE
French Embassy, London

F—English 1974 16pp

Facts, Figures France: no. A/99/6/74. Details of the
Government's defence policy covering the army, navy and
air force.

1199 FRENCH RAILWAYS — A NEW HIGH SPEED LINE ON
THE SOUTH-EASTERN NETWORK
French Embassy, London

F—English 1974 8pp

Facts, Figures France: no. A/98/5/74. Description of the
new line planned for 1980 to achieve Paris to Lyons in two
hours, and Paris to Marseille in under five hours.

1200 FRENCH RAILWAYS: AN INVESTMENT PROGRAMME
FOR ENERGY CONSERVATION
French Embassy, London

F—English 1975

Facts, Figures France: no. A/105/1/75. Summary of the
Government's investment and development plans for French
railways.

1201 FRENCH REGIONAL DEVELOPMENT RESULTS 1969-70
French Embassy, London

F—English 1971

Facts, Figures France: no. B/62/4/71. Commentary and
statistics on regional development.

1202 THE FRENCH SOCIAL SECURITY SYSTEM
French Embassy, London

F—English

Facts, Figures France: no. A/64/12/8. Summary of the
social security services in France.

1203 FRENCH WORKER PARTICIPATION IN PROFIT-
SHARING
French Embassy, London

F—English 1970

Facts, Figures France: no. B/57/4/70. Review of profit-
sharing in French industries.

1204 GAZ DE FRANCE
Gaz de France

F—Français annual

Annual statistics covering the production and distribution of
gas, including data on: industrial, commercial and domestic
usage; service; prices; labour; regional administration.

1205 LES GRANDS AMENAGEMENTS DE LA REGION
MARSEILLE
Chambre de Commerce et d'Industrie de Marseille

F—Français 1974 72pp

Marseille's Chamber of Commerce study on the regional
development and expansion of Marseille.

1206 THE HEART OF FRANCE: SURVEY OF PARIS
The Economist

F—English 17 Jan. 1976 18pp

An economic and social survey of Paris.

1207 HINTS TO BUSINESSMEN — FRANCE
British Overseas Trade Board

F—English 1976

Practical guide to travelling executives covering: general
information; travel; hotels; restaurants and tipping; postal
and telephone facilities; economic factors; import and
exchange control regulations; methods of doing business;
government and commercial organisations; reading lists; maps.

1208 IMMIGRATION ET CROISSANCE URBAINE
Chambre de Commerce et d'Industrie de Marseille

F—Français 1974 76pp

An economic study of immigration and migrant workers in
Provence - Côte d'Azur.

1209 IMMIGRATION ET ECONOMIE: LE TRAVAILLEUR
MIGRANT DANS LES BOUCHES-DU-RHONE
Chambre de Commerce et d'Industrie de Marseille

F—Français 1973 92pp

An economic study of the migrant worker in the Rhône
provinces.

1210 L'INDUSTRIE FRANCAISE DU PETROLE
Union des Chambres Syndicales de l'Industrie du Pétrole

F—Français annual

Annual statistics on the consumption and production of
petroleum products.

1211 INDUSTRIE LAINIERE FRANCAIS: STATISTIQUES DE
PRODUCTION
Comité Central de la Laine et de l'Industrie Lainière

F—Français annual

Annual statistics of wool production.

1212 INDUSTRIE LAINIERE FRANCAISE: STATISTIQUES DU
COMMERCE EXTERIEUR DE PRODUITS LAINIERE
Comité Central de la Laine et de l'Industrie Lainière

F—Français annual

Annual statistics on foreign trade in woollen products.

1213 INDUSTRIES ELECTRONIQUES
Fédération Nationale des Industries Electroniques

F—Français 11 issues per year

Electronics industry; each issue contains detailed tables of
imports and exports of electronic equipment.

1214 INFORMATIONS RAPIDES
Institut National de la Statistique et des Etudes Economiques

F—Français

Complementary to "Tendances de la Conjoncture" (no. 1276)
this regular bulletin contains the provisional results of surveys
conducted by the Institute into various aspects of industry
and commerce.

1215 A LOOK AT FRANCE
La Documentation Française

F—Français 1973 31pp

Commentary and statistics on: population; education and
culture; scientific research; social institutions; standard of
living; EEC; agriculture; industrial production; internal and
foreign trade; regional development; tourist sites.

1216 LYONS: SPECIAL REPORT
The Times

F—English 18 Apr. 1975 6pp

Special report in the Times Newspaper on the development
of Lyons as an international banking and commercial centre.

1217 MAJOR FRENCH COMMERCIAL PORTS
French Embassy, London

F—English 1976 12pp

Facts, Figures France: no. A/115/11/76. Government policy
towards ports; details of the following ports: Bordeaux - Le
Verdon; Dunkirk; Le Havre and Rouen; Marseille - Fos;
Nantes - St. Nazaire.

1218 MARKETING IN FRANCE
US Department of Commerce

F—English 1976 30pp

Overseas Business Report no. OBR 76-25. Contents: market
analysis for selected products; industry trends; distribution
and sales channels; government procurement; transportation
and ports; credit; import-export regulations; investment in
France; employment; taxation.

1219 MARSEILLE
Chambre de Commerce et d'Industrie de Marseille

F—Français 1972 70pp

An economic and commercial portrait of Marseille.

1220 MARSEILLE - FOS: RENCONTRE D'UN SITE ET D'UNE
IDEE
Chambre de Commerce et d'Industrie de Marseille

F—Français 1971 54pp

Report by the Marseille Chamber of Commerce on the
development of the industrial port complex at Marseilles -
Fos.

1221 MUNICIPAL ORGANIZATION IN FRANCE
French Embassy, London

F—English 1972

Facts, Figures France: no. A/86/2/72. Description of local
government organisation in France.

1222 THE NEW INVESTMENT INCENTIVE SCHEME
French Industrial Development Board

F—English 1976 17pp

Details of the new cash grants available to companies
establishing manufacturing facilities in the French regions,
introduced by the French Government on April 15, 1976.

1223 **NUMERO SPECIAL DU BULLETIN "STATISTIQUES DE LA CONSTRUCTION"**
Ministère de L'Aménagement du Territoire, de l'Equipement, du Logement et du Tourisme, Direction du Bâtiment et des Travaux Publics et de la Conjoncture (Institut National de la Statistique et des Etudes Economiques)

F—Français quarterly

Quarterly economic and statistical survey on housing, the building trade and public works.

1224 **OECD ECONOMIC SURVEYS — FRANCE**
Organisation for Economic Co-operation and Development

F—English/Français 1976 68pp

Individual analysis of the French economy, covering recent developments in demand, output, employment, prices and incomes and the broad lines of economic policies affecting fiscal, employment, industrial restructuring and prices and incomes.

1225 **AN OUTLINE OF FRENCH TRADE UNIONISM**
French Embassy, London

F—English 1975 10pp

Facts, Figures France: no. A/108/5/75. Summary of the role and position of trade unions in France.

1226 **PANORAMA OF A FRANCE REBORN**
DATAR

F—English 1975 8pp

Personal assessment by John Ardagh of the growth and development of the French economy.

1227 **THE PARIS REGION: PLANNING AND DEVELOPMENT**
French Embassy, London

F—English 1974

Facts, Figures France: no. A/103/9/74. Details of the Government's regional development plans for Paris.

1228 **THE PASTEUR INSTITUTE**
French Embassy, London

F—English 1971

Facts, Figures France: no. B/65/10/71. Description of the organisation and objectives of the Pasteur Institute.

1229 **THE PORT OF DUNKIRK AND ITS DEVELOPMENT**
French Embassy, London

F—English 1971

Facts, Figures France: no. B/63/8/71. Details of the redevelopment plans for Dunkirk.

1230 **PROBLEM REGIONS OF EUROPE: THE FRANCO-BELGIAN BORDER REGION**
Oxford University Press

F/B—English 1975 48pp

One of a series of studies which identifies and analyses the need and problems of regional planning including: agriculture; industry; population; towns and urbanization; transport and communications.

1231 **PROBLEM REGIONS OF EUROPE: THE LOWER RHONE AND MARSEILLE**
Oxford University Press

F—English 1975 48pp

One of a series of studies which identifies and analyses the need and problems of regional planning, including: agriculture; industry; population; towns and urbanization; transport and communications.

1232 **PROBLEM REGIONS OF EUROPE: THE MASSIF CENTRAL**
Oxford University Press

F—English 1973 48pp

One of a series of studies which identifies and analyses the need and problems of regional planning, including: agriculture; industry; population; towns and urbanization; transport and communications.

1233 **PROBLEM REGIONS OF EUROPE: THE PARIS BASIN**
Oxford University Press

F—English 1973 48pp

One of a series of studies which identifies and analyses the need and problems of regional planning including: agriculture; industry; populations; towns and urbanization; transport and communications.

1234 **PRODUCTION ET DISTRIBUTION DE L'ENERGIE ELECTRIQUE EN FRANCE**
Direction du Gaz, de l'Electricité et du Charbon (Ministère du Développement Industriel et Scientifique)

F—Français annual

Annual details of electricity production and distribution for each region of France.

1235 **PRODUCTION OF FRUIT AND VEGETABLES IN OECD MEMBER COUNTRIES**
Organisation for Economic Co-operation and Development

F/B/L—Français/English 1970

Survey of fruit and vegetable production in France, Belgium and Luxembourg.

1236 **PUBLIC ENTERPRISE IN FRANCE**
French Embassy, London

F—English 1972

Facts, Figures France: no. A/87/5/72. The encouragement of public enterprise in France.

1237 **QUARTERLY ECONOMIC REVIEW — FRANCE**
Economist Intelligence Unit

F—English quarterly with annual supplement

Analysis of current economic trends including: government; population; employment; exchange rates; national accounts; agriculture; mining; fuel and power; manufacturing industries; transport and communications; finance.

1238 QUELQUES DONNEES STATISTIQUES SUR
L'INDUSTRIE FRANCAISE DES PATES, PAPIERS ET
CARTONS
Centre d'Etude et de Productivité des Industries des Papiers,
Cartons et Celluloses

F—Français annual c30pp

Statistics of the French pulp, paper and box industries;
contains data on: production; foreign trade; supply and stock
of pulp and paper products; consumption of wood and
power.

1239 RECENSEMENT DE LA DISTRIBUTION
Institut National de la Statistique et des Etudes Economiques

F—Français 1966

Census of distribution; data on: persons employed in types
of enterprises; wages and salaries; investment; numbers of
enterprises of different types. Information is given nationally,
regionally and for each Department of France.

1240 RECENSEMENT DE LA DISTRIBUTION DE 1966:
HOTELS, CAFES, RESTAURANTS — AUTRES SERVICES
Institut National de la Statistique et des Etudes Economiques

F—Français 1968

Statistics for the service industry taken from the 1967 trade
census.

1241 RECENSEMENT DE L'INDUSTRIE 1963: RESULTATS
POUR 1962
Institut National de la Statistique et des Etudes Economiques

F—Français 5 vols

Census of industry. Vol. 1: Enterprises employing less than
10 employees. Vol. 2: Enterprises employing more than 10
employees; for the whole country, by types of business and
size. Vol. 3: Total enterprises by type of business and size.
Vol. 4: Total enterprises by regions; type of business and
size. Vol. 5: Total number of establishments by types of
business and size.

1242 RECENSEMENT GENERAL DE LA POPULATION
Institut National de la Statistique et des Etudes Economiques

F—Français 1968

Statistics from the census of population. Includes information
on towns of over 2,000 inhabitants.

1243 LA REGION ET LE CHANGEMENT 1975
Chambre de Commerce et d'Industrie de Marseille

F—Français 1975 72pp

Details of regional and industrial redevelopment in Provence -
Côte d'Azur.

1244 THE REGIONS AND REGIONAL REFORM IN FRANCE
French Embassy, London

F—English 1974

Facts, Figures France: no. A/95/2/74. Details of the
Government's regional reform and redevelopment plans.

1245 REPORT ON CONSUMER RESEARCH IN FRANCE
Marplan Ltd.

F—English 1975 2 vols

A companion study to Confremca's survey of the French
Market for wallcoverings, comprising a detailed survey
of French consumer demand in this field.

1246 RESULTATS DE L'EXPLOITATION DES PORTS
MARITIMES
Ministère de l'Aménagement du Territoire, de l'Equipement,
du Logement et du Tourisme, Direction des Ports Maritimes
et des Voies Navigables (Institut National de la Statistique et
des Etudes Economiques)

F—Français annual

Annual statistics of trade through the French ports.

1247 RESULTATS TECHNIQUES D'EXPLOITATION
Ministère du Développement Industriel et Scientifique
Electricité de France

F—Français annual

Contains information on production, distribution and
consumption of electrical energy in France.

1248 REVUE ECONOMIQUE
Banque National de Paris

F—Français monthly

Articles and commentary on the French economic situation.

1249 SELLING IN FRANCE
British Embassy in Paris/Department of Trade

F—English 1972 20pp

Statistics and commentary on the French market for British
exports.

1250 THE SEVENTH PLAN FOR ECONOMIC AND SOCIAL
DEVELOPMENT (1976-80)
French Embassy, London

F—English 1976 16pp

Facts, Figures France: no. A/116/11/76. Sets out the major
objectives for 1980 and contains the firm financial commitments
relating to 25 priority programmes.

1251 LA SITUATION DE L'AGRICULTURE
Assemblée Permanente des Chambres d'Agriculture

F—Français annual c80pp

The agricultural situation; supplement to the journal
"Chambre d'Agriculture"—data on: agricultural production;
crops; livestock; milk; honey; foreign trade; finances; sales.

1252 THE SIXTH PLAN (1971-75)
French Embassy, London

F—English 1972

Facts, Figures France: no. A/85/1/72. Describes the
Government's economic and financial objectives for the
period 1971-75.

1253 SPOTLIGHT ON OVERSEAS TRADE — SELLING TO FRANCE
Midland Bank International

F—English 1976 4pp

Contents: economic situation; market opportunities; regulations and documentary requirements; company formation in France. UK exports to France.

1254 STATISTICAL SUMMARY
French Embassy, London

F—English 1974

Facts, Figures France: no. A/97/4/74. Statistical summary of the French economy.

1255 STATISTIQUE AGRICOLE
Ministère de l'Agriculture

F—Français annual 2 vols

Agricultural statistics; contains data on: climate; education; technical centres; wages; distribution of land; production of crops; number and production of animals; prices and value of agricultural production; fertilizers; tools; tractors; food manufacturing industry; insurance and investment.

1256 STATISTIQUE DE L'INDUSTRIE MINERALE
Ministère de l'Industrie

F—Français annual c150pp

Statistics of the mineral industry; data on: mineral production; mineral sales; mining.

1257 STATISTIQUE DE L'INDUSTRIE MINIERE
Ministère du Développement Industriel et Scientifique, Direction des Mines

F—Français annual

Annual data and commentary of the mining industry in France.

1258 STATISTIQUE GENERALE DE L'INDUSTRIE TEXTILE FRANCAISE
Union des Industries Textiles

F—Français annual c90pp

General statistics of the French textile industry; data on: number of enterprises and factories; wages; production; foreign trade; consumption; wholesale and retail price index numbers.

1259 STATISTIQUES DE LA CONSTRUCTION
Ministère de l'Aménagement du Territoire, de l'Equipement, du Logement et du Tourisme, Direction du Bâtiment et des Travaux Publics et de la Conjoncture (Institut National de la Statistique et des Etudes Economiques)

F—Français monthly

Statistics on housing, building trade and public works.

1260 STATISTIQUES DU COMMERCE EXTERIEUR DE LA FRANCE: ANNUAIRE ABREGE
Direction Générale des Douanes

F—Français annual c300pp

Statistics of the foreign trade of France: abridged yearbook; a condensed version of items.

1261 STATISTIQUES DU COMMERCE EXTERIEUR DE LA FRANCE: COMMENTAIRES ANNUELS
Ministère de l'Economie et des Finances (Direction Générale des Douanes)

F—Français annual

Statistics of the foreign trade of France: annual commentary; data on foreign trade, with graphs and statistical tables showing trends over the past five years.

1262 STATISTIQUES DU COMMERCE EXTERIEUR DE LA FRANCE: COMMENTAIRES TRIMESTRIELS
Ministère de l'Economie et des Finances (Direction Générale des Douanes)

F—Français quarterly

Statistics of the foreign trade of France: quarterly commentary; quarterly analysis by geographic zones, principal countries, and products of the structure and importance of foreign trade.

1263 STATISTIQUES DU COMMERCE EXTERIEUR DE LA FRANCE: IMPORTATIONS-EXPORTATIONS EN NGP
Ministère de l'Economie et des Finances (Direction Générale des Douanes)

F—Français quarterly

Statistics of the foreign trade of France: imports and exports by commodities; tables of imports and exports arranged by BTN classification and subdivided by countries of origin and destination. Also contains tables of imports and exports by commodity groups and by country.

1264 STATISTIQUES DU COMMERCE EXTERIEUR DE LA FRANCE: IMPORTATIONS-EXPORTATIONS EN NOMENCLATURE CTCI
Ministère de l'Economie et des Finances (Direction Générale des Douanes)

F—Français annual

Statistics of the foreign trade of France: imports and exports by SITC; details of imports and exports classified by SITC and subdivided by countries of origin and destination. Also tables of imports and exports arranged by countries of origin and destination and subdivided by the main commodity groups.

1265 STATISTIQUES DU COMMERCE EXTERIEUR DE PRODUITS LAINIERS
Comité Central de la Laine et de l'Industrie Lainière

F—Français annual

Data on foreign trade in woollen products.

1266 STATISTIQUES DU COMMERCE EXTERIEUR, TABLEAU GENERAL DES TRANSPORTS
Ministère de l'Economie et des Finances (Direction Générale des Douanes)

F—Français annual

Details of imports and exports arranged by country, commodity and mode of transport.

1267 STATISTIQUES ET ETUDES FINANCIERES
Ministère de l'Economie et des Finances

F—Français monthly

Graphs and statistics on national accounts and other financial information. Monthly supplements examine specific financial topics.

1268 STATISTIQUES ET INDICATEURS DES REGIONS FRANCAISES
Institut National de la Statistique et des Etudes Economiques

F—Français annual c300pp

French regional statistics and indicators; tables and maps covering: population; active population; agriculture; industry and services; foreign trade; housing; education; tourism; communications; revenues; finance for particular regions of France.

1269 STATISTIQUES INDUSTRIELLES PAR REGIONS ET PAR ACTIVITES
Ministère du Développement Industriel et Scientifique

F—Français annual 2 vols

Statistics of production and labour, in two volumes.

1270 STATISTIQUES OFFICIELLES DE L'INDUSTRIE GAZIERE EN FRANCE
Direction du Gaz, de l'Electricité et du Charbon (Ministère du Développement Industriel et Scientifique)

F—Français annual

Annual statistics on production, distribution, transport and supply and utilization of gas in France.

1271 STRUCTURE OF THE PUMP, VALVE AND FABRICATED PROCESS PLANT INDUSTRIES: FRANCE AND WEST GERMANY
National Economic Development Office

F/D—English 1973

A comparative analysis and assessment of industry structures in both countries; also indentifies the major companies and individual product suppliers.

1272 LES STRUCTURES INDUSTRIELLES FRANCAISES
Ministère du Développement Industriel et Scientifique SCSII, and Centre National d'Information pour la Productivité des Entreprises CNIPE

F—Français 1968

Industrial structure of France; results of an enquiry into the structure of particular industries, including: iron mining; steel; non-ferrous metals; machine tools; transport; electrical and electronic manufacturers; perfumes; furniture.

1273 STUDY OF FRENCH MARKET CARRIED OUT FOR BWMA STRUCTURAL AND COMPONENTS SECTION
Building Management and Marketing Consultants Ltd.

F—English 1973 2 vols

A detailed survey of the French market for timber structures and components concentrating in particular on Glulam beams and roof trusses. Includes a brief survey of the French construction industry.

1274 A SURVEY OF THE AUTOMATIC BATTERY MARKET IN EUROPE
Product and Marketing Research Ltd.

F/B/D/NL/I—English 1975 6 vols

Report prepared for the British Battery Makers' Society, in six volumes. Reports on five Common Market countries (Belgium, France, Germany, Holland and Italy) and a summary volume.

1275 TABLEAUX DE L'ECONOMIE FRANCAISE
Institut National de la Statistique et des Etudes Economiques

F—Français annual c160pp

A picture of the French economy; contains tables and charts giving detailed indicators of the general economic development; an abridged version of "Annuaire Statistique de la France".

1276 TENDANCES DE LA CONJONCTURE: GRAPHIQUES MENSUELS
Institut National de la Statistique et des Etudes Economiques

F—Français monthly

Economic trends; in two parts. Part 1: Graphs and indices of trends in industrial production, consumption, internal trade, industrial investment, housing, foreign trade. Part 2: Textual comments on the contents in Part 1.

1277 TOWN PLANNING IN FRANCE
French Embassy, London

F—English 1972

Facts, Figures France; no. A/88/6/72. Commentary on central and local government town planning in France.

1278 LE TRANSPORT DU COMMERCE EXTERIEUR
Ministère de l'Economie et des Finances (Direction Générale des Douanes et Droits Indirects)

F—Français annual

Annual survey and analysis of transportation in connection with French foreign trade.

1279 TRANSPORT IN FRANCE
French Embassy, London

F—English 1973

Facts, Figures France: no. A/91/10/73. Summary of the French transport system.

1280 LES TRANSPORTS DANS LA REGION DU SUD-EST
Chambre de Commerce et d'Industrie de Marseille

F—Français 1973 82pp

Commentary and statistics on transport in South East France, including road, rail, air and ports.

1281 TWENTY-FIVE YEARS OF SOCIAL SECURITY IN FRANCE (1945-70)
French Embassy, London

F—English 1971

Facts, Figures France: no. B/61/2/71. Review and commentary on the French social security service.

1282 **L'USINE NOUVELLE: LES INFORMATIONS**
      Usine Publications, SA

      F—Français 1975 142pp

      A-Z directory of over 100 towns in France, with populations
      between 50,000 — 200,000, giving details of population,
      consumer spending, facilities and also includes company
      information of firms and manufacturing establishments in
      each town.

1283 **VALVES IN FRANCE**
      Metra Consulting Group Ltd.

      F—English 1975

      Begins with a brief survey of the French economy and the
      French valve industry. A detailed survey of French valve-
      using industries, including a profile of the industry concerned,
      the types of valve it uses, purchasing requirements and supply
      structure, and expenditure on valves.

1284 **WEST EUROPEAN MARKETS FOR LABORATORY**
      ANALYTICAL INSTRUMENTS: VOLUME 2:
      CONTINENTAL EUROPE
      Sira Institute

      F/INT—English 1975

      Volume 2 of two volume study, (Volume 1 covers the
      United Kingdom) covers ten West European countries giving
      data on production, imports and exports. Contains more
      detailed surveys of West Germany, France and Italy, with
      market size analysed by product group and by market
      sector, with forecasts of growth to 1979. Includes sections
      on major suppliers plus a profile of the country concerned in
      economic and statistical terms.

1285 **WINE GROWING IN FRANCE**
      French Embassy, London

      F—English 1970

      Facts, Figures France: no. A/71/11/9. Review including
      statistics on the French wine growing industry.

GB-GREAT BRITAIN

1350 ABSTRACT OF REGIONAL STATISTICS
Central Statistical Office HMSO

GB—English annual c170pp £2.70

Main economic and social statistics available for regions
of the UK. Includes: area; climate; population; social
services; education; production; employment; investment;
construction; transport and distribution; incomes and
household surveys.

1351 ACCOMMODATION FOR THE LOWER PRICED MARKET
National Economic Development Office

GB—English 1975 £2.00

Discusses whether low-priced accommodation units
operated at low tariffs can be as profitable as
conventional hotels.

1352 ADVERTISER'S ANNUAL
Kelly's Directories Ltd.

GB—English annual c1610pp £10.50

Classified trade directory for those engaged in
advertising and selling.

**1353 THE ADVERTISING AGENCY'S ROLE IN
DEVELOPING INTERNATIONAL MARKETS**
Institute of Practitioners in Advertising

GB—English 1968 12pp £0.25

Booklet reviewing the advertising agency's functions
and objectives in developing international markets.

**1354 ADVERTISING ASSOCIATION: ADVERTISING
EXPENDITURE 1960-1972**
Advertising Association

GB—English 1974 16pp £0.75

Statistics of advertising expenditure during the period
1960-72, including an index of media rates. Reprinted
from 'Advertising Quarterly' issue No. 36, Summer 1973.

1355 THE AGE OF US AND UK MACHINERY
National Economic Development Office

GB—English 1974 52pp £0.90

NEDO Monographs No. 3.
Estimates the length of life and age of machine tools
in the US and UK and analyses the results within the
framework of an economic growth model.

**1356 AGRICULTURAL AND FOOD STATISTICS: A
GUIDE TO OFFICIAL SOURCES**
Central Statistical Office HMSO

GB—English 1974 90pp £2.00

Studies in Official Statistics Series No. 23.
A comprehensive guide to sources of agricultural,
food and fisheries statistics.

1357 AGRICULTURAL STATISTICS: ENGLAND AND WALES
Ministry of Agriculture, Fisheries and Food HMSO

GB—English annual c190pp £2.30

Statistics covering: acreage and production of crops;
numbers of livestock; agricultural holdings and
workers in each county; agricultural machinery.

1358 AGRICULTURAL STATISTICS: SCOTLAND
Department of Agriculture, Scotland

GB—English annual c120pp £1.90

Statistics on: acreage; yields and production of crops;
labour employed; numbers of livestock; types of
farming; prices of produce.

1359 AGRICULTURAL STATISTICS: UNITED KINGDOM
Ministry of Agriculture, Fisheries and Food HMSO

GB—English annual c100pp £1.75

Statistics on: acreage and production of crops;
numbers of livestock; agricultural holdings and
agricultural workers in the UK. Separate figures
are given for England and Wales, Scotland, GB and
Northern Ireland. Also includes monthly and annual
price indices.

1360 AGRICULTURE IN SCOTLAND 1974
Cmnd 5998 HMSO

GB—English 1975 96pp £0.80

Report and review of production, prices and marketing.

Includes statistics on: agricultural output; incomes; production costs; land sales; economics.

1361 AGRICULTURE REPORT FOR NORTHERN IRELAND
Department of Agriculture, Northern Ireland

GB—English annual c180pp £1.35

Annual report and statistics on: acreage; livestock production; value of gross and net output. Updates the Report on Agricultural Statistics (No. 1645).

1362 AGRICULTURE'S IMPORT SAVING ROLE
National Economic Development Office HMSO

GB—English 1968 130pp £1.00

Study of the UK agricultural output and the technical feasibility of expanding it.

1363 AIR INCLUSIVE TOUR MARKETING
Economist Intelligence Unit

GB/D—English 1975 £10.00

Study analysing the impact of air inclusive tours on the development of the retail travel trade in the UK and West Germany.

1364 THE ANATOMY OF PURCHASING CLOTHING MACHINERY
National Economic Development Office

GB—English 1974 £0.60

A survey of the reasons and attitudes which have influenced clothing manufacturers to select types of advanced machinery.

1365 ANATOMY OF UK FINANCE 1970-75
The Financial Times

GB—English 1976 175pp £25.50

Study of recent financial developments in the UK economy. It uses the flow of funds type of analysis to examine the effect of the interrelation of the major sectors on such issues as company profits, money supply, finance for industry, the public sector deficit, the pound, the effects of inflation.

1366 ANNUAL ABSTRACT OF STATISTICS
Central Statistical Office HMSO

GB—English annual c480pp £5.80

Contents: statistics on: area; climate; population; social conditions; social security; health; housing; crime; justice; education; labour; production; transport and communications; retail distribution; external trade; balance of payments; national income and expenditure; personal income; expenditure and wealth; central and local government finance; banking; investment; insurance.

1367 ANNUAL ESTIMATES OF THE POPULATION OF SCOTLAND
General Register Office, Scotland

GB—English annual c10pp £0.18

Mid-yearly annual estimates of the population of Scotland.

1368 ANNUAL REPORT OF THE COMMISSIONERS OF HM CUSTOMS AND EXCISE
HM Customs and Excise HMSO

GB—English annual c150pp £1.75

Annual report and review of the year's activity. Includes an appendix giving description and statements of Customs and Excise receipts.

1369 ANNUAL REPORT OF THE REGISTRAR GENERAL FOR SCOTLAND
General Register Office, Scotland

GB—English annual

Part 1: Mortality tables (c400pp £5.60)
Part 2: Population and vital statistics (c160pp £2.50)

1370 ANNUAL REPORT OF THE REGISTRAR GENERAL NORTHERN IRELAND
General Register Office, Northern Ireland

GB—English annual c200pp £2.45

Detailed analyses of the births, marriages and deaths for each local authority area.

1371 ANNUAL REVIEW OF AGRICULTURE
Cmnd 5977 HMSO

GB—English annual 50pp £0.55

Main features of the general economic climate and prospects for the agricultural industry.

1372 ANNUAL STATEMENT OF OVERSEAS TRADE OF THE UNITED KINGDOM
HM Customs and Excise HMSO

GB—English annual 5 vols

Vol. 1: Summaries of imports and exports by areas and countries classified by SITC (c350pp £11.00)
Vol. 2: Detailed data on imports (671pp £20.00)
Vol. 3: Similar coverage for exports (582pp £18.00)
Vol. 4: Total import and export for each country with principal commodities in these totals (c271pp £11.00)
Vol. 5: Detailed data on commodity traffic through UK ports and airports (c162pp £10.00)

1373 ANNUAL STATISTICAL SURVEY OF THE ELECTRONICS INDUSTRY
National Economic Development Office

GB—English annual 59pp £1.00

Statistics on employment, trade, investment and profitability.

1374 ATTITUDES TO PRICE INCREASES AND PAY CLAIMS
National Economic Development Office

GB—English 1974 77pp £1.70

NEDO Monographs No. 4.
Study of the effect of price increases on public attitudes and wage claims.

1375 BANKERS' ALMANAC AND YEARBOOK
Thomas Skinner Directories

GB—English annual c2310pp £20.00

Basic reference data, arranged A-Z for financial organisations, including banks, discount houses, bullion brokers etc. Also gives information on international banks and similar companies, branches of banks throughout Britain, insurance companies, amalgamations and liquidations.

1376 BANK OF ENGLAND QUARTERLY BULLETIN
Bank of England

GB—English quarterly c130pp free

The Bank's regular review covering current financial topics of interest and including reference statistics.

1377 BANK OF ENGLAND STATISTICAL ABSTRACT
Bank of England

GB—English annual 193pp free

Financial statistics on: banking; credit; external finance; capital markets; exchange and interest rates; central government accounts.

1378 BASIC ECONOMIC PLANNING DATA
Institute of Marketing

GB—English 1970 25pp £12.50

Analysis by standard region and county of certain key UK statistics:- population; employment; income; retail trade.

1379 BASIC ROAD STATISTICS
British Road Federation

GB—English annual c50pp £0.50

Road and road traffic statistics including: motor vehicle data; road traffic; road accidents; road transport; mileage; road finance and expenditure; motor taxation.

1380 BRITAIN 1977: AN OFFICIAL HANDBOOK
Central Office of Information HMSO

GB—English 1977 520pp £5.00

Basic survey of the administration and national economy of Britain, including: government; EEC; justice; defence; social welfare; environmental planning; housing; industry; energy; agriculture; transport and communications; employment; finance; trade; arts; sciences; sport.

1381 BRITAIN'S QUOTED INDUSTRIAL COMPANIES
Jordan Dataquest

GB—English annual £12.50

Provides detailed financial data on over 17200 companies, ranked by size, basic reference information A-Z and other tables and ratios.

1382 BRITAIN'S TOP 1000 FOREIGN OWNED COMPANIES
Graham and Trotman Ltd.

GB—English annual c130pp £9.00

Basic reference data plus examination of standard financial information with 'turnover league table'.

1383 BRITAIN'S TOP 1000 PRIVATE COMPANIES
Jordan Dataquest Ltd.

GB—English annual c95pp £12.00

Basic reference data for the companies arranged A-Z, together with examination of balance sheet information, 'league tables', key ratios and tables of selected data.

1384 BRITISH AID STATISTICS
Foreign and Commonwealth Office HMSO

GB/INT—English annual c150pp £3.00

Statistics and details of UK overseas economic aid; aid programmes to developing countries; public expenditure and persons financed.

1385 BRITISH BUREAU OF TELEVISION ADVERTISING: INDEPENDENT TELEVISION IN THE UNITED KINGDOM: FACTS AND FIGURES
British Bureau of Television Advertising

GB—English 1974 23pp free

Details and statistics on independent television advertising in the United Kingdom.

1386 BRITISH BUREAU OF TELEVISION ADVERTISING: SELLING WITH TELEVISION IN THE UNITED KINGDOM: HOW BBTA CAN HELP
British Bureau of Television Advertising

GB—English 1974 15pp free

Concise booklet showing how the BBTA can assist companies with their television marketing campaigns.

1387 BRITISH EXPORTS
Kompass Publishers Ltd.

GB—English annual c1600pp £15.00

Directory of manufacturers A-Z with details of: address; telephone numbers; telex; export sales executives; overseas agents; trade names. Also includes separate classified product index.

1388 BRITISH HOUSEHOLDS
IPC Marketing Services Department

GB—English 1975 £7.00

Guide to British households and their health, homes, holidays, food and the ways household income is allocated.

1389 BRITISH LABOUR STATISTICS: HISTORICAL ABSTRACT 1886-1968
Department of Employment HMSO

GB—English 1971 436pp £7.00

Detailed selection of the principal labour statistics in Britain covering the period 1886-1968.

1390 BRITISH LABOUR STATISTICS YEARBOOK
Department of Employment HMSO

GB—English annual c400pp £12.00

Tables and graphs on all the main British labour
statistics including: wage rates and normal hours;
earnings and hours actually worked; employment;
unemployment; retail prices; summary data on family
expenditure surveys; trade union memberships;
industrial disputes; industrial accidents; cost per unit
of output; output per person employed.

1391 BRITISH MACHINE TOOLS IN EUROPE
National Economic Development Office

GB/INT—English 1972 73pp £1.00

A study by the Machine Tools EDC on the effect of
EEC entry on the UK machine tools industry. (See
also No. 1723)

1392 BUSINESS ATLAS OF GREAT BRITAIN
Gower Economic Publications, Teakfield

GB—English 1974 186pp £8.50

Data in map, graph and tabular form on population
and land use; consumer standards; communications;
foreign trade; industrial development; labour; fuels;
major industries; retail distribution; construction;
wholesale distribution; banking and finance.

1393 BUSINESS MONITOR: MISCELLANEOUS SERIES
Department of Industry HMSO

GB—English

Series of reports covering the following:
M1: Motor vehicle registration (monthly £7.35 p.a.)
M2: Cinemas (annual: £0.25)
M3: Company finance (annual £0.50)
M4: Overseas transactions (annual £0.50)
M5: Insurance companies and private pensions funds
investment (quarterly £0.50 p.a.)
M6: Overseas travel and tourism (quarterly £0.50)
M7: Acquisitions and mergers of companies (quarterly
£0.50)
M8: Nationality of vessels in sea-borne trade (annual
£0.50)
M9: 1975 Survey of the United Kingdom aerospace
industries (£1.05)
M10: 1975 Overseas trade analysed in terms of
Industries (£0.30)
M11: Survey of standby electricity generating plant in
industry (£0.54)

1394 BUSINESS MONITORS: PRODUCTION SERIES
Department of Industry HMSO

GB—English monthly and quarterly, by subscription only;
monthly issues: £1.40; quarterly issues: £0.52; complete
set, monthly and quarterly issues £35 p.a.

Series of 169 periodicals covering the following industries:
PM33.36 Engineering (volume indices of sales and orders)
PQ102 Stone and slate quarrying and mining;
PQ103 Chalk, clay, sand and gravel extraction;
PQ104 Petroleum and natural gas;
PQ109.2 Miscellaneous mining and quarrying;
PQ109.3 Salt; PQ211 Grain milling;
PQ212 Bread and flour confectionery; PQ213 Biscuits;
PQ215 Milk and milk products; PQ216 Sugar;
PQ217 Cocoa, chocolate and sugar confectionery;
PQ219 Animal and poultry foods; PQ221 Vegetable &
animal oils & fats; PQ229.1 Margarine; PQ229.2 Starch

and miscellaneous foods; PQ231 Brewing and malting;
PQ232 Soft drinks; PQ239.1 Spirit distilling and
compounding; PQ239.2 British wines, cider and perry.
PQ240 Tobacco; PQ262 Mineral oil refining; PQ262
Lubricating oils and greases;PQ271 General chemicals;
PQ271.2 Organic chemicals; PQ272 Pharmaceutical
chemicals and preparations. PQ273 Toilet preparations;
PQ274 Paint; PQ275 Soap and detergents; PQ276.1
Synthetic resins and plastics materials; PQ277 Dye-
stuffs/pigments PQ277.1 Colours; PQ278 Fertilizers;
PQ279.1 Polishes; PQ279.2 Formulated adhesives,
gelatine, etc; PQ279.5 Printing ink; PQ279.6 Surgical
bandages, etc; PQ279.7 Photographic chemical materials;
PQ321 Aluminium and aluminium alloys; PQ322 Copper,
brass & other copper alloys; PQ323 Miscellaneous base
materials; PQ331 Agricultural machinery (except
tractors); PM332 Metal-working machine tools: orders
and deliveries; PQ332 Metal-working machine tools;
PQ333 Pumps, valves, compressors and fluid power
equipment; PQ334 Industrial engines; PQ335 Textile
machinery and accessories; PQ336 Construction and
earth moving equipment; PQ337 Mechanical handling
equipment; PQ338 Office machinery; PQ339.1 Mining
machinery; PQ339.2 Printing, bookbinding & paper
goods machinery; PQ339.3 Refrigerating machinery,
space-heating, ventilating and air-conditioning equipment;
PQ339.5 Scales and weighing machinery and portable
power tools; PQ339.7 Food and drink processing machinery
& packaging & bottling machinery; PQ339.9 Miscellaneous
(non-electrical) machinery; PQ341.1 Ball, roller, plain and
other bearings; PQ349.2 Precision chains and other
mechanical engineering products; PQ351 Photographic and
document copying equipment; PQ352 Watches and clocks;
PQ353 Surgical instruments and appliances; PQ354 Scientific
and industrial instruments and systems; PQ361 Electrical
machinery; PQ362 Insulated wires and cables; PQ363
Telegraph and telephone apparatus and equipment;
PQ364 Radio and electronic components; PQ365.1
Gramophone records and tape recordings; PQ366 Electronic
computers; PQ367 Radio, radar & electronic capital goods;
PQ368 Electric appliances primarily for domestic use;
PQ369.1 Electrical equipment for motor vehicles, cycles &
aircraft; PQ369.2 Primary and secondary batteries;
PQ369.4 Electric lamps, electric light fittings, wiring
accessories; PQ370 Ships, boats and marine engineering;
PQ380 Wheeled tractors; PQ381 Cars and commercial
vehicles; PQ381.I Road vehicles; PQ381.2 Trailers, caravans
and freight containers; PQ382 Motor cycles and pedal cycles;
PQ383 Aerospace products; PQ384 Locomotives, railway
track equipment, railway carriages, wagons and trams;
PQ390 Engineers' small tools and gauges; PQ391 Hand tools
and implements; PQ392 Cutlery, spoons, forks, tableware
and safety razors; PQ393 Bolts, nuts, screws, rivets, etc.
PQ394 Wire and wire manufactures; PQ395 Cans & metal
boxes; PQ396.2 Jewellery; PQ399.1 Metal furniture;
PQ399.2 Metal windows; PQ399.3 Safes, locks, latches,
keys and springs; PQ399.5 Drop forgings, etc; PQ399.6
Metal hollow-ware; PQ399.8 Needles, pins, fish-hooks &
other metal small-ware; PQ399.9 Domestic gas appliances;
PQ399.10 Metallic closures; PQ399.11 Metal finishing;
PQ399.12 Miscellaneous metal goods; PQ411 Production
of man-made fibres; PQ412 Spinning and doubling other
cotton and flax systems; PQ413 Weaving of cotton, linen
and man-made fibres; PQ414 Woollen and worsted; PQ415
Jute; PQ416 Rope, twine & net; PQ417.1 Hosiery and other
knitted goods; PQ417.2 Warp knitting; PQ418 Lace;
PQ419 Carpets; PQ421 Narrow fabrics; PQ422.1 Household textiles and handkerchiefs; PQ422.2 Canvas goods and
sacks and other made-up textiles; PM423 Foam backing, foam
laminating and fabric to fabric bonding; PQ423 Textile
finishing; PQ429.1 Asbestos; PQ429.2 Miscellaneous textile
industries; PQ431 Leather & fellmongery; PQ432 Leather
goods; PQ433 Fur; PQ440 Made-up clothing (sales volume
indices); PQ441 Weatherproof outerwear; PQ442 Men's &
boys' tailored outerwear; PQ443 Women's and girls'
tailored outerwear; PQ444 Overalls and men's shirts, under-
wear etc; PQ445 Women's and girls' light outerwear,
lingerie, infants' wear, etc; PQ446 Hats, caps and millinery;
PQ449.1 Corsets and miscellaneous dress industries;
PQ449.2 Gloves; PQ450 Footwear; PQ461.1 Refractory

goods; PQ461.2 Clay building bricks and other non-refractory goods; PQ462 Pottery; PQ463 Glass; PQ464 Cement; PQ469.1 Abrasives; PQ469.2 Miscellaneous building materials and mineral products; PQ471 Timber (sawmilling, etc and builders' woodwork): PM471.1 Wood chipboard; PQ472 Wooden furniture & upholstery; PQ473 Bedding and soft furnishings; PQ474 Shop & office fitting; PQ475 Wooden containers and baskets; PM476 Imported timber; PQ479 Miscellaneous wood and cork manufactures; PQ480 Packaging; PQ481 Paper and paper making materials; PQ481Paper and board; PQ482.1 Cardboard boxes, cartons & fibreboard packing cases; PQ482.2 Miscellaneous packaging products of paper and film; PQ483 Manufactured stationery; PQ484.1 Wallcoverings; PQ484.2 Miscellaneous manufactures of paper and board; PQ485 Newspapers and periodicals; PQ489 General printing & publishing; PQ491 Rubber: consumption and stocks; PQ491 Rubber; PQ492 Plastic floorcoverings, leathercloth etc.; PQ493 Brushes and brooms; PQ494.1 Toys, games & children's carriages; PQ494.3 Sports equipment; PQ495 Miscellaneous stationers' goods; PQ496 Plastic products; PQ499.1 Musical instruments; PQ499.2 Miscellaneous manufacturing industries; PQ602 Electricity; PQ603 Water supply; PQ1000 Index to commodities (annual).

1395 BUSINESS MONITORS: SERVICE AND DISTRIBUTIVE SERIES
Department of Industry HMSO

GB—English

Regular series of reports covering the following:
SD1: Food shops (monthly £2.80 p.a.)
SD2: Clothing and footwear shops (monthly £2.80 p.a.)
SD3: Durable goods shops (monthly £2.80 p.a.)
SD4: Miscellaneous non-food shops (monthly £2.80 p.a.)
SD5: Catering trades (monthly £0.80 p.a.)
SD6: Instalment credit business of finance houses (monthly £1.40 p.a.)
SD7: Assets and liabilities of finance houses (quarterly £0.50 p.a.)
SD8: Instalment credit business of retailers (monthly £1.40)
SD9: Computer services (quarterly £0.50 p.a.)

1396 CAPITAL TRANSFER TAX: CONSEQUENCES FOR PRIVATE LIMITED COMPANIES
Confederation of British Industry

GB—English 1976 9pp £0.50

Examines the ways in which the capital transfer tax could affect a private limited company. Contains examples, tables of rates, details of reliefs available and areas where further professional advice should be sought.

1397 CENSUS 1971: ADVANCE ANALYSIS, GREAT BRITAIN
Office of Population, Censuses and Surveys HMSO

GB—English 1972 296pp £4.50

Information on Great Britain, England and Wales (Standard Regions, conurbations and subdivisions) and for Scotland (the Clydeside conurbation and planning sub-regions). Also includes tables giving data on households for the same areas and on birthrates for Great Britain, England and Wales, Scotland and the standard regions.

1398 CENSUS 1971: AGE, MARITAL CONDITIONS AND GENERAL TABLES, GREAT BRITAIN
Office of Population, Censuses and Surveys HMSO

GB—English 1974 94pp £1.55

Definitive statistics on population, household numbers, age, sex, marital conditions. Also includes selected statistics showing changes since the first census 1801, with breakdowns to regional, sub-regional and county level.

1399 CENSUS 1971: COUNTRY OF BIRTH TABLES (GREAT BRITAIN)
Office of Population, Censuses and Surveys HMSO

GB—English 1974 228pp £3.65

Population analyses by country of birth and year of entry into the United Kingdom. Cross classified by age, sex and marital condition.

1400 CENSUS 1971: ENGLAND AND WALES; AVAILABILITY OF CARS
Office of Population, Censuses and Surveys HMSO

GB—English 1974 92pp £1.30

Relationship between car availability, household size, composition and tenure in England and Wales as a whole and regions and local authority areas in 1971.

1401 CENSUS 1971: GREAT BRITAIN, ECONOMIC ACTIVITY
Office of Population, Censuses and Surveys HMSO

GB—English 1974; Part 1: (100%) 128pp £1.90
1975: Part 2: (10% sample) 260pp £5.45
1975: Part 3: (10% sample) 361pp £7.65
1975: Part 4: (10% sample) 308pp £9.50

Details of numbers in employment, seeking work, students and the retired or economically inactive for other reasons. Analyses by age.

1402 CENSUS 1971: GREAT BRITAIN SUMMARY TABLES (1% SAMPLE)
Office of Population, Censuses and Surveys HMSO

GB—English 1973 228pp £3.60

Statistics on demography, economic activity and household composition. Figures are estimated based on a small sample of the Census returns.

1403 CENSUS 1971: HOUSEHOLD COMPOSITION TABLES
Office of Population, Censuses and Surveys HMSO

GB—English 1975

Statistics on household compositions - 10 per cent sample.
Part 1: 213pp £4.55
Part 2: 249pp £5.30
Part 3: 277pp £5.90

1404 CENSUS 1971: HOUSING SUMMARY TABLES, GREAT BRITAIN
Office of Population, Censuses and Surveys HMSO

GB—English 1974 60pp £0.95

Analyses by occupation and tenure of households classified by number of occupants.

1405 CENSUS 1971: HOUSING TABLES
Office of Population, Censuses and Surveys HMSO

GB—English 1974

Part 1: Households (382pp £4.55)
Part 2: Amenities Part 3: Dwellings (212pp £3.40)
Part 4: Density of Occupation (278pp £4.50)

1406 CENSUS 1971: MIGRATION TABLES, GREAT BRITAIN, PART 1 (10% SAMPLE)
Office of Population, Censuses and Surveys HMSO

GB—English 1975 196pp £3.15

Data on migrants, analysed by sex, age, marital status, area of former usual residence and area of usual residence at the Census.

1407 CENSUS 1971: NEW LOCAL AUTHORITY AREAS OF ENGLAND AND WALES. REPORT FOR COUNTY OF ... AS CONSTITUTED ON 1 APRIL 1974
Office of Population, Censuses and Surveys HMSO

GB—English

Series of new county reports in which results of the 1971 Census are re-grouped to provide adjusted statistics for the new counties and districts. Reports vary from 52 to 100 pages with prices typicallyly between £1.10 and £2.10.

1408 CENSUS 1971: NON-PRIVATE HOUSEHOLDS, GREAT BRITAIN
Office of Population, Censuses and Surveys HMSO

GB—English 1974 220pp £3.50

Extension of the tables on non-private households published after the 1961 and 1966 Censuses. Includes analyses of those living in non-private households by age, sex and marital condition, status in establishment and type of establishment.

1409 CENSUS 1971: NORTHERN IRELAND, SUMMARY TABLES
General Register Office, Northern Ireland

GB—English 1975 140pp £0.26

Statistical summary tables of the 1971 population census.

1410 CENSUS 1971: PERSONS OF PENSIONABLE AGE, GREAT BRITAIN
Office of Population, Censuses and Surveys HMSO

GB—English 1974 340pp £5.45

Statistical tables relating to people of pensionable age in Britain, analysed by: sex; marital condition; household size; composition of rooms; amenities of tenure. Also includes pensioners in non-private establishments.

1411 CENSUS 1971: REPORT ON THE WELSH LANGUAGE IN WALES
Office of Population, Censuses and Surveys HMSO

GB—English 1975 92pp £1.35

Tables showing number of people in Wales (aged three and over) who speak, read or write Welsh.

Covering age, sex and whether English also spoken. Numbers are given for wards, civil parishes and local authority areas also counties and county boroughs.

1412 CENSUS 1971: SCOTLAND, HOUSEHOLD COMPOSITION TABLES
General Register Office, Scotland

GB—English 1975 388pp £5.75

Estimated statistics on household composition in Scotland based on a 10% sample from the 1971 Census.

1413 CENSUS 1971: SCOTLAND, HOUSING REPORT
General Register Office, Scotland

GB—English 1975 276pp £6.35

Analyses of housing in Scotland with details of households, amenities and density of occupation.

1414 CENSUS 1971: SCOTLAND, POPULATION TABLES
General Register Office, Scotland

GB—English 1974 228pp £3.70

Statistical tables on population, households and economic activity.

1415 CENSUS 1971: SCOTLAND, SCOTTISH POPULATION SUMMARY
General Register Office, Scotland

GB—English 1973 20pp £0.35

Brief statistical summaries of area populations, economic activity and households.

1416 CENSUS 1971: USUAL RESIDENCE TABLES
Office of Population, Censuses and Surveys HMSO

GB—English 1974 88pp £1.40

Comparison of the enumerated and usually resident population of areas in Great Britain down to 1971 local authority level. Also gives data on visitors to England and Wales at the time of the 1971 Census by age, sex, marital condition, area of usual residence and area of enumeration.

1417 CENSUS 1971: WALES, SUMMARY TABLES
Office of Population, Censuses and Surveys HMSO

GB—English 1975 209pp £4.90

Population of Wales classified by: age; birthplace; amenities; overcrowding; availability of cars; household size; number of pensioners.

1418 CENTURY OF AGRICULTURAL STATISTICS, GREAT BRITAIN, 1866-1966
Ministry of Agriculture, Fisheries and Food HMSO

GB—English 1968 140pp £0.97½

Detailed agricultural statistics for the period 1866-1966.

1419 CHANNELS AND COSTS OF DISTRIBUTION IN THE N.E. REGION
National Economic Development Office HMSO

GB—English 1971 £0.70

A study of distribution patterns in the North East of England.

1420 CHANNELS AND COSTS OF GROCERY DISTRIBUTION
Retail Outlets Research Unit Manchester Business School

GB—English 1973 £6.00

Research Report 8:
Study carried out for the Economic Development Committee for the Distributive Trades and the Institute of Grocery Distribution, and was intended to demonstrate the inter-relationship of physical distribution activity with the changing market conditions of food retailing.

1421 CHEMICAL INDUSTRY DIRECTORY AND WHO'S WHO
Benn Bros. Ltd.

GB—English 1976 c435pp £15.00

Basic directory of reference data for manufacturers, suppliers, merchants, consultant chemists, parent companies, societies, institutes, trade names etc. Contains a Who's Who Section.

1422 CHEMICALS MANPOWER IN EUROPE
National Economic Development Office HMSO

GB/F/D/NL—English 1973 67pp £0.70

Comparisons of the French, West German and Dutch chemical industries with the UK in terms of manpower, productivity, industrial relations. Also covers worker participation laws.

1423 THE CITY DIRECTORY 1976-77; AN INVESTORS CHRONICLE GUIDE TO FINANCIAL AND PROFESSIONAL SERVICES ALLIED TO THE CITY OF LONDON
Woodhead-Faulkner Ltd.

GB—English 1976 340pp £8.50 hardback/£5.95 paperback

Directory of nearly 5000 entries covering organisations involved in the following activities within the City of London: banking; money market; stock market; funds; insurance; building societies; financial services; commodity and bullion markets; export-import houses; shipbrokers and airbrokers; advertising and public relations; financial press; professional bodies.

1424 CIVIL SERVICE STATISTICS
Civil Service Department HMSO

GB—English annual c40pp £1.10

Statistics on the Civil Service based on figures available in January of the year of publication and details of changes which occurred during the previous year.

1425 COMPANY FINANCIAL RESULTS 1970/71 - 1974/75
National Economic Development Office

GB—English 1976 c75pp £1.50

Key financial data, including cash flow and profits, from nearly 400 mechanical engineering companies.

1426 CONFEDERATION OF BRITISH INDUSTRY ECONOMIC SITUATION REPORT
Confederation of British Industry

GB—English monthly £50.00 p.a.

Summary reports of the CBI's view of economic trends with data on: official economic indicators; short term forecasts for the UK economy; economic developments in Europe. Full reports appear at least eight times a year.

1427 CONFEDERATION OF BRITISH INDUSTRY EDUCATION AND TRAINING BULLETIN
Confederation of British Industry

GB—English quarterly £5.00

Quarterly publication covering education and training developments of industrial interest.

1428 CONFEDERATION OF BRITISH INDUSTRY INDUSTRIAL TRENDS SURVEY
Confederation of British Industry

GB—English four times a year £50.00 p.a.

Four surveys a year give current trends in output, orders, employment, investment plans, stocks of raw materials, costs, prices, export orders and deliveries. Results are given for each of 33 different manufacturing industries, for four size groups, and for Scottish industry.

1429 CONFEDERATION OF BRITISH INDUSTRY REVIEW
Confederation of British Industry

GB—English quarterly c30pp £5.00 p.a.

Quarterly review designed to activate discussion on issues and problems of concern to business management.

1430 CONSOLIDATED FUND AND NATIONAL LOANS FUND ACCOUNTS
HM Treasury HMSO

GB—English annual c20pp £0.26

Details of the transactions of the Consolidated Fund and National Loans Fund.

1431 CONSTRUCTION AND BUILDING MATERIALS REVIEW 1975-76
Gower Economic Publications, Teakfield

GB—English 1974 440pp £25.00

Costs, prices and analytical data of interest to civil engineers, building contractors and material manufacturers.

1432 CONSTRUCTION FORECASTING SERVICE
National Economic Development Office HMSO

GB—English annual subscription £3.00

Forecasts of building and civil engineering output covering the next two to three years.

1433 CONSTRUCTION INDUSTRY PROSPECTS TO 1979
National Economic Development Office

GB—English 1971 229pp £0.25

Forecast of construction output by sectors of the industry.

1434 CONSTRUCTION INTO THE EARLY 1980s
National Economic Development Office HMSO

GB—English 1976 58pp £2.00

Studies the possible effects of different patterns and levels of demand, on manpower and materials in the construction industry.

1435 CONSUMER CREDIT
Department of Trade & Industry

GB—English 1971 £15.00

Surveys on consumer credit carried out by NOP Market Research Ltd. for the Committee on Consumer Credit.

1436 COSTING OF HANDLING AND STORAGE IN WAREHOUSING
Department of Industry HMSO

GB—English 1970/72

Part 1: Conventional warehouses; (104pp £2.00)
Part 2: High-bay warehouses; (88pp £2.00)

1437 THE COUNTER-INFLATION POLICY: PAY - THE SECOND YEAR (1 AUGUST 1976-31 JULY 1977)
Confederation of British Industry

GB—English 1976 11pp £1.00

Guidance on the second stage of the Government pay policy covering legal basis and pay limits and intervals. Appendix includes a pro forma for pay settlement notification and guidance on the policy's effect on proposed occupational pension scheme improvements.

1438 CRAWFORD'S DIRECTORY OF CITY CONNECTIONS
Crawford Publications Ltd.

GB—English 1976 c425pp £21.00

Basic directory on public companies, arranged A-Z. Also gives: their principal stockbrokers and bankers; A-Z of stockbrokers who publish surveys (with subject index).

1439 CYCLICAL FLUCTUATIONS IN THE UNITED KINGDOM ECONOMY
National Economic Development Office

GB/INT—English 1976 £1.00

Compares the UK economy with other advanced economies and studies in detail the fluctuations of the last ten to fifteen years.

1440 THE DEMAND FOR NEW CARS
National Economic Development Office

GB—English 1974 £1.85

Description of an isometric model designed to forecast new car registrations in the UK.

1441 THE DENSITY OF CASH AND CARRY WHOLESALING: 18 MONTHS OF CHANGE, A STUDY OF COMPARATIVE MARKET POTENTIAL
Retail Outlets Research Unit, Manchester Business School

GB—English 1971 £9.60

Research Report 4.
Report is based on an intensive examination of the characteristics of grocery cash and carry depots in Great Britain. Analysis of possible future developments is included and comparisons made on a regional basis.

1442 DIGEST OF ENERGY STATISTICS
Department of Energy HMSO

GB—English annual c180pp £9.00

Statistics of UK energy consumption and production. Separate sections deal with the production and consumption of individual fuels, oil and gas reserves, fuel prices and foreign trade in fuels.

1443 DIGEST OF HOUSING STATISTICS FOR NORTHERN IRELAND
Department of Housing, Local Government and Planning, Northern Ireland

GB—English quarterly c15pp £0.30

Details of approvals for new houses, those under construction and completed by regions. Also includes details of improvement grants and slum clearance.

1444 DIGEST OF STATISTICS, NORTHERN IRELAND
Department of Finance, Northern Ireland

GB—English quarterly c90pp £3.20

Main economic and social statistics of Northern Ireland, including: national accounts; total numbers employed; new earnings survey; road vehicles.

1445 DIGEST OF TOURIST STATISTICS
The British Travel Association

GB—English 1974 88pp £3.50

Statistics of foreign tourists visiting the UK giving details of: numbers, mode of transport, expenditure, purpose of visit.

1446 DIGEST OF WELSH STATISTICS
Welsh Office HMSO

GB—English annual c200pp £3.90

Main economic and social statistics for Wales covering: population and vital statistics; social conditions; education; labour; production; transport and communication; finance; climate and area.

1447 DIRECTORY AND YEARBOOK OF INDUSTRIAL MARKETING RESEARCH IN EUROPE
European Marketing Association and European Council for Industrial Marketing

GB—English 1976 c190pp £12.00

Basic reference data on market research organisations and consultants in Europe. Also includes geographical, subject and services indexes.

1448 DIRECTORY OF BRITISH IMPORTERS
Trade Research Publications

GB—English 1975 c425pp £11.50

Basic reference data on companies importing and those offering import services, arranged A-Z. Also includes indexes of products and countries involved.

1449 DIRECTORY OF CONTRACTORS AND PUBLIC WORKS ANNUAL
Biggar & Co. (Publishers) Ltd.

GB—English annual c210pp £7.00

Classified list of contractors, civil engineers, architects, local authority surveyors and architects, nationalised bodies, government departments, societies etc.

1450 DIRECTORY OF DIRECTORS 1977
Thomas Skinner Directories

GB—English 1977 c1300pp £10.00

Directory of c40,000 members of the boards of the principal companies in the UK, giving names, addresses and appointments.

1451 DIRECTORY OF SHIPOWNERS, SHIPBUILDERS AND MARINE ENGINEERS
IPC Industrial Press Ltd.

GB—English annual 1330pp £10.00

Directory covering: shipowners; container shipping; tugs; shipping associations; government departments and officials.

1452 DISTRIBUTIVE TRADES STATISTICS
National Economic Development Office HMSO

GB—English 1970 45pp £0.65

Guide to sources of official statistics on the distributive trades.

1453 DUTCH COMPANIES WITH THEIR UK AGENTS, REPRESENTATIONS
Netherlands—British Chamber of Commerce

GB—English 1975 c70pp £6.20

Basic reference data on Dutch companies with representation in UK.

1454 EARNINGS IN GB 1974
National Economic Development Office

GB—English 1975 £3.25

Wages and salaries, classified by industry and national agreements presented in a wallchart form.

1455 ECONOMIC REVIEW
Trades Union Congress

GB—English annual 88pp £0.25

General review and commentary on the economic situation and the future outlook.

1456 ECONOMIC REVIEW FOR THE FURNITURE INDUSTRY
Furniture Industry Research Association

GB—English annual 87pp £6.00

Annual survey covering the key economic aspects of the furniture industry.

1457 ECONOMIC TRENDS
Central Statistical Office HMSO

GB—English monthly 100pp £28.72 p.a.

Monthly summary with a selection of tables and charts. It provides a broad background to trends in the UK economy. The annual supplement (£1.15) gives quarterly figures for all the main series.

1458 EDUCATION FOR MANAGEMENT A STUDY OF RESOURCES
National Economic Development Office HMSO

GB—English 1972 £1.35

Detailed examination of the range of British management education and training facilities available.

1459 EMPLOYMENT GAZETTE
Department of Employment HMSO

GB—English monthly c1150pp £15.40

Monthly journal of the Department of Employment with data on: employment; unemployment; hours worked; manpower; earnings; wage rates; stoppages; disputes; industrial accidents; output; retail prices.

1460 EMPLOYMENT PRACTICES IN EEC CLOTHING INDUSTRIES
National Economic Development Office

GB/INT—English 1974 free

Report on employer and employee organisations in five EEC countries visited by a NEDO group.

1461 ENERGY CONSERVATION IN THE UK
National Economic Development Office HMSO

GB—English 1974 106pp £3.40

Methods of saving energy, for industry, commerce and domestic users.

1462 ENERGY FOR INDUSTRY; THE EXECUTIVE'S GUIDE TO FUEL SUPPLIES, PRICING AND SUITABILITY
Cambridge Information and Research Services Ltd.

GB/INT—English annual 192pp £9.50—with quarterly updating service £19.50

Annual survey of the demand, supply and pricing conditions of oil, gas, electricity and coal in the British market. Also includes information on the world energy profile.

1463 THE ENERGY MARKETS TO 1990
Cambridge Information and Research Services Ltd.

GB—English 1977 80pp £16.25

Contents: energy forecasts to 1990; market demand

projections; conservation; energy supply prospects; matching energy demand and supply; energy forecast implications.

1464   ENERGY POLICY AND THE MOTOR INDUSTRY
Society of Motor Manufacturers and Traders

GB—English 1974 36pp £1.00

Special study by the Society of Motor Manufacturers and Traders Energy Steering Committee.

1465   ENGINEERING INDUSTRIES ASSOCIATION: CLASSIFIED DIRECTORY AND BUYERS GUIDE
Northern Advertising Agency (Bradford) Ltd.

GB—English

Basic reference data for member companies, arranged regionally. Also includes classified index.

1466   ENGINEERING INDUSTRIES REVIEW 1973/4
Gower Economic Publications, Teakfield

GB—English 1973 350pp £15.00

A survey of the mechanical and electrical engineering industries in the UK. Contains detailed surveys of particular sectors of the engineering industries, and includes information on output, labour, distribution, exports etc. Has a list of the top two hundred engineering companies and directory information on one hundred companies.

1467   EXPORT DATA
Benn Bros., Ltd.

GB/INT—English annual c400pp £15.00

Monthly updating service giving details of changes in export procedure throughout the world. Also includes data on: EEC; Commonwealth preference regulations; ATA Carnet scheme; VAT and exporters; Containers and unit loads services operating out of UK ports.

1468   EXTEL BRITISH COMPANY INFORMATION SERVICE
Extel Statistical Services

GB—English prices on application

Basic reference and financial data on over 4,250 companies in Britain. Standard financial performance information - balance sheet, profit and loss account etc. - supplied on an updating card system.

1469   EXTEL HANDBOOK OF MARKET LEADERS
Extel Statistical Services

GB—English twice a year annual subscription £50.00

Gives basic reference data on the companies included in FT Actuaries Index A-Z. Also standard financial performance, balance sheet, profit and loss etc

1470   EXTEL PROSPECTUSES
Extel Statistical Services

GB—English 2-4 volumes p.a. prices on application

Prospectuses and new issues arranged in chronological order with all relevant financial details arranged A-Z.

1471   EXTEL UNQUOTED COMPANIES SERVICE
Extel Statistical Services

GB—English prices on application

Basic reference and financial data on over 2,400 major, unquoted public and private companies. Standard financial performance information is updated weekly.

1472   FAIR TRADING - GUIDANCE FOR INDUSTRY AND COMMERCE
Confederation of British Industry

GB—English 1976 £2.00

Booklet giving concise and straightforward outline of the current Fair Trading law.

1473   FAMILY EXPENDITURE SURVEY
Department of Employment HMSO

GB—English annual c160pp £3.50

Provides economic and social data on household expenditure on food, housing, clothes, services, transport, fuel. Indicates how expenditure patterns vary in different kinds of households and provides reliable analyses of earnings of broad groups of individual members of private households.

1474   FARM CLASSIFICATION IN ENGLAND AND WALES
Ministry of Agriculture, Fisheries and Food HMSO

GB—English annual c120pp £1.38

Annual distribution of agricultural holdings, crop acreages, livestock numbers, workers, by farming type and size of business.

1475   FARM INCOMES IN ENGLAND AND WALES
Ministry of Agriculture, Fisheries and Food HMSO

GB—English annual c130pp £1.60

Statistics of farm incomes in England and Wales which includes comparison with the previous year and selected references to earlier years.

1476   FARM PRODUCTIVITY: A REPORT ON FACTORS AFFECTING PRODUCTIVITY AT THE FARM LEVEL
National Economic Development Office HMSO

GB—English 1973 15pp £0.50

Discusses factors directly associated with productivity levels including: farmer's age; planning a work force; management; husbandry skills.

1477   FERTILIZER STATISTICS
Fertilizer Manufacturers' Association

GB—English annual c25pp £1.00

Annual statistics of fertilizer production and related information.

1478   FINANCE AND PROFITABILITY IN THE WOOL TEXTILE INDUSTRY 1970-71—1973-74
National Economic Development Office

GB—English 1975 £2.50

Gives information on overall size, structure and performance of the textile industry with financial data on over 450 companies.

1479 FINANCE FOR INVESTMENT
National Economic Development Office

GB/INT—English 1975 207pp £5.00

Studies manufacturing industry finance, its problems, methods of financing, suppliers and users of finance with comparisons with EEC, Japanese and U.S. systems.

1480 FINANCE FOR INVESTMENT: APPENDICES
National Economic Development Office

GB/INT—English 1975 £5.00

Includes comparisons with UK of EEC, Japanese and U.S. tax treatment of capital gains, calculation of capital. Also stock market data.

1481 FINANCIAL PERFORMANCE IN THE ELECTRONICS INDUSTRY
National Economic Development Office

GB—English 1974 118pp £1.00

Study of companies with annual turnover in excess of £0.5 million. It covers some 300 companies.

1482 FINANCIAL RESULTS OF UK CHEMICAL COMPANIES 1971/72 - 1974/75
National Economic Development Office

GB—English 1976 98pp £3.60

First report on the 230 companies, employing more than 150 people, which make up 90% of the chemical industry in UK. The data covers performance, funds and income in the industry.

1483 FINANCIAL STATEMENT, NORTHERN IRELAND
Department of Finance, Northern Ireland

GB—English annual c10pp £0.15

Annual statement and details of the Northern Ireland Government finance, revenue and expenditure.

1484 FINANCIAL STATISTICS
Central Statistical Office HMSO

GB—English monthly 158pp £42.93 p.a.

Key financial and monetary statistics of the UK, including: central and local government; public corporations; banking and other financial institutions; companies. Also includes data on: money; credit; stock market; exchange rates; interest rates; securities. Separate annual supplement is issued with notes and definitions on the monthly statistics.

1485 A FINANCIAL STUDY OF BRITISH MACHINE TOOL COMPANIES
National Economic Development Office

GB—English 1974 £1.55

A study aimed at helping companies—by indicating the factors behind the financial success of certain selected companies—to compare with their own results.

1486 FINANCIAL TABLES FOR THE CLOTHING INDUSTRY 1973/74
National Economic Development Office

GB—English 1975 92pp £1.75

Analyses the performance of the clothing industry.

1487 FIRST DESTINATION OF UNIVERSITY GRADUATES
University Grants Commission HMSO

GB—English annual c80pp £1.35

Results of the annual survey covering Great Britain on the first employment taken by university graduates.

1488 FOCUS ON PHARMACEUTICALS
National Economic Development Office HMSO

GB—English 1972 129pp £1.85

The UK pharmaceutical industry studied in detail, with information on its economics, problems and prospects.

1489 FOLLOW-UP REPORT TO 'THE FREIGHT FORWARDER'
National Economic Development Office

GB—English 1973 20pp free

Describes the changes, since 1970, in the freight forwarding industry (see also No. 1498)

1490 FOLLOW-UP REPORT TO 'SHORT SEA SHIPPING'
National Economic Development Office only

GB—English 1972 free

Discusses the effect of the Economic Development Committee's recommendations. (See also No. 1675)

1491 FOOD INDUSTRIES REVIEW 1975-76
Gower Economic Publications, Teakfield

GB—English 1975 350pp £30.00

Reviews the following major sectors of the food industry: dairy; chocolate; sugar; bread and flour; cakes and biscuits; fruit and vegetables; meat and fish; cereals; drink; tobacco. Contains trading summaries on the top 100 companies.

1492 FOOD PROCESSING AND PACKAGING DIRECTORY
IPC Business Press Ltd.

GB—English annual c825pp £12.00

Directory listing all the known UK food processors, research organisations, government departments, trade associations, plant equipment and packaging manufacturers; materials and suppliers.

1493 FOOD TRADES DIRECTORY AND FOOD BUYER'S YEARBOOK
Newman Books Ltd.

GB/INT—English annual c1067pp £16.00

Directory of food suppliers, manufacturers, importers and merchants. Also includes details of UK and overseas food producers.

1494 FOOTWEAR INDUSTRY STATISTICAL REVIEW
British Footwear Manufacturers Association

GB—English annual

Annual statistical review of the footwear manufacturing
industry.

1495 FOOTWEAR 1980: A MARKET FORECAST
British Footwear Manufacturers Federation

GB—English 1970

Survey of the UK footwear industry in 1970, with data
on: consumption; prices; imports; exports; production;
forecasts to 1980. Also includes a section on possible
markets for UK exports and future changes in international trading relationships.

**1496 FORECASTING THE DEMAND FOR TOURISM IN
SCOTLAND AND THE REGIONS OF SCOTLAND**
Business and Economic Planning/Scottish Tourist Board

GB—English 1975 179pp £12.00

Detailed report of a research survey investigating the
demand, problems and potential for tourism in Scotland.

1497 FORECASTS OF THE UNITED KINGDOM ECONOMY
Econtel Research Ltd.

GB—English annual c20pp £15.00

Annual estimates of economic indicators, including:
prices; wages; interest rates; unemployment; consumer
credit; forecasting five years ahead.

1498 THE FREIGHT FORWARDER
National Economic Development Office/HMSO

GB—English 1970 44pp £0.50

Study and recommendations on freight forwarding in the
UK (See also No. 1489).

1499 FT ACTUARIES SHARE INDICES
The Financial Times Ltd.

GB—English 56pp £30.50

A fortnightly record of the FT Actuaries share indices
from their inception in April 1962 up to date, inclusive
of quarterly updates.

1500 FUTURE PATTERN OF SHOPPING
National Economic Development Office HMSO

GB—English 1971 £1.25

Study of the pattern of shopping by 1980.

1501 GAS DIRECTORY AND WHO'S WHO
Benn Bros. Ltd.

GB—English annual 280pp £10.00

Comprehensive guide to the British Gas Corporation with
maps and references; index to undertakings in the UK and
Ireland with names of principal officers; EEC and overseas
undertakings; buyers' guide and trade names; list of
approved gas appliances.

**1502 GERMAN/ENGLISH GLOSSARY OF TERMS USED IN
FREIGHT FORWARDING**
National Economic Development Office

GB/D—English 1971 48pp free

Short glossary based on the German freight forwarders'
standard terms and conditions.

**1503 GUIDE TO GOVERNMENT DEPARTMENTS AND OTHER
LIBRARIES AND INFORMATION BUREAUX**
The British Library

GB—English 1976 c70pp £3.00

Basic reference data of selected sources of information.

1504 GUIDE TO OFFICIAL STATISTICS
Central Statistical Office HMSO

GB—English 1976 391pp £7.50

Covers all official and the major non-official sources of
statistics for the UK and the Isle of Man (but excluding
the Channel Islands); each entry contains a contents
description.

**1505 GUIDE TO THE CLASSIFICATION FOR OVERSEAS
TRADE STATISTICS**
HM Customs and Excise HMSO

GB—English annual c550pp £4.00

Sets out in detail the descriptions and code numbers under
which imports and exports to and from the UK and the
Channel Islands are classified for overseas trade statistics.

1506 A HANDBOOK FOR MARKETING MACHINERY
National Economic Development Office HMSO

GB—English 1970 100pp £1.35

Survey aimed at improving marketing techniques in the
engineering industry, based on machine tool experience.

1507 HANDBOOK OF ELECTRICITY SUPPLY STATISTICS
The Electricity Council

GB—English annual c120pp free

Electricity supply statistics covering: power stations data;
the National Grid; distribution systems; electricity
generation; financial and commercial information;
earnings; employment.

**1508 HEALTH AND PERSONAL SOCIAL SERVICES
STATISTICS FOR ENGLAND (WITH SUMMARY
TABLES FOR GREAT BRITAIN)**
Department of Health and Social Security HMSO

GB—English annual c180pp £3.00

Details of: population; finance; manpower; hospital
administration; health services. Statistics give
historical trends.

**1509 HEALTH AND PERSONAL SOCIAL SERVICES
STATISTICS FOR WALES**
Welsh Office HMSO

GB—English annual c150pp £3.35

Detailed statistics on: finance; manpower; hospital
administration; executive councils; community health;
maternity and child health; personal social services.

1510   HOSIERY AND KNITWEAR IN THE 1970s
National Economic Development Office HMSO

GB—English 1970 £2.25

The hosiery and knitwear industry and the changes in the
social, economic and technological fields which will
affect it up to 1978.

1511   HOTELS AND GOVERNMENT POLICIES
National Economic Development Office

GB—English 1974 £0.75

An examination of taxation of the hotel industry. Also
discusses VAT, regional incentives and industrial
building allowances.

1512   HOTELS AND THE BUSINESS TRAVELLER
National Economic Development Office HMSO

GB—English 1970 48pp £0.40

A study of the hotel needs of the businessman.

1513   HOUSEHOLD FOOD CONSUMPTION AND EXPENDITURE
(REPORT OF THE NATIONAL FOOD SURVEY
COMMITTEE)
Ministry of Agriculture, Fisheries and Food HMSO

GB—English annual c250pp £2.30

Food consumption patterns with comparisons between
varying income groups, different sized families and
regions. Also gives details of the estimates of the average
energy value and nutrient content of the diet in various
types of household.

1514   HOUSING AND CONSTRUCTION STATISTICS
Department of the Environment HMSO

GB—English quarterly c100pp £12.06 p.a.

Gives statistics on: output; orders; prices; finance in
construction; housebuilding; building materials. Includes
some regional analyses. The annual subscription also
includes the annual supplement (c.3Opp) which gives
notes and definitions supplementing the quarterly
statistics.

1515   HOUSING MARKETS REVIEW 1974
Gower Press Ltd., Teakfield

GB—English 1973 176pp £6.50

A survey of housing in the UK. Contains information on
both a national and regional basis. Includes an analysis
of trends in house building in both the public and private
sectors, house prices, land and construction costs, the
building societies, government attitudes and future
prospects for the industry. There is a list of principal
housebuilding companies.

1516   THE HUNDRED CENTRE GUIDE TO COMMERCIAL
PROPERTY DEVELOPMENT 1975-76
Gower Economic Publications, Teakfield

GB—English 1975 414pp £12.50

Survey shop and office development opportunities.
Includes data on: site costs and availability; local
economy and transport infrastructure. Also shows
regional centre selection tables and city plans indicating
site locations. (See also No. I525)

1517   HYDRAULIC EQUIPMENT IN THE EEC—
IMPLICATIONS FOR THE UK INDUSTRY
National Economic Development Office

GB/INT—English 1975 £25.00

Studies the key factors and strategies of market success
in the UK and EEC both for hydraulic equipment and
other industries.

1518   ICC FINANCIAL SURVEYS
Inter Company Comparisons Ltd.

GB—English annual £22.00 - £30.00

Individual surveys for over 125 sectors of British industry;
each survey covers a large number of private and public
companies, giving: comparative figures for two years' turnover; profits before tax; payments to directors; total
assets; current liabilities.

1519   THE IMPACT OF KNITWEAR IMPORTS
National Economic Development Office

GB—English 1970 free

Survey of buyers' attitudes to imported knitwear.

1520   IMPACT OF THE EMPLOYMENT PROTECTION ACT
ON PART-TIME EMPLOYMENT IN RETAILING
National Economic Development Office

GB—English 1975 free

Studies the changes affecting part-time workers which
were brought about by the 1975 Employment Protection
Act. Includes statistics on part-time employment in
retailing, and interviews with relevant organisations.

1521   IMPORTED MANUFACTURES
National Economic Development Office HMSO

GB—English 1965 £0.17½

An examination of the causes and reasons for the
dramatic increase in imports of goods in the late 1950s
and early 1960s.

1522   THE INCREASED COST OF ENERGY—IMPLICATIONS
FOR UK INDUSTRY
National Economic Development Office HMSO

GB—English 1974 £3.40

The energy situation and its effect on the UK economy
and manufacturing industry in particular.

1523   THE INCREASED COST OF ENERGY—SUPPLEMENTARY
CALCULATIONS OF ITS EFFECTS
National Economic Development Office HMSO

GB—English 1975 free

Revised estimates of industrial products price increases
using additional data thus supplementing the original
report.

1524   INDEXATION AND INFLATION
The Financial Times Ltd.

GB—English 1975 c170pp £50.35

A report on the likely effect of indexation within the UK
economy and its relevance to the control of inflation.

1525   INDUSTRIAL DEVELOPMENT GUIDE 1975-76
Gower Economic Publications, Teakfield

GB—English 1974 660pp £12.50

Companion volume to the 'Hundred Centre Guide'
(No. 1516) charts current industrial distribution with
expansion opportunities. Surveys development
attitudes and prospects in 11 regions of the UK.

1526   INDUSTRIAL DIRECTORY OF WALES
Development Corporation for Wales

GB—English 1975 c205pp £4.00

Basic reference data on companies in Wales arranged
A-Z. Also includes information on those with overseas
connections.

1527   INDUSTRIAL EXPANSION HANDBOOK
Regional Reference Press, JHS Management (Holdings) Ltd.

GB—English 1976 124pp £2.50

Reference guide to government departments and
organisations dealing with industrial development in
the regions and new towns.

1528   INDUSTRIAL FUEL MARKETS 1973-74
Gower Economic Publications Teakfield

GB—English 1973 350pp £12.50

Surveys the UK supply and demand patterns for coal,
gas, oil and electricity by domestic and industrial
users. Assesses the effect of price changes.

**1529   INDUSTRIAL PERFORMANCE ANALYSIS: A
FINANCIAL ANALYSIS OF UK INDUSTRY AND
COMMERCE**
Inter Company Comparisons Ltd.

GB—English 1976 111pp £9.50

Summarises the progress achieved by sectors of British
industry over the three year period ending in 1975.
Includes: construction industry; chemical and plastics;
drinks; electrical and electronic; engineering and
metals; food; motor; paper and printing; textiles.

**1530   INDUSTRIAL RESTRUCTURING: SOME MANPOWER
ASPECTS**
National Economic Development Office

GB—English 1976 £1.50

Attempts to give guidelines for future industrial re-
organisation by examining various industry-wide
restructuring schemes and their manpower aspects.

1531   INDUSTRIAL REVIEW TO 1977
National Economic Development Office

GB—English 1973 £1.00

Studies the effects of both a 3.5% and a 5.0% growth
rate on the economy and the 11 key industries,
making up 60% of UK manufacturing, in particular.

1532   INDUSTRIAL REVIEW TO 1977: CASTINGS
National Economic Development Office

GB—English 1974 £0.50

Discusses the growth, prospects and problems of the
UK foundry industry.

1533   INDUSTRIAL REVIEW TO 1977: CHEMICALS
National Economic Development Office

GB—English 1973 38pp £0.50

Examines growth, prospects, opportunities and
problems for the UK chemical industry.

1534   INDUSTRIAL REVIEW TO 1977: CLOTHING
National Economic Development Office

GB—English 1974 £0.50

Gives factors affecting growth in a study of the
economy of the clothing industry to 1977.

**1535   INDUSTRIAL REVIEW TO 1977: ELECTRICAL
ENGINEERING**
National Economic Development Office

GB—English 1974 35pp £0.50

Factors affecting growth are examined in this
economic study of the electrical engineering
industry.

1536   INDUSTRIAL REVIEW TO 1977: ELECTRONICS
National Economic Development Office

GB—English 1973 31pp £0.50

Prospects, in summary form, for the industry's markets,
exports, imports, output and resources.

**1537   INDUSTRIAL REVIEW TO 1977: MECHANICAL
ENGINEERING**
National Economic Development Office

GB—English 1974 £0.50

Gives possible developments and future implications
in the industry's competitive position. (See also No. 1695)

1538   INDUSTRIAL REVIEW TO 1977: MOTORS
National Economic Development Office

GB/INT—English 1973 £0.50

Study of demand, trade, output, competitiveness, problems,
manpower issues, pay structure and labour force of UK
motor industry.

1539   INDUSTRIAL REVIEW TO 1977: TEXTILES
National Economic Development Office

GB—English 1974 £0.50

UK textile industry, studied as a whole, in an attempt to
assess medium-term prospects.

1540 INFLATION AND COMPANY ACCOUNTS IN
      MECHANICAL ENGINEERING
      National Economic Development Office

      GB—English 1973 £1.00

      Covers the mechanical engineering industry 1965-71, its
      financial position and the consequences of adjusting
      for inflation effects on company accounts.

1541 INLAND REVENUE STATISTICS
      Board of Inland Revenue HMSO

      GB—English annual c190pp £3.00

      Statistical tables on taxation, incomes, capital and
      valuation. Includes results of the Surveys of Personal
      Income and estimates of personal wealth not published
      elsewhere. Some separate figures are given for England
      and Wales, Scotland and Northern Ireland.

1542 INNOVATIVE ACTIVITY IN THE PHARMACEUTICAL
      INDUSTRY
      National Economic Development Office HMSO

      GB/INT—English 1973 38pp £0.50

      Study of the level and effectiveness of innovative
      activity in the UK, including a comparison with other
      countries.

1543 INPUT-OUTPUT TABLES FOR THE UK 1968
      Central Statistical Office HMSO

      GB—English 1973 128pp £7.30

      Studies in Official Statistics Series No. 22. Data based
      largely on the census of production results, showing how
      the tables were constructed. Includes full details of the
      tables of industry and commodity groups in domestic
      production.

1544 INPUT-OUTPUT TABLES FOR THE UK 1970
      Central Statistical Office HMSO

      GB—English 1974 102pp £1.00

      Updates and complements the volume of 1968 tables.
      Also a comprehensive guide to the structure of the
      UK economy.

1545 INSURANCE DIRECTORY AND YEARBOOK
      Buckley Press Ltd.

      GB—English annual c450pp £7.00

      Basic reference data on insurance companies in UK and
      Ireland. Also includes: geographical classification of
      brokers, loss adjustors; societies; institutes.

1546 INTERNATIONAL PRICE COMPARISON
      National Economic Development Office

      GB/D/F/I—English 1972 free

      Compares French, West German, Japanese and Italian
      pharmaceutical prices with those in UK.

1547 INVESTMENT APPRAISAL IN THE CLOTHING INDUSTRY
      National Economic Development Office HMSO

      GB—English 1973 £1.35

Guide to investment techniques for clothing company
managers, including illustrated examples.

1548 INVESTMENT IN THE CHEMICAL INDUSTRY
      National Economic Development Office

      GB—English 1972 93pp £0.85

      Covers cash flow and investment requirements to 1978.

1549 IPC INDUSTRIAL MARKETING MANUAL OF THE
      UNITED KINGDOM
      IPC Marketing Services Dept.

      GB—English 1975 c450pp

      Reference data on UK industry.

1550 IPC SOCIOLOGICAL MONOGRAPHS
      IPC Marketing Services Dept.

      GB—English 1975 Available as a set (£50) or
      individually

      In 12 volumes
      Vol. 1 Patterns of population change (£3.00)
      Vol. 2 Current housing conditions in Great Britain (£3.00)
      Vol. 3 Structure and content of educational development
      (£5.00)
      Vol. 4 Household spending (£5.00)
      Vol. 5 The structure of employment (£3.00)
      Vol. 6 Employment: Work and society (£3.00)
      Vol. 7 Employment: Working conditions and rewards
      (£3.00)
      Vol. 8 Women at work (£5.00)
      Vol. 9 The mass media—the audience (£5.00)
      Vol. 10 The mass media—the content (£5.00)
      Vol. 11 The mass media—uses and gratifications (£5.00)
      Vol. 12 Leisure (£12.00)

      A series of reports on trends and developments in key social
      areas.

1551 IRON AND STEEL INDUSTRY ANNUAL STATISTICS
      FOR THE UNITED KINGDOM
      British Steel Corporation

      GB—English annual c120pp £5.00

      Annual statistics of the iron and steel industry including:
      supply of steel; production of iron ore; oxygen consumption;
      fuel; minerals and refractories; detailed statistics on
      various types of iron and steel. Also gives data on: prices;
      imports and exports; labour.

1552 JORDAN DATAQUEST: INDUSTRIAL SURVEYS
      Jordan Dataquest Ltd.

      GB—English 1976

      Detailed analyses of the financial performance of major companies
      in the industrial and services sectors, over a four-year period.
      Includes basic reference data.

1553 KELLY'S MANUFACTURERS AND MERCHANTS
      DIRECTORY, INCLUDING INDUSTRIAL SERVICES
      Kelly's Directories Ltd.

      GB/IRL—English annual 2 vols c4000pp £10.85

      A-Z and classified listings of manufacturers, merchants
      in England, Scotland, Wales, London and suburbs,
      Northern Ireland, Irish Republic. Also includes
      classified lists of importers and exporters in each area.

1554   KEY BRITISH ENTERPRISES: I
Dun and Bradstreet Ltd.

GB—English annual c1200pp £40.00

Gives details on 11,000 large firms and companies in
the UK engaged in manufacturing and distributive trades,
transport and communications and specialist service
organisations. Lists companies A-Z with details of:
address; telephone numbers; products and services;
employees; directors; capital; trade names. Also includes
separate classified index and list of company subsidiaries.

1555   KEY BRITISH ENTERPRISES: II
Dun and Bradstreet Ltd.

GB—English annual c600pp £30.00

Formerly 'British Middle Market Directory'. Selection
of c11,000 UK firms and companies, in four sections:
1: Businesses A-Z; 2: Classified listing of companies by
trade SIC; 3: A-Z products and services classified by
SIC; 4: Group affiliations.

1556   KNOW MORE ABOUT OIL: WORLD STATISTICS
Institute of Petroleum

GB/INT—English 1976 8pp free

Concise guide to world oil statistics, compiled by the
Information Department of the Institute of Petroleum.

1557   KOMPASS REGISTER OF BRITISH INDUSTRY AND
COMMERCE
Kompass Publishers Ltd.

GB—English annual 2 vols 2000pp £25.00

The official register of the Confederation of British
Industry it lists the products and services of 28,000
UK companies, giving details of: address; telephone
numbers; directors; executives; capital; number employees;
products; trade names; subsidiaries; branches; overseas
agents. Vol. 2 also includes systematic product charts
giving a breakdown of over 33,000 products and services
classified under 30 trade groups. It is fully indexed in
English, French, German, Spanish and Italian. Regional
sections available separately £4.50 (£3.50 7 or more).

1558   KOMPASS UK TRADE NAMES
Kompass Publishers Ltd.

GB—English c400pp £20.00

Listing of c70,000 trade names, A-Z, with details of:
manufacturer, address, type of product.

1559   LEISURE INDUSTRIES REVIEW 1975/6
Gower Economic Publications, Teakfield

GB—English 1975 262pp £19.50

Economic survey of the leisure industry in the UK
covering: brewing; hotels; catering; gaming and betting;
holidays and sports equipment. Examines prospects by
sector and includes a review of the major companies.

1560   LLOYDS BANK REVIEW
Lloyds Bank Ltd.

GB—English quarterly 50pp free

Quarterly review and commentary on economic,
industrial and social topics.

1561   LOCAL AUTHORITY FINANCIAL RETURNS,
NORTHERN IRELAND
Department of Housing, Local Government and
Planning, Northern Ireland

GB—English annual c100pp £1.05

Annual statistics giving details of: income; expenditure;
loan debt; classified by type of service.

1562   LOCAL FINANCIAL RETURNS, SCOTLAND
Scottish Office

GB—English annual c20pp £0.75

Information on financial transactions of counties,
cities, burghs and district councils, joint boards and
committees, local harbour and dock authorities and
district fishery boards.

1563   LOCAL GOVERNMENT FINANCIAL STATISTICS
ENGLAND AND WALES
Department of the Environment (Housing and Local
Government) HMSO

GB—English annual c70pp £1.05

Analyses of local government income and expenditure.
Gives separate tables for England and Wales.

1564   LOCAL HOUSING STATISTICS ENGLAND AND WALES
Department of the Environment (Housing and Local
Government)HMSO

GB—English quarterly c50pp £1.40

Quarterly statistics of new housing construction, slum
clearance and renovation grants, by regions.

1565   LONDON GAZETTE
HMSO

GB—English 4 times weekly various pp £55.90 p.a.

Gives monthly figures of Consolidated Fund transactions,
analyses by borrowing authority and borrowing and
repayment of debt by type of security. Once a week
lists assets and liabilities of the Bank of England.

1566   LONG TERM DEMAND STUDIES 1963-75
National Economic Development Office

GB—English 7 vols £10.00 each

Detailed studies of seven key industries: valves; shell
boilers; process plant; pumps; fluid power; construction
equipment; agricultural machinery. Available on a
restricted circulation basis from the Secretary,
Mechanical Engineering EDC at NEDO.

1567   LOW-COST WORK AIDS FOR THE CLOTHING AND
GARMENT INDUSTRIES
National Economic Development Office

GB—English 1974 £2.50

Aims to show ways of quick, inexpensive and effective
methods of improving productivity or quality.

1568   MADE TO MEASURE
National Economic Development Office

GB—English 1971 free

Gives details on 75 research and management service organisations available to clothing manufacturers.

1569 MAJOR SUBURBAN SHOPPING CENTRES
Retail Outlets Research Unit, Manchester
Business School

GB—English 1971

Research Report 1:
Vol. 1: Statistical handbook
Vol. 2: Atlas.
A statistical and geographical survey of the major shopping centres in Great Britain in 1970.

1570 MANAGEMENT TRAINING IN INDUSTRIAL RELATIONS
National Economic Development Office

GB—English 1975 £2.30

Report assessing the current situation in management training in industrial relations and containing recommendations for improvement.

1571 MANPOWER AND PAY IN RETAIL DISTRIBUTION
National Economic Development Office

GB—English 1974 76pp £1.10

Factors affecting retail distribution including labour, pay, conditions and problems of low pay.

1572 MANPOWER POLICY IN THE HOTELS AND RESTAURANT INDUSTRY—RESEARCH FINDINGS
National Economic Development Office

GB—English 1975 76pp £2.60

Gives details of: staff turnover, recruitment, training, terms and conditions, management and employee relations.

1573 MANPOWER POLICY IN THE HOTELS AND RESTAURANT INDUSTRY - SUMMARY AND RECOMMENDATIONS
National Economic Development Office

GB—English 1975 free

Research findings in summary form with recommendations for policymakers.

1574 MANPOWER 75
Road Transport Industry Training Board

GB—English 1975 182pp £4.50

Study of manpower and training needs in the road transport industry 1967-80.

1575 THE MARKET FOR CLOVES AND CLOVE PRODUCTS IN THE UNITED KINGDOM
Tropical Products Institute

GB—English 1975 37pp £0.60

This study explores the UK market for the following materials: clove buds; the oleoresin extracted from the buds; the clove oil, which is generally distilled in this country, and the stem and leaf oils which are imported.

1576 THE MARKET FOR TABLE WINE IN THE UNITED KINGDOM
International Trade Centre

GB—English 1974

Surveys the current market situation, giving statistical information on local production and imports, consumer patterns, trade channels and practices, trade regulations and promotion.

1577 MARKETING IN A SMALL BUSINESS
National Economic Development Office

GB—English 1970 free

Booklet examining modern marketing techniques for the independent hotelier/restaurateur.

1578 MARKETING MANUAL OF THE UNITED KINGDOM
IPC Marketing Services Department

GB—English 1976 c450pp £21.00

Three main sections give; social and economic data, market place data with summaries of product fields, media and advertising data. Includes maps, over 300 tables and index.

1579 MEAL DIGEST OF ADVERTISING EXPENDITURE
Media Expenditure Analysis Ltd.

GB—English monthly on subscription

Expenditure by brand of good on press and television with the name of the agency handling the account.

1580 THE MEASUREMENT AND INTERPRETATION OF SERVICE OUTPUT CHANGES
National Economic Development Office

GB—English 1972 181pp free

Covers the difficulties of assessing changes in productivity and real output.

1581 THE MECHANICAL ENGINEERING INDUSTRY— DIGEST OF STATISTICAL INFORMATION 1971
National Economic Development Office

GB—English 1971 68pp £0.60

Facts and figures on the mechanical engineering industry.

1582 MERCHANT BANKING: ANNUAL REVIEW
reprinted from 'The Banker' Dec. issue

GB—English 1974 c65pp £0.25

Includes basic reference data on merchant banks with foreign exchange authorisation, arranged A-Z.

1583 METALWORKING PRODUCTION'S SURVEY OF MACHINE TOOLS AND PRODUCTION EQUIPMENT IN BRITAIN
Morgan Grampian Ltd.

GB—English 1971 186pp £5.00

Short articles and detailed statistics on the machine tool and production equipment industries.

1584   MIDLAND BANK REVIEW
Midland Bank Ltd.

GB—English quarterly c20pp free

Quarterly review and commentary of economic,
industrial and social topics.

1585   MINES INSPECTORATE REPORTS
HMSO

GB—English annual 5 parts

Annual official report of HM Inspectors of Mines and
Quarries, in five regional parts:
North and South Midlands Districts; (c60pp £0.95)
South Wales Districts; (c45pp £0.85)
Southern Districts; (c50pp £0.85)
West Midlands and North Western Districts; (c50pp
£0.95)
Yorkshire Districts; (c45pp £0.95)

1586   MONTHLY BULLETIN OF CONSTRUCTION INDICES
Department of the Environment (Property Services
Agency)/HMSO

GB—English monthly 3 parts

Statistics and costs of labour and materials for use
with National Economic Development price adjustment
formula; In 3 parts:
Building Works; (annual sub. £7.38)
Civil Engineering Works (annual sub. £4.98)
Specialist Engineering Installations (annual sub. £6.18)

1587   MONTHLY DIGEST OF STATISTICS
Central Statistical Office HMSO

GB—English monthly c170pp £27.86

Monthly and quarterly statistics on: national income and
expenditure; population; labour; social services; production;
transport; agriculture and food; energy; metal;
engineering; vehicles; textiles; construction; retailing;
external trade; wages and prices.

1588   MONTHLY STATISTICAL REVIEW
Society of Motor Manufacturers and Traders

GB—English monthly £18.00 p.a.

Monthly statistical review of the motor industry.

1589   THE MOTOR INDUSTRY OF GREAT BRITAIN
Society of Motor Manufacturers and Traders

GB—English annual c360pp £1.50

Annual review with statistics and commentary on the
motor industry.

1590   MULTINATIONAL BUSINESS
Economist Intelligence Unit

GB/INT—English quarterly c55pp £70.00 p.a.

Current data and statistics on key aspects of the multinational business climate and performance, including
company, country, sectoral and industry case studies.
Record of recent company acquisitions and mergers
is maintained.

**1591   MULTIPLE SHIFTWORK: A PROBLEM FOR DECISION
BY MANAGEMENT AND LABOUR**
National Economic Development Office HMSO

GB—English 1970 28pp £0.40

NEDO Monographs No. 1.
Examines the economic advantages of shiftworking.

1592   THE MUNICIPAL BUYERS' GUIDE
The Municipal Journal Ltd., London

GB—English annual c372pp

Companion volume to the Municipal Year Book,
compiled for local government purchasers listing 4000
companies selling to local authorities; also includes an
A-Z product index and a separate A-Z list of companies.

**1593   THE MUNICIPAL YEAR BOOK AND PUBLIC
SERVICES DIRECTORY**
The Municipal Journal Ltd.

GB—English annual cl2I5pp £13.50

In 3 parts: Part 1: Introduction with general index to
local authorities
Part 2: Annual reviews with facts and figures on thirty
topics e.g. architecture and building; civil aviation;
education; finance
Part 3: Main directory of government departments,
local authorities, parishes, development corporations,
political composition of councils, officers of local
authorities.

1594   NATIONAL INCOME AND EXPENDITURE
Central Statistical Office HMSO

GB—English annual c150pp £2.20

'Blue Book' - detailed statistics of national product,
income and expenditure for the UK over a ten-year
period with summary tables for earlier years.

1595   NATIONAL INSTITUTE ECONOMIC REVIEW
National Institute of Economic and Social Research

GB—English quarterly c70-118pp £10.00

Quarterly economic forecasts covering the UK and world
outlook plus a limited number of special articles.

1596   NATIONAL WESTMINSTER BANK QUARTERLY REVIEW
National Westminster Bank Ltd.

GB—English quarterly c60pp free on application

Quarterly review and commentary on economic,
industrial and social topics.

**1597   NEW CONTRIBUTIONS TO ECONOMIC STATISTICS;
7th SERIES**
Central Statistical Office HMSO

GB—English 1975 156pp £2.65

Studies in Official Statistics Series No. 24. Selection of
articles reprinted from Economic Trends Dec. 1971-1973,
including: national accounts; input-output; production;
finance; cars.

1598   NEW EARNINGS SURVEY
Department of Employment HMSO

GB—English annual 6 parts £6.80 p.a.

A sample survey of employees in industry:
Part A: Report: general and selected key results.
Part B: Analyses by agreement.
Part C: Analyses by industry.
Part D: Analyses by occupation.
Part E: Analyses by region and age group.
Part F: Hours; holidays with pay; earnings of
part-time workers.

**1599   THE NEW EUROPEAN PATENT SYSTEM AND ITS
INPLICATIONS FOR INDUSTRY**
Confederation of British Industry

GB/INT—English 1974 44pp £2.50

Booklet reproducing conference papers which studied the
new European patent system and its implications for
industry affecting the UK and the 14 nations that signed
the 1973 treaty.

1600   NEW REGISTRATION OF NEW MOTOR VEHICLES
Society of Motor Manufacturers and Traders Ltd.

GB—English quarterly

Details of new registrations of new cars, vans, other goods
vehicles by make and, for cars only, by model. Includes
British and imported vehicles.

1601   NORTHERN IRELAND FAMILY EXPENDITURE SURVEY
Department of Finance, Northern Ireland

GB—English annual c80pp £1.00

Tables showing pattern of household expenditure on food,
clothing, housing, services and other items by income and
distribution of households.

1602   NORTH SEA OIL INFORMATION SOURCES
Kogan Page

GB—English 1975

Basic reference data on all relevant government, public
authority, stockbroking sources.

**1603   NORWEGIAN CHAMBER OF COMMERCE IN LONDON:
YEARBOOK**
Norwegian Chamber of Commerce

GB—English annual 244pp £1.00

Directory of members A-Z with details of town and
business activity. Also includes a separate classified list
of members with addresses and products.

**1604   OFFSHORE SUPPLIERS GUIDE: UNITED KINGDOM
1976**
IPC Business Press Ltd.

GB—English 1976 c185pp £6.50

Buyers guide to equipment, products and services
relevant to the offshore industries.

1605   OIL—CONSUMPTION AND REFINERY PRODUCTION
Institute of Petroleum

GB—English annual 20pp free

Annual review of the oil industry covering consumption
and production of refineries.

1606   ON-SHORE BRITAIN 1976-77
Gower Press, Teakfield

GB—English 1976 401pp £18.50

Summary by region and town of developments relating
to the off-shore industries. Also includes a directory of
addresses for supporting services.

1607   OPEC FUNDS AND THE UK
Economist Intelligence Unit

GB—English 1975 c80pp £15.00

Study assessing the UK's need for OPEC funds, size of
OPEC surpluses and potential proportion that may be
invested in the UK. Also examines investment
opportunities in the UK for OPEC investment managers,
with an analysis of how UK domestic policy will
influence the flow of OPEC funds.

1608   OVERSEAS ADVERTISING
Institute of Practitioners in Advertising

GB—English 1973 11pp £0.50

Booklet covering methods of handling overseas advertising
and facilities of the IPA available to members.

**1609   OVERSEAS BUYERS' GUIDE TO RAW MATERIALS,
TOPS AND YARNS**
'Wool Record', Bradford/National Wool Textile Export
Corporation

GB—English 1975 76pp £1.25

Classified trade guide for overseas buyers in the textile
industry.

1610   OVERSEAS TRADE STATISTICS
Department of Trade HMSO

GB—English monthly c550pp £6.50 per issue

Statistics of imports and exports, classified by SITC and
presented by country of origin and destination.

1611   PACKING FOR PROFIT
National Economic Development Office HMSO

GB—English 1973 £1.40 2 vols.

Describes the economic advantages of utilising break bulk
cargo and detailing various unit load techniques with a
guide to the services and equipment available.

1612   PACKAGING REVIEW DIRECTORY AND BUYERS GUIDE
IPC Business Press Ltd.

GB—English 1976 250pp £12.00

Guide to suppliers of materials, equipment products and
services available within the UK packaging industry.

1613   PAPER AND PACKAGING BULLETIN
Economist Intelligence Unit

GB/INT—English quarterly c70pp £90.00 p.a.

Quarterly analysis of trends in packaging materials—
paper and plastic, and printing papers, for consumers
and producers. Includes statistics for the UK and the
EEC on: production; exports of pulp and paper by
grades; imports; consumption; stocks. Also includes
a guide to UK paper prices.

1614   PASSENGER TRANSPORT IN GREAT BRITAIN
Department of the Environment (Transport) HMSO

GB—English annual c40pp £0.82

Base source covering road traffic and rail travel.

1615   PERSONAL SAVINGS AND WEALTH IN BRITAIN
Financial Times Ltd.

GB—English 1975 103pp £50.50

Survey of the assets of 13,000 adults; an analysis of
the saver, the savings, the shareowners and the changing
pattern of investment. (See also No. 1671)

1616   THE PHARMACEUTICAL INDUSTRY
Economists Advisory Group/Dun & Bradstreet

GB—English 1973 50pp £60.00

A statistical profile of the UK pharmaceutical industry.
Includes data on structure of the industry, profitability,
companies and foreign trade.

1617   PHYSICAL DISTRIBUTION MANAGEMENT
National Economic Development Office

GB—English 1976 free

Newsletter concentrating on the economic factors
involved in physical distribution.

1618   THE PLASTICS INDUSTRY AND ITS PROSPECTS
National Economic Development Office HMSO

GB—English 1972 148pp £1.60

In-depth study of the UK plastics industry, its markets,
growth prospects to 1980 and the resources needed.

1619   PLASTICS INTO THE 1980s
National Economic Development Office

GB—English 1972 free

Summary version of 'The plastics industry and its
prospects'.

**1620   POPULATION PROJECTIONS 1974-2014, UNITED
KINGDOM**
Office of Population Censuses and Surveys HMSO

GB—English annual 1975 90pp £1.55

Population projections based on the 1974 mid-year
estimates by sex and age. Also includes some marital
condition projections. Detailed discussion of the
projections including derivation, method used and
variations from earlier projections.

1621   POPULATION TRENDS
Office of Population Censuses and Surveys HMSO

GB—English quarterly c60pp £8.56

Contains regular series of tables on population,
components of change, vital statistics, live births,
marriages, divorces, migration, deaths, abortions.

**1622   PRACTICAL EMPLOYEE PARTICIPATION IN
SMALLER FIRMS**
Confederation of British Industry

GB—English 1976 17pp £0.50

Details of the CBI's proposals on employee
participation in firms with less than 500 employees.
Outlines four main types of participation with a
framework establishing Company Councils and a
working checklist for assessing companies' positions
and progress.

1623   PRICE PROPAGATION IN AN INPUT-OUTPUT MODEL
National Economic Development Office HMSO

GB—English 1975 18pp £1.75

A booklet setting out the algebra for determining the
implications of higher energy costs for industrial
prices.

1624   PRINTING TRADES DIRECTORY
Benn Bros. Ltd.

GB—English 1976 34pp £15.00

Directory of printing and allied industries with over
30,000 entries including details of 6,000 printers,
with details of type of work undertaken, arranged
A-Z and geographically. Also includes data on printers'
specialities, manufacturers and suppliers, machinery,
materials.

1625   PRIVATE CONTRACTORS' CONSTRUCTION CENSUS
Department of the Environment HMSO

GB—English annual 40pp £0.77

Structure of the construction industry, with data on:
firms; output; type of work and crafts; size; trade.

1626   PROCESS INDUSTRIES INVESTMENT FORECASTS 11
National Economic Development Office

GB—English 1976 £1.50

Annual investment forecast by the Process Plant
Working Party.

**1627 PRODUCT CHANGES IN INDUSTRIAL COUNTRIES'
TRADE: 1955-1968**
National Economic Development Office

GB/INT—English 1971 58pp free

NEDO Monographs No. 2.
Analyses changes in the major industrial countries'
commodity patterns of trade.

**1628 PRODUCTION OF AGGREGATES IN GREAT BRITAIN
1972 & 1973**
**Department of the Environment (Public Buildings and
Works) HMSO**

GB—English 1975 20pp £0.34

Production statistics for sand and gravel and crushed
rock. Also includes statistics for clay and shales used
in aggregate form in construction.

**1629 PROFITABILITY AND LIQUIDITY IN THE
DISTRIBUTIVE TRADES**
National Economic Development Office

GB—English 1975 £2.20

Shows the effect of the retail and wholesale industries
on the economy as a whole with data from company
accounts and its implications for profit, investment and
employment.

**1630 PROFITABILITY IN THE HOSIERY AND KNITWEAR
INDUSTRY**
National Economic Development Office

GB—English 1971 104pp £0.45

Data drawn from a study of selected company accounts,
giving profitability and efficiency ratios.

1631 PROPERTY MARKET REVIEW 1975/6
Gower Economic Publications, Teakfield

GB—English 1975 320pp £25.00

Surveys the market in the UK, with individual regional
reviews as well as an overall analysis. Includes a
directory of major companies.

**1632 PROSPECTS FOR THE PLASTICS PACKAGING
INDUSTRY**
National Economic Development Office

GB—English 1976 54pp £1.80

Examines current performance and future prospects for
the industry up to 1980, based on financial details for
certain selected companies.

**1633 QUALIFIED MANPOWER IN THE ELECTRONICS
INDUSTRY: A PRELIMINARY REPORT**
National Economic Development Office

GB—English 1971 44pp free

Studies factors affecting the supply and demand of
scientific and technological manpower.

1634 QUARTERLY ECONOMIC REVIEW—UNITED KINGDOM
Economist Intelligence Unit

GB—English quarterly c30pp (with annual supplement)

Analysis of current economic trends, including: government
economic policies; population; employment; currency;
national accounts; agriculture; industry; fuel and power;
transport and communications; tourism; finance; foreign
trade data.

1635 RAILWAY DIRECTORY AND YEAR BOOK
IPC Transport Press

GB—English annual c825pp £8.00

Gives comprehensive statistical and general reference data.
Includes information on major systems throughout the
world.

1636 REACHING WORLD MARKETS
National Economic Development Office

GB/INT—English 1971 free

Survey of international marketing in the pharmaceutical
industry.

**1637 RECENT DEVELOPMENTS IN THE UK AND WORLD
ECONOMY**
National Economic Development Office

GB/D/F/S—English 1976 £1.50

Gives statistics, charts, graphs and commentaries for
UK, USA, French, West German, Swedish and Japanese
short-term economic developments. Figures are at half-
yearly intervals over three years.

1638 REGIONAL CONSTRUCTION FORECASTS TO 1977
National Economic Development Office

GB—English 1974 4 vols

Vol. 1: South East, East Midlands and East Anglia.
132pp £2.60
Vol. 2: Wales, West Midlands and South West. £2.60
Vol. 3: North, North West and Humberside. 116pp £2.60
Vol. 4: Scotland. £1.50

**1639 REGIONAL POPULATION PROJECTIONS: NEW
STANDARD REGIONS OF ENGLAND AND WALES**
Office of Population Censuses and Surveys HMSO

GB—English 1975 16pp £0.34

Projections of home population of New Standard
Regions of England (boundaries at 1st April 1974)
based on the mid-year estimates of 1973. Includes
adjustments for projected inter-regional and overseas
migration. Results by sex and broad age group for
selected years to 1991.

**1640 REGISTER OF DEFUNCT AND OTHER COMPANIES
REMOVED FROM THE STOCK EXCHANGE OFFICIAL
YEAR BOOK**
Thomas Skinner & Company (Publishers) Ltd.

GB—English annual c570pp £5.00

Details of companies that have ceased trading and were
previously listed in the Stock Exchange Official Year Book.

1641 REGISTRAR GENERAL'S ANNUAL ESTIMATES OF THE POPULATION OF ENGLAND AND WALES AND OF LOCAL AUTHORITY AREAS
Office of Population Censuses and Surveys HMSO

GB—English annual c30pp £0.50

Estimates of population (male and female combined) of each Administrative area, including members of the Armed Forces stationed in the area.

1642 REGISTRAR GENERAL'S RETURN OF BIRTHS, DEATHS AND MARRIAGES: NORTHERN IRELAND
General Register Office, Northern Ireland

GB—English quarterly c30pp £1.60

Details of registered births, marriages and deaths. Also notifications of infectious diseases.

1643 REGISTRAR GENERAL SCOTLAND, RETURNS OF BIRTHS, DEATHS AND MARRIAGES
General Register Office, Scotland

GB—English quarterly £4.16 p.a.

Details of registered births, deaths and marriages. Also notifications of infectious diseases.

1644 REPORT OF THE CHIEF REGISTRAR OF FRIENDLY SOCIETIES
Registry of Friendly Societies HMSO

GB—English annual

Annual statistical report in four parts:
Part 1: General Incorporating the report of the Industrial Assurance Commissioner. (73pp £1.30)
Part 2: Building societies. (49pp £1.40)
Part 3: Industrial and Provident Societies. (26pp £0.60)
Part 4: Trade Unions. (39pp £0.70)

1645 REPORT ON THE AGRICULTURAL STATISTICS OF NORTHERN IRELAND 1961/62-1966/67
Department of Agriculture, Northern Ireland

GB—English 1970 178pp £1.00

Statistical details of acreage, livestock and production by county. (See also No. 1361)

1646 REPORT ON THE CENSUS OF DISTRIBUTION AND OTHER SERVICES 1966
Department of Industry HMSO

GB—English 1970/71 2 vols

Vol. 1: Main tables on the retail trade and service trades. (164pp £1.18)
Vol. 2: Transport costs; floor space; special forms of trading; other tables; standard errors. (220pp £1.20)

1647 REPORT ON THE CENSUS OF DISTRIBUTION AND OTHER SERVICES 1971
Department of Industry HMSO

GB—English 1975-76 13 parts

Published individually in 13 parts in the Business Monitor Series Nos. SD10-22:

SD10 Part 1: Retail outlets (Establishment tables) 1975 (140pp £1.60)
SD11 Part 2: Area Tables Scotland; 1975 (87pp £1.70)
SD12 Part 3: Area Tables Wales; 1975 (46pp £1.20)
SD13 Part 4: Area Tables North Region; 1976 (68pp £1.50)
SD14 Part 5: Yorkshire and Humberside Region; 1976 71pp £1.50
SD15 Part 6: Area Tables East Midlands Region; 1975 49pp £1.20
SD16 Part 7: Area Tables East Anglia Region; 1975 29pp £1.05
SD17 Part 8: Area Tables, London & SE Region; 1976 265pp £4.80
SD18 Part 9: Area Tables South West Region; 1975 52pp £1.20
SD19 Part 10: Area Tables, West Midlands Region; 1976 78pp £1.70
SD20 Part 11: Area Tables, North West Region; 1975 117pp £2.25
SD21 Part 12: Area Summary Figures; 1976 105pp £2.00
SD22 Part 13: Retail Organisation Tables and Service Trades £2.95

1648 REPORT ON THE CENSUS OF PRODUCTION 1972
Department of Trade HMSO

GB—English 1974

Latest census for which the full series of some 170 sub-industry reports are available. Price per report normally between £0.35 and £1.00.

1649 REPORT ON THE CENSUS OF PRODUCTION 1974
Department of Trade HMSO

GB—English 1976

Reports are issued as part of the Business Monitor series. Released, so far:
PA 500: Construction £0.76
PA 1000: Provisional results £1.10
PA 1007: Minerals 1974 and 1975 £0.95

1650 REPORT ON THE SEA AND INLAND FISHERIES OF NORTHERN IRELAND
Department of Agriculture, Northern Ireland

GB—English annual c30pp £0.35

Includes statistics on the landings and disposals of fresh, frozen and cured fish.

1651 THE RESPONSIBILITIES OF THE BRITISH PUBLIC COMPANY
Confederation of British Industry

GB—English 1976 48pp £1.00

A final report, with recommendations, which examines many aspects of the responsibilities of private enterprise in general and of the joint-stock company in particular.

1652 RETAIL BUSINESS
Economist Intelligence Unit

GB—English monthly c100pp £95.00 p.a.

Covers the economic aspects of the retail trade, with emphasis on consumer goods, market research, distribution patterns and sales trends. Subscription includes a quarterly economic review on the UK economy and its effect on the retail trade, plus a comprehensive annual index.

1653 RETAIL DIRECTORY
Newman Books

GB—English annual c1250pp £20.00

Basic directory on all types of stores and shops in the UK.
Includes details on hypermarkets, mail order firms, check
traders etc. Shopping street surveys identify the locations
of the principal shops in selected centres.

**1654 RETAIL TRADE DEVELOPMENTS IN GREAT
BRITAIN 1976-77**
Gower Economic Publications, Teakfield

GB—English 1976 360pp £19.00

Economic analysis of trading and company performance,
including a survey of shopping developments in the
planning regions and city centres. Includes data on:
regional growth rates; local shopping schemes; national
consumer trends. Maps of major centres show current
and future retail development and indicate the sites of
the major retail organisations.

1655 REVIEW OF NON-FERROUS METALS
British Metal Corporation

GB—English annual

Annual review with statistics of the non-ferrous metal
industry.

1656 REVIEW OF THE LINEN INDUSTRY
Department of Commerce, Northern Ireland

GB—English annual c100pp free

Annual review with statistics of the linen industry
in Northern Ireland.

1657 ROADS IN ENGLAND
Department of the Environment (Transport) HMSO

GB—English annual c90pp £1.90

Contents: expenditure on road construction,
improvement and maintenance by class of road and
Central or Local Authority Funds for England, Scotland,
Wales and Great Britain; mileage of roads by type;
major schemes of new construction; motorway progress
report.

**1658 RUBBER AND THE AUTOMOTIVE INDUSTRY IN
THE UK AND USA**
Economist Intelligence Unit

GB—English quarterly 1976 50pp £10.00

Study which examines in detail effects of the oil crisis
on the UK and US motor manufacturing sectors in terms
of volume of output, markets and actions taken to
adjust to the new environment. Also includes an analysis
of the impact on tyre manufacturers, with a review of
trends and prospects.

1659 SCOTLAND TO 1980
The Financial Times Ltd.

GB—English 1975 £50.35

Report examining Scotland as an environment for
investment with the development of North Sea oil,
and the political and historical background of the
country.

1660 SCOTTISH ABSTRACT OF STATISTICS
Scottish Office

GB—English annual c180pp £2.40

Main economic and social statistics available for
Scotland, with some explanatory notes, covering:
population and vital statistics; social conditions;
labour; personal income and expenditure;
production; transport; trade; finance.

1661 SCOTTISH AGRICULTURAL ECONOMICS
Department of Agriculture, Scotland

GB—English annual c70pp £0.50

Details of agricultural output and expenditure;
farm incomes; grants and subsidies; hours and
wages; rents; land sale prices.

1662 SCOTTISH CONSTRUCTION INTO THE EARLY 1980s
National Economic Development Office HMSO

GB—English 1976 £2.00

Forecasts of material and manpower supply and demand.

1663 SCOTTISH ECONOMIC BULLETIN
Scottish Office

GB—English twice yearly c40pp £0.90

Information on: employment; average weekly earnings;
hours worked; household expenditure; housing; trade
through Scottish sea and airports.

1664 SCOTTISH HEALTH STATISTICS
Scottish Home and Health Department

GB—English annual c200pp £4.60

Statistical information arranged in ten main sections
covering: population; vital statistics; mortality;
morbidity; diagnostic; general medical; dental;
ophthalmic services; manpower; costs.

**1665 SCOTTISH NATIONAL REGISTER OF CLASSIFIED
TRADES**
Sell's Publications

GB—English annual c450pp £6.50

Scottish firms classified under 3,000 different trade
headings giving basic reference data for each. Also
includes separate A-Z of firms.

1666 SCOTTISH SEA FISHERIES STATISTICAL TABLES
Department of Agriculture, Scotland

GB—English annual c50pp £0.65

Tables of statistics for: landings and value of fish;
by fishing method; district and area of catch.

1667 SCOTTISH SOCIAL WORK STATISTICS
Scottish Education Department

GB—English annual c130pp £2.30

Statistics covering: care of children; families; disabled;
elderly; mentally disordered. Also includes data on
staffing and finance.

1668 SEA FISHERIES STATISTICAL TABLES
Ministry of Agriculture, Fisheries and Food HMSO

GB—English annual c50pp £0.40

Data for England and Wales on: landings of fish;
consumption estimates; fishermen and fishing vessels;
fish imports and exports.

1669 SELL'S BRITISH EXPORTERS
Sell's Publications Ltd.

GB—English annual c350pp £7.00

(Amalgamation of 'British Marketing', 'GB Commart'
and 'Sell's British Export Register'.) Lists British
exporters A-Z and also classified under trade headings.
Separate trade marks and brands section also included.

1670 SELL'S DIRECTORY OF PRODUCTS AND SERVICES
Sell's Publications Ltd.

GB—English 1976 2 vols c1200pp £12.00

Vol. 1: A-Z list of (60,000) firms in two sections:
London; country;
Vol. 2: Classified index of (30,000) products and
services, cross-referenced by simple codes to a company
data section including full details of listed firms with
named executives to contact.

1671 THE SHARE-OWNERS
The Financial Times Ltd.

GB—English 1975 c345pp £200.55

A supplementary volume to 'Personal Savings and Wealth
in Britain' (No.1615), which contains detailed
tabulations in two sections: 1 - a survey of 500
investors in stock exchange and other securities;
2 - covers 3,700 holders of all 21 financial assets covered
in the report.

1672 SHIFTWORKING IN THE MOTOR INDUSTRY
National Economic Development Office

GB/INT—English 1974 £1.50

Major study of shiftwork in the UK and other European
motor industries. Covers health and social aspects, shift
premia, operating problems, financial evaluation, and
discusses the advantages and disadvantages of different
shift systems from both the employer and employee
standpoints. Also examines UK and continental shift
practices, presenting new information on a range of
topics including accident rates, earnings and productivity.

1673 SHIFTWORKING IN THE MOTOR INDUSTRY—SUMMARY
National Economic Development Office

GB—English 1974 £0.40

Summary version of the main report.

1674 SHIRTS IN THE SEVENTIES
National Economic Development Office HMSO

GB—English 1970 £1.05

Follow-up report to 'Your future in clothing'. It
examines prospects for the shirt industry for the next
five years and gives recommendations for action.

1675 SHORT SEA SHIPPING
National Economic Development Office

GB—English 1970 £0.40

Survey of the UK coastal and short sea shipping
industry. (See also No. 1490)

1676 SHORT TERM TRENDS
National Economic Development Office

GB—English quarterly free

Data on the mechanical engineering industry
including prospects, orders, deliveries.

1677 SOCIAL AND ECONOMIC TRENDS IN NORTHERN IRELAND
Department of Finance, Northern Ireland

GB—English annual c90pp £2.50

New series, commencing 1975, replacing N. Ireland
Economic Report. Commentary and statistics provide
a broad background to trends in the N. Ireland economy.

1678 SOCIAL SECURITY STATISTICS
Department of Health and Social Security HMSO

GB—English annual c250pp £3.65

Detailed tables cover each of the social security benefits,
National Insurance contributions and finance. Tables
showing trends over several years and more detailed
analyses for the most recent years.

1679 SOCIAL TRENDS
Central Statistical Office HMSO

GB—English annual c280pp £4.90

Key social and demographic statistics with charts and
tables and detailed commentary on social topics.
Includes data on: population; employment; leisure;
personal income and wealth; education; housing;
health; justice; public expenditure.

1680 SOURCES OF FINANCE FOR INDUSTRY AND COMMERCE
Confederation of British Industry

GB—English 1975 56pp £1.50

Examines the characteristics, advantages and disadvantages
of the main forms and sources of industrial and
commercial finance.

1681 SOURCES OF UK MARKETING INFORMATION
Benn Bros. Ltd.

GB—English 1976 c155pp £15.00

Details of published sources, methods, market research firms
A-Z, degree courses, periodicals.

1682 STATISTICAL AND ECONOMIC REVIEW OF THE PACKAGING INDUSTRIES 1972-76 WITH OUTLOOK 1977-78
Pira

GB—English c170pp £70.00

Comprehensive survey of the UK packaging industry.
Gives data on structure of the industry, production
prices, consumption, raw material availability, by
particular type of packaging product.

**1683 STATISTICAL DIGEST FOR THE CLOTHING
INDUSTRY**
National Economic Development Office

GB—English 1975 free

Statistics covering the clothing industry, its output,
trade, employment and social and economic factors.

**1684 STATISTICAL DIGEST FOR THE FURNITURE
INDUSTRY**
Furniture Industry Research Association

GB—English annual 111pp £6.00

Annual digest of statistics for the furniture industry
with data on: industry structure; employment; prices;
costs; population; timber supplies; consumer expenditure;
credit; overseas trade; housing.

**1685 STATISTICAL NEWS: DEVELOPMENTS IN BRITISH
OFFICIAL STATISTICS**
Central Statistical Office HMSO

GB—English quarterly 72pp £3.64 p.a.

Articles and reviews on new developments and new
publications in the UK Government Statistical Service -
updating the 'List of Principal Statistical Series and
Publications'.

**1686 A STATISTICAL SURVEY OF INDUSTRIAL FUEL
AND ENERGY USE**
Confederation of British Industry

GB—English 1976 36pp £2.00

Statistics and commentary resulting from a survey
carried out by the CBI in conjunction with the
Department of Energy.

1687 STATISTICAL TABLES
British Man-Made Fibres Association

GB—English monthly

Monthly statistical data on the man-made fibre industry.

1688 STATISTICS: EUROPE
CBD Research

GB—English 1976 c470pp £15.00

An extensive guide to a wide variety of available sources
giving publishers, libraries, government departments and
other organisations. Also includes indexes of titles,
subjects and organisations.

1689 STATISTICS FOR TOWN AND COUNTRY PLANNING
Department of the Environment (Housing and Local
Government) HMSO

GB—English 1974 16pp £0.50

Analysis of applications in England and Wales by class
of development and decision taken by planning
authority. Includes regional figures.

1690 STEAM BOILERS AND BOILERHOUSE PLANT
National Economic Development Office

GB—English 1972 128pp £1.20

Effect of UK entry into the EEC: a marketing data
handbook.

**1691 STEEL TIMES ANNUAL REVIEW OF THE STEEL
INDUSTRY**
Fuel and Metallurgical Journals Ltd.

GB—English annual c150pp £2.00

Annual review with commentary on specific topics
of concern to the steel industry.

1692 STOCK EXCHANGE OFFICIAL YEARBOOK
Thomas Skinner Directories

GB—English annual c2500pp 2 vols £27.00

Directory of public companies whose securities are
dealt in on the London Stock Exchange. Broadly
classified with details of: address; telephone numbers;
telex; directors; brief company history; capital;
financial results. Index of companies A-Z and their
subsidiaries. Also lists broker members of the London
and provincial stock exchanges.

**1693 STUBBS' BUYERS' NATIONAL GUIDE; INCORPORATING
STUBBS' DIRECTORY**
Stubbs Ltd.

GB—English 1976 1250pp £12.00

Comprehensive buyers' guide to professional and
commercial products and services, including a classified
directory of London, England, Scotland, Wales, Northern
Ireland, Republic of Ireland. Also includes separate
classified lists of exporters, offshore oil services, brand
names and trade marks.

1694 A STUDY OF TWO LOCAL LABOUR MARKETS
National Economic Development Office

GB—English 1975 free

Studies the patterns of unemployment, features and
problems of the labour markets in Liverpool and
Manchester. Includes tentative suggestions for remedying
the situations.

**1695 SUMMARY OF THE FINDINGS AND RECOMMENDATIONS
OF THE 'INDUSTRIAL REVIEW TO 1977'**
National Economic Development Office

GB—English 1974 free

Summary of the mechanical engineering industrial
review. (See also No. 1537)

1696 SURVEY OF BUYING POWER OF UNITED KINGDOM
Comart Research Ltd.

GB—English 1974 121pp £18.75

Provides information for tackling consumer sales and
marketing problems which involve assessment of area
potential. Includes data on retail sales and population
by area and assess the marketing potential of each region
by means of buying power index.

1697   A SURVEY OF MANUFACTURING CAPACITY
National Economic Development Office

GB—English 1971 free

Survey of present and planned capacity of certain
sectors of the process plant manufacturing industry.

**1698   SURVEY OF THE UNITED KINGDOM AEROSPACE
INDUSTRY 1975**
Business Statistics Office HMSO

GB—English 1975 45pp £1.05

Survey of current and future prospects of the UK
aerospace industry.

1699   TAXATION IN WESTERN EUROPE
Confederation of British Industry

GB/INT—English 1976 200pp £7.50

The 11th edition presenting a summary of the taxation
structure of the UK and the following West European
countries: Austria; Belgium; Denmark; Finland; France;
Federal Republic of Germany; Gibraltar; Greece; Guernsey;
Iceland; Republic of Ireland; Isle of Man; Italy; Jersey;
Luxembourg; Malta; Netherlands; Norway; Portugal;
Spain; Sweden; Switzerland.

1700   TECHNOLOGY AND THE GARMENT INDUSTRY
National Economic Development Office HMSO

GB—English 1971 £1.50

Programmes Analysis Unit report: covers technology's
influence on machine makers and clothing manufacturers.

1701   TELETEXT: DATA TRANSMISSION BY TELEVISION
The Financial Times Ltd.

GB—English 1975 187pp £80.50

Report on the cost and operation of teletext, the
opportunities and the commercial implications in its
future development.

1702   TEXTILE TRENDS
National Economic Development Office

GB—English 1976 64pp £1.80

Report presenting statistical information on the UK
textile and clothing industries. Examines future trends
and charts industrial performance over the last ten years.

1703   THIS IS THE DISTRIBUTIVE TRADES EDC
National Economic Development Office

GB—English 1975 free

An explanatory brochure on the Distributive Trades
Economic Development Committee.

1704   TIMBER TRADES DIRECTORY
Benn Bros. Ltd.

GB—English 1977 c450pp £15.00

Revised edition of the reference guide to the UK
timber, board and woodworking industries; detailed
information is indexed A-Z, geographically and by trades.

1705   TIMBER STATISTICS YEARBOOK
Timber Trade Federation

GB—English annual 40pp £2.50

Yearbook of timber statistics.

1706   THE TIMES 1000 1976-77
The Times Newspapers Ltd.

GB—English annual c130pp £6.00

Current data on the 1000 largest UK industrial
companies, giving data on: activities; turnover; capital;
net profit; employees; equity; also gives information
on the 500 leading European companies and the 100
leading American, Japanese, Canadian, Australian, South
African and Irish companies.

1707   TOTAL MARKET SIZES
Institute of Practitioners in Advertising

GB—English 1974 29pp £5.00

Third revised edition giving statistics on consumption
and consumer goods.

1708   TOURISM POLICY IN BRITAIN
Economist Intelligence Unit

GB—English 1974 35pp £5.00

E.I.U. special report examining the national
tourism situation for domestic and overseas tourists.
Comments on the current official approach to
tourism and suggests the actions necessary to establish
a national tourism policy.

1709   TOWN VARIATIONS
IPC Marketing Services Department

GB—English 1974 £5.50

Ready reference to the principal local deviations
from the national norm on key marketing indicators
such as age structure.

1710   TRADE AND INDUSTRY
Department of Trade HMSO

GB—English weekly c75pp £25.00 p.a.

Weekly journal with special articles and reports of
interest to all sections of industry, especially exporters.
Contains regular statistics and commentary on:
wholesale prices; capital expenditure and stocks;
retail sales; catering and motor trade turnover; hire
purchase; overseas trade.

**1711   TRADE BALANCE IN THE 1970s—THE ROLE OF
MECHANICAL ENGINEERING**
National Economic Development Office

GB—English 1971 35pp free

Discusses the future of the mechanical engineering
industry, particularly import and export trends, with
recommendations.

1712   TRADE MARKS: REPORT ON A SURVEY AMONG HOUSEWIVES
Confederation of British Industry

GB—English 1976 51pp £2.75

Details of a quantitative research carried out among 1,000 housewives assessing the importance of trade marks and brand names and their value to the consumer under practical shopping conditions.

1713   THE TRAINING OF BRITISH MANAGERS
National Economic Development Office HMSO

GB—English 1972 210pp £2.00

Examines managerial training in government, industry and hospital services. It covers policies and practices and includes interviews with individuals and training boards.

1714   TRANSPORT STATISTICS, GREAT BRITAIN 1964-74
Department of Transport HMSO

GB—English 1976 235pp £5.25

Replaces 'Highway Statistics and Passenger Transport in GB'.
Gives statistics on: road vehicle fleet, numbers of motor vehicles; miles of road of different standards; road expenditure; estimates of road use; taxation paid; number of current driving licences.

1715   TRENDS IN CATERING
National Economic Development Office only

GB—English annual subscription £35.00

A series of one annual and four quarterly reports providing current information and analysis of the catering market.

1716   TRENDS IN TEXTILE TECHNOLOGY
National Economic Development Office

GB/INT—English 1976 free

Data from a survey of the ITMA, Milan 1975 covers technological changes likely over the next 10 years and trends in supply and demand for textile machinery.

1717   THE UK AND WEST GERMAN MANUFACTURING INDUSTRY 1954-72
National Economic Development Office

GB/D—English 1976 103pp £4.50

Differences in manufacturing industries in the UK and West Germany covering structure, performance, economic problems and prospects.

1718   UK BALANCE OF PAYMENTS
Central Statistical Office HMSO

GB—English annual c90pp £2.00

'Pink Book' - detailed statistics on the nation's balance of payments, including details on visible and invisible trade, investment, official financing, assets and liabilities.

1719   UK CHEMICAL INDUSTRIES REVIEW 1974-75
Gower Economic Publications, Teakfield

GB—English 1974 336pp £25.00

An overview of the UK chemical industry in terms of growth, productivity and profits. Also presents an in-depth analysis of the five principal sectors: general chemicals; pharmaceuticals; plastics and synthetic resins; paints; agrochemicals. Profiles and comparative data on the top 100 UK companies are given.

1720   UK CHEMICAL INDUSTRY STATISTICS
Chemical Industries Association Ltd.

GB—English annual 165pp £5.00

Annual statistics on the UK chemical industry.

1721   UK CHEMICALS 1975-85
National Economic Development Office

GB—English 1976 100pp £2.50

Reviews prospects to 1985 with emphasis on increasing the industry's share of world markets and contribution to the balance of payments.

1722   THE UK DAIRY INDUSTRY SINCE 1970
Institute of Economic Affairs

GB—English 1975 18pp £0.30

A supplement to research monograph 21 'The marketing of milk' by L. Whetstone. Updates statistics on the UK dairy industry 1970-1975.

1723   UK—EEC MACHINE TOOL COMPETITION IN 1971
National Economic Development Office

GB/INT—English 1973 £1.00

This publication is a follow-up to 'British machine tools in Europe' (No. 1391), and analyses developments in relative UK—EEC competitiveness in 1971.

1724   UK FARMING AND THE COMMON MARKET
National Economic Development Office

GB/INT—English 1973/4 c17-85pp free

Series of studies examining UK agriculture and the EEC. Subjects include apples, beef, cereals, glasshouse crops, grass, nursery plants, hills and uplands, pears, milk, pigs, potatoes and soft fruit.

1725   UK MOTOR MANUFACTURERS AND IMPORTERS
Extel Statistical Services Ltd.

GB—English 1975 40pp £50.00

An Extel sector study giving comprehensive data on UK motor manufacturers and importers.

1726   UK OFFSHORE OIL AND GAS YEARBOOK
Kogan Page

GB—English annual c350pp £15.00

Contents: UK offshore industry progress and prospects; European continental shelf; guide to localities concerned with oil and gas related activities; directory of organisations, services and manufacturers.

**1727 UK PETROLEUM INDUSTRY STATISTICS:
CONSUMPTION AND REFINERY PRODUCTION**
Institute of Petroleum

GB—English 1975 9pp

Consumption and refinery production statistics published
by the Institute of Petroleum from data independently
collated on behalf of the UK Petroleum Industry
Advisory Committee.

1728 THE UK TEXTILE INDUSTRY 1968-1970
National Economic Development Office

GB—English 1972 £1.25

Illustrates flow of raw materials through to finished
product in wall chart form.

**1729 ULSTER YEARBOOK: THE OFFICIAL HANDBOOK OF
NORTHERN IRELAND**
Northern Ireland Information Service

GB—English annual c300pp £1.00

Official yearbook of Ulster with data on: population;
government; justice; social welfare; protective services;
education; housing; transport and communication;
industry and trade; agriculture; labour; central and
local government finance; the arts; science; the media;
sport.

1730 UNITED KINGDOM AIR CARGO
National Economic Development Office

GB—English 1975 £1.25

Studies important aspects of UK air cargo industry
and new developments which may influence its
competitiveness in the Continental market up to 1980.

1731 UNITED KINGDOM DAIRY FACTS AND FIGURES
Federation of United Kingdom Milk Marketing Boards

GB—English 1974 199pp £1.25

Statistics and brief commentary on the dairy industry
including: production; consumption; retrospective
statistics.

**1732 UNITED KINGDOM INTERNATIONAL TRADE
1980-1985**
National Ports Council

GB—English 1976 173pp £35.00

Report in three parts:
Part 1: Summary and interpretation of results with
brief description of forecasting methods used;
Part 2: Commentary on each commodity, describing
its main characteristics;
Part 3: Describes the econometric model of international trade developed and used with the
market research data and analyses;
Appendices contain the matrices of the 1980 and 1985
forecasts together with the 1973 actual figures used for
reference purposes.

1733 UNLOCKING PRODUCTIVITY POTENTIAL
National Economic Development Office

GB—English 1975 £1.20

Study of seven companies illustrating what productivity
improvements can be achieved using technology available
to clothing manufacturing firms.

**1734 US DIRECT INVESTMENT IN THE UK: HAS THE
OPTIMISM BEEN JUSTIFIED?**
Economist Intelligence Unit

GB—English 1975 70pp £15.00

Examines the record of US direct investment in the UK
since 1965. Indicates factors that US and other foreign
direct investors should consider when preparing future
investment plans.

1735 VALUE ADDED TAX
National Economic Development Office HMSO

GB—English £1.00

A NEDO report on the implications of the introduction
of Value Added Tax.

**1736 WAGE PAYMENT SYSTEMS IN THE CLOTHING
INDUSTRY**
National Economic Development Office

GB—English 1972 free

Study of the clothing industry's wages systems with
guidance and case studies.

1737 WEALTH TAX
Confederation of British Industry

GB—English 1976 £0.50

A report by the CBI Wealth Tax Working Party which
examines and discusses aspects of the proposed new tax.

**1738 WELSH ECONOMIC TRENDS (TUEDDIADAU'R
ECONOMI)**
Welsh Office HMSO

GB—English annual c80pp £2.00

Gives latest statistics available on: population; regional
and household income and expenditure; employment;
industrial activity; output; agriculture; construction;
capital and public expenditure; traffic through Welsh ports.

1739 WEST EUROPEAN LIVING COSTS 1976
Confederation of British Industry

GB/INT—English 1976 32pp £6.00

Covers 13 countries including the UK giving data on:
prices of accommodation; clothing; consumer goods;
entertainment; food; salaries; services; office services;
postal charges; social security; transport; taxation.

1740 WHAT THE GIRLS THINK
National Economic Development Office

GB—English 1972 free

The effect of employees attitudes on the clothing
industry's labour turnover.

1741 WHICH COMPANY? (DAILY TELEGRAPH GUIDE TO JOB OPPORTUNITIES AND EMPLOYERS)
Kogan Page

GB—English annual c175pp £3.75 (£1.25 paperback)

Reference data on about seven hundred 'key employers' with articles on certain major companies as well as ones covering aspects of job changing.

1742 WHO MAKES WHAT IN NORTHERN IRELAND
HMSO

GB—English 1975 387pp £1.50

A directory of goods produced in Northern Ireland with the names of the firms making them. Also provides details of companies offering textile and engineering services.

1743 WHO OWNS WHOM (UK EDITION): A DIRECTORY OF PARENT, ASSOCIATE AND SUBSIDIARY COMPANIES
Who Owns Whom Ltd.

GB—English annual 2 vols £32.00

Vol. 1: UK parent and senior associate companies in Great Britain and Eire; Overseas parent and senior associate companies in the UK and Eire; Consortia; (c900pp)
Vol. 2: Index to subsidiaries and associate companies listed in volume 1. (c1550pp)

1744 WHY GROUP TECHNOLOGY?
National Economic Development Office

GB—English 1975 36pp free

Booklet covering the benefits and possible problems and solutions involved in group technology.

1745 WORKER PARTICIPATION IN BRITAIN
The Financial Times Ltd.

GB—English 1974 144pp £20.25

Report by Social Policy Research, in collaboration with John C. Wood, examining worker participation in Britain. It uses material from 21 private and nationalised British companies together with six extensive case studies.

1746 WORKWEAR: THE CHANGING SCENE
National Economic Development Office HMSO

GB—English 1971 £2.00

Examination of the prospects facing the British overall manufacturing industry.

1747 THE YOUNGER WORKER IN AGRICULTURE: PROJECTIONS TO 1980
National Economic Development Office

GB—English 1972 free

Discussion document to the future prospects for younger workers in agriculture.

I-ITALY

1800 ADVERTISING CONDITIONS IN ITALY
Institute of Practitioners in Advertising

I—English 1975 20pp

Contents: basic facts—geography and demography; the media—press, outdoor, cinema, fairs, direct mail, advertising agencies and services; advertising and related organisations.

1801 ANNUARIO DI STATISTICA AGRARIA
Istituto Centrale di Statistica

I/INT— Italiano annual c350pp

Yearbook of agricultural statistics; data on: crop cultivation; food production; wages and prices; machinery used; fertilizer consumption; petrol; oil; electricity. Also includes a section on world agriculture.

1802 ANNUARIO DI STATISTICA FORESTALE
Istituto Centrale di Statistica

I—Italiano annual

Statistical yearbook of forestry; data on: forestry statistics; climate; production; cultivation; consumption of forest products; also includes some international statistics.

1803 ANNUARIO DI STATISTICHE DEL LAVORO E DELL'
EMIGRAZIONE
Istituto Centrale di Statistica

I—Italiano annual

Statistical yearbook of labour and emigration; tables and graphs on: population; employment; unemployment; consumer prices; emigration.

1804 ANNUARIO DI STATISTICHE INDUSTRIALI
Istituto Centrale di Statistica

I—Italiano annual c280pp

Yearbook of industrial statistics; data on: industrial production and consumption; co-operative production; machinery installed; wages and prices; foreign trade.

1805 ANNUARIO DI STATISTICHE PROVINCIALI
Istituto Centrale di Statistica

I—Italiano annual c400pp

Yearbook of provincial statistics; similar in contents to "Annuario Statistico Italiano" but with regional information.

1806 ANNUARIO STATISTICO DEL COMMERCIO INTERNO
Istituto Centrale di Statistica

I—Italiano annual c500pp

Annual statistics of internal trade; detailed data on the wholesale and retail trade and also the tourist and hotel industries.

1807 ANNUARIO STATISTICO DELL' ATTIVITA EDILIZIA
DELLE OPERE PUBBLICHE
Istituto Centrale di Statistica

I—Italiano annual

Statistical yearbook of building and public works.

1808 ANNUARIO STATISTICO ITALIANO
Istituto Centrale di Statistica

I—Italiano annual c450pp

Italian statistical yearbook; annual summary of economic and social statistics; main sections: geography and climate; population; housing census; health and social services; education and culture; justice; elections; agriculture; forestry; hunting and fishing; industry; building and public works; internal trade; transport and communications; credit; insurance; banking; prices (including cost of living index); employment; consumption; finance; foreign trade; public administration; national accounts; international statistics.

1809 L'AUTO ESTERA IN ITALIA
Unione Nazionale Rappresentanti Autoveicoli Esteri

I—Italiano annual

Annual statistics on the import and registration of foreign cars. Includes details of the number of vehicles by make and cubic capacity.

1810 AUTOMOBILE IN CIFRE
Associazione Nazionale fra Industrie Automobilistiche

I—Italiano annual

Annual statistics of the Italian automobile industry.

1811 BANCA D'ITALIA—ABRIDGED VERSION OF THE
REPORT FOR THE YEAR
Banca d'Italia

I/INT—English annual c220pp

Statistical tables and commentary on: international economy;
Italian economy—domestic demand; employment; wages;
prices; distribution of incomes; money and financial
markets.

1812 BANCA NAZIONALE DEL LAVORO—ANNUAL REPORT
Banca Nazionale del Lavoro

I—English annual c40pp

Annual report with commentary and statistics on: mortgage
credit; industrial credit; hotel and tourist credit; financing of
public works and utilities; credit to co-operatives; motion
picture credit; theatre credit.

1813 BARCLAYS' COUNTRY REPORT—ITALY
Barclays Bank

I—English 1975 2pp

Brief economic summary covering: balance of payments; prices
and wages; external position; economic outlook.

1814 BASIC DATA ON THE ECONOMY OF ITALY
US Department of Commerce

I—English 1970 19pp

Overseas Business Report no. OBR 70-59: General report on
the Italian economy covering: basic structure; industrial
sectors; labour market; trade; finance; economic outlook.

1815 BOLLETTINO MENSILE DI STATISTICA
Istituto Centrale di Statistica

I—Italiano monthly

Monthly bulletin of statistics including data on: climate;
population; health and social services; industry; internal trade;
foreign trade; transport and communications; banking; prices
and cost of living; public finance; national accounts; some
international statistics; separate supplements on specific
topics are issued from time to time.

1816 BOLLETTINO STATISTICO
Associazione Nazionale fra Industrie Automobilistiche

I/INT—Italiano monthly

Monthly statistics on the automobile industry, giving data on:
vehicle production; imports and exports for Italy and foreign
countries.

1817 BOLLETTINO STATISTICO: SULLE FONTI DI ENERGIA
E SULLA PRODUZIONE INDUSTRIALE
Ministero dell' Industria e del Commercio

I—Italiano twice a year

Statistics on energy production and supply and on industrial
production in general.

1818 CATALOGO DELLE PUBBLICAZIONI
Istituto Centrale di Statistica

I—Italiano annual c100pp

Catalogue of publications; current publications of ISTAT in
subject order, including a description of contents. Also
includes a subject index.

1819 CENSIMENTO GENERALE DELL'AGRICOLTURA 1970
Istituto Centrale di Statistica

I—Italiano every 10 years

General census of agriculture. Vol. 1: Provisional results.
Vol. 2: Sections dealing with each of the 92 provinces of
Italy. Vol. 3: Cultivation. Vol. 4: Stock. Vol. 5: Plant and
machinery. Vol. 6: General summary. Vol. 7: Explanation of the
methodology of the census.

1820 CENSIMENTO GENERALE DELLA POPOLAZIONE
Istituto Centrale di Statistica

I—Italiano every 10 years 10 vols

General census of population. Vol. 1: Summary data of
population and housing. Vol. 2: Principal characteristics of
the population: sex, age, education and financial status.
Vol. 3: Sections dealing with each of the 92 provinces of
Italy. Vol. 4: Families and family units. Vol. 5: Data by sex,
age, civil state, place of birth. Vol. 6: Data on professions.
Vol. 7: Data on education. Vol. 8: Housing information.
Vol. 9: General summary. Vol. 10: Methodology of the
census.

1821 CENSIMENTO GENERALE DELL'INDUSTRIA E DEL
COMMERCIO
Istituto Centrale di Statistica

I—Italiano every 10 years

General census of industry and commerce; data on: industrial
establishments, trade and services, transport and
communications, for the whole of Italy and individual
provinces.

1822 COMPENDIO STATISTICO ITALIANO
Istituto Centrale di Statistica

I—Italiano annual c400pp

Italian statistical abstract; abridged version of "Annuario
Statistico Italiano".

1823 CONGIUNTURA ITALIANA: RASSEGNA MENSILE
Istituto Nazionale per lo Studio della Congiuntura

I—Italiano monthly

Monthly review of Italian economic trends.

1824 LA CONJUNCTURA . . .
Banco di Sicilia

I—Italiano annual c100pp

Statistical data on: the Italian economic situation; agriculture;
fisheries; industry; employment; banking and credit; tourism.

1825 CONTI ECONOMICI TERRITORIALI PER GLI ANNI 1951-69
Istituto Centrale di Statistica

I—Italiano 1970

Supplement to "Bollettino Mensile di Statistica", no. 19, September 1970, giving financial statistics for the whole of Italy and for the regions. Also includes appendices giving data on national accounts and occupational structure in the regions.

1826 CURRENT STATISTICAL INFORMATION ON ITALY'S ECONOMY
Banco Nazionale del Lavoro

I—English monthly

Monthly commentary with statistics on the Italian economy.

1827 L'ECONOMIA INDUSTRIALE ITALIANA
Ministero dell'Industria e del Commercio

I—Italiano annual 2 vols

Industrial economy of Italy. Vol. 1: detailed data on each major industry. Vol. 2: statistics of foreign trade of the major industries covered in Vol. 1.

1828 ECONOMIA NAZIONALE PRODUZIONE E SCAMBI CON L'ESTERO NELL'INDUSTRIA
Ministero dell'Industria e del Commercio

I—Italiano

Economic statistics on: production; imports and exports; industrial products.

1829 ELECTRON MICROSCOPES
British Overseas Trade Board

I—English 1972

This report summarises the electron microscope market in Italy, and outlines the market prospects for British instruments.

1830 ESTABLISHING A BUSINESS IN ITALY
US Department of Commerce

I—English 1971 10pp

Overseas Business Report no. OBR 71-034: Concise information on setting up a business in Italy, including, factors affecting investment; organisation of businesses; employment; taxation.

1831 EURO-COOPERAZIONE: STUDI ECONOMICI EUROPEI
Banco di Roma

I/INT—Italiano quarterly

Quarterly survey with statistics on the European economy.

1832 THE EUROPEAN MARKET FOR DEEP-FROZEN FRUIT AND VEGETABLES
Istituto per la Ricerche e le Informazioni di Mercato e la Valorizzazione della Produzione Agricola

I—Italiano(contents list in English) 1971 2 vols

A study of the European deep-frozen food industry, giving information and statistics for various periods up to 1970. Covers production, distribution, structure of the industry, foreign trade, prices and consumption figures with forecasts to 1980. (Volume 2 is a statistical appendix)

1833 FINANCIAL TIMES SURVEY: ITALY
Financial Times

I—English 12 April 1976 p13-24

Contents: economy; political scene; foreign policy; foreign trade; motors; chemicals; energy; state industry; the media; research; steel industry; agriculture; tourism; fashion and fabrics.

1834 A GUIDE FOR FOREIGN INVESTORS IN ITALY
Banco Nazionale del Lavoro

I—English

Details on the Italian economy of interest to potential foreign investors.

1835 HINTS TO BUSINESSMEN—ITALY
British Overseas Trade Board

I—English 1976 54pp

Practical guide to travelling executives covering: general information; travel; hotels; restaurants and tipping; postal and telephone facilities; economic factors; import and exchange regulations; methods of doing business; government and commercial organisations; reading list; map.

1836 INDAGINE SULLA STRUTTURA DELLE AZIENDE AGRICOLE, 1967
Istituto Centrale di Statistica

I—Italiano 1970 2 vols

Results of the inquiry in 1967 into the structure of Italian agriculture.

1837 INDEX: BOLLETTINO MENSILE DI INFORMAZIONI
Centro per la Statistica Aziendale

I—Italiano monthly

Monthly statistics giving wholesale and retail price indices and data on materials used in various sectors of industry.

1838 INDICATORI MENSILI
Istituto Centrale di Statistica

I—Italiano monthly

Monthly summary of the main economic indicators covering: wages, prices, industrial production, building construction.

1839 INDUSTRIA COTONIERA
Associazione Cotoniera Italiana

I—Italiano monthly

Monthly review for the cotton and textile industries on topics of economic, technical and social interest.

1840 L'INDUSTRIA TESSILE: UN'INDAGINE SUI SETTORI
COTONIERO E LANIERO IN ITALIA
Istituto Mobiliare Italiano

I—Italiano

Commentary, graphs and statistics on the structure of the
cotton and textile industries in Italy.

1841 ITALIAN ECONOMIC SURVEY
Association of Italian Joint Stock Companies

I—English/Italiano monthly

Monthly review with articles on aspects of the Italian
economy and including data on trade, cost of living and
banking.

1842 THE ITALIAN ECONOMY: FACTS AND FIGURES
Banco Nazionale del Lavoro

I—English

Concise summary with statistics of the main Italian economic
indicators.

1843 THE ITALIAN STOCK MARKET
Banco Nazionale del Lavoro

I—English monthly 6pp

Monthly bulletin giving a commentary and detailed statistics
of shares and prices quoted on the Italian Stock Exchange.

1844 ITALIAN TRENDS
Banco Nazionale del Lavoro

I—English monthly c6pp

Monthly financial newsletter with economic and statistical
data on: industrial production; cost of living; foreign trade.

1845 LETTERE D'AFFARI
Centro per la Statistica Aziendale

I—Italiano monthly

Monthly review of the main economic events.

1846 MARKETING IN ITALY
US Department of Commerce

I—English 1976 24pp

Overseas Business Report no. OBR.76-04: Contents: market
analysis for selected products; industry trends; distribution
and sales; government procurement; transportation and ports;
credit; import-export regulations; investment in Italy;
employment; taxation.

1847 MOVIMENTO DELLA NAVIGAZIONE NEI PORTI
ITALIANI
Istituto Centrale di Statistica

I—Italiano annual

Supplement to "Bollettino Mensile di Statistica", giving
statistics of foreign shipping movements in Italian ports.

1848 MOVIMENTO VALUTARIO
Istituto Nazionale per il Commercio Estero

I—Italiano quarterly

Quarterly financial review which includes balance of
payments statistics.

1849 NOTIZIARIO ISTAT—SERIES 1
Istituto Centrale di Statistica

I—Italiano 10 parts

Gives up-to-date statistical information in advance of
publication in "Bollettino Mensile di Statistica". The 10 parts
cover: agriculture; forestry; industrial production; public
works; building; foreign trade; insurance; sea and rail traffic
and road accidents; air traffic; tourism.

1850 NOTIZIARIO ISTAT—SERIES 2
Istituto Centrale di Statistica

I—Italiano 4 parts

Gives up-to-date statistical information in advance of
publication in "Bollettino Mensile di Statistica". Covers
various aspects of prices and wages.

1851 NOTIZIARIO ISTAT—SERIES 3
Istituto Centrale di Statistica

I—Italiano 5 parts

Gives up-to-date statistical information in advance of
publication in "Bollettino Mensile di Statistica". Covers:
demography; justice; health; labour force; culture.

1852 NOTIZIE ECONOMICHE
Banco di Roma

I—Italiano monthly

Monthly commentary and statistics on economic trends.

1853 OCCUPAZIONI IN ITALIA NEGLI ANNI 1967-69:
INDUSTRIA
Istituto Centrale di Statistica

I—Italiano 1970

Supplement to "Bollettino Mensile di Statistica", containing
the results of a census carried out to determine the
occupational structure of Italian industry.

1854 PANORAMA ECONOMICA
24 Ore—Il Sole

I—Italiano annual

Articles and statistics on financial and economic issues for
the past year.

1855 PREVISIONI A BREVE TERMINE
Centro per la Statistica Aziendale

I—Italiano monthly

Statistical series on the general economic situation.

1856 PREVISIONI DI SVILUPPO DELL'INDUSTRIA ITALIANA
Confederazione Generale dell'Industria Italiana

I—Italiano annual

Annual statistics showing the growth of Italian industry
projected over a four year period.

**1857 LE PROSPETTIVE DELL'INDUSTRIA ITALIANA: NEL
QUADRIENNIO 1972-75**
Confederazione Generale dell'Industria Italiana

I—Italiano annual

Economic forecast of industrial prospects in Italy for the
period 1972-75.

**1858 QUADERNI DI INFORMAZIONE PER I QUADRI
INTERMEDI DELL'INDUSTRIA TESSILE**
Associazione Cotoniera Italiana

I—Italiano 6 issues a year

Technical articles on current topics of interest to supervisors
and technicians in the cotton industry.

1859 QUARTERLY ECONOMIC REVIEW
Istituto Mobiliare Italiano

I—English quarterly

Quarterly review of general articles on the Italian economy
and specific commentaries on individual industries.

1860 QUARTERLY ECONOMIC REVIEW—ITALY
Economist Intelligence Unit

I—English quarterly with annual supplement

Analysis of current economic trends including: government;
population; employment; exchange rates; national accounts;
agriculture; mining; fuel and power; manufacturing industries;
transport and communications; finance.

1861 QUARTERLY REVIEW
Banco Nazionale del Lavoro

I—English quarterly

Detailed review of current economic trends.

1862 RELAZIONE ANNUALE
Associazione Cotoniera Italiana

I—Italiano annual

Annual review of the Italian cotton industry, covering the
home, national and international situations.

1863 REPORT ON CONSUMER RESEARCH IN ITALY
Marplan Ltd.

I—English 1975 2 vols

A companion study to Market Datasearch's survey.
Comprises detailed research on consumer demand for
wallcoverings in Italy.

1864 REVIEW OF THE ECONOMIC CONDITIONS IN ITALY
Banco di Roma

I—English 6 issues a year

Reviews and statistics on the current Italian economic
climate.

1865 REVIEWS OF NATIONAL SCIENCE POLICY: ITALY
Organisation for Economic Co-operation and Development

I—English/Français 1969

Review and commentary on the Government's national
policy for science.

1866 RILIEVI STATISTICI SUL MERCATO ITALIANO
Ogilvy and Mather SpA

I—Italiano 1968

Statistical report and commentary on the Italian market.

1867 SCIENTIFIC INSTRUMENTS IN ITALY
British Overseas Trade Board

I—English 1972

A survey of the market for scientific instruments in Italy
identifying opportunities for British manufacturers.

1868 SELLING IN ITALY
US Department of Commerce

I—English 1969 12pp

Overseas Business Report no. OBR 69-76. Contents: import
requirements; commercial practices; marketing; government
procurement; notes for business travellers.

**1869 SINTESI GRAFICA DELLA VITA ECONOMICA
ITALIANA**
Istituto Centrale di Statistica

I—Italiano monthly

Graphs of the Italian economy; diagrams and graphs covering:
population; agriculture; industry; internal trade; tourism;
transport; cost of living and price indices; labour; finance;
banking; foreign trade.

1870 SOME ITALIAN STATISTICS (TIEC)
The Italian Economic Corporation

I—English monthly

Brief general statistical data on: population; national accounts;
money; balance of payments; agriculture; industry; foreign
trade.

**1871 LE SPESE PER GLI INVESTIMENTI FISSI
NELL'INDUSTRIA, ANNI 1967 E 1968**
Istituto Centrale di Statistica

I—Italiano 1970

Supplement to "Bollettino Mensile di Statistica" giving the
cost of fixed investment in industry for 1967 and 1968.

1872 **SPOTLIGHT ON OVERSEAS TRADE—SELLING TO
ITALY**
Midland Bank International

I—English 1971 4pp

Contents: economic situation; market opportunities;
regulations and documentary requirements; company
formation in Italy; UK exports to Italy.

1873 **STATISTICA ANNUALE DEL COMMERCIO CON
L'ESTERO**
Istituto Centrale di Statistica

I—Italiano annual 2 vols

Annual statistics of foreign trade: Vol. 1: Summary data on
imports and exports by countries of origin and destination
subdivided by commodity groups; transit trade. Vol. 2:
Detailed tables of imports and exports arranged by
commodity classifications (BTN) and subdivided by
countries of origin and destination; tables of re-imports;
re-exports.

1874 **STATISTICA DEL TURISMO: BOLLETTINO TECHNICO
TRIMESTRALE DEL ENTE NAZIONALE ITALIANO
PER IL TURISMO**
Ente Nazionale Italiano per il Turismo

I—Italiano quarterly and annual

Contains statistics of tourists arriving in Italy, arranged by
province and divided by country of origin of visitor.

1875 **STATISTICA DELLA NAVIGAZIONE MARITTIMA**
Istituto Centrale di Statistica

I—Italiano annual

Annual statistics of foreign trade shipping movements into
Italian ports.

1876 **STATISTICA MENSILE DEL COMMERCIO CON
L'ESTERO**
Istituto Centrale di Statistica

I/INT—Italiano monthly

Monthly statistics of foreign trade: tables showing exports
and imports arranged by commodity classification (BTN)
subdivided by countries of origin and destination. Other
tables show imports and exports within the EEC.

1877 **STATISTICHE COTONIERE**
Associazione Cotoniera Italiana

I—Italiano annual

Annual statistics of the cotton and cotton textile industries
covering, production and imports and exports.

1878 **STATISTICHE SUI CONSUMI DEI TABACCHI**
Amministrazione Autonoma dei Monopoli di Stato

I—Italiano annual

Tobacco production and consumption statistics for the
whole country and for each province.

1879 **SURVEY ON THE WALLCOVERINGS MARKET IN
ITALY**
Market Datasearch Ltd.

I—English 1974

Surveys the Italian market for wallcoverings. Contains data
on market size and trends, supply, retail trade, consumption
and distributive structure of the industry. A consumer survey
was conducted separately by Marplan. Includes a list of
major manufacturers and distributors.

1880 **TAVOLA INTERSETTORIALE DELL'ECONOMIA
ITALIANA PER L'ANNO . . .**
Istituto Centrale di Statistica

I—Italiano

Supplement to "Bollettino Mensile di Statistica", giving
detailed trade input-output tables.

1881 **USEFUL INFORMATION FOR INVESTING CAPITAL IN
ITALY**
Credito Italiano

I—English c95pp

Contents: economic information; general regulations
governing companies; Italian corporate law; Italian banking
system; employment regulations; regulations governing
investment of foreign capital in Italy.

1882 **WOOL IN ITALY**
Bureau of Agricultural Economics

I—English 1966

A study of the Italian wool textile industry.

IRL-IRELAND

1900 AGRICULTURAL OUTPUT
Central Statistics Office

IRL—English annual

Annual statistics of agricultural production, issued in stencilled form.

1901 ANIMALS EXPORTED BY SEA AND AIR
Central Statistics Office

IRL—English monthly

Monthly statistics, issued in stencilled form.

1902 BARCLAYS COUNTRY REPORTS—THE IRISH REPUBLIC
Barclays Bank

IRL—English 1976 2pp

Brief economic summary covering: GNP; government economic policy; economic development; balance of payments; economic outlook.

1903 CENSUS OF DISTRIBUTION AND SERVICES
Central Statistics Office

IRL—English 1970 2 vols

Vol. 1: Retail trade; comprehensive information taken from the 1966 census on: volume of sales and purchases; levels of stocks held; persons engaged by sex and status; wages and salaries and gross margin for 31 types of business. Also gives data on: geographical patterns; size of business; numbers of employees; legal status; number of establishments owned; commodity sales. Vol. 2: Wholesale trade and services.

1904 CENSUS OF INDUSTRIAL PRODUCTION
Central Statistics Office

IRL—English annual

Results of the annual census of industrial production are published in the "Irish Statistical Bulletin". Over 50 industries are reported separately and analyses include data on: gross and net output; wages and salaries; number employed.

1905 CENSUS OF POPULATION OF IRELAND
Central Statistics Office

IRL—English 1966 7 vols

Vol. 1: Data on population of district electoral divisions, towns and larger units. Vol. 2: Data on ages and conjugal conditions (classified by areas). Vol. 3: Data on industries. Vol. 4: Data on occupations. Vol. 5: Data on occupations and industries (classified by ages and conjugal conditions). Vol. 6: Data on housing and households. Vol. 7: Data on education. Refer to "Statistical Abstract of Ireland" for more up-to-date population figures.

1906 CENTRAL BANK OF IRELAND – ANNUAL REPORT
Central Bank of Ireland

IRL—English annual c200pp

Includes a general review of the Irish economy, with details of monetary developments in Ireland, international developments and details of the Central Bank accounts. Also includes a statistical appendix of economic and financial information.

1907 CONSUMER PRICE INDEX
Central Statistics Office

IRL—English quarterly

Quarterly statistics issued in stencilled form.

1908 CROPS AND LIVESTOCK ENUMERATION
Central Statistics Office

IRL—English twice a year

Issued in stencilled form, statistics of crops and livestock enumerated in January and June of each year.

1909 DIRECTORY OF STATE SERVICES
Government Publications Sales Office

IRL—English annual c120pp

Lists government departments with details of address, telephone numbers, lists of staff.

1910 ECONOMIC REPORT — REPUBLIC OF IRELAND
Lloyds Bank Ltd.

IRL—English 1975 27pp

Contents: British trade with Ireland; Anglo-Irish Free Trade
Agreement (AIFTA); Ireland in the EEC; foreign trade;
exports; establishing a business in Ireland; agriculture;
industry; mineral resources; tourism; price indices.

1911 ECONOMIC SERIES
Central Statistics Office

IRL—English monthly

A series of monthly booklets of statistical information on
economic subjects.

1912 EXTERNAL TRADE — PROVISIONAL TOTAL FIGURES
Central Statistics Office

IRL—English monthly

Issued in stencilled form, in advance of "Trade statistics of
Ireland".

1913 EXTERNAL TRADE STATISTICS
Central Statistics Office

IRL—English annual c380pp

Gives data on: imports and exports by country of origin and
destination and by trading areas according to SITC
classification. Also includes historical statistics on external
trade in total and for trade with principal countries.

1914 FAISNÉIS RÁITHIÚL
Central Bank of Ireland

IRL—English quarterly

Quarterly bulletin containing statistical data on: money;
interest rates; credit; savings; external trade; consumer prices
and indices; index value of retail sales; index numbers of
wholesale trade; unemployment.

**1915 HINTS TO BUSINESSMEN — THE REPUBLIC OF
IRELAND**
British Overseas Trade Board

IRL—English 1975 52pp

Practical guide for travelling executives covering: general
information; travel; hotels; restaurants and tipping; postal and
telephone facilities; economic factors; import and exchange
control regulations; methods of doing business; government
and commercial organisations; reading list; map.

1916 HIRE PURCHASE AND CREDIT SALES
Central Statistics Office

IRL—English annual

Annual statistics issued in stencilled form.

1917 HOUSEHOLD BUDGET INQUIRY
Central Statistics Office

IRL—English 1965/66 210pp

Gives detailed information on the average weekly income
and expenditure of urban households taken from a large-scale
sample inquiry. The results are classified by size of household, composition, income, social group, location.

1918 INDEX NUMBERS OF RETAIL SALES
Central Statistics Office

IRL—English monthly

Monthly survey in stencilled form designed to measure trends
in the level of the value of retail sales.

**1919 INDUSTRIAL DEVELOPMENT OPPORTUNITIES —
IRELAND**
Industrial Development Authority

IRL—English 1970 30pp

Facts and figures for the British industrialist considering
setting up a manufacturing undertaking in Ireland.

1920 INVESTMENT IN IRELAND
First National City Bank

IRL—English 48pp

Contains information on: general economy; taxes; industrial
investment; labour and training; setting up a business;
exchange control; grants and financing.

1921 IRELAND AND THE EEC: 1975
Business and Finance Supplement

IRL—English 1975 40pp

Contents: producers and consumers; marketing problems of
agricultural products in Europe; marketing dairy products;
Irish meat.

1922 IRELAND IN FIGURES
Allied Irish Banks

IRL—English 1976 8pp

Details on the Republic of Ireland and Northern Ireland,
including statistics for: standard of living; national income;
population; transport; agriculture; industry; trade.

1923 IRELAND'S NATURAL RESOURCES
Business and Finance Supplement

IRL—English 1975 60pp

Series of articles reviewing Ireland's mineral and other
natural resources. Includes: mineral deposits; oil; energy; gas;
mining; offshore developments.

1924 IRISH ECONOMIC STATISTICS
Central Bank of Ireland

IRL—English 1976 6pp

Small booklet including data on: national production;
industrial production; building and construction; agriculture;
transport; manpower; incomes; prices; external trade; balance
of payments; government finance; interest rates; purchasing
power of the £.

1925 IRISH ECONOMIC STATISTICS
Institute of Public Administration

IRL—English 1968 180pp

Guide to the sources of collections, presentations and analyses of the major economic statistic series of Ireland.

1926 IRISH EXPORT BOARD: ANNUAL REPORT
Irish Export Board

IRL—English annual c30pp

The annual report and accounts of the Irish Export Board which includes a general review of trade and statistics on exports.

1927 IRISH EXPORT DIRECTORY
Irish Export Board

IRL—English c450pp

Lists manufacturers A-Z with details of their addresses, telephone numbers and products. Also includes a separate classified index.

1928 IRISH EXPORTERS ASSOCIATION: ANNUAL DIRECTORY
Irish Exporters Association

IRL—English annual c60pp

Includes members A-Z with details of their addresses. Also includes a separate classification listing with details of members' addresses, telephone numbers, products and services. Lists Irish representatives overseas and gives shipping facilities at Irish ports.

1929 IRISH INDUSTRIAL YEARBOOK
McEvoy Press

IRL—English c370pp

Lists manufacturers, arranged geographically, with details of: addresses, telephone numbers, date established, directors, products, capital, number of employees. Also includes two separate indexes: firms A-Z and classified.

1930 IRISH STATISTICAL BULLETIN
Central Statistics Office

IRL—English quarterly

Quarterly features include: report on industrial production; economic indicators; external trade reviews; employment and unemployment; wages; wholesale and retail price indices; agricultural prices and price indices.

1931 KELLY'S MANUFACTURERS AND MERCHANTS DIRECTORY, INCLUDING INDUSTRIAL SERVICES
Kelly's Directories Ltd.

GB/IRL—English annual 2 vols c400pp

A-Z and classified listings of manufacturers, and merchants in England, Scotland and Wales, London and suburbs, Northern Ireland, Irish Republic. Also includes classified lists of importers and exporters in each area.

1932 MARKETING IN IRELAND
Business and Finance Supplement

IRL—English 1976 28pp

Collection of articles of interest to the potential exporter to Ireland. Includes: consumers; marketing to Ireland; new product development; research; Marketing Institute of Ireland; who's who in Irish public relations agencies.

1933 MARKETING IN IRELAND
US Department of Commerce

IRL—English 1974 20pp

Overseas Business Report no. OBR 74-56. Contents: market profile; industry trends; distribution and sales channels; government procurement; advertising and research; credit; trade representation; investment in Ireland; guidance for businessmen abroad.

1934 NATIONAL INCOME AND EXPENDITURE
Central Statistics Office

IRL—English annual c80pp

Includes data on national income and expenditure, personal income and expenditure, Gross National Product.

1935 OECD ECONOMIC SURVEY: IRELAND
Organisation for Economic Co-operation and Development

IRL—English/Français 1976 57pp

Individual analyses of the Irish economy, covering recent developments in demand, output, employment, prices and incomes, and the broad lines of economic policies affecting fiscal, employment, industrial restructuring and prices and incomes.

1936 O'NEILLS COMMERCIAL WHO'S WHO AND INDUSTRIAL DIRECTORY OF IRELAND
General Publications Ltd.

IRL—English c950pp

Includes companies broadly classified with details of: address, telephone numbers, directors, products and services, trade names. Also gives information on: newspapers and periodicals; securities quoted on the Dublin stock exchange; members of the Dublin, Cork and Belfast stock exchanges.

1937 PRODUCTION OF FOOTWEAR
Central Statistics Office

IRL—English monthly

Monthly up-to-date data on the production of footwear.

1938 PUBLICATIONS
Central Statistics Office

IRL—English c12pp free on application

A list of publications compiled by the CSO.

1939 QUARTERLY ECONOMIC REVIEW — IRELAND
Economist Intelligence Unit

IRL—English quarterly with annual supplement £25.00

Analysis of current economic trends including: government; population; employment; currency; national accounts; agriculture; industry; fuel and power; transport and communications; tourism; finance; foreign trade payments and agreements.

1940 QUARTERLY INDUSTRIAL INQUIRY
Central Statistics Office

IRL—English

The results of the enquiries, two series: Series 1: Volume of production, employment, earnings and hours of work. Series 2: Earnings and hours of work by men and women.

1941 REPORT OF THE ELECTRICITY SUPPLY BOARD
Electricity Supply Board

IRL—English annual

Annual report which includes details and statistics on: production, generation and electricity capacity.

1942 REPORT OF THE IRISH TOURIST BOARD
Bord Fáilte Eireann

IRL—English annual

Annual report and survey of the Irish tourist industry.

1943 REPORT OF THE NATIONAL BUILDING AGENCY
National Building Agency Ltd.

IRL—English annual

Annual report which includes statistics on: industrial housing, housing for state employees, private housing, local authority housing.

1944 REVIEW OF EXTERNAL TRADE
Central Statistics Office

IRL—English quarterly

Quarterly statistical summary, in stencilled form, each issue reviewing the situation for the previous quarter.

1945 SIGNPOST: INDUSTRY IN THE SEVENTIES
The Confederation of Irish Industry

IRL—English 1971 39pp

Review of the opportunities and prospects for Irish industry in the 1970s.

1946 SMALL INDUSTRY IN IRELAND
Business and Finance Supplement

IRL—English 1976 24pp

Series of articles reviewing the prospects for small enterprises in Ireland and the generous scale of grant assistance available under the small industries programme.

1947 STATISTICAL ABSTRACT OF IRELAND
Central Statistics Office

IRL—English annual c400pp

Annual abstract of statistics. Main sections: area and climate; population; forestry and fisheries; agriculture; land purchase; industrial production; internal trade; foreign trade; social statistics; education; justice; defence; finance; transport and communications; prices. Also includes an appendix on Northern Ireland

1948 STATISTICS IN IRELAND
Institute of Public Administration

IRL—English 1970 70pp

Guide to official Irish statistics covering: agriculture; employment and unemployment; internal and external trade; national income and expenditure; vital statistics; census of population.

1949 STATISTICS OF WAGES, EARNINGS AND HOURS OF WORK
Central Statistics Office

IRL—English every 3 years

Comprehensive data on wages, earnings and hours of work in certain occupations and certain town districts.

1950 TRADE STATISTICS OF IRELAND
Central Statistics Office

IRL—English monthly

Includes tables showing statistics of imports and exports classified by commodities. Also gives data on: trade with principal countries; trade by principal commodities with different areas; exports and imports. Trade with the UK is shown separately.

IS-ICELAND

1975 BARCLAYS COUNTRY REPORT — ICELAND
Barclays Bank

IS—English 1976 2pp

Brief economic summary covering: prices and wages; external position; economic outlook.

1976 BASIC DATA ON THE ECONOMY OF ICELAND
US Department of Commerce

IS—English 1967 13pp

Overseas Business Report no. OBR 67-11. General report on the Icelandic economy covering; basic structure; industrial sectors; labour market; trade; finance; economic outlook.

1977 BÚNAĎARSKÝRSLUR
Hagstofa Íslands

IS—Icelandic(English headings) c140pp

Agricultural production statistics; data on: agricultural and livestock production; milk processing; wages; agricultural machinery; investment.

1978 CENTRAL BANK OF ICELAND — ANNUAL REPORT
Central Bank of Iceland

IS—English annual c80pp

Annual report and summary of: production; wages and prices; balance of payments; central government finance; investment credit funds; pension funds; credit market; exchange rates; also includes a detailed statistical appendix.

1979 DIRECTORY OF ICELAND
Icelandic Year Book Ltd.

IS—English annual c300pp

Lists firms A-Z in Reykjavik, then in other towns A-Z with addresses and brief trade description. Also lists societies and organisations. Separate classified sections of firms and exporters.

1980 FINANCIAL TIMES SURVEY: ICELAND
The Financial Times

IS—English 1 Dec. 1976 p.17-20

Survey in the Financial Times newspaper covering: the economy; energy industry; fishing industry; tourism.

1981 FJÁRMALÁTÍĎINDI
Sedlabanki Íslands

IS—Icelandic 3 issues per year

Economic review; journal of the Central Bank of Iceland giving statistics and commentary on the economic and banking situations.

1982 FOREIGN TRADE REGULATIONS OF ICELAND
US Department of Commerce

IS—English 1971 8pp

Overseas Business Report no. OBR 71-008. Contents: trade policy; import tariff system; special customs provisions; internal taxes; shipping documentation; non-tariff and import controls; Icelandic export controls.

1983 HAGTÍĎINDI
Hagstofa Íslands

IS—Icelandic monthly

Monthly statistical bulletin, with data on: the fish catch; foreign trade by countries; imports by broad SITC groups; cost of living index; banking statistics.

1984 HINTS TO BUSINESSMEN — ICELAND
British Overseas Trade Board

IS—English 1975 44pp

Practical guide to travelling executives covering: general information; travel; hotels; restaurants and tipping; postal and telephone facilities; economic factors; imports and exchange control regulations; methods of doing business; government and commercial organisations; reading list; map.

1985 ÍBÚASKRÁ REYKJVÍKUR 1 DES ÁR HVERT
Hagstofa Íslands

IS—Icelandic annual c1300pp

A complete list of the population of the capital on December 1st each year according to the National Registry.

1986 ICELAND'S 50 MILES AND THE REASONS WHY
The Government of Iceland, Reykjavik

IS—English 1973 16pp

States the Icelandic Government's case for extending its
fishery limits to fifty miles on 1st September 1972.

1987 IŎNAŎARSKÝRSLUR
Hagstofa Íslands

IS—Icelandic(English headings) c80pp

Industrial production statistics; sample survey which gives
data on: number of establishments and workers; industrial
income and expenditure; wages; salaries; cost of goods
consumed; payments for services.

1988 MANNTAL
Hagstofa Íslands

IS—Icelandic

The final report of the population census.

1989 MARKETING IN ICELAND
US Department of Commerce

IS—English 1975 16pp

Overseas Business Report no. OBR 75-10. Contents: market
analysis for selected products; industry trends; distribution
and sales channels; government procurement; transportation
and ports; credit; import-export regulations; investment in
Iceland; employment; taxation.

1990 OECD ECONOMIC SURVEYS — ICELAND
Organisation for Economic Co-operation and Development

IS—English/Français 1976 60pp

Individual analyses of the Icelandic economy, covering recent
developments in demand; output; employment; prices and
incomes; and the broad lines of economic policies affecting

fiscal, employment, industrial restructuring and prices and
incomes.

1991 STATISTICAL BULLETIN
Hagstofa Íslands

IS—English quarterly

An abridged version of ''Hagtíðindi''.

1992 TOLFROEŎIHANDBOK
Hagstofa Íslands

IS—Icelandic/English 1967 383pp

Statistical abstract of Iceland. Main sections: geography and
meteorology; population and housing; national accounts;
balance of payments; agriculture; fisheries; manufacturing
industries; foreign trade; transport and communications;
social insurance; prices and wages; consumption; education
and culture; justice; elections.

1993 VERZLUNARSKÝSLUR
Hagstofa Íslands

IS—Icelandic(English headings) annual c220pp

External trade; main tables give imports and exports arranged
by BTN commodity classification subdivided by countries of
origin and destination. Also gives data on: value of imports
and exports by SITC; value of imports and exports by
country of origin and destination subdivided by SITC groups;
imports and exports by customs area; consumption of sugar,
coffee, tobacco and alcoholic beverages.

**1994 VIŎSKIPTASKRÁIN ATVINNU — OG KAUPSÝSLUSKRA
ISLANDS**
Steindorsprent HF

IS—Icelandic(English headings) c750pp

Commercial and industrial directory for Iceland. Contents:
government departments; companies by towns; classified
directory; streets directory of Reykjavik; register of Icelandic
ships; geographical, political and economic survey.

L-LUXEMBOURG

2000 ANNUAIRE STATISTIQUE
Service Centrale de la Statistique et des Etudes Economiques

L—Français annual 350pp

Statistical yearbook; gives data on: geography and climate; population; agricultural and industrial production; transport; public finance; prices; wages; cost of living; health; education; tourism. Also includes some international statistics.

2001 BARCLAYS COUNTRY REPORT — LUXEMBOURG
Barclays Bank

L—English

Brief summary covering: payments; prices and wages; external positions; economic outlook.

2002 BUDGETS FAMILIAUX
Service Centrale de la Statistique et des Etudes Economiques

L—Français

Report of an enquiry into family budgets.

2003 BULLETIN DE SERVICE CENTRAL DE LA STATISTIQUE ET DES ETUDES ECONOMIQUES
Service Centrale de la Statistique et des Etudes Economiques

L—Français monthly

Data on: cost of living indices; prices; agriculture; industry; transport and communications; employment; finance.

2004 COMPTES NATIONAUX
Service Centrale de la Statistique et des Etudes Economiques

L—Français annual c120pp

National accounts statistics and details for the previous financial year. Also includes retrospective figures.

2005 ECONOMIC REPORT - BELGIUM AND LUXEMBOURG
Lloyds Bank Ltd.

B/L—English 1975 31pp

Current economic and financial survey on UK and foreign trade with the B.L.E.U. Also information on: marketing; import regulations; purchasing power; major industries; recent economic trends; advice on establishing a business in Belgium or Luxembourg.

2006 L'ECONOMIE INDUSTRIELLE DE LUXEMBOURG 1948-66
Service Centrale de la Statistique et des Etudes Economiques

L—Français 1967 c200pp

The industrial economy of Luxembourg 1948-66. Economic survey which includes analyses by industry and by region, of the industrial economy.

2007 EMPLOYMENT IN LUXEMBOURG
Luxembourg Embassy, London

L—English

Details of work permits, contracts, collective agreements, workers delegations and legal conciliation procedures.

2008 FACTS ABOUT LUXEMBOURG
Luxembourg Embassy, London

L—English

Summary and data on the history, the economy and the position of Luxembourg in Europe.

2009 FOREIGN TRADE REGULATIONS OF BELGIUM/ LUXEMBOURG
US Department of Commerce

B/L—English

Overseas Business Report no. 73-26. Contents: trade policy; import tariff system; special customs provisions; internal taxes; shipping documentation; non-tariff and import controls; Belgium/Luxembourg export controls.

2010 THE GRAND DUCHY OF LUXEMBOURG — POLITICAL HISTORY
Ministère d'Etat, Service Presse et Information

L—English

Political introduction and history of Luxembourg.

2011 HINTS TO BUSINESSMEN — BELGIUM/LUXEMBOURG
British Overseas Trade Board

B/L—English 1976 72pp

Practical guide to travelling executives covering: general
information; travel; hotels; restaurants and tipping; postal
and telephone facilities; economic factors; import and
exchange control regulations; methods of doing business;
government and commercial organisations; reading list; maps.

**2012 INDICATEURS RAPIDES: NOTES TRIMESTRIELLES DE
CONJONCTURE**
Service Centrale de la Statistique et des Etudes Economiques

L—Français quarterly

Quick indicators: quarterly notes. Analytical commentaries
based on the data given in the monthly statistical series with
the same title.

2013 INDICATEURS RAPIDES: STATISTIQUES
Service Centrale de la Statistique et des Etudes Economiques

L—Français monthly

Quick indicators: statistics; six series of current data on:
A: Cost of living indices. B: Indices of industrial production
and consumption. C: Employment; steel production; finance.
D: Motor vehicles registration. E: Vital statistics. F: Road
accidents.

**2014 THE INSTITUTIONS OF THE GRAND DUCHY OF
LUXEMBOURG**
Ministère d'Etat, Service Presse et Information

L—English 1970

Details of the institutions of Luxembourg, including the
government, Council of State, Law Courts, public
administration and communes.

2015 LUXEMBOURG — FINANCIAL TIMES SURVEY
The Financial Times

L—English 17 Feb. 1976 p.14-18

Survey in the Financial Times newspaper covering: the
economy; steel industry; banking and finance.

2016 LUXEMBOURG — SURVEY
Investors Chronicle

L—English 29 Nov. 1974 6pp

Survey in the Investors Chronicle journal discussing the
prospects of Luxembourg becoming the EEC's financial
centre.

2017 LE RECENSEMENT DE LA POPULATION
Service Centrale de la Statistique et des Etudes Economiques

L—Français 1962-68 6 vols

Census of population in 1960. Vol. 1: General results.
Vol. 2: personal characteristics. Vol. 3: Economic characteristics. Vol. 4: Housing. Vols 5 & 6: Family units, methodology and legislation.

**2018 RECENSEMENT DE LA POPULATION AU 31 DECEMBRE
1966**
Service Centrale de la Statistique et des Etudes Economiques

L—Français 1969 189pp

Sample census of population taken on the 31st December
1966 giving tables showing personal characteristics, age,
marriage, economic population. Also gives statistics and
household tables.

**2019 SOCIAL SERVICES IN THE GRAND DUCHY OF
LUXEMBOURG**
Luxembourg Embassy, London

L—English

Details of social services including: accident and health
insurance; pensions; family allowances; unemployment
benefit.

**2020 SOCIETE DE LA BOURSE DE LUXEMBOURG
RAPPORTS ET BILAN**
Société de la Bourse de Luxembourg

L—Français annual c30pp

Annual report of the Luxembourg Stock Exchange including
commentary and statistics on share dealings and price trends.

**2021 SPOTLIGHT ON OVERSEAS TRADE - SELLING TO
LUXEMBOURG**
Midland Bank International

L—English 1975 4pp

Contents: economic situation; market opportunities;
regulations and documentary requirements; company
formation in Luxembourg; UK exports to Luxembourg.

2022 TAXATION OF LUXEMBOURG COMPANIES
Luxembourg Embassy, London

L—English

Information on the taxation of companies, their officers,
associates, shareholders and directors.

**2023 THE THIRTY MOST IMPORTANT LUXEMBOURG
COMPANIES**
Luxembourg Embassy, London

L—English

Statistics and commentary on the top 30 most important
companies in Luxembourg.

N - NORWAY

2050 ALDERS - OG YRKESSTRUKTUREN I JORDBRUKET: EIN ANALYSIS PÅ GRUNNLAG AV JORDBRUKSTELIJUNGANE I 1949 OG 1959
Statistisk Sentralbyrå

N—Norsk(English headings) 1965

Land holders by age and occupational status; an analysis based on the censuses of agriculture in 1949 and 1959.

2051 ALKOHOLSTATISTIKK
Statistisk Sentralbyrå

N—Norsk(English headings) annual c40pp

Alcohol statistics; data on production and consumption, imports and exports of alcoholic beverages.

2052 ARBEIDSMARKEDSTATISTIKK
Statistisk Sentralbyrå

N—Norsk(English headings) annual

Manpower statistics; data on: employment; unemployment; vacancies; labour conflicts; government measures taken to promote employment.

2053 BARCLAYS COUNTRY REPORT — NORWAY
Barclays Bank

N—English 1976 2pp

Brief economic summary covering: prices and wages; external position; economic outlook.

2054 BASIC DATA ON THE ECONOMY OF NORWAY
US Department of Commerce

N—English 1970 15pp

Overseas Business Report no. OBR 70-5. General report on the Norwegian economy covering: basic structure; industrial sectors; labour market; trade; finance; economic outlook.

2055 BIL- OG VEISTATISTIKK
Opplysningsrådet for Biltrafikken den Norske Veiforening

N—Norsk

Detailed motoring statistics.

2056 BYGGE- OG ANLEGGSSTATISTIKK
Statistisk Sentralbyrå

N—Norsk(English headings) annual

Annual construction statistics; data on: employment; value of work; receipts and gross fixed capital formation for the construction industry.

2057 BYGGEAREALSTATISTIKK
Statistisk Sentralbyrå

N—Norsk annual

Detailed analysis of building statistics.

2058 COMMERCIAL BANKS IN NORWAY
A.S. Økonomisk Literatur

N—Norsk/English annual c250pp

Data on Norwegian commercial banks, including name, address, board members, executives, profit and loss accounts, employees, stock holders, branch offices.

2059 COMMODITY LIST FOR EXTERNAL TRADE STATISTICS: NORWAY
Statistisk Sentralbyrå

N—English 1973

Definitions of Norwegian commodity numbers and SITC equivalents.

2060 ECONOMIC BULLETIN
Norges Bank

N—English quarterly c40pp

Quarterly bulletin of short articles on the economic situation. Also includes an appendix of financial statistics.

2061 ECONOMIC REPORT: NORWAY
Lloyds Bank Ltd.

N—English 1973 19pp

Contents: export opportunities; import and export trade; general economic summary and prospects.

2062 ELEKTRISITETSSTATISTIKK
Statistisk Sentralbyrå

N—Norsk(English headings) annual

Annual electricity statistics; data on consumption and
supply of the larger public supply undertakings and private
plants producing electricity.

2063 ESTABLISHING A BUSINESS IN NORWAY
US Department of Commerce

N—English 1968 12pp

Overseas Business Report no. OBR 68-81. Concise
information on setting up a business in Norway, including:
factors affecting investment; organisation of businesses;
employment; taxation.

2064 FIGURES IN A NUT-SHELL
Den Norske Creditbank

N—English

Brief booklet on the Norwegian economy, mainly financial
statistics.

2065 FINANCIAL TIMES SURVEY: NORWAY
The Financial Times

N—English 14 May 1976 p.17-20

Survey in the Financial Times newspaper which examines:
effect of North sea oil on the Norwegian economy; shipping
industry; foreign trade.

2066 FISKERISTATISTIKK
Fiskeridirektoratet

N—Norsk(English headings) annual c90pp

Fishery statistics; data on: quantity and value of landings of
different kinds of fish; disposition of landings; prices;
subsidies; costs and earnings of fishermen; vessels; exports
and imports of fish and fishery products.

2067 FISKERITELLING 1 NOVEMBER 1960
Statistisk Sentralbyrå

N—Norsk(English headings) 1962-66 3 vols

Fishery census taken on 1st November 1960.

2068 FLYTTESTATISTIKK
Statistisk Sentralbyrå

N—Norsk(English headings) annual

Migration and immigration statistics; data on migrants by
counties, sex, age, trade districts; immigrants and emigrants
by sex, age and country.

2069 FOLKEMENGDEN ETTER ALDER
Statistisk Sentralbyrå

N—Norsk(English headings) annual

Population statistics arranged by age and sex for counties,
municipalities, trade areas and trade districts.

2070 FOLKETALLET I KOMMUNENE
Statistisk Sentralbyrå

N—Norsk(English headings) annual

Population by municipalities; data on population and
population changes for the past three years. Also gives details
of population in trade districts.

2071 FOLKETELLING 1960
Statistisk Sentralbyrå

N—Norsk(English headings) 1964 8 vols

Population census taken in 1960. Vol. 1: Population and
area by administration divisions, densely populated areas in
rural municipalities; inhabited islands. Vol. 2: Population
by sex, age and marital status. Vol. 3: Population by industry,
occupation and status. Vol. 4: Education. Vol. 5: Households
and family units. Vol. 6: Housing. Vol. 7: Fertility of
marriages. Vol. 8: Religions and denominations; place of
birth; citizenship; private car owners; dwelling units with
telephone.

2072 FORBRUKSUNDERSØKELSE
Statistisk Sentralbyrå

N—Norsk(English headings) 1967 3 vols

Survey on consumer spending. Vol. 1: General results and
methods. Vol. 2: Detailed analysis of household expenditure;
consumption; size and composition. Vol. 3: Expenditure on
various commodity groups according to assessed incomes.

2073 FOREIGN TRADE REGULATIONS OF NORWAY
US Department of Commerce

N—English 1969 8pp

Overseas Business Report no. OBR 69-83. Contents: trade
policy; import tariff system; special customs provisions;
internal taxes; shipping documentation; non-tariff and import
controls; Norwegian export controls.

2074 FRAMSKRIVING AV FOLKERNENGDEN TIL 1990
Statistisk Sentralbyrå

N—Norsk(English headings) 1969

Population projections to 1990; estimates on sex, age and
regional distribution of population up to 1990.

2075 HINTS TO BUSINESSMEN — NORWAY
British Overseas Trade Board

N—English 1976 44pp

Practical guide to travelling executives covering: general
information; travel; hotels; restaurants and tipping; postal and
telephone facilities; economic factors; import and exchange
control regulations; methods of doing business; government
and commercial organisations; reading list; map.

2076 HISTORISK STATISTIKK
Statistisk Sentralbyrå

N—Norsk 1968 646pp

Historical coverage of a wide range of economic and social
statistical studies, as in "Statistisk Arbok"; issued every
ten years.

2077 HOUSING AND THE EUROPEAN COMMUNITY
National Building Agency

N/INT—English 1973 5 vols

Provides a detailed analysis of the housing market in nine
EEC countries plus Norway, in a series of national surveys.
Examines the size of the market, importance of the public
and private sectors, the types of dwelling, housing standards
and average prices, regional distribution of housing: the
housing stock and its conditions: and surveys the structure of
the building industry with information on labour, number
and size of firms, costs, materials used.

2078 INDUSTRISTATISTIKK
Statistisk Sentralbyrå

N—Norsk(English headings) annual c170pp

Industrial statistics; data on: production; investment; stocks;
consumption of raw materials and fuel; labour; mining and
manufacturing industries.

2079 INVESTORS CHRONICLE SURVEY: NORWAY
Investors Chronicle

N—English 25 July 1975 10pp

Economic survey in the Investors Chronicle journal covering:
consumption; GNP; foreign investment.

**2080 IRON AND METAL WORKS INDUSTRY, ENGINEERING
WORKS**
A.S. Økonomisk Literatur

N—Norsk(English headings) 1976

Data on the Norwegian primary metal industries, machinery
industry, electrotechnical industry, transport industry.

2081 JORDBRUKSSTATISTIKK
Statistisk Sentralbyrå

N—Norsk(English headings) annual c110pp

Annual agricultural statistics; data on: agriculture;
horticulture; livestock; milk yield; fertilizers and seed; labour
force; prices.

2082 KREDITTMARKEDSSTATISTIKK
Statistisk Sentralbyrå

N—Norsk annual

Annual statistics on the credit market.

2083 LAKS- OG SJOAUREFISKE
Statistisk Sentralbyrå

N—Norsk annual

Annual statistics on salmon and sea trout fisheries.

2084 LØNNSSTATISTIKK
Statistisk Sentralbyrå

N—Norsk(English headings) annual

Wage statistics; annual data on: changes in wage rate; wage
statistics for different groups of wage earners.

2085 MARKETING IN NORWAY
US Department of Commerce

N—English 1974 27pp

Overseas Business Report no. OBR 74-54. Contents: market
analysis for selected products; industry trends; distribution
and sales channels; government procurement; transportation
and ports; credit; import-export regulations; investment in
Norway, employment; taxation.

**2086 THE NORDIC MARKET FOR SELECTED PRODUCTS OF
EXPORT INTEREST TO DEVELOPING COUNTRIES**
International Trade Centre UNCTAD/GATT

S/DK/N/SF—English 1970 503pp

The potential export markets of Sweden, Denmark, Norway
and Finland for: toys and games; sporting goods; musical
instruments; handtools and domestic utensils; leather goods;
preserved fruits; tropical sawnwood; veneer, plywood and
parquet flooring; cork products; dyeing and tanning extracts.

2087 NORDIC SHIPPING AND SHIPBUILDING
The Financial Times

S/DK/N/SF—English 26 March 1974 p.14-17

Discusses the importance of shipping to the Nordic economy;
also covers: shipbuilding; the marine equipment market;
Baltic ferries.

2088 NORGES BANK – ANNUAL REPORT AND ACCOUNTS
Norges Bank

N—English annual c100pp

Annual report including a commentary on the Norwegian
economy, credit and foreign exchange policies. Also includes
a detailed statistical appendix.

2089 NORWAY: SPECIAL REPORT
The Times

N—English 24 Feb.1975 p.11-13

Report in the Financial Times newspaper covering: shipping;
oil; farming and fishing; potential of the Arctic.

2090 NORWAY – THE NEXT RICHEST NATION
The Economist

N—English 15 Nov.1975 30pp

Special survey by the Economist journal which examines why
Norway, once the poorest country in Western Europe could
have the world's richest economy by 1980.

2091 THE NORWEGIAN ECONOMY AT YOUR FINGER TIPS
Andresens Bank

N—English 1976 10pp

Brief statistics on: standard of living; economic conditions;
labour; wages; prices; trade; imports; exports; fixed capital
by industry; GNP; investment; employment by industry;
production; public finance.

2092 NORWEGIAN FURNITURE INDUSTRY
A.S. Økonomisk Literatur

N—Norsk/English 1976

Data on Norwegian furniture industry: name, address,
board members, executives, production, sales, employees.

**2093 NORWEGIAN PAPER AND PULP INDUSTRY
WALLBOARD AND CHIPBOARD PLANT**
A.S. Økonomisk Literatur

N—Norsk/English 1975 228pp

Data on Norwegian paper and pulp makers, wallboard and
chipboard plants, carton and box manufacturers. Also gives
table of production statistics.

2094 NORWEGIAN TEXTILE AND CLOTHING INDUSTRY
A.S. Økonomisk Literatur

N—Norsk/English 1976

Data on Norwegian textile manufacturers: name, address,
board members, executives, production, sales, employees.

2095 OECD ECONOMIC SURVEYS — NORWAY
Organisation for Economic Co-operation and Development

N—English/Français 1976 60pp

Individual analyses of the Norwegian economy, covering
recent developments in demand, output, employment, prices
and incomes and the broad lines of economic policies
affecting fiscal, employment, industrial restructuring and
prices and incomes.

2096 QUARTERLY ECONOMIC REVIEW — NORWAY
Economist Intelligence Unit

N—English quarterly with annual supplement

Analysis of current economic trends including: government;
population; employment; exchange rates; national accounts;
agriculture, mining, fuel and power; manufacturing industries;
transport and communications; finance.

2097 SAVINGS BANKS IN NORWAY
A.S. Økonomisk Literatur

N—Norsk(English headings) annual c525pp

Contents; data on savings banks: name; address; board
members; executives; profit and loss accounts; employees;
branch offices.

2098 SELLING IN NORWAY
US Department of Commerce

N—English 1972 12pp

Overseas Business Report no. OBR 72-043. Contents: import
requirements; commercial practices; marketing; government
procurement; notes for business travellers.

2099 SKOGSTATISTIKK
Statistisk Sentralbyrå

N—Norsk(English headings) annual c100pp

Annual forestry statistical data on: forest area and property;
production; forest conservation; machinery and equipment;
prices; labour force.

**2100 SPOTLIGHT ON OVERSEAS TRADE — SELLING TO
NORWAY**
Midland Bank International

N—English 1974 4pp

Contents: economic situation; market opportunities;
regulations and documentary requirements; company
formation in Norway; UK exports to Norway.

2101 STATISTISK ARBOK
Statistisk Sentralbyrå

N—Norsk(English headings) annual c450pp

Statistical yearbook; data on: geography and climate;
population; health; labour market; national accounts; balance
of payments; agriculture; livestock; forestry; fishing; sealing
and whaling; mining and quarrying; electricity and gas supply;
construction; transportation and communication; internal
and external trade; credit; prices; justice; education; culture.
Also includes some international statistics.

2102 STATISTISK MÅNEDSHEFTE
Statistisk Sentralbyrå

N—Norsk(English headings) monthly

Monthly bulletin of statistics; data on: labour; national
accounts; balance of payments; agricultural production;
fishing; industrial production; investment; building
construction; internal and external trade; transport and
communications; public finance; money and credit; prices
and wages; justice; crime. Also includes some international
data.

2103 THE THOUSAND LARGEST COMPANIES IN NORWAY
A.S. Økonomisk Literatur

N—English/Norsk 1976 150pp

Lists the top 1000 companies with data on: ranking by sales;
capital; assets; invested capital; invested capital as a
percentage of assets; profit; sales per employee. Also contains
special economic surveys.

2104 UTENRIKSHANDEL
Statistisk Sentralbyrå

N—Norsk(English headings) annual 2 vols

External trade statistics. Vol. 1: Imports and exports
classified by BTN and subdivided by countries of origin
and destination. Vol. 2: Imports and exports arranged by
country of origin and destination subdivided by commodities
(SITC & BTN).

2105 VAREHANDELSSTATISTIKK
Statistisk Sentralbyrå

N—Norsk(English headings) annual c90pp

Wholesale and retail trade statistics; data on: sales
establishments; persons employed and sales by industry.

NL-NETHERLANDS

2150 ADVERTISING CONDITIONS IN THE NETHERLANDS
Institute of Practitioners in Advertising

NL—English 1972 22pp

Contents: basic facts; geography and demography; the media—
press, outdoor, cinema, fairs, direct mail; advertising agencies
and services; research; taxes; laws and regulations;
advertising and related organisations.

2151 ALGEMENE VOLKSTELLING
Centraal Bureau voor de Statistiek

NL—Nederlands(English headings) 1960

Population census. Vol. 1: General results. Vol. 2: Population
of the municipalities and their territorial subdivisions.
Vol. 3: Data on place of birth and period of settlement in the
present place of residence. Vol. 4: Sex, age and marital status.
Vol. 5A: General introduction. Vol. 5B: Households, families
and dwellings. Vol. 6: Existing marriages and marital fertility.
Vo. 7: Religion. Vol. 7A: General introduction. Vol. 7B:
Regional data for each municipality. Vol. 8-9: Education.
Vol. 10-11: Economically active population. Vol. 12:
Population living in institutions. Vol. 13: Population living
permanently on inland vessels and in caravans. Vol. 14:
Principal key figures for each municipality.

2152 AMRO STOCK MARKET NEWS
Amsterdam-Rotterdam Bank NV

NL—English bimonthly

Regular bulletin giving the latest news on the Stock Market.

2153 AMSTERDAM
The Financial Times

NL—English 20 May 1975 p.32-33

Special report in The Financial Times newspaper reviewing
the city's history, recent development, its current economic
and social problems and its potential for the future.

2154 AMSTERDAM: SURVEY
The Financial Times

NL—English 31 May 1974 p.14-19

Survey in the Financial Times newspaper on: Amsterdam as

a financial centre; the port and airport; transportation;
property; tourism; the arts.

2155 ANNUAL NETHERLANDS BRITISH TRADE DIRECTORY
Netherlands-British Chamber of Commerce

NL—English annual

Annual directory giving general and specific commercial data
on the Netherlands.

2156 BARCLAYS COUNTRY REPORT—THE NETHERLANDS
Barclays Bank

NL—English 1976 2pp

Brief economic summary covering: balance of payments;
prices and wages; external position; economic outlook.

**2157 BEREKENINGEN OMTRENT DE TOEKOMSTIGE LOOP
DER NEDERLANDSE BEVOLKING 1970-2000**
Centraal Bureau voor de Statistiek

NL—Nederlands/English 1971

Population projections for the Netherlands for the period
1970-2000.

2158 BEVOLKING DER GEMEENTEN VAN NEDERLAND
Centraal Bureau voor de Statistiek

NL—Nederlands annual c70pp

Population of the municipalities of the Netherlands.

**2159 BRITISH CHAMBER OF COMMERCE IN THE
NETHERLANDS: YEAR BOOK**
British Chamber of Commerce

NL—English annual c180pp

Directory of member firms listed A-Z in two sections: 1—in
the Netherlands; 2—in the UK, giving details of name, address
and telephone and telex numbers. Also includes a classified
index.

2160 BUSINESS COMMENTS FROM THE NETHERLANDS
Algemene Bank Nederland

NL—English monthly

Monthly economic surveys and trends.

2161 CAPITAL GOODS FROM HOLLAND
ABC voor Handel en Industrie CV

NL—Nederlands/English c130pp

Lists manufacturers A-Z including details of: name, address,
telephone numbers, date established, capital, directors,
number of employees, products. Also includes a separate
classified index.

2162 CENTRAAL ECONOMISCH PLAN
Centraal Planbureau

NL—Nederlands annual

Annual review with articles on industrial conditions, company
news and economic statistics.

2163 CONJUNCTUURTEST
Centraal Bureau voor de Statistiek

NL—Nederlands monthly

Business trends; current monthly forecasts on the
manufacturing and building industry, with data on: activity;
stocks of unsold products; orders received; order position for
consumer goods, capital goods and other goods.

2164 THE DEMAND FOR BUTTER IN THE NETHERLANDS
University of Reading, Department of Agricultural Economics

NL—English 1974 16pp

Contents: Butter consumption in the Netherlands; butter
smuggling; cold store butter; margarine market; statistical
tables on supply and demand.

2165 THE DUTCH ECONOMY IN FIGURES
Amsterdam-Rotterdam Bank NV

NL—English 1976 8pp

Small booklet with data on: population and employment;
national production and expenditure; industrial production;
prices; wages; foreign trade; central government finance;
money and the capital market; foreign currencies.

2166 DUTCH PROPERTY
The Financial Times

NL—English 9 May 1974 p.28-31

Special report in the Financial Times newspaper on Dutch
property, including: increasing British investment; speculative
industrial building; office buildings.

2167 ECONOMETRISCHE ANALYSE VAN DE VRAAG
NAAR WONINGEN
Centraal Bureau voor de Statistiek

NL—Nederlands 1970

An econometric analysis of the demand for housing,
including statistics and an economic commentary.

2168 ECONOMIC QUARTERLY REVIEW
Amsterdam-Rotterdam Bank NV

NL—English quarterly

Contains articles on various aspects of the Dutch economy
plus a statistical appendix with data on: national income and
expenditure; population; employment; investment;
consumption; prices and wages; foreign trade; balance of
payments.

2169 ECONOMIC REPORT—THE NETHERLANDS
Lloyds Bank Ltd.

NL—English 1975 24pp

Current economic and financial survey on UK and foreign
trade with the Netherlands covering: marketing; import
regulations; purchasing power; recent economic trends;
advice on establishing a business in the Netherlands.

2170 ECONOMISCH OVERZICHT VAN DE NEDERLANDSE
KATOEN-, RAYON-, LINNEN- EN JUTE INDUSTRIE
Centraal Bureau van de Katoen-, Rayon-, en Linnen-Industrie

NL—Nederlands annual c60pp

Annual economic survey of the cotton, rayon, linen and jute
industry; giving data on: import of raw materials; spinning;
weaving; investment; production; exports.

2171 ESTABLISHING A BUSINESS IN THE NETHERLANDS
US Department of Commerce

NL—English 1967 17pp

Overseas Business Report no. OBR 67-31. Concise
information on setting up a business in the Netherlands,
including: factors affecting investment; organisation of
businesses; employment; taxation.

2172 FEDERATIE VOOR DE NEDERLANDSE EXPORT
(FENEDEX): LIJST VAN AANGESLOTEN
ONDERNEMINGEN
FENEDEX

NL—Nederlands c30pp

Federation for Dutch exports; list of affiliated members, A-Z
with brief details of names and addresses.

2173 FOREIGN TRADE REGULATIONS OF THE
NETHERLANDS
US Department of Commerce

NL—English 1973 11pp

Overseas Business Report no. OBR 73-58. Contents: trade
policy; import tariff system; special customs provisions;
internal taxes; shipping documentation; non-tariff and import
controls; Netherlands export controls.

2174 GIDS BIJ DE PRIJSCOURANT VAN DE VEREENIGING
VOOR DEN EFFECTENHANDEL TE AMSTERDAM
Uitgeverij J H de Bussy NV

NL—Nederlands annual c1350pp

Securities guide of the Amsterdam association of stockbrokers; lists major companies, broadly classified, giving
details of: name, address, date established, financial data.
Also includes a separate index of companies A-Z.

2175 GIDS VOOR DE KAMERS VAN KOOPHANDEL EN FABRIEKEN IN NEDERLAND
NV Drukkerij H P de Swart & Zn

NL—Nederlands c150pp

Directory of chambers of commerce and industry in the Netherlands.

2176 HINTS TO BUSINESSMEN—NETHERLANDS
British Overseas Trade Board

NL—English

Practical guide to travelling executives covering: general information; travel; hotels; restaurants and tipping; postal and telephone facilities; economic factors; import and exchange control regulations; methods of doing business; government and commercial organisations; reading list and map.

2177 HOLLAND ENERGY REPORT
The Petroleum Times

NL—English 26 Nov. 1976 31pp

Special supplement by the Petroleum Times journal on the Dutch offshore industry.

2178 THE INFORMATION YOU NEED WHEN PLANNING A BUSINESS IN THE NETHERLANDS
Algemene Bank Nederland NV

NL—English 1975 24pp

Contents: legal structure; financing of new establishments; labour; social security; insurance; taxes; foreign exchange regulations; foreign trade; EEC.

2179 IN TOUCH
Netherlands-British Chamber of Commerce

NL/UK—English monthly

Monthly bulletin covering aspects of trade between the Netherlands and Britain.

2180 INVESTMENT CENTRES OF THE WORLD: AMSTERDAM
The Times

NL—English 15 May 1975 p.21-23

Special report in The Times newspaper reviewing the Amsterdam Stock Exchange and the numerous financial services.

2181 JAARCIJFERS VOOR NEDERLAND
Centraal Bureau voor de Statistiek

NL—Nederlands(English headings)

Statistical yearbook of the Netherlands; summary of economic and social statistics with indications of general trends. Data on: area and climate; population; public health; housing; politics; religion; education; economically active population; establishments and enterprises; agriculture; fisheries; distribution; foreign trade; transport and communications; money; banking.

2182 JAARVERSLAG N.V. NEDERLANDSE SPOORWEGEN
N.V. Nederlandse Spoorwegen

NL—Nederlands annual c50pp

Annual report of the Netherlands Railways. Contents: annual report and accounts; statistical data and tables on: railway lines; equipment; rolling stock; passenger and goods traffic; finances.

2183 KOMPASS—INFORMATIEWERK OVER HET NEDERLANDSE BEDRIJFSLEVEN
Kompass Nederland NV

NL—Nederlands/English/Deutsch/Español/Français c2400pp

Kompass register of Netherlands industry and commerce; companies classified geographically, giving details of: name; address; telephone numbers; capital; employees; directors; products. Also includes systematic product charts and separate products index.

2184 LANDBOUWCIJFERS
Landbouw-Economisch Instituut: Centraal Bureau voor de Statistiek

NL—Nederlands annual

Agricultural data; detailed annual statistics on: land utilisation; agricultural production; prices; consumption of food and agricultural products; foreign trade.

2185 LANDBOUWTELLING
Centraal Bureau voor de Statistiek

NL—Nederlands/English 1970 2 vols

Census of agriculture, taken every ten years.

2186 MAANDCIJFERS VAN DE INVOER, UITVOER EN ASSEMBLAGE VAN MOTORRIJTUIGEN
Centraal Bureau voor de Statistiek

NL—Nederlands monthly

Monthly bulletin on the import, export and assembly of motor vehicles; monthly statistics of motor vehicles, including tractors, by make and countries of origin and destination. Also assembly and production of new motor vehicles by make and type according to country of origin.

2187 MAANDCIJFERS VAN DE VISSERIJ
Centraal Bureau voor de Statistiek

NL—Nederlands(English headings) monthly

Monthly bulletin of fishery statistics; contains more up-to-date information on similar subjects as in the annual "Statistiek van de Visserij".

2188 MAANDSCHRIFT VAN HET CENTRAAL BUREAU VOOR DE STATISTIEK
Centraal Bureau voor de Statistiek

NL—Nederlands(English headings) monthly

Monthly bulletin of the Central Bureau of Statistics; statistics on the range of topics of general interest found in "Statistisch Zakboek" and "Jaarcijfers voor Nederland"; also includes the most important monthly and quarterly series of tables and a guide to recent publications issued by the CBS.

2189 MAANDSTATISTIEK BOUWNIJVERHEID
Centraal Bureau voor de Statistiek

NL—Nederlands monthly

Monthly bulletin of construction statistics; data on: building
permits; new construction of dwellings; building materials;
employment; deliveries.

**2190 MAANDSTATISTIEK INTERNATIONAAL
ZEEHAVENVERVOER**
Centraal Bureau voor de Statistiek

NL—Nederlands(English headings) monthly

Monthly statistical bulletin of international port traffic;
details of foreign trade by principal commodity groups, means
of transport and port of arrival or departure.

2191 MAANDSTATISTIEK VAN DE BINNENLANDSE HANDEL
Centraal Bureau voor de Statistiek

NL—Nederlands(English headings) monthly

Monthly bulletin of distribution statistics; data on the
wholesale and retail trade and consumption of principal
commodities; also includes wholesale, retail and import
price indices.

**2192 MAANDSTATISTIEK VAN DE BUITENLANDSE HANDEL
PER GOEDERENSOORT**
Centraal Bureau voor de Statistiek

NL—Nederlands(English headings) monthly

Monthly statistical bulletin of foreign trade by commodities;
data on imports and exports by commodities (BTN
classification) and subdivided by countries of origin and
destination.

**2193 MAANDSTATISTIEK VAN DE BUITENLANDSE HANDEL
PER LAND**
Centraal Bureau voor de Statistiek

NL—Nederlands(English headings) monthly

Monthly statistical bulletin of foreign trade by countries;
detailed data on imports and exports subdivided by
commodities arranged by SITC commodity classification.
Also totals of storage in, and removal from, bonded warehouses by countries.

2194 MAANDSTATISTIEK VAN DE INDUSTRIE
Centraal Bureau voor de Statistiek

NL—Nederlands(English headings) monthly

Monthly statistical bulletin of manufacturing; monthly and
quarterly production figures for various sectors of Dutch
industry; also includes index numbers of industrial production
and special surveys of specific industries.

2195 MAANDSTATISTIEK VAN DE LANDBOUW
Centraal Bureau voor de Statistiek

NL—Nederlands(English headings) monthly

Monthly bulletin of agricultural statistics.

2196 MAANDSTATISTIEK VAN HET FINANCIEWEZEN
Centraal Bureau voor de Statistiek

NL—Nederlands(English headings) monthly

Monthly bulletin of financial statistics; monthly and some
quarterly data on: banking; capital market; stock exchange;
insurance; public finance; balance of payments.

2197 MAANDSTATISTIEK VAN VERKEER EN VERVOER
Centraal Bureau voor de Statistiek

NL/INT—Nederlands(English headings) monthly

Monthly bulletin of transport statistics; data on: international
goods traffic; inland shipping; international inland shipping;
sea-going shipping; rail traffic; road traffic; tourist traffic.

2198 MARKETING IN THE NETHERLANDS
US Department of Commerce

NL—English 1976 33pp

Overseas Business Report no. OBR 76-31. Contents: market
analysis for selected products; industry trends; distribution
and sales channels; government procurement; transportation
and ports; credit; import-export regulations; investment in
the Netherlands; employment; taxation.

2199 NATIONALE REKENINGEN
Centraal Bureau voor de Statistiek

NL—Nederlands annual c130pp

National accounts; text and tables relating to national income
and expenditure; gross capital formation; gross domestic
product; gross national product; balance of payments.

2200 NEDERLANDS ABC VOOR HANDEL EN INDUSTRIE
ABC voor Handel en Industrie CV

NL—Nederlands 2 vols c2500pp

Netherlands ABC for commerce and industry. Vol. 1:
manufacturers and wholesalers; separate products index; A-Z
list of firms; A-Z list of foreign firms with Dutch agents.
Vol. 2: manufacturers and wholesalers broadly classified,
subdivided to towns, giving data on: address, telephone
numbers, date established, capital, employees, products,
subsidiaries.

**2201 NEDERLANDSE CENTRALE ORGANISATIE VOOR
TOEGEPAST NATUURWETENSCHAPPELIJK
ONDERZOEK WEGWIJZER TNO**
Nederlandse Centrale Organisatie voor T.N.O.

NL—Nederlands c100pp

Netherlands organisation for applied scientific research:
directory; lists TNO institutes with details of: address,
telephone numbers, director, scope, departments,
publications.

**2202 DE NEDERLANDSE ENERGIEHUISHOUDING:
UITKOMSTEN VAN MAAND- EN
KWARTAALTELLINGEN**
Centraal Bureau voor de Statistiek

NL—Nederlands quarterly

Energy supply in the Netherlands; results of monthly and
quarterly enquiries on energy supply.

2203 THE NETHERLANDS
The Financial Times

NL—English 11 Nov. 1975 p.15-18

Reports in the Financial Times newspaper on: the
Netherlands economy; energy; industry; transport; finance.

2204 THE NETHERLANDS
The Times

NL—English 4 April 1974 4pp

Special report in The Times newspaper, covering: the swing
from oil to natural gas; agriculture; industrial production;
tourism.

2205 THE NETHERLANDS BUSINESS CORPORATION CODE
Commerce Clearing House Inc.

NL—English 1977 78pp

A "Common Market Report" feature covering
various aspects of the Netherlands Corporation
code, its workings and applications in
practice.

2206 THE NETHERLANDS IN FIGURES
Algemene Bank Nederland

NL—English 1974 8pp

Brief data on: population; national income and expenditure;
industrial production; agricultural production; housing;
tourism; prices; wages; foreign trade; imports and exports;
balance of payments; banks.

2207 THE NETHERLANDS: INVESTORS CHRONICLE SURVEY
Investors Chronicle

NL—English 12 July 1974 22pp

Survey in the Investors Chronicle journal, covering: politics;
investment; banking; property; energy situation.

2208 THE NORTHERN NETHERLANDS
IBN

NL—English Nov. 1973 15pp

Survey prepared by IBN, The Industrialization Authority
for the northern part of the Netherlands providing current
information for industrialists looking for a favourable location
inside the Common Market countries. Contents: industrial
sites; housing; transport; utilities; Investment Incentives,
taxation; employment.

2209 OECD ECONOMIC SURVEY: NETHERLANDS
Organisation for Economic Co-operation and Development

NL—English/Français 1976 60pp

Covers recent developments in demand, output, employment,
prices and incomes, and the broad lines of economic policies
affecting fiscal, employment, industrial restructuring and
prices and incomes.

**2210 PROBLEM REGIONS OF EUROPE: RANDSTAD,
HOLLAND**
Oxford University Press

NL—English 1973 48pp

One of a series of studies which identifies and analyses the
need and problems of regional planning, including:
agriculture; industry; population; towns and urbanisation;
transport and communications.

2211 PRODUKTIESTATISTIEKEN
Centraal Bureau voor de Statistiek

NL—Nederlands(English headings) annual

Production statistics; published in separate annual volumes
for each industry, giving data on: sales, production,
consumption of raw materials and semi-finished products,
fuel consumption, stocks and unit value of selected products
sold. Volume titles: earthenware; motor cars and bodies;
bricks; narrow fabrics; concrete products; cocoa bean
processing and cocoa extractive factories; chemical industry;
clothing; roofing tiles industry; wire industry, forging from
bars, etc; printing; electrical engineering; steel furniture;
vegetable and fruit processing industry; wood products;
sand-lime bricks; synthetic materials processing industry;
leather industry; leather goods; mechanical and
constructional engineering; margarine works; flour mills;
compound feeds industry; paper industry; paper goods,
corrugated paper and cardboard; hardware, hollow-ware,
stoves, etc; bicycles, bicycle parts and accessories; rubber
industry; shipbuilding; footwear industry; spinning and
weaving; strawboard industry; tobacco products; carpet
industry; textile bleaching, dyeing and printing; hosiery and
other knitted goods; dairy industry.

**2212 PYTTERSEN'S NEDERLANDSE ALMANAK—HANDBOEK
VAN PERSONEN EN INSTELLINGEN IN NEDERLAND,
DE NEDERLANDSE ANTILLEN EN SURINAME**
Kon. Drukkerij Van de Garde NV

NL—Nederlands(English headings) annual c750pp

Pyttersen's Dutch Almanack—handbook of people and
institutions in the Netherlands, the Netherlands Antilles and
Surinam. Lists government departments, diplomatic service,
legal institutions, local government areas, universities,
schools, institutions, learned societies. Also includes a separate
A-Z list of organizations.

2213 QUARTERLY ECONOMIC REVIEW—NETHERLANDS
Economist Intelligence Unit

NL—English quarterly with annual supplement

Analysis of current economic trends including: government;
population; employment; exchange rates; national accounts;
agriculture; mining fuel and power; manufacturing industries;
transport and communications, finance.

2214 QUARTERLY STATISTICS
De Nederlandsche Bank NV

NL—English quarterly

Quarterly data on: bank statistics; money; saving deposits;
monetary and financial developments; balance of payments;
capital; interest rates; share prices; foreign currencies.

2215 RETAIL DISTRIBUTION IN THE NETHERLANDS
The Netherlands-British Chamber of Commerce

NL—English 1974 71pp

Survey of retail distribution in supermarkets and large
multiples. Contents: general economic data; the retail trade;
consumer market; major statutory regulations; approaching
Dutch retailers; directory of the important Dutch
organisations and companies in the retail grocery trade.

2216 ROTTERDAM EUROPORT
The Financial Times

NL—English 24 Aug. 1973 p.24-29

Survey in the Financial Times newspaper on the Rotterdam
port complex.

2217 ROTTERDAM: FINANCIAL TIMES SURVEY
The Financial Times

NL—English 19 Sept. 1974 p.31-34

Special survey in the Financial Times newspaper on
Rotterdam covering: the oil centre; Maasvlakte development;
property; labour.

2218 SOCIALE MAANDSTATISTIEK
Centraal Bureau voor de Statistiek

NL—Nederlands(English headings) monthly

Monthly bulletin of social statistics; data covers cost of living;
employment; unemployment; working hours; wages and
labour conditions; social insurance; consumption; savings.

**2219 SPOTLIGHT ON OVERSEAS TRADE—SELLING TO THE
NETHERLANDS**
Midland Bank International

NL—English 1976 4pp

Contents: economic situation; market opportunities;
regulations and documentary requirements; company
formation in the Netherlands; UK exports to the Netherlands.

**2220 STAATSALMANAK VOOR HET KONINKRIJK DER
NEDERLANDEN**
Staatsdrukkerij en Uitgeverijbedrijf

NL—Nederlands c650pp

State almanack for the Kingdom of the Netherlands;
government departments; classified, with details of address,
telephone numbers, functions, chief officers. Also lists local
authorities A-Z, with names of mayors and officials. Also
includes separate subject and persons indexes.

2221 STATISTICAL YEARBOOK OF THE NETHERLANDS
Centraal Bureau voor de Statistiek

NL—English annual c400pp

Contents: area; territory and climate; population; health;
housing; education; agriculture and fisheries; manufacturing
industries; distribution; foreign trade; traffic and transport;
money and banking; national accounts; balance of payments;
public finance; income and wealth; consumption; prices;
social affairs; justice and prisons.

**2222 STATISTIEK DER LONEN VAN ARBEIDERS IN DE
NIJVERHEID OKTOBER 1966**
Centraal Bureau voor de Statistiek

NL—Nederlands 1969

Statistics of wages in manufacturing industries; a general
survey of the wage structures including data on: earnings
according to age, sex, occupation, hours of work and size
of establishment.

2223 STATISTIEK DER MOTORRIJTUIGEN
Centraal Bureau voor de Statistiek

NL—Nederlands annual

Statistics on motor vehicles; annual data on: motor vehicles;
motorcycles; scooters and invalid carriages.

2224 STATISTIEK DER RIJKSFINANCIEN: 1967-72
Centraal Bureau voor de Statistiek

NL—Nederlands 1974

Statistics of central government finance for the years
1967-72.

**2225 STATISTIEK HANDBOEK: METAAL- EN ELEKTRO-
TECHNISCHE INDUSTRIE**
Federatie Metaal- en Elektrotechnische Industrie

NL—Nederlands annual c260pp

Statistical handbook of the metal and electrical industries;
giving data on: national accounts; production; orders;
employment; structure of the industries; investment; imports
and exports; price indices.

2226 STATISTIEK VAN DE BINNENVLOOT
Centraal Bureau voor de Statistiek

NL—Nederlands annual

Analysis of inland fleet by size, capacity, province, carrying
capacity and year of construction.

2227 STATISTIEK VAN DE BUITENLANDSE MIGRATIE
Centraal Bureau voor de Statistiek

NL—Nederlands(English headings) biennial c150pp

External migration statistics; detailed tables and graphs on
immigration and emigration to and from the Netherlands,
subdivided by nationals and aliens.

**2228 STATISTIEK VAN DE ELEKTRICITEITSVOORZIENING
IN NEDERLAND**
Centraal Bureau voor de Statistiek

NL—Nederlands(English headings) annual c60pp

Statistics on the electricity supply in the Netherlands; giving
data on electricity production and supply to the public.

**2229 STATISTIEK VAN DE GASVOORZIENING IN
NEDERLAND**
Centraal Bureau voor de Statistiek

NL—Nederlands(English headings) annual c50pp

Statistics of gas supply in the Netherlands; data on
production, distribution, supply and demand of gas.

2230 STATISTIEK VAN DE INVESTERINGEN IN VASTE ACTIVA IN DE INDUSTRIE
Centraal Bureau voor de Statistiek

NL—Nederlands(English headings) annual c45pp

Statistics on fixed capital formation in industry; data on the major industries, including mining and quarrying, manufacturing, construction, electricity, gas, water.

2231 STATISTIEK VAN DE KOOPVAARDIJVLOOT
Centraal Bureau voor de Statistiek

NL/INT—Nederlands annual c30pp

Statistics of the merchant marine; annual data on the merchant marine of the Netherlands, its overseas territories and the world merchant marine fleet.

2232 STATISTIEK VAN DE LUCHTVAART
Centraal Bureau voor de Statistiek

NL—Nederlands(English headings) c60pp

Civil aviation statistics, covering: Dutch air transport; world air transport; aircraft by type; investments; profit and loss accounts of KLM and Schiphol airport; aircraft movements; passengers transported; goods transported.

2233 STATISTIEK VAN DE PACHT- EN KOOPPRIJZEN VAN LANDBOUWGRONDEN
Centraal Bureau voor de Statistiek

NL—Nederlands(English headings) c50pp

Statistics of rents and prices of farmlands.

2234 STATISTIEK VAN DE VISSERIJ
Centraal Bureau voor de Statistiek

NL—Nederlands(English headings) annual

Fishery statistics; commentary and data on: fishing craft; manpower in the fishing industry; production of fish; processing; prices; sales; consumption; imports and exports; price indices; total output; gross value and net product in the fishery industry.

2235 STATISTIEK VAN HANDEL, NIJVERHEID EN VERKEER
Rotterdam Chamber of Commerce and Industry

NL—Nederlands annual

Statistics of trade, industry and traffic; data on: shipping; goods and passenger traffic; shipping trade and industry in Rotterdam.

2236 STATISTIEK VAN HET AUTOPARK
Centraal Bureau voor de Statistiek

NL—Nederlands 1973

Motor vehicle statistics; giving data on: passenger and commercial vehicles produced and registered and analyses by make of vehicles.

2237 STATISTIEK VAN HET INTERNATIONAAL GOEDERENVERVOER
Centraal Bureau voor de Statistiek

NL—Nederlands annual c250pp

Statistics of international goods traffic; annual cumulation of statistics contained in the monthly bulletin, giving data on: total transport; sea-going shipping; inland shipping; road, rail and air transport; transit trade with transhipment.

2238 STATISTIEK VAN HET INTERNATIONAAL ZEEHAVENVERVOER
Centraal Bureau voor de Statistiek

NL—Nederlands(English headings) quarterly

Statistics of international port traffic; data on: imports, exports, transit trade and goods loaded and unloaded, for seaborne shipping, inland shipping, railways, road transport, civil aviation.

2239 STATISTIEK VAN HET PERSONENVERVOER
Centraal Bureau voor de Statistiek

NL—Nederlands annual c45pp

Statistics on passenger transport; data on: transport by bus, train and tram, inter-urban passenger transport; number of enterprises by type of transport; railways; civil aviation; sea transport.

2240 STATISTIEK VAN LAND- EN TUINBOUW
Centraal Bureau voor de Statistiek

NL—Nederlands(English headings) annual c120pp

Statistics on agriculture and horticulture; data on: land utilisation; agricultural production; prices; agricultural income; imports and exports of agricultural products; market supplies; consumption of food and agricultural products.

2241 STATISTIEK VREEMDELINGENVERKEER
Centraal Bureau voor de Statistiek

NL—Nederlands c80pp

Tourism statistics; data on: foreign tourists in hotels, regionally and by town.

2242 STATISTISCH ZAKBOEK
Centraal Bureau voor de Statistiek

NL—Nederlands annual

Statistical pocket yearbook giving data on the same range of subjects as "Jaarcijfers voor Nederland"—the statistical yearbook, but in less detail.

2243 SYSTEMATISCH OVERZICHT VAN DE CBS PUBLIKATIES, 1946 73
Centraal Bureau voor de Statistiek

NL—Nederlands annual 97pp

Systematic survey of publications, 1945-73; Comprehensive bibliography of the CBS publications, kept up-to-date by a monthly list.

2244 TRADE BULLETIN
Netherlands-British Chamber of Commerce

NL—English every two months

Regular bulletin dealing mainly with trade enquiries of opportunities for business in the UK and the Netherlands.

2245 TUINBOUWCIJFERS
Centraal Bureau voor de Statistiek and Landbouw-
Economisch Instituut

NL—Nederlands

Detailed horticultural statistics.

2246 VAN OSS' EFFECTENBOEK
Uitgeverij J H de Bussy NV

NL—Nederlands annual 2 vols c1400pp

Van Oss' stocks and shares book. Vol. 1: Dutch quoted
companies with details of: address, date established, directors,
capital, activities. Vol. 2: Foreign quoted companies, similar
data.

2247 VERKEERSTELLINGEN
Centraal Bureau voor de Statistiek

NL—Nederlands 1970 3 vols

Traffic census. Part 1: General census results. Part 2: Results
by provinces. Part 3: Results for primary roads.

2248 WATER POLLUTION CONTROL IN WEST GERMANY AND
THE NETHERLANDS: THE MARKET FOR TREATMENT
PLANT AND INSTRUMENTS
Sira Institute

NL/D—English 1973 2 vols

This study is concerned firstly with instruments for
measuring and controlling water pollution in West Germany
and the Netherlands but also gives coverage of markets for
water and effluent treatment plant. Three market sectors are
distinguished in each country: public sewage treatment and
surface water control; drinking supply; effluent treatment in
industry. In each sector structural information and market
size data are presented for the base years (1971-2) with
forecasts for 1977.

2249 ZEVENTIG JAREN STATISTIEK IN TIJDREEKSEN,
1899-1969
Centraal Bureau voor de Statistiek

NL—Nederlands 1970 189pp

Historical data on the key Dutch economic indicators.

2250 ZUIVELSTATISTIEK
Centraal Bureau voor de Statistiek

NL—Nederlands(English headings) annual

Dairy statistics; annual data on: production; imports and
exports; consumption; prices of dairy produce.

P-PORTUGAL

2275 ANUARIO ESTATISTICA: VOLUME 1, CONTINENTE E ILHAS ADJACENTES
Instituto Nacional de Estatística

P—Português/Français annual c440pp

Statistical yearbook; covering Portugal and adjacent islands; data on: geography and climate; demography; public health; social security; co-operative organisations; education; sport; culture; justice; production and consumption; property; commerce; prices and wages; transport; tourism; finance; balance of payments; public administration.

2276 BANCO DE PORTUGAL—ANNUAL REPORT
Banco de Portugal

P—English annual c180pp

Annual report including an economic and financial survey with data on: employment; wages; prices; external balance of payments; foreign trade; public finance; investment.

2277 BARCLAYS COUNTRY REPORT—PORTUGAL
Barclays Bank

P—English

Brief summary covering: payments; prices and wages; external position; economic outlook.

2278 BASIC DATA ON THE ECONOMY OF PORTUGAL
US Department of Commerce

P English 1071 12pp

Overseas Business Report no. OBR 71-036. General report on the Portuguese economy covering: basic structure; industrial sectors; labour market; trade; finance; economic outlook.

2279 BETWEEN AFRICA AND EUROPE: SURVEY OF PORTUGAL
The Economist

P—English 26 Feb. 1972 28pp

Extensive survey on the political and economic questions then facing the country.

2280 BOLETIN MENSAL DE ESTATISTICA
Instituto Nacional de Estatística

P/INT—Português/Français monthly

Monthly bulletin of statistics; data on: demography; production and consumption; trade; prices and wages; transport and communications; banking; credit; property; public finance. Also includes a section on international statistics and special studies and commentaries.

2281 ESTATISTICAS AGRICOLAS E ALIMENTARES
Instituto Nacional de Estatística

P—Português annual c200pp

Agricultural and food statistics; data on: climate; population; agricultural exploitation; fruit and olive groves; production and development; agricultural, forestry and livestock production; finance and wages; prices; fire insurance; education; hygiene.

2282 ESTATISTICAS DA EDUCACAO
Instituto Nacional de Estatística

P—Português annual

Annual official statistics on education.

2283 ESTATISTICAS DA ENERGIA
Instituto Nacional de Estatística

P—Português/Français annual c50pp

Statistics of energy; contains data on: general data and statistics of production, consumption and labour in the power industries—coal, oil, electricity; also includes statistics of production of primary and secondary power; and consumption of certain types of power.

2284 ESTATISTICAS DA PESCA
Instituto Nacional de Estatística

P—Português/Français annual c60pp

Fishery statistics; includes data on: production; trade; prices; consumption; active population in the fishing industry.

2285 **ESTATISTICAS DAS CONTRIBUICOES E IMPOSTES**
Instituto Nacional de Estatística

P—Português annual

Annual tax statistics.

2286 **ESTATISTICAS DAS SOCIEDADES**
Instituto Nacional de Estatística

P—Português annual c160pp

Statistics of companies; includes data on the number of companies in each industry and the financial state of the industries.

2287 **ESTATISTICAS DEMOGRAFICAS**
Instituto Nacional de Estatística

P—Português annual

Annual publication of demographic statistics.

2288 **ESTATISTICAS DO COMERCIO EXTERNO**
Instituto Nacional de Estatística

P—Português annual 2 vols

Statistics of foreign trade: Vol. 1: Tables of imports and exports arranged by commodities, subdivided by countries of origin and destination; also includes less detailed retrospective tables of foreign trade for the past years. Vol. 2: Tables of imports and exports and transit trade arranged by countries of origin and destination, subdivided by commodities.

2289 **ESTATISTICAS DO TURISMO**
Instituto Nacional de Estatística

P—Português annual

Annual official statistics on tourism.

2290 **ESTATISTICAS FINANCEIRAS**
Instituto Nacional de Estatística

P—Português annual

Financial statistics covering national income and expenditure; banking; balance of payments; industrial income and expenditure; loans to agricultural establishments.

2291 **ESTATÍSTICAS INDUSTRIAIS**
Instituto Nacional de Estatística

P—Português/Français annual c500pp

Industrial statistics; census of industrial production under 100 headings containing data on: number of establishments; production and consumption of materials; machinery and equipment; fuel and power; persons employed in each industrial sector.

2292 **ESTATISTICAS MONETARIAS E FINANCEIROS**
Instituto Nacional de Estatística

P—Português annual

Annual official financial and monetary statistics.

2293 **ESTIMATIVA DE PRODUCTO BRUTO FLORESTAL NO CONTINENTE, 1938, 1947 A 1963**
Instituto Nacional de Estatística

P—Português 1964

Statistics on the production and value of forest products for three selected years.

2294 **FOLHA MENSAL DO ESTADO DOS CULTURAS E PREVISAO DE COLHEITAS**
Instituto Nacional de Estatística

P—Português monthly

Monthly report on the state of cultivation.

2295 **FOREIGN INVESTMENT CODE**
Banco Português do Atlântico

P—English 1976 30pp

Translation of Decree Law no. 239/76, April 6, 1976, which established new regulations on foreign investment in Portugal.

2296 **THE FOREIGN INVESTOR IN PORTUGAL**
Banco Português do Atlântico

P—English

Guide for the potential foreign investor giving information on the economic background and advice on establishing and operating a business in Portugal.

2297 **A GUIDE TO INVESTMENTS AND BUSINESS IN PORTUGAL**
Banco Espirito Santo e Comercial di Lisboa

P—English c100pp

Investment and business guide including data on: banking; foreign exchange regulations; taxes; company law; licencing; investment.

2298 **INDICADORES ESTATÍSTICOS A CURTO PRAZO**
Instituto Nacional de Estatística

P—Português monthly

Short-term statistical indicators in the form of tables and graphs.

2299 **INDICES DE SALARIOS PROFISSIONAIS, POR RAMOS DE ACTIVIDADE E PARA A CIDADE DE LISBOA**
Instituto Nacional de Estatística

P—Português

Charts and tables showing indices of salaries and wages of workers in the Lisbon area.

2300 **INFORME ECONOMICO**
Banco de Bilbao

P—Português annual c350pp

Commentary and statistics on the Portuguese economy.

2301 INVENTARIO DES ESTATISTICAS DISPONIVEIS NO CONTINENTE E ILHAS ADJACENTES
Instituto Nacional de Estatísticas

P—Português c280pp

Inventory of statistical information for Portugal and adjacent islands; listing of statistical publications arranged by subject.

2302 MARKET REPORT: PORTUGAL
Department of Trade and Industry

P—English 12 Nov. 1976 p.444-447

Special report in Trade and Industry journal on the potential for British exporters following the government's new economic plan.

2303 MARKETING IN PORTUGAL
US Department of Commerce

P—English 1974 59pp

Overseas Business Report no. OBR 74-52. Contents: market analysis for selected products; industry trends; distribution and sales channels; government procurement; transportation and ports; credit; import-export regulations; investment in Portugal; employment; taxation.

2304 OECD ECONOMIC SURVEYS—PORTUGAL
Organisation for Economic Co-operation and Development

P—English/Français

Individual analyses of the Portuguese economy, covering recent developments in demand, output, employment, prices and incomes and the broad lines of economic policies affecting fiscal, employment and industrial restructuring, and prices and incomes.

2305 OPPORTUNITIES IN PORTUGAL AND HER OVERSEAS PROVINCES
British National Export Council

P—English 1970 10pp

Contents: exports and imports; Common Market; market opportunities; links between British and Portuguese manufacturers.

2306 PORTUGAL: FINANCIAL TIMES SURVEY
The Financial Times

P—English 7 July 1975 p.17-22

Survey in the Financial Times newspaper reviewing the political and economic problems in Portugal.

2307 PORTUGAL: INVESTORS CHRONICLE SURVEY
Investors Chronicle

P—English 1 June 1973 22pp

Survey in the Investors Chronicle covering: banking potential; Portuguese coins; foreign investment; tourism; building; wine; the stock exchange.

2308 THE PORTUGUESE ECONOMY
Banco Pinto e Sotto Mayor

P—English c70pp

Booklet giving information on: main economic features of Portugal; foreign trade; foreign investment; also includes data on Angola and Mozambique.

2309 PORTUGUESE INDUSTRY AND FINANCE
The Financial Times

P—English 11 Dec. 1975 p.28-33

Special report covering: economic problems; decolonisation; shipbuilding; tourism; farming; wine; chemicals; textiles.

2310 PORTUGUESE PROPERTY AND TOURISM
The Financial Times

P—English 30 Jan. 1974 p. 23-25

Survey on tourism in the Algarve.

2311 PORTUGUESE SHIPBUILDING AND REPAIRING
The Financial Times

P—English 11 Jan. 1974 p.14-15

Newspaper report showing how shipbuilding was boosting the Portuguese economy.

2312 PRODUCTION OF FRUIT AND VEGETABLES IN OECD MEMBER COUNTRIES: PORTUGAL
Organisation for Economic Co-operation and Development

P—English/Français 1967

Information on production, utilisation and trade in fruit and vegetables in Portugal.

2313 QUARTERLY ECONOMIC REVIEW—PORTUGAL
Economist Intelligence Unit

P—English quarterly with annual supplement

Analysis of current economic trends including government; population; employment; exchange rates; national accounts; agriculture; mining, fuel and power; manufacturing industries; transport and communications; finance.

2314 RECENSEAMENTO GERAL DA POPULACAO NO CONTINENTE E ILHAS ADJACENTES
Instituto Nacional de Estatística

P—Português/Français 1960 6 vols

General census of population of the mainland and adjacent islands. Vol. 1: Population; retrospective figures 1864-1960. Vol. 2: Families, collective households, resident population. Vol. 3: Part 1: Age. Part 2: Education. Vol. 4: Foreigners, orphans, the blind and deaf mutes. Vol. 5: Conditions of work and status. Vol. 6: Domestic housing.

2315 SOME DATA ABOUT PORTUGAL
Banco Português do Atlântico

P—English 1975/6 3 parts

Booklet 1: Territory; climate; transport (20pp). Booklet 2: Population; education; health (12pp). Booklet 3: Foreign trade; tourism; emigration; balance of external payments; reserves (34pp).

2316 STRUCTURE AND GROWTH OF THE PORTUGUESE
       ECONOMY
       European Free Trade Association

       P—English 1964

       Economic survey covering: agriculture; industrial structure
       and growth and foreign trade.

2317 SUMMARY OF FOREIGN EXCHANGE REGULATIONS
       IN PORTUGAL
       Banco Português do Atlântico

       P—English 1975 52pp

       Contents: foreign trade operations; private capital import
       and export operations; opening of accounts in escudos to
       non-residents; opening of accounts in foreign currencies;
       bank guarantees; monetary directives.

S-SWEDEN

2325 ADVERTISING CONDITIONS IN SWEDEN
Institute of Practitioners in Advertising

S—English 1976 20pp

Contents: geography and demography; the media—press, outdoor, cinema, fairs, direct mail, advertising agencies and services; research; taxes, laws and regulations; advertising and related organisations.

2326 ALLMÄN MÅNADSSTATISTIK
Statistiska Centralbyrån

S—Svensk(English headings) monthly

Monthly digest of Swedish statistics; data on: population; labour; agriculture and fisheries; mining; manufacturing; transport and communications; building; retail trade; external trade; wages and prices

2327 ARBETSKRAFTSUNDERSÖKNINGARNA 1961-1969
Statistiska Centralbyrån

S—Svensk(English headings)

Survey of the Swedish labour force based on the quarterly figures collected by the Survey Research Institute of the Statistiska Centralbyrån.

2328 BARCLAYS COUNTRY REPORT—SWEDEN
Barclays Bank

S—English July 1976 2pp

Brief economic summary covering: balance of payments; prices and wages; external positions; economic outlook.

2329 BASIC FACTS ABOUT SWEDEN
Skandinaviska Enskilda Banken

S—English 1974 7pp

Small brochure giving statistics on: population; labour; consumption; industrial output; transportation; banks; prices and wages; taxation; foreign trade.

2330 BEFOLKNINGSFRAMRÄKNING FÖR RIKET 1963-2000
Statistiska Centralbyrån

S—Svensk(English headings) 1965

Population projections to 2000 including data on the number of people by age, sex and marital status.

2331 CONSUMER POLICY IN SWEDEN
The National Swedish Board for Consumer Policies

S—English 1975 78pp

Papers presented at a French/Swedish symposium on consumer affairs in December 1974, including: activities of the consumer ombudsman; laws and institutions in the field of consumer protection; treatment of private disputes; viewpoints on the consumer-government-business relationship.

2332 THE CORPORATE INCOME TAX IN SWEDEN
Skandinaviska Enskilda Banken

S/INT—English c60pp

Survey of the corporate income tax system covering: basic principles; ordinary deductions; other deductions; taxes other than income tax; international aspects of the Swedish corporate income tax.

2333 ESTABLISHING A BUSINESS IN SWEDEN
US Department of Commerce

S—English 1971 17pp

Overseas Business Report no. OBR 71-042. Concise information on setting up a business in Sweden, including: factors affecting investment; organisation of business; employment; taxation.

2334 FACT SHEETS ON SWEDEN
The Swedish Institute

S—English 1976 2pp

A series of fact sheets, including: foreign policy; industry and the economy; labour market; education; research; Sweden in general.

2335 FISKE
Statistiska Centralbyrån

S—Svensk(English headings) annual

Fishery statistics on landings; catches, fishermen, sales; imports and exports and average prices of fish.

2336 FOREIGN TRADE REGULATIONS OF SWEDEN
US Department of Commerce

S—English 1973

Overseas Business Report no. OBR 73-35. Contents: trade
policy; import tariff system; special customs provisions;
internal taxes; shipping documentation; non-tariff and import
controls; Swedish export controls.

2337 FÖRETAGENS. . .EKONOMISK REDOVISNING
Statistiska Centralbyrån

S—Svensk(English headings) annual

Annual data on income, expenditure and profits of business
enterprises in Sweden.

2338 HINTS TO BUSINESSMEN: SWEDEN
British Overseas Trade Board

S—English 1976 52pp

Practical guide to travelling executives covering: general
information; travel; hotels; restaurants and tipping; postal
and telephone facilities; economic factors; import and
exchange regulations; methods of doing business; government
and commercial organisations; reading list; map.

2339 INDUSTRI
Statistiska Centralbyrån

S—Svensk(English headings) annual

Manufacturing; statistical survey of the manufacturing
industries, including mining and quarrying. Data on: number
of establishments, production, cost of production, raw
materials consumption, fuel and power, number of employees.

2340 INVESTORS CHRONICLE SURVEY—SWEDEN
Investors Chronicle

S—English 25 July 1975 16pp

Survey covering: the economy and the balance of payments;
state ownership; Swedish banking system; industry review.

2341 JORDBRUGSSTATISTISK ÅRSBOK
Statistiska Centralbyrån

S—Svensk(English headings) annual

Agricultural statistical abstract of Sweden; data on:
agricultural enterprises; types of land, population and labour
force; real estate and buildings; machinery; crop farming;
vegetables; food consumption; foreign trade in agricultural
products.

2342 JORDBRUKSEKONOMISKA MEDDELANDEN
National Swedish Agricultural Marketing Board

S/INT—Svensk monthly

Monthly review with market surveys and reports and
statistical notes on Swedish and foreign agriculture.

2343 KONSUMENTPRISER OCH INDEXBERÄKNINGAR
Statistiska Centralbyrån

S—Svensk(English headings) annual

Annual statistics on consumer prices.

**2344 KONSUMENTPRISINDEX SAMT FRAMSKRIVNA
ALDRE INDEXSERIER**
Statistiska Centralbyrån

S—Svensk(English headings)

Index of consumer prices.

2345 LÖNER
Statistiska Centralbyrån

S—Svensk/English annual 2 parts

Statistics on wages, in two parts: Part 1: wages of salaried
employees in mining and manufacturing, wholesale and retail
trade. Part 2: wages of agricultural and industrial workers.

2346 MARKETING IN SWEDEN
US Department of Commerce

S—English 1975 26pp

Overseas Business Report no. OBR 75-41. Contents: market
analysis for selected products; industry trends; distribution
and sales channels; government procurement; transportation
and ports; credit; import-export regulations; investment in
Sweden; employment; taxation.

2347 PLANNING AND PRODUCTIVITY IN SWEDEN
Croom Helm

S—English 1976 212pp

Describes how state and industry work together through the
Labour Market Board in an effort to produce the optimum
level and rate of investment in plant and equipment.

2348 QUARTERLY ECONOMIC REVIEW—SWEDEN
Economist Intelligence Unit

S—English quarterly with annual supplement

Analysis of current economic trends including: government;
population; employment; exchange rates; national accounts;
agriculture; mining, fuel and power; manufacturing industries;
transport and communications; finance.

**2349 REPORT ON THE ACTIVITIES OF THE STOCKHOLM
STOCK EXCHANGE**
The Stockholm Stock Exchange

S—English/Svensk annual c15pp

Annual report including details on: stock exchange securities;
share values; bonds; price trends.

2350 SKOGSSTATISTISK ÅRSBOK
National Board of Private Forestry

S—Svensk annual

Forestry statistics yearbook with data on: timber production;
pulp and paper; number of agricultural units under private
enterprises; labour; prices; industrial accidents.

2351 SOME DATA ABOUT SWEDEN 1975-76
Skandinaviska Enskilda Banken

S—English biennial 96pp

Brief outline of Sweden's economic and social structure
including: geography and population; political system;
labour; production; agriculture; energy; transportation;
investment; housing; foreign investment; foreign trade;
exports; foreign exchange controls.

2352 SOME PROMINENT SWEDISH COMPANIES
PA Norstedt and Söner

S—English

Contains the annual reports of some 170 Swedish companies
which are registered on the Swedish Stock Exchange.

**2353 SPOTLIGHT ON OVERSEAS TRADE—SELLING TO
SWEDEN**
Midland Bank International

S—English 1976 4pp

Contents: economic situation; market opportunities;
regulations and documentary requirements; company
formation in Sweden; UK exports to Sweden.

2354 STARTING A BUSINESS IN SWEDEN
Svenska Handelsbanken

S—English c20pp

Advice on starting a business including: foreign exchange
regulations; legal aspects; taxes; labour market; social
benefits.

2355 STATISTISK ÅRSBOK
Statistiska Centralbyrån

S/INT—Svensk(English headings) annual

Statistical yearbook; data on: geography and climate;
population; households; agriculture; forestry; fisheries;
manufacturing; internal and external trade; transport and
communications; money and credit; insurance; cost of living;
housing; labour; wages and salaries; health; education; justice;
national accounts. Also includes some international statistics.

2356 STATISTISKA MEDDELANDEN
Statistiska Centralbyrån

S—Svensk(English headings) annual

Statistical economic reviews, each issue deals with a single
aspect of the Swedish economy.

2357 SVENSK INDUSTRIKALENDER
Sveriges Industriförbund

S—Svensk(English headings)

Directory of c4000 firms with data on: nature of business;
products; share capital; directors; also includes a classified
product index with details of suppliers.

2358 SVENSKA AKTIEBOLAG
PA Norstedt & Söner

S—Svensk(English headings)

Directory of c3500 Swedish limited companies classified by
activity. Includes data on production and financial
information for the past five years. For companies listed on

the Swedish Stock Exchange a ten-year financial summary is
given.

2359 SVERIGES JÅRNVÅGER
State Railways Board

S—Svensk annual

Annual commentary and statistics on the State and private
railways, with data on: investment; financial results; capital;
employment; accidents; road and ferry boat services.

2360 SVERIGES RIKSBANK—ANNUAL REPORT
Sveriges Riksbank

S—English/Svensk annual c100pp

Annual report including commentary and statistics on:
credit policy; credit market; interest rates; balance of
payments.

**2361 SVERIGES RIKSBANK—STATISTICAL APPENDIX TO
THE ANNUAL REPORT**
Sveriges Riksbank

S—English/Svensk annual c180pp

Separate publication to the "Annual Report", containing
detailed charts and statistics on: the Riksbank; commercial
banks; other banks; insurance and pensions institutions;
mortgage institutions and credit companies; government;
local authorities; business sector; bonds and shares; credit
market; interest rates; balance of payments; foreign exchange
market.

**2362 SWEDEN'S CHEMICAL INDUSTRY: DIRECTORY OF
MANUFACTURERS AND PRODUCTS**
Sveriges Kemiska Industrikontor

S—English

Survey with statistical tables; basic information on major
chemical manufacturers; also includes classified product
index and index of trade names.

2363 SWEDEN'S ECONOMY
Svenska Handelsbanken

S—English

Economic commentary including statistics on production,
labour, trade and finance.

2364 THE SWEDISH BUDGET 1976/77
Ministry of Finance

S—English 1976 137pp

Summary of the draft budget for fiscal 1976-77 with an
abbreviated version of the budget statement including details
of central government revenue and expenditure. Also gives
short descriptions of the Swedish civil service; the
constitution; proposed budget reform; taxation system.

2365 THE THOUSAND LARGEST COMPANIES IN SWEDEN
Ekonomisk Litteratur

S—English/Svensk 1976 150pp

Lists the top 1000 companies with data on: ranking by sales;
capital; assets; invested capital; invested capital as a

percentage of assets; profit; sales per employee. Also contains special economic surveys.

2366 UTRIKESHANDEL
Statistiska Centralbyrån

S—Svensk(English headings) annual 2 vols

Foreign trade statistics. Vol. 1: detailed tables of imports and exports classified by commodities BTN, subdivided by countries of origin and destination. Vol. 2: Analyses by countries of origin and destination, subdivided by SITC, and customs districts.

2367 UTRIKESHANDEL MÅNADSSTATISTIK
Statistiska Centralbyrån

S—Svensk(English headings) monthly

Foreign trade monthly bulletin, including import and export statistics by SITC and BTN, by countries and by trading area.

2368 VEM AGER VAD I SVENSKT NÄRINGSLIV
Almquist and Wiksell Forlag AB

S—Svensk(English headings)

Swedish "Who owns whom" including companies listed and not listed on the Swedish Stock Exchange.

2369 YEAR BOOK
Swedish Chamber of Commerce in the UK

S/GB—English annual

Contents: annual commentary with statistics on Anglo-Swedish trade; businessman's guide to Sweden and Britain; list of members.

SF-FINLAND

2400 ALCOHOL STATISTICS
Alko Oy Ab

SF—English annual

Extract from Alko statistical yearbook which includes data for the production, sales, export and import of alcoholic beverages, and consumption of alcoholic beverages.

2401 BANK OF FINLAND MONTHLY BULLETIN
Bank of Finland

SF—English monthly

Monthly data and statistics on: national income and expenditure; foreign trade by main commodity groups; and by countries; balance of payments; indices of prices; wages and production.

2402 BANK OF FINLAND—YEAR BOOK
Bank of Finland

SF—English annual c65pp

Contents: economic development; central bank policy; monetary and foreign exchange; balance sheet and income statement of the Bank of Finland; charts and statistical tables on: unemployment; prices; wages and salaries; balance of payments; state finance; rates of interest; exchange rates; foreign exchange reserves.

2403 BARCLAYS COUNTRY REPORTS—FINLAND
Barclays Bank

SF—English 1976 2pp

Brief economic summary, covering: current economic situation; industrial scene; trade; future economic outlook.

2404 BRIEF FACTS ABOUT FINNISH INDUSTRY
Federation of Finnish Industries

SF—English

Short statistical review of industry and commerce.

2405 A BUSINESSMAN'S GUIDE TO FINLAND
Scan Edit A/S

SF—English

Basic introduction and information on many aspects of Finnish business.

2406 DIRECTORY OF FINNISH RESEARCH LIBRARIES
Suomen Tieteellisten Kirjastojen Lautakunta

SF—English

Libraries are classified by subject specialisations with names in Finnish and English, with details of address, telephone numbers, hours, services, publications. Also includes separate A-Z index of libraries.

2407 ECONOMIC REPORT—FINLAND
Lloyds Bank

SF—English 1976 22pp

Contents: opportunities for exporters; principal British exports; trading and economic associations; EFTA; EEC; USSR; import trade; foreign investment; background to the economy; agriculture; fishing; forestry; transport; incomes; prices and employment; balance of payments; international reserves.

2408 ECONOMIC REVIEW
Kansallis-Osake-Pankii

SF—English quarterly

Quarterly economic review including statistical tables. First issue of each year reviews the economic development of Finland for the preceding year. Third issue of each year contains a detailed review of the first half of the current year. Second and Fourth issues of each year contain features, articles and a statistical section with data on: national income; index of industrial production; agriculture; internal and external trade; prices and wages; employment.

2409 ECONOMIC SURVEY
Valtion Painatuskeskus

SF—Suomalainen/English/Svensk annual c120pp

Issued by the Economic Department, Ministry of Finance, contains data on: international developments; foreign trade; production; employment; income; costs and prices; financial markets; public finance.

2410 ESTABLISHING A BUSINESS IN FINLAND
Commission for Foreign Investment and the Bank of Finland

SF—English 1970 40pp

Contents: introduction to the market; legislation; resources
for new investment; labour; energy and raw materials;
industrial sites and building; monetary system and banking;
price level and structure; establishing a business; foreign
exchange regulations.

2411 ESTABLISHING A BUSINESS IN FINLAND
US Department of Commerce

SF—English 1969 14pp

Overseas Business Report no. OBR 69-54. Contents:
investment climate; legislation governing investment; business
organisation; industrial property protection; employment;
availability of capital; bibliography.

2412 FACTS ABOUT FINLAND 1976
Union Bank of Finland

SF—English 1976 13pp

Contents: brief statistics on: area; population; press;
communications; standard of living; currency; economy;
prices and wages; distribution of national income; private
consumption; state revenues and expenditure; foreign trade;
imports and exports.

**2413 THE FIFTEEN HUNDRED LARGEST COMPANIES IN
FINLAND**
A.S. Yritystieto Oy

SF—English/Soumalainen/Svensk 1975 124pp

Lists the top 1500 companies in Finland with data on:
ranking by sales; invested capital; invested capital as a
percentage of assets; profit; sales per employee; exports.
Also includes special surveys on current and future economic
trends.

2414 FINLAND—FINANCIAL TIMES SURVEY
The Financial Times

SF—English 10 June 1976 p.11-15

Survey in the Financial Times newspaper; Contents:
problems of the coalition government; exports; importance
of the Russian market for metals; forestry industry; energy
policy.

2415 FINLAND HANDBOOK
Finnish Tourist Board

SF—English c40pp

Useful compilation of general information helpful to foreign
visitors.

2416 FINLAND IN FIGURES
Kansallis-Osake-Pankki

SF—English

Booklet with statistics on: population; media; transport;
national economy; standard of living.

2417 FINLAND—TRAVEL FACTS
Finnish Tourist Board

SF—English annual c40pp

Introducing Finland to the foreign visitor. Contents: travel;
tours; accommodation; food and drink; entertainment;
special events; sports facilities.

2418 FINLANDS STATSKALENDER
Weilin and Göös Oy Ab

SF—Svensk c950pp

Official yearbook of Finland: includes details of government
departments; national organisations; public officers; institutes
and societies. Separate index of organisations A-Z.

2419 FINNCELL
Suomen Selluloosayhdistys

SF—English

Sales organisation for the wood pulp industry; contains
statistics of production, domestic consumption of various
materials covered by the wood pulp industry.

2420 FINNFACTS
Finnfacts Institute

SF—English 8 issues a year c16pp

Newsletter covering: overseas trading; imports and exports;
forestry industry; metals and engineering; electronics;
furniture; food; banking news.

2421 FINNISH FOREIGN TRADE DIRECTORY
The Finnish Foreign Trade Association

SF—English c550pp

A-Z listing of manufacturing, exporting and importing
companies with details of: address, date established, directors;
products, capital. Also separate classified trade section and
list of trade associations.

2422 FINNISH PAPER AND TIMBER
Finnish Forest Industries

SF—Suomalainen/English

Journal on the timber industry which also includes statistics
on: production and exports; foreign trade.

2423 FINNISH PULP AND PAPER
The Financial Times

SF—English 22 October 1975 p.23-27

Article in the Financial Times newspaper discussing the
critical importance of pulp and paper to the Finnish
economy.

2424 FINNISH SHIPPING
The Times

SF—English 26 Feb. 1976 p.17-19

Reviews the growth of the Finnish shipbuilding industry.
Comments on prospects for the highly specialised yards which
can produce vessels ranging from ice-breakers to oil rigs.

2425 FINNISH TRADE REVIEW
The Finnish Foreign Trade Association

SF—English

Commercial and industrial news and product features.

2426 HELSINKI
The Times

SF—English 24 May 1976 p.8-9

Article in The Times newspaper which examines the facilities Helsinki has to offer as an international conference centre.

2427 HINTS TO BUSINESSMEN—FINLAND
British Overseas Trade Board

SF—English 1975 44pp

Practical guide for travelling executives covering: general information; travel; hotels; restaurants and tipping; postal and telephone facilities; economic factors; import and exchange control regulations; methods of doing business; government and commercial organisations; reading list; map.

2428 INDEXATION IN AN INFLATIONARY ECONOMY: A CASE STUDY OF FINLAND
Political and Economic Planning

SF—English Apr. 1975 111pp

One of a series from PEP's study of inflation. Contents: purposes and methods of indexing; anti-inflationary policy in Finland; indexation of wage agreements in Finland; Finnish bank deposit accounts; bonds issued by the Finnish government or industry; social security pensions and insurance; commercial and property contracts; legislation on index-linking in Finland; evaluation of indexation; index-linking in Britain; references and select bibliography.

2429 LOOK AT FINLAND
Finnish Tourist Board & Ministry of Foreign Affairs, Press Section

SF—English 5 times a year c60pp

Regular journal with articles of general interest on Finland.

2430 MAATALOUS: MAATALOUDEN VUOSITILASTO
Maataloushallituksen Tilastotoimisto

SF—Suomalainen/Svensk(English headings) annual c60pp

Agriculture: annual statistics of agriculture. Data on: agricultural land; arable land; agricultural yield; consumption of agricultural products; number of animals slaughtered; number of days of working input by various categories of agricultural workers.

2431 MAATALOUSTILASTOLLINEN KUUKAUSIKATSAUS
Maataloushallituksen Tilastotoimisto

SF—Suomalainen monthly

Monthly bulletin of agricultural statistics, published by the State Office of the Board of Agriculture.

2432 MARKETING IN FINLAND
US Department of Commerce

SF—English 1975 24pp

Overseas Business Report no. OBR 75-04. Contents: foreign trade outlook; Finland market profile; industry trends; distribution and sales channels; government procurement; advertising and research; credit; trade representation; investment in Finland; guidance for businessmen abroad.

2433 METAL INDUSTRIES YEARBOOK
Association of Finnish Metal and Engineering Industries

SF—Suomalainen/English annual

Report on the metal and engineering industries including data on: gross value of production and value added in the main Finnish industries; labour and imports and exports of metal and engineering products.

2434 MISTÄ MITÄKIN SAA—SININEN KIRJA TUOTEHAKEMISTO
Sininen Kirja Oy

SF— Suomalainen(English index and headings) c550pp

Who supplies what in Finland. Classified listing of manufacturers giving details of: address, telephone numbers, trade description in Finnish. Separate products index.

2435 OECD ECONOMIC SURVEYS: FINLAND
Organisation for Economic Co-operation and Development

SF—English/Français 1976 60pp

Regular survey of the Finnish economy, covering recent developments in demand, output, employment, prices and incomes, money, the capital market, the balance of payments.

2436 QUARTERLY ECONOMIC REVIEW—FINLAND
Economist Intelligence Unit

SF—English quarterly with annual supplement c20pp

Analysis of current economic trends including: government; population; employment; currency; national accounts; agriculture; industry; fuel and power; transport and communications; tourism; finance; foreign trade payments and agreements.

2437 THE SCANDINAVIAN MARKET
Nord-Finanz-Bank

SF—English annual

Annual survey of Finland and the other Nordic markets for the businessman.

2438 SININEN KIRJA: SUOMEN TALOUSELAMAN HAKEMISTO
Sininen Kirja Oy

SF—Suomalainen(English index) c1500pp

The blue book: economic directory of Finland. Contents: businesses A-Z under towns arranged in economic regions. Details are given of company address, date established, directors, capital, number of employees, turnover. Separate indexes of firms A-Z and classified by products.

2439 SPOTLIGHT ON OVERSEAS TRADE—SELLING TO FINLAND
Midland Bank

SF—English July 1974 22pp

Contents: economic situation; the Finnish market; export opportunities; approaching the market; import regulations; setting up in Finland; statistics of UK exports to Finland.

2440 SUOMEN PANKIT JA OSAKEYHTIÖT
Kustannus Oy Liiketieto

SF—Suomalainen/Svensk c1800pp

Finnish banks and companies; lists banks, insurance companies and industrial companies in A-Z order with details of: address, date established, directors, activities, capital, financial statistics, number of employees. Separate listing of important associations A-Z with detailed information.

2441 SUOMEN TIETEELLISTEN KIRJASTOJEN OPAS
Suomen Tieteellisten Kirjastojen Lautakunta

SF—Suomalainen c150pp

Guide to research libraries in Finland. Lists libraries, classified by subject specialisations with details of address, telephone numbers, hours, services, publications. Also includes separate A-Z index of libraries.

2442 SUOMEN TILASTOLLINEN VUOSIKIRJA
Tilastollinen Päätoimisto

SF—Suomalainen/Svensk(English headings) annual c500pp

Statistical yearbook of Finland; contents: area and climate; geography; agriculture; fishing; forestry; industry; buildings; dwellings; external and internal trade; banking and credit; insurance; transport and communications; state finance; income and property; consumption and prices; wages and salaries; health and medical care; justice and crime; elections; international statistics.

2443 SUOMEN VIRALLISEN TILASTON LUETTELO 1971
Tilastollinen Päätoimisto

SF—Suomalainen/English/Français 1972 33pp

List of official statistics of Finland 1971. Reprint from the Statistical Yearbook of Finland.

2444 SURVEY FINLAND
Investors Chronicle

SF—English 29 August 1975 10pp

Article reviewing the current economic situation including—imports and exports, credit restrictions, shipbuilding.

2445 SUUNTA JA SUHDANNE, KUVIOITA JA TAULUKOITA TALOUDELLISISTA AIKASARJOISTA
Suomen Pankki Taloustieteellinen Tutkimuslaitos

SF—Suomalainen/English quarterly

Economic indicators and charts covering the money market; state finances; wages and prices; production; employment; forestry; agriculture; internal trade; house construction; foreign trade.

2446 TEOLLISUUSTILASTO
Tilastollinen Päätoimisto

SF—Suomalainen/English/Svensk annual 2 vols

Industrial statistics. Vol. 1: census of production with data on: industrial activity by regions and by communes; activity in major groups of industry; number of establishments and personnel; gross value of production; wages, salaries and hours worked; fixed capital; power; fuel consumed; value and costs of production. Vol. 2: detailed information of production and consumed raw materials by kinds of commodity manufactured.

2447 TILASTOKATSAUKSIA
Tilastollinen Päätoimisto

SF—Suomalainen/Svensk/English monthly

Bulletin of statistics; covers: population; migration; production; commerce; banking; credit and finance; prices and wages; labour market; other economic statistics; state finance; crime; health. Also lists recent statistical publications.

2448 TILASTOTIE DOTUS: KANSANTALOUDEN TILINPITO
Tilastollinen Päätoimisto

SF—Suomalainen/English/Svensk annual c60pp

Statistical review of national finances including data on: GNP; GDP; gross domestic capital formations; government and private financial transactions; distribution of national income; private consumption expenditure; wages and salaries by industrial sectors.

2449 ULKOMAANKAUPPA KUUKAUSIJULKAISU: UTRIKESHANDEL MÅNADSPUBLIKATION
Tullihallituksen Tilastotoimisto

SF—Suomalainen/Svensk(English headings) monthly

Foreign trade monthly bulletin showing exports and imports by BTN and SITC commodity classifications.

2450 ULKOMAANKAUPPA VUOSIJULKAISU: UTRIKESHANDEL ARSPUBLIKATION
Tullihallituksen Tilastotoimisto

SF—Suomalainen/Svensk(English headings) annual 2 vols

Foreign trade. Vol. 1: detailed tables of imports and exports classified by commodities (BTN) subdivided by countries of origin and consumption. Vol. 2: annual report of the Customs Department with tables showing breakdown of imports and exports by SITC.

2451 UNITAS: ECONOMIC REVIEW OF FINLAND
Pohjoismaiden Yhdyspankki

SF—Suomalainen/Svensk/Deutsch/English quarterly

Quarterly economic review issued by a commercial bank covering the economic situation in Finland. Includes statistical tables of: national income; production; indices of consumer prices; cost of living; cost of building; wholesale prices.

2452 YLEINEN VAESTOLASKENTA
Tilastollinen Päätoimisto

SF—Suomalainen/Svensk/English 13 vols 1962-65

General census of population in 13 volumes. Vol. 1: Housing. Vol. 2: Population by age, marital status, main languages. Vol. 3: Economically active population by industry and industrial status. Vol. 4: Population by industry and industrial status. Vol. 5: Families. Vol. 6: Population by socio-economic status; location of working places. Vol. 7: Households and housing conditions. Vol. 8: Population by birthplace and by education; displaced population. Vol. 9: Occupation and vocational training. Vol. 10: Buildings.

Vol. 11: Non-administrative urban settlements and their boundaries. Vol. 12: Supplementary volume. Vol. 13: List of tables.

PART TWO

THE PUBLISHING BODIES

THE PUBLISHING BODIES

INT – INTERNATIONAL

AGRA EUROPE (LONDON) LTD
16 Longdale Gardens
Tunbridge Wells
Kent TN1 1PD
England
Tel: Tunbridge Wells (0892) 33813
Telex: 95114

Entry: 005

ASSOCIAZIONE NAZIONALE DELL' INDUSTRIA CHIMICA
Via Fatebene Fratelli 10
20121 Milano
Italy
Tel: 66 62 02

Entry: 041

AXEL SPRINGER VERLAG
ZENTRALE ANZEIGEN MARKETING
Kaiser - Wilhelm Strasse 6
2000 Hamburg 36
West Germany
Tel: 3 47 - 1
Telex: 212621

Entries: 021 025 176

G G BAKER AND ASSOCIATES
54 Quarry Street
Guildford
Surrey GU1 3UA
England
Tel: 048 68 6653

Entry: 037

BANCO DI ROMA
Via de Corso 307
Roma
Italy
Available in UK through:
BANCO DI ROMA
14-18 Eastcheap
London EC3M 1JY
Tel: 01 623 1681
Telex: 888074

Entry: 073

BARCLAYS BANK LTD
54 Lombard Street
London EC3P 3AH
England
Tel: 01 627 1567
Telex: 884970

Entry: 036

BENN BROTHERS LTD
Directories Department
Sovereign Way
Tonbridge
Kent TN9 1RW
England
Tel: Tonbridge (0732) 364422
Telex: 27844

Entries: 034 095 103 105 152 200 205 236

BOWKER PUBLISHING CO LTD
Erasmus House
Epping
Essex CM16 4BU
England
Tel: Epping (0378) 77333
Telex: 81410

Entries: 233 269

BRITISH INSTITUTE OF MANAGEMENT
Management House
32 Parker Street
London WC2B 5PT
England
Tel: 01 405 3456

Entries: 109 110 111 112

BRITISH OVERSEAS TRADE BOARD
50 Ludgate Hill
London EC4M 7HU
England
Tel: 01 248 5757
Telex: 886143

Entry: 147 Publication available through HMSO

THE BRITISH PETROLEUM CO LTD
Britannic House
Moor Lane
London EC2Y 9BU
England
Tel: 01 920 8000
Telex: 27971

Entry: 027

BRITISH STEEL CORPORATION
Statistical Services
12 Addiscombe Road
Croydon
Surrey CR9 3JH
England
Tel: 01 686 9050 ext 494
Telex: 946372

Entries: 153 243

**BUILDING MANAGEMENT AND MARKETING
CONSULTANTS LTD**
Waldorf House
18 Exeter Street
London WC2E 7DU
England
Tel: 01 836 9484

Entry: 170

BUSINESS INTERNATIONAL SA
Chemin Rieu 12-14
1208 Genève
Switzerland
Tel: 47 53 55
Telex: 22669

Entry: 237

CALLUND AND COMPANY
46 St. James's Place
London SW1A 1NS
England
Tel: 01 493 7971

Entry: 070

CBD RESEARCH
154 High Street
Beckenham
Kent BR3 1EA
England
Tel: 01 650 7745

Entries: 049 086 247

COMMONWEALTH SECRETARIAT
Marlborough House
Pall Mall
London SW1Y 5HX
England
Tel: 01 839 3411
Telex: 27678

Entries: 124 125 131 132 138 177 197 228 272

CONFEDERATION OF BRITISH INDUSTRY
21 Tothill Street
London SW1H 9LP
England
Tel: 01 930 6711
Telex: 21332

Entries: 256 277

**THE COVENTRY AND DISTRICT ENGINEERING
EMPLOYERS' ASSOCIATION**
18 Davenport Road
Coventry
Warwickshire CV5 6PX
England
Tel: Coventry (0203) 74333

Entry: 163

D A F S A
125 Rue Montmartre
75081 Paris
Cedex 02
France
Tel: 236 43 86
Telex: 220963

Entry: 028

DEPARTMENT OF TRADE & INDUSTRY
    1 Victoria Street
    London SW1H 0ET
    England
    Tel: 01 215 7877
    Telex: 25955

Entry: 064
Publication available through HMSO

DIRECTION GENERALE DE L'AGRICULTURE
    Direction Economie et Structure Agricole
    30 Rue Joseph II
    1040 Bruxelles
    Belgium

Entry: 168

DUN & BRADSTREET LTD
    26 Clifton Street
    London EC2P 2LY
    England
    Tel: 01 247 4377

Entry: 078

ECONOMIC COMMISSION FOR EUROPE
    Palais des Nations
    1211 Genève 10
    Switzerland
    Tel: 34 60 11
    Telex: 289 696

**Entries: 009 010 020 032 058 061 062 172
        208 227**
Publications available in the UK through HMSO

ECONOMIST INTELLIGENCE UNIT LTD
    27 St. James's Place
    London SW1A 1NT
    England
    Tel: 01 493 6711
    Telex: 266353

**Entries: 047 066 067 068 080 102 145 154
        156 164 173 184 199 206 211 218
        229 231 253 280 295**

ECONTEL RESEARCH LTD
    c/o World Economics Ltd
    10 Charles II Street
    London SW1Y 4AA
    England
    Tel: 01 839 1921

Entry: 281 290 291

EMPLOYMENT CONDITIONS ABROAD LTD
    Devonshire House
    13 Devonshire Street
    London W1N 1FS
    England
    Tel: 01 637 7604

Entry: 297

EUROMONITOR PUBLICATIONS LTD
    PO Box 67
    London SW1Y 5DY
    England
    Tel: 01 930 1445

Entries: 045 096 151

EUROPA PUBLICATIONS LTD
    18 Bedford Square
    London WC1B 3JN
    England
    Tel: 01 580 8236

Entry: 074

EUROPEAN COMMUNITIES COMMISSION
    Official Publications Office
    Rue du Commerce
    PO Box 1003
    Luxembourg
    Tel: 49 01 91
    Telex: 2731 PUBLOF LU

**Entries: 050 075 127 128 133 141 158 159 160
        221 222 223 224 249 254 255 266**

**EUROPEAN COMMUNITIES INFORMATION
SERVICE**
    20 Kensington Palace Gardens
    London W8 4QQ
    England
    Tel: 01 727 8090
    Telex: 23208

Entry: 085

EUROPEAN DATA AND RESEARCH LTD
    Eurodatex Division
    77 George Street
    London W1H 5PL
    England
    Tel: 01 486 7621

Entry: 079

EUROPEAN FREE TRADE ASSOCIATION
9-11 Rue de Varembé
1211 Genève 20
Switzerland
Tel: 34 90 00
Telex: 22660 EFTA CH

Entries: 017 065 213 261 271
Publications available in UK through:
Gothard House Publications Ltd
Gothard House
Henley on Thames
Oxon RG9 1AJ
England
Tel: Henley (049 12) 3602

EUROPEAN INTELLIGENCE LTD
Agroup House
16 Lonsdale Gardens
Tunbridge Wells
England
Tel: Tunbridge Wells (0892) 33811
Telex: 95114

Entry: 094

EUROPOTENTIALS AND PLANNING LTD
29 Old Bond Street
London W1X 3AB
England
Tel: 01 637 4920

Entry: 175

EXTEL STATISTICAL SERVICES LTD
37/45 Paul Street
London EC2A 4PB
England
Tel: 01 253 3400
Telex: 23721

Entry: 107

FEARNLEY AND EGERS CHARTERING CO LTD
Rådhusgt 23
PO Box 355
Oslo 1
Norway
Tel: 41 70 00
Telex: 16666

Entry: 225

FRANK FEHR & CO LTD
Prince Rupert House
64 Queen Street
London EC4R 1ER
England
Tel: 01 248 5066
Telex: 883074

Entry- 018

THE FINANCIAL TIMES LTD
10 Bolt Court
London EC4A 3HL
England
Tel: 01 836 5444
Telex: 27368

**Entries: 003 004 024 029 040 072 076 115 116
117 118 119 186 201 210 230 273 274
275 276 296**

FOOD AND AGRICULTURAL ORGANIZATION
Viale delle Terme di Caracalla
Roma
Italy
Tel: 5797

**Entries: 006 007 051 182 209 212 241 259 264
285 287**
Publications available in UK through HMSO

FURNITURE INDUSTRY RESEARCH ASSOCIATION
Maxwell Road
Stevenage
Hertfordshire SG1 2EW
England
Tel: Stevenage (0438) 3433

Entry: 060

GARNSTONE PRESS LTD
59 Brompton Road
London SW3 1DS
England
Tel: 01 584 0911

Entry: 260

GOWER PRESS, TEAKFIELD LTD
1 Westmead
Farnborough
Hampshire GU14 7RU
England
Tel: Farnborough (0252) 41196
Telex: 858193

**Entries: 002 033 039 054 071 083 088 089 090
092 100 104 137 140 150 238 263 286**

GRAHAM & TROTMAN LTD
Bond Street House
14 Clifford Street
London W1X 1RD
England
Tel: 01 493 6351

Entries: 057 081 091 202 203 239

HMSO
The Government Bookshop
PO Box 569
London SE1 9NH
England
Tel: 01 928 6977
Telex: 266455

Entries: 126 244

FRANCIS HODGSON
FH Books Ltd
PO Box 74
Guernsey
C I
Tel: Guernsey 24332

Entry: 055

INSTITUT INTERNATIONAL DE STATISTIQUE
2 Oostduinlaan
Den Haag
The Netherlands

Entry: 012

INSTITUTE OF PETROLEUM
61 New Cavendish Street
London W1M 8AR
England
Tel: 01 636 1004
Telex: 264 380

Entry: 195

INSTITUTE OF PRACTITIONERS IN ADVERTISING
44 Belgrave Square
London SW1X 8QZ
England
Tel 01 235 7020
Telex 918352

Entries: 139 144 174

INSTITUTE OF PUBLIC ADMINISTRATION
59 Lansdowne Road
Dublin
Ireland
Tel: 68 62 33

Entry: 084

INTERNATIONAL AIR TRANSPORT ASSOCIATION
1000 Sherbrooke St West
Montreal
Quebec H3A 2R4
Canada
Tel: 844 86311
Telex: CNP 5267627

Entry: 282

INTERNATIONAL CIVIL AVIATION ORGANIZATION
International Aviation Building
1000 Sherbrooke West
Montreal
Quebec
Canada
Tel: 285 8219
Telex: CNP 524513

Entry: 011

INTERNATIONAL COTTON ADVISORY COMMITTEE
South Agriculture Building
Indep Av 12th/14th SW
Washington DC 20250
USA
Tel: RE7 4142

Entry: 048

INTERNATIONAL MONETARY FUND
19th and H Streets NW
Washington DC 20431
USA
Tel: EX3 - 6362
Telex: WU1 64111

Entries: 022 053 149

INTERNATIONALE SELBSTBEDIENUNGS-ORGANISATION
Burgmaner 53
5 Köln 1
West Germany

Entry: 234

INTERNATIONAL SUGAR ORGANIZATION
28 Haymarket
London SW1Y 4SP
England
Tel: 01 930 4038

Entries: 242 251

INTERNATIONAL TEA COMMITTEE
    Sir John Lyon House
    Upper Thames Street
    London EC4V 3NH
    England
    Tel: 01 248 4672

Entry: 015

INTERNATIONAL TRADE CENTRE
    Villa le Bocage
    Palais des Nations
    Genève
    Switzerland
    Tel: 33 10 01

Entry: 129

**INTERNATIONAL UNION OF OFFICIAL TRAVEL
ORGANISATIONS**
    Rue de Varembé 1
    Genève
    Switzerland
    Tel: 34 14 80

Entry: 157

INTERNATIONAL WHEAT COUNCIL
    Haymarket House
    Haymarket
    London SW1Y 4SS
    England
    Tel: 01 930 4128
    Telex: 916128

Entries: 267 268

**INTERNATIONALER VERBAND DES
GEWERBSGARTENBAUES**
    Stadhoudersplantsoen 12-18
    Postbus 361
    Den Haag
    The Netherlands

Entry: 250

IPC BUSINESS PRESS LTD
    40 Bowling Green Lane
    London EC1R 0NE
    England
    Tel: 01 837 3636
    Telex: 23839

Entries: 026 035 038 082 099 187 219

**ISTITUTO PER LE RICERCHE E LE INFORMAZIONI
DI MERCATO E LA VALORIZZAZIONE DELLA
PRODUZIONE AGRICOLA**
    43 Via Castelfidardo
    Roma
    Italy
    Tel: 48 20 41

Entry: 179

JOHN I JACOBS & CO LTD
    Winchester House
    77 London Wall
    London EC2N 1BX
    England
    Tel: 01 588 1255
    Telex: 888081

Entry: 298

JANE'S YEARBOOKS
    Paulton House
    8 Shepherdess Walk
    London N1 7LW
    England
    Tel: 01 437 0686

Entry: 161

KOGAN PAGE LTD
    116a Pentonville Road
    London N1 9JN
    England
    Tel: 01 837 7851

Entries: 043 044 098 135 189 190 196

LLOYD'S REGISTER OF SHIPPING
    71 Fenchurch Street
    London EC3M 4BS
    England
    Tel: 01 709 9166
    Telex: 24305

Entry: 019

McGRAW-HILL
    Book Orders
    Princetown Road
    Highstown
    NJ
    USA
    Tel: 609 448-1700

Entry: 283

MACKINTOSH CONSULTANTS CO LTD
33 Bruton Street
London W1X 7DD
England
Tel: 01 499 0605

Entry: 165

MARKET RESEARCH SOCIETY
39 Hertford Street
London W1Y 7TG
Tel: 01 499 1913

Entry: 146

METAL BULLETIN LTD
46 Wigmore Street
London W1H 0BJ
England
Tel: 01 486 4141

Entry: 180

MIDLAND BANK LTD
Poultry
London EC2P 2BX
England
Tel: 01 606 9911
Telex: 8811822

Entries: 113 240

MIELKE & CO
21 Hamburg 90
PO Box 153
West Germany
Tel: 7 60 20 81

Entry: 194

MINISTRY OF AGRICULTURE AND FISHERIES OF THE NETHERLANDS
Eerste v d Boschstr 4
Den Haag
The Netherlands

Entry: 232

MOTOR VEHICLE MANUFACTURERS ASSOCIATION OF THE UNITED STATES
320 New Center Building
Detroit
Michigan 48202
USA
Tel: 873 4311

Entry: 293

NATIONAL BUILDING AGENCY
NBA House
7 Arundel Street
London WC2R 3DZ
England
Tel: 01 836 4488

Entries: 030 136

NATIONAL ECONOMIC DEVELOPMENT OFFICE
Millbank Tower
Millbank
London SW1P 4QX
England
Tel: 01 211 3000

Entry: 069

NOYES DATA CORPORATION
Noyes Building
Mill Road at Grand Avenue
Park Ridge
New Jersey 07656
USA
Tel: 201 391 8484

Entry: 093

A S ØKONOMISK LITERATUR
Ebbellsgt 3
Oslo 1
Norway

Entry: 087
Available in UK from:
CAMBRIDGE INFORMATION & RESEARCH SERVICES LTD
8 Market Passage
Cambridge CB2 3PF

ORGANIZATION FOR ECONOMIC AND DEVELOPMENT PUBLISHING OFFICE
2 Rue André Pascal
Paris 16
France
Tel: 524 8200
Telex: 620160

Entries: 008 046 059 063 114 120 121 122
155 162 166 167 169 178 181 188
191 193 198 214 215 220 226 248
257 270
Publications available in UK through HMSO

PAN AMERICAN COFFEE BUREAU
    1350 6th Ave
    New York
    NY
    USA
    Tel: 489 8050
    Telex: ITT 421871

Entry: 016

POLITICAL AND ECONOMIC PLANNING/ROYAL INSTITUTE OF INTERNATIONAL AFFAIRS

POLITICAL AND ECONOMIC PLANNING
    12 Upper Belgrave Street
    London SW1X 8BB
    England
    Tel: 01 235 5271
ROYAL INSTITUTE OF INTERNATIONAL AFFAIRS
    Chatham House
    10 St James's Square
    London SW1Y 4LE
    England
    Tel: 01 930 2233

Entries: 101 108 123 143 262 265

READER'S DIGEST ASSOCIATION LTD
    25 Berkeley Square
    London W1X 6AB
    England
    Tel: 01 629 8144
    Telex: 264631

Entry: 252

SHELL BRIEFING SERVICE
    Royal Dutch Shell Group
    Shell Centre
    London SE1 7NA
    England
    Tel: 01 934 1234 Ext 4918
    Telex: 919651

Entry: 192

SIRA INSTITUTE
    South Hill
    Chislehurst
    Kent
    England
    Tel: 01 467 2636
    Telex: 896649

Entries: 097 278

THOMAS SKINNER DIRECTORIES
    Stuart House
    41/43 Perrymount Road
    Haywards Heath
    West Sussex RH16 3BS
    Tel: Haywards Heath (0444) 59188

Entries: 023 279

SOCIETE BELGE D'ECONOMIE ET MATHEMATIQUE APPLIQUEES SA
    207 Boulevard du Souverain
    Bruxelles 16
    Belgium

Entry: 142

STATISTISCHES BUNDESAMT
    Gustav - Stresemann - Ring 11
    Postschliessfach 828
    Wiesbaden
    West Germany
    Telex: 4186511

Entry: 207

SWEET & MAXWELL LTD
    116 Chancery Lane
    London WC2A 1PP
    England
    Tel: 01 405 5711

Entry: 134

TEXTILE ECONOMICS BUREAU INC
    489 5th Ave
    New York
    NY 10016
    USA
    Tel: 661 5166

Entry: 258

THETA TECHNOLOGY CORPORATION
    Peer Building
    530 Silas Desne Highway
    Wethersfield
    Conn 06109
    USA

Entry: 300

THE TIMES
Marketing Department
New Printing House Square
Grays Inn Road
London WC1N 2JD
England
Tel: 01 837 1234
Telex: 264971

Entry: 077

UNITED NATIONS CONFERENCE ON TRADE AND DEVELOPMENT
Palais des Nations
Av de la Paix 8-14
1211 Genève 10
Switzerland
Tel: 34 60 11

Entry: 235

UNITED NATIONS EDUCATIONAL SCIENTIFIC AND CULTURAL ORGANIZATION
9 Pl de Fontenoy
75007 Paris
France
Tel: 566 57 57

Entry: 246
Publication available in UK through HMSO

UNITED NATIONS PUBLICATIONS
Palais des Nations
Av de la Paix 8-14
1211 Geneve 10
Switzerland
Tel: 34 60 11

Entries: 013 014 042 052 056 183 185 204 216
           217 245 288 289 301 302 303

UNIVERSITY OF SUSSEX
Science Policy Research Unit
Lewes Road
Falmer
Brighton
Sussex BN1 9QT
England
Tel: Brighton 686758
Telex: 877191

Entry: 292

URWICK ORR & PARTNERS LTD
50 Doughty Street
London WC1N 2LS
England
Tel: 01 405 4683

Entry: 106

US BUREAU OF INTERNATIONAL COMMERCE
14th E/Constitution Ave NW
Washington DC
USA
Tel: ST 3-9200
Telex: RCA 248475

Entry: 294

US DEPARTMENT OF COMMERCE
14th E/ Constitution Ave NW
Washington DC
USA
Tel: ST 3-9200
Telex: RCA 248475

Entries: 148 171 299

VERLAG MODERNE INDUSTRIE AG
Dorlistrasse 73
8050 Zurich
Switzerland
Tel: 468140
Telex: 57547

Entry: 130
Available in the UK from
CAMBRIDGE INFORMATION AND RESEARCH SERVICES LTD
8 Market Passage
Cambridge
CB2 3PF

WOODHEAD FAULKNER (PUBLISHERS) LTD
8 Market Passage
Cambridge CB2 3PF
England
Tel: Cambridge (0223) 51472

Entry: 001

WORLD BANK GROUP
1818 H
Washington DC
USA
Tel: EX 3-6360

Entry: 284

A – AUSTRIA

AUSTRIA TODAY LTD
Neue Hofburg
Heldenplatz
PO Box 47
Wien A-1014
Tel: 57 21 84

Entry: 403

AUSTRIAN TRADE DELEGATION
1 Hyde Park Gate
London SW7 5ER
England
Tel: 01 584 6938
Telex: 25668

Entry: 407

BRITISH HOSIERY AND KNITWEAR EXPORT GROUP
Now: **BRITISH KNITTING EXPORT COUNCIL**
Academy House
26 Sackville Street
London W1X 1DA
England
Tel: 01 734 6277

Entry: 451

BRITISH OVERSEAS TRADE BOARD
1 Victoria Street
London SW1H 0ET
England
Tel: 01 215 7877
Telex: 27366

Entry: 429

BUNDESMINISTERIUM FÜR HANDEL, GEWERBE UND INDUSTRIE
Stubenring 1
1010 Wien
Tel: 57 56 55
Telex: 11145

Entry: 433

BUNDESMINISTERIUM FÜR LAND-FORSTWIRTSCHAFT
Stubenring 1
1010 Wien
Telex: 11780

Entry: 412

BUNDESMINISTERIUM FÜR VERKEHR UND VERSTAATLICHTE UNTERNEHMUNGEN
Elisabethstrasse 9
1010 Wien
Tel: 57 56 41
Telex: 11800

Entry: 411

COMPASS-VERLAG
Wipplingerstrasse 32
1013 Wien
Tel: 63 66 16

Entries: 418 425 432 447

CREDITANSTALT-BANKVEREIN
Schottengasse 6
1010 Wien
Tel: 63 69 0
Telex: 74793

Entries: 408 414 446

DRUCK UND VERLAG DER ÖSTERREICHISCHEN STAATSDRUCKEREI
Rennweg 12a
1030 Wien

Entry: 444

ECONOMIST INTELLIGENCE UNIT
Spencer House
27 St. James's Place
London SW1A 1NT
England
Tel: 01 493 6711
Telex: 266353

Entry: 450

FACHVERBAND DER TEXTILINDUSTRIE ÖSTERREICHS
13 Bauermarkt
Wien 1
Tel: 63 57 63 0

Entry: 443

FEDERAL PRESS SERVICE
Ballhausplatz 2
A-1014 Wien

Entry: 401

THE FINANCIAL TIMES LTD
  10 Bolt Court
  London EC4A 3HL
  England
  Tel: 01 836 5444
  Telex: 27368

Entries: 402 404 405 406 461

GIROZENTRALE UND BANK DER ÖSTERREICHISCHEN SPARKASSEN AG
  Schubertring 5-7
  Postfach 255
  1010 Wien
  Tel: 72 94 0
  Telex: 12591

Entry: 434

GOF-VERLAG GUSTAV O FRIEDL
  Stoss-im-Himmel 3
  Wien
  Tel: 63 86 19

Entry: 421

HEROLD VEREINIGTE ANZEIGENGES. GmbH
  Wipplingerstrasse 14
  1010 Wien
  Tel: 63 26 26

Entries: 427 428

INTERCONTINENTAL BOOK AND PUBLISHING CO
  5708 Jeanne Mance
  Montreal 8
  Canada

Entry: 463

JUPITER VERLAGSGES. GmbH
  Robertgasse 2
  1020 Wien
  Tel: 24 22 94

Entry: 426

KAMMER FÜR ARBEITER UND ANGESTELLTE IN WIEN
  4 Prinz Eugenstrasse 20-22
  Wien
  Tel: 65 37 65
  Telex: 11690

Entry: 465

LLOYDS BANK LIMITED
  Overseas Department
  Export Promotion Section
  6 Eastcheap
  London EC3P 3AB
  England
  Tel: 01 283 1000
  Telex: 888301

Entry: 415

ORGANISATION FOR ECONOMIC CO-OPERATION AND DEVELOPMENT
  Publications Office
  2 Rue André Pascal
  Paris 16
  France
  Tel: 524 8200
  Telex: 62160

Entries: 431 441 448

ÖSTERREICHISCHE LÄNDERBANK
  Am Hof 2
  Wien A-1010
  Tel: 63 16 31
  Telex: 75561

Entries: 436 453

ÖSTERREICHISCHE NATIONALBANK
  Otto Wagner-Platz 3
  1090 Wien
  Tel: 43 600
  Telex: 74669

Entry: 442

ÖSTERREICHISCHE NATIONALBIBLIOTHEKEN
  Josefsplatz 1
  Wien
  Tel: 52 16 84
  Telex: 12624

Entry: 424

ÖSTERREICHISCHER BUNDESVERLAG FÜR UNTERRICHT WISSENSCHAFT UND KUNST
  1 Schwarzenbergstr 5
  Wien
  Tel: 52 25 61

Entry: 422

ÖSTERREICHISCHES INSTITUT FÜR WIRTSCHAFTSFORSCHUNG
Postanschrift 1103
Postfach 91
Arsenal
Wien 3
Tel: 65 66 61 - 0

Entry: 440

ÖSTERREICHISCHES STATISTISCHES ZENTRALAMT
Neue Hofburg
Heldenplatz
1014 Wien
Tel: 524686
Telex: 12600

Entries: 410 416 417 420 430 437 445 449 454
455 456 457 458 459 462 466

SOCIETE GENERALE ALSACIENNE DE BANQUE AG
Allgemeine Elsässische Bank AG
Schwarzenbergplatz 1
1010 Wien
Tel: 75 51 03
Telex: 13766

Entry: 413

US BUREAU OF INTERNATIONAL COMMERCE
Government Printing Office
Washington DC 20402
USA
Tel: 783 3238
Telex: TWX 710 8229274

Entries: 409 419

US DEPARTMENT OF COMMERCE
Government Printing Office
Washington DC 20402
USA
Tel: 783 3238
Telex: TWX 710 8229274

Entries: 438 452

VERBAND ÖSTERREICHISCHER BANKEN UND BANKIERS
Am Hof 4
Wien 1

Entry: 439

VEREINIGUNG DER KOOPERATIVEN FORSCHUNGSINSTITUTE DER GEWERBLICHEN WIRTSCHAFT
Dirmoserstrasse 6
Wien
Tel:. 65 57 05

Entry: 435

VERLAG HEINREICH, VERLAG DR ADOLF HEINREICH
Akademienstrasse 3
1010 Wien
Tel: 52 64 74

Entry: 423

WIENER BÖRSEKAMMER
Wipplingerstrasse 34
A-1011
Wien 1
Tel: 63 37 66
Telex: 74693

Entry: 464

WIRTSCHAFTSFÖRDERUNGSINSTITUTE DER BUNDESHANDELSKAMMER
Hoher Markt 3
Wien
Tel: 63 57 63-0

Entry: 460

ZENTRALVERBAND ÖSTERREICHISCHER AKTIENGESELLSCHAFTEN
Biberstrasse 2
1010 Wien

Entry: 400

B – BELGIUM

ABNEI
7 Rue des Israélites
Anvers
Tel: 37 66 71

Entry: 510

ADMINISTRATION CENTRALE DES CONTRIBUTIONS
Bureau de Vente des Publications
Rue d'Arlon 80
B-1040 Bruxelles
Tel: 512 58 00

Entry: 531

ADMINISTRATION DE L'ENERGIE
Ministère des Affaires Economiques
Rue J A de Mot 26
Bruxelles B4
Tel: 230 00 20

Entries: 580 599 600

ANNUAIRE GENERAL DE LA BELGIQUE
62 Rue de La Caserne
Bruxelles 1
Tel: 11 64 49

Entry: 503

L'ASSOCIATION NATIONALE DES TISSEURS DE LIN
Casinoplein 10
Kortrijk

Entry: 582

BANQUE DE BRUXELLES
Rue de la Régence 2
B-1000 Bruxelles
Tel: 513 62 50
Telex: 21421

Entries: 519 523 527

BANQUE NATIONALE DE BELGIQUE
5 Bd de Berlaimont
B-1000 Bruxelles
Tel: 219 46 10
Telex: 21516

Entries: 511 532

BARCLAYS BANK
Group Economic Intelligence Unit
54 Lombard Street
London EC3 3AH
England
Tel: 01 283 8989
Telex: 887591

Entry: 512

BELGIAN CHAMBER OF COMMERCE
Rue de Trèves 112
B-1040 Bruxelles
Tel: 12 01 47

Entry: 566

BELGIAN CHAMBER OF COMMERCE
6 Belgrave Square
London SW1X 8PH
England
Tel: 01 235 3255

Entries: 575 618

THE BOURSE
Palais de la Bourse
Place de la Bourse
Bruxelles
Tel: 511 26 44

Entry: 525

BOURSE INDUSTRIELLE DE BELGIQUE
10 Rue de la Presse
Bruxelles 1
Tel: 217 13 14

Entry: 522

BRITISH CHAMBER OF COMMERCE
30 Rue Joseph II
Bruxelles 4
Tel: 219 07 88

Entry: 524

BRITISH OVERSEAS TRADE BOARD
1 Victoria Street
London SW1H 0ET
England
Tel: 01 215 7877
Telex: 27366

Entry: 558

CENTRAL ADMINISTRATION OF THE TVA
Tour Madou
1 Place Madou
B-1030 Bruxelles

Entry: 593

CENTRE DE RECHERCHES ECONOMIQUES SOCIALES
ET POLITIQUES
   Katholieke Universiteit
   B-3000 Leuven

Entry   589

CENTRE NATIONAL DE DOCUMENTATION
SCIENTIFIQUE ET TECHNIQUE
   4 Boulevard de l'Empereur
   B-1000 Bruxelles

Entry: 564

CHAMBRE DE COMMERCE DE BRUXELLES
   112 Rue de Trèves
   Bruxelles 4
   Tel: 511 46 28
   Telex: 22082

Entry: 538

CHAMBRE D'INDUSTRIE D'ANVERS
   9-12 h Markgravestr 12
   Anvers 1
   Tel: 32 22 19

Entry: 539

CHAMBRE SYNDICATE DU COMMERCE AUTOMOBILE
DE BELGIQUE
   Bd de la Woluwe 46
   Bruxelles 20
   Tel: 771 00 80

Entry: 552

COMMERCE CLEARING HOUSE INC
   5 Charterhouse Buildings
   London EC1M 7AN
   England
   Tel: 01 253 8815

Entry: 542

CONSEIL CENTRAL DE L'ECONOMIE
   17-21 Avenue de la Joyeuse Entrée
   Bruxelles 4

Entry: 576

DEPARTMENT D'ECONOMIE APPLIQUEE DE
L'UNIVERSITE LIBRE DE BRUXELLES
   Rue de Chatelain 49
   B-1050 Bruxelles
   Tel: 49 91 65

Entry: 537

DIRECTION GENERALE DES ETUDES ET DE LA
DOCUMENTATION
   Rue de l'Industrie 6
   4e Etage
   B-1040 Bruxelles

Entry: 578

ECONOMIST INTELLIGENCE UNIT
   Spencer House
   27 St. James's Place
   London SW1A 1NT
   England
   Tel: 01 493 6711
   Telex: 266353

Entry: 581

EDITIONS MERTENS & ROZEZ
   14 Boulevard de l'Empereur
   Bruxelles 1
   Tel: 11 80 26

Entry: 502

ETS EMILE BRUYLANT
   67 Rue de la Regence
   Bruxelles 1
   Tel: 12 98 45

Entries: 501 589

ETUDES FINANCIERES ET ECONOMIQUES
   Rue de la Loi 28
   1040 Bruxelles
   Tel: 511 54 81

Entry: 555

EUROPEAN COMMUNITIES COMMISSION
   Official Publications Office
   Rue du Commerce
   PO Box 1003
   Luxembourg
   Tel: 49 01 91
   Telex: 2731 PUBLOF LU

Entry: 545

FEDERATION BELGE DES INDUSTRIES DE L'AUTOMOBILE ET DU CYCLE
22 Rue du Luxembourg
Bruxelles

Entry: 601

FEDERATION DE L'INDUSTRIE DU GAZ
4 Av Palmerston
Bruxelles
Tel: 733 82 32

Entry: 507

FEDERATION DES INDUSTRIES BELGES
Rue Ravenstein 4
B-1000 Bruxelles
Tel: 11 58 80

Entries: 514 528 560 562 584

FEDERATION DES INDUSTRIES CHIMIQUES DE BELGIQUE
49 Square Marie-Louise
1040 Bruxelles
Tel: 735 40 80
Telex: 23167

Entry: 553

FEDERATION NATIONALE DES CHAMBRES DE COMMERCE
40 Rue du Congrès
Bruxelles 1
Tel: 217 36 71

Entry: 554

FEDERATION PROFESSIONELLE DE PRODUCTEURS ET DISTRIBUTEURS D'ELECTRICITE DE BELGIQUE
Rue Belliard 31
1040 Bruxelles
Tel: 12 99 46

Entry: 505

THE FINANCIAL TIMES LTD
10 Bolt Court
London EC4A 3HL
England
Tel: 01 836 5444
Telex: 27368

Entries: 515 518 620

HALLET SPRL
27 Boulevard de la 2e Armée Britannique
Bruxelles 19
Tel: 44 50 14

Entry: 592

INSTITUT BELGE D'INFORMATION ET DE DOCUMENTATION
Rue Montoyer 3
B-1040 Bruxelles
Tel: 511 63 76
Telex: 21716

Entry: 571

INSTITUT NATIONAL DE STATISTIQUE
44 Rue de Louvain
B-1000 Bruxelles
Tel: 513 13 68

Entries: 505 508 530 535 540 543 544 550 585
          587 588 596 597 602 603 604 605 606
          607 608 609 610 611 612 614 615 616

INSTITUTE OF PRACTITIONERS IN ADVERTISING
44 Belgrave Square
London SW1X 8QZ
England
Tel: 01 235 7020
Telex: 918352

Entry: 500

INTERCONTINENTAL BOOK & PUBLISHING CO LTD
5708 Jeanne Mance
Montreal 8
Canada

Entry: 619

KOMPASS BELGIUM SA
Ave Molière 256
B-1060 Bruxelles
Tel: 345 19 83
Telex: 26903

Entry: 567

KREDIETBANK
Rue Arenberg 7
B-1000 Bruxelles
Tel: 513 80 50
Telex: 21123

Entries: 513 516 536 561 617

LASALLE & CIE
3 Rue Carmes
Liège
Tel: 23 66 17

Entry: 504

LLOYDS BANK LTD
Overseas Department
International Trade Promotion Section
6 Eastcheap
London EC3 3AB
Tel: 01 283 1000
Telex: 888301

Entry: 547

MINISTERE DE L'EMPLOI ET DU TRAVAIL
Rue Lambermont 2
B-1000 Bruxelles
Tel: 513 40 90
Telex: 22937

Entry: 594

MINISTERE DES AFFAIRES ECONOMIQUES
Rue de l'Industrie 6
4e Etage
B-1040 Bruxelles
Tel: 12 79 50

Entries: 509 548 565 568 584 591

**MINISTERE DES AFFAIRES ECONOMIQUES
ADMINISTRATION DES MINES**
Rue J A de Mot 24-26
B-1040 Bruxelles
Tel: 35 80 50

Entries: 533 613

**MINISTERE DES AFFAIRES ETRANGERES ET DU
COMMERCE EXTERIEUR**
Rue des Quatre Bras 2
B-1000 Bruxelles
Tel: 513 62 40
Telex: 23979

Entries: 520 574 579

**NETHERLANDS CHAMBER OF COMMERCE FOR
BELGIUM & LUXEMBOURG**
PO Box 4
93 Koningsstraat
1000 Bruxelles
Tel: 219 1174

Entry: 595

OFFICE BELGE DU COMMERCE EXTERIEUR
Bd E Jacqmain 162
Bruxelles
Tel: 219 45 50
Telex: 21502

Entries: 517 541

**OFFICE BELGE POUR L'ACCROISSEMENT DE LA
PRODUCTIVITE**
60 Rue de la Concorde
Bruxelles 5
Tel: 511 81 55

Entry: 546

OFFICE NATIONAL DE L'EMPLOI
Boulevard de l'Empereur 7
B-1000 Bruxelles
Tel: 513 85 60

Entries: 534 570 586 621

**ORGANISATION FOR ECONOMIC CO-OPERATION
AND DEVELOPMENT**
Publications Office
2 Rue André Pascal
Paris 16e
France
Tel: 524 82 00
Telex: 62160

Entry: 577

REVUE DE L'ADMINISTRATION BELGE
64 Avenue de l'Opale
Bruxelles 4
Tel: 33 30 30

Entry: 557

**SERVICE BELGE DES ECHANGES
INTERNATIONAUX**
80 Rue des Tanneurs
Bruxelles 1
Tel: 511 74 63

Entry: 569

SOCIETE GENERALE DE BANQUE
Montagne du Parc 3
B-1000 Bruxelles
Tel: 513 66 00
Telex: 22203

Entries: 529 551 563

STOCK EXCHANGE PRESS COMMITTEE
    Palais de la Bourse
    Place de la Bourse
    Bruxelles
    Tel: 511 26 44

Entry: 526

THE TIMES
    Marketing Department
    New Printing House Square
    Grays Inn Road
    London WC1N 2JD
    England
    Tel: 01 837 1234
    Telex: 264971

Entry: 521

UNION BELGE DES ANNONCEURS
    4 Rue de la Chancellerie
    Bruxelles
    Tel: 513 47 62

Entry: 559

UNIVERSITE LIBRE DE BRUXELLES
    Institut de Sociologie
    Centre d'Economie Politique
    44 Avenue Jeanne
    Bruxelles 5
    Tel: 648 81 58

Entry: 549

US DEPARTMENT OF COMMERCE
    Government Printing Office
    Washington DC 20402
    USA
    Tel: 783 3238
    Telex: TWX 710 8229274

Entries: 556 572

J WALTER THOMPSON CO LTD
    40 Berkeley Square
    London W1X 6AD
    England
    Tel: 01 629 9496
    Telex 22871

Entry: 573

CH – SWITZERLAND

ARTHUR ANDERSEN & CO AG
    Todistrasse 47
    8000 Zurich
    Tel: 02 70 20
    Telex: 53800

Entry: 718

BANQUE NATIONALE SUISSE
    Börsenstrasse 15
    8022 Zürich
    Tel: 23 47 40
    Telex: 52400

Entries: 654 659

BARCLAYS BANK
    Group Economic Intelligence Unit
    54 Lombard Street,
    London EC3 3AH
    England
    Tel: 01 283 8989
    Telex: 887591

Entry: 715

BOURSE DE BALE
    Freie Strasse 3
    CH-4001 Basle
    Tel: 25 11 50
    Telex: 62719

Entries: 656 658

BOURSE DE ZÜRICH
    Bleicherweg 5
    8001 Zürich
    Tel: 27 14 70
    Telex: 57065

Entry: 726

BRITISH HOSIERY AND KNITWEAR EXPORT GROUP
Now: **BRITISH KNITTING EXPORT COUNCIL**
Academy House
26 Sackville Street
London W1X 1DA
England
Tel: 01 734 6277

Entry: 695

BRITISH OVERSEAS TRADE BOARD
1 Victoria Street
London SW1H 0ET
Tel: 01 215 7877
Telex: 27366

Entry: 679

BUNDESKANZLEI
3000 Bern
Tel: 61 11 11

Entry: 702

BUREAU FEDERALE DE STATISTIQUE
Hallwylstrasse 15
CH-3000 Berne
Tel: 61 88 11

**Entries: 651 661 668 669 671 683 684 688 691
693 706 710 711 719 721**

CREDIT SUISSE
Paradeplatz 8
CH 8021 Zürich
Tel: 29 28 11
Telex: 58412

Entry: 712

DEPARTEMENT FEDERAL DE L'ECONOMIE PUBLIQUE
Bundesgasse 8
3003 Berne
Tel: 61 21 11

Entry: 724

DIRECTION GENERALE DES DOUANES
Monbijoustrasse 40
Berne
Tel: 61 61 11

Entries: 704 705 707

ECONOMIST INTELLIGENCE UNIT
Spencer House
27 St James's Place
London SW1A 1NT
England
Tel: 01 493 6711
Telex: 266353

Entry: 689

EDITIONS KOMPASS SUISSE SA
Neuhausstrasse 4
8044 Zürich
Tel: 47 80 00

Entry: 680

EIDGENÖSSISCHES STATISTISCHES AMT
Hallwylstr 15
Berne
Tel: 61 91 11

Entries: 692 694 696 698 722

THE FINANCIAL TIMES LTD
10 Bolt Court
London EC4A 3HL
England
Tel: 01 836 5444
Telex: 27368

Entry: 716

INTERCONTINENTAL BOOK & PUBLISHING CO
5708 Jeanne Mance
Montreal 8
Canada

Entry: 725

INTERNATIONAL CHAMBER OF COMMERCE
38 Cours Albert 1er
75008 Paris
France

Entry: 713

LLOYDS BANK LTD
Overseas Department
International Trade Promotion Section
6 Eastcheap
London EC3 3AB
Tel: 01 283 1000
Telex: 888301

Entry: 665

MOSSE-ANNONCEN AG
    Limmatquai 94
    8023 Zürich
    Tel: 47 34 00
    Telex: 55235

Entries: 650 723

ORELL FÜSSLI VERLAG
    Nüschelerstrasse 22
    8001 Zürich
    Tel: 25 36 36

Entry: 700

**ORGANISATION FOR ECONOMIC
CO-OPERATION AND DEVELOPMENT**
    Publications Office
    2 Rue André Pascal
    Paris 16e
    France
    Tel: 524 8200
    Telex: 62160

Entries: 685 687

**SCHWEIZ. VEREINIGUNG FÜR
DOKUMENTATION**
    Hallwylstrasse ·13
    3003 Bern

Entry: 652

SCHWEIZERISCHER BANKVEREIN
    Aeschenvorstadt 1
    4002 Basle
    Tel: 23 23 23
    Telex: 62773

Entries: 678 699

**SCHWEIZERISCHER HANDELS - UND
INDUSTRIE - VEREIN**
    Börsenstrasse 26
    Postfach 235
    8022 Zürich
    Tel: 23 27 07
    Telex: 58294

Entry: 657

**SWISS OFFICE FOR THE DEVELOPMENT OF
TRADE**
    Dreikönigstrasse 8
    8022 Zürich
    Tel: 25 77 40

Entry: 662

THE TIMES
    Marketing Department
    New Printing House Square
    Grays Inn Road
    London WC1N 2JD
    England
    Tel: 01 837 1234
    Telex: 264971

Entry: 672

UNION DE BANQUES SUISSES
    Bahnhofstrasse 45
    Zürich
    Tel: 29 44 11
    Telex: 57715

**Entries: 653 660 663 664 666 667 673 675
        676 677 686 703 709 714 717 720**

**UNION SUISSE DU COMMERCE ET DE
L'INDUSTRIE**
    Börsenstrasse 26
    8001 Zürich

Entry: 690

US DEPARTMENT OF COMMERCE
    Government Printing Office
    Washington DC 20402
    USA

Entries: 655 670 674 681 682 701

VERLAG SCHWABE & CO
    Steinentorstrasse 13
    4000 Basel
    Tel: 24 58 35

Entry: 696

D - GERMANY

ABC DER DEUTSCHEN WIRTSCHAFT
    Verlag mbH
    ABC Verlagshaus
    Berliner Allee 8
    Postfach 40 34
    61 Darmstadt
    Tel: 8 62 42 - 44
    Telex: 419257

Entries: 750 751 752

ADRESSBUCHVERLAG GEORG HARTMANN KG
  Dorotheenstrasse 239
  53 Bonn
  Tel: 3 67 80

Entry: 808

AMERICAN EMBASSY
  Economic Affairs Section
  532 Bonn — Bad Godesberg
  Tel: 89 55

Entry: 810

ATLANTIK-BRÜCKE
  65 Sanderskoppel 15
  Hamburg
  Tel: 5 36 60 43

Entry: 840

AXEL SPRINGER VERLAG AG
  Kaiser - Wilhelm - Strasse 6
  2000 Hamburg 36
  Tel: 3 47 1

Entries: 761 770 790 823 835 836 837 841 852
      875

BARCLAYS BANK LTD
  Group Economic Intelligence Unit
  54 Lombard Street
  London EC3 3AH
  England
  Tel: 01 283 8989
  Telex: 887591

Entry: 797

BETRIEBSBERATUNG GASTOWERBE GmbH
  Pampelforter Str 47
  Düsseldorf
  Tel: 35 39 06

Entry: 786

BEUTH-VERTRIEB GmbH
  Uhlandstrasse 175
  1 Berlin 15
  Tel: 91 92 76

Entry: 885

BRITISH OVERSEAS TRADE BOARD
  1 Victoria Street
  London SW1H 0ET
  England
  Tel: 01 215 7877
  Telex: 27366

Entries: 817
        832—Available from:
**THE FAIRS & PROMOTIONS BRANCH OF THE
DEPARTMENT OF TRADE**
  1 Victoria Street
  London SW1H 0ET
  England
  Tel: 01 638 1717
  Telex: 887358

BRITISH PLASTICS FEDERATION
  47 Piccadilly
  London W1V 0DN
  England
  Tel: 01 734 2041

Entry: 847

BUNDESANSTALT FÜR ARBEIT
  Regenburger Str 104
  8500 Nurnberg
  Telex: 22348

Entry: 756

**BUNDESMINISTERIUM FÜR ARBEITS- UND
SOZIALORDNUNG**
  Bonner Strasse 85
  5300 Bonn-Duisdorf
  Tel: 74 - 1
  Telex: 886377

Entry: 759

**BUNDESMINISTERIUM FÜR ERNÄHRUNG
LANDWIRTSCHAFT UND FORSTEN**
  Rochusstr 1
  5300 Bonn
  Tel: 75 35 05
  Telex: 886844

Entry: 865

BUNDESMINISTERIUM FÜR WIRTSCHAFT
  Villemombler St 76
  5300 Bonn-Duisdorf
  Tel: 37 67 67
  Telex: 886747

Entries: 767 788 900

**BUNDESVERBAND DES DEUTSCHEN
VERSANDHANDELS**
    Johann-Klotz-Strasse 12
    6 Frankfurt/Main 71
    Tel: 67 50 47

Entry: 883

BUSINESS INTERNATIONAL SA
    Chemin Rieu 12-14
    1208 Genève
    Switzerland
    Tel: 47 53 55
    Telex: 22669

Entry: 806

COMMERZBANK AG
    Grosse Gallusstrasse 17-19
    Postfach 2534
    D-6000 Frankfurt-am-Main
    Tel: 28621
    Telex: 411246

Entry: 891

CONTIMART LTD
Available through:
RSGB LTD
    Crown House
    London Road
    Morden
    Surrey
    England
    Tel: 01 540 8991

Entry: 896

DEUTSCHE BUNDESBANK
    50 Wilhelm-Epstein Strasse 14
    PO Box 3611
    6 Frankfurt-am-Main 1
    Tel: 1 58 1
    Telex: 41227

Entries: 762 843 854 892 904

**DEUTSCHER ADRESSBUCH-VERLAG FÜR
WIRTSCHAFT UND VERKEHR GmbH**
    DAV-Verlagshaus
    61 Darmstadt
    Tel: 8 40 11
    Telex: 419548

Entries: 779 783 784

DEUTSCHER BÜCHEREIVERBAND
    Gitschiner Strasse 97-103
    1 Berlin 61
    Tel: 18 02 61

Entry: 816

DEUTSCHER FACHVERLAG GmbH
    Schumannstrasse 27
    Postfach 2625
    6 Frankfurt/Main
    Tel: 74331
    Telex 0411862

Entries: 838 839 873

DEUTSCHER INDUSTRIE- UND HANDELSTAG
    Adenauerallee 148
    53 Bonn
    Tel: 1 04 1

Entry: 819

**DEUTSCHER VERBAND TECHNISCH-
WISSENSCHAFTLICHER VEREINE**
    Graf Reckerstrasse 84
    4 Düsseldorf
    Tel: 6 21 41

Entry: 782

**DEUTSCHES INSTITUT FÜR
WIRTSCHAFTSFORSCHUNG**
    Königin-Luise-Strasse 5
    1000 Berlin 33
    Tel: 82 91 1
    Telex: 183247

Entries: 768 787 886 903

**DIVO INMAR GESELLSCHAFT FÜR
MARKTFORSCHUNG MARKTPLANUNG UND
MARKETINGBERATUNG mbH**
    Am Eisernen Schlag 31
    Frankfurt-am-Main

Entry: 893

DRESDNER BANK
    Gallusanlage 7
    6 Frankfurt-am-Main 1
    Tel: 26 31
    Telex: 41230

Entry: 798

ECONOMIST INTELLIGENCE UNIT
 27 St James's Place
 London SW1A 1NT
 England
 Tel: 01 493 6711
 Telex: 266353

Entry: 850

ECONTEL RESEARCH LTD
 c/o World Economics Ltd
 10 Charles II Street
 London SW1Y 4AA
 England
 Tel: 01 839 1921

Entry: 775

EMBASSY OF THE FEDERAL REPUBLIC OF GERMANY
 23 Belgrave Square
 London SW1X 8PZ
 England
 Tel: 01 235 5033

Entry: 826

EUROPEAN COMMUNITIES COMMISSION
 Official Publications Office
 Rue du Commerce
 PO Box 1003
 Luxembourg
 Tel: 49 01 91
 Telex: 2731 PUBLOF LU

Entry: 777

FESTLAND VERLAG GmbH
 Meckenheimer Allee 126
 53 Bonn
 Tel: 63 41 21

Entry: 869

FINANZ- UND KORRESPONDENZ-VERLAG
 Dr Gisela Mossner
 Taunusstrasse 3
 1 Berlin 33
 Tel: 89 45 14

Entry: 814

FRANKFURTER ALLGEMEINE ZEITUNG
 Hellerhof Strasse 2-4
 Frankfurt-am-Main
 Tel: 75 91 1
 Telex: 41223

Entry: 789

GEMEINSCHAFTSVERLAG GmbH
 Spreestrasse 9
 61 Darmstadt
 Tel: 84727

Entry: 766

THE GERMAN CHAMBER OF INDUSTRY AND COMMERCE IN THE UK
 11 Grosvenor Crescent
 London SW1X 7EU
 England
 Tel: 01 235 9947

Entries: 771 772 809 858

GESAMTVERBAND DER TEXTILINDUSTRIE IN DER BUNDESREPUBLIK DEUTSCHLAND
 Schaumainkai 87
 6000 Frankfurt-am-Main
 Tel: 638 035 - 39
 Telex: 411034

Entry: 874

GFK
 Burgschmiedestrasse 2
 8500 Nürnberg
 Tel: 3 95 1

Entry: 849

GRUNER UND JAHR & CO AG
 Klaus-Groth-Str 11
 Postfach 129
 2210 Itzehoe
 Tel: 2210

Entries: 791 801 804 805 830 831 834 876 895
    897

CARL HEYMANNS VERLAG KG
 Gereonstrasse 18-32
 5 Köln 1
 Tel: 23 45 55
 Telex: 8881888

Entry: 774

HOUSE INFORMATION SERVICES LTD
 1 Creswell Park
 Blackheath
 London SE3 9RG
 England
 Tel: 01 852 6177

Entry: 778

IFO - INSTITUT FÜR WIRTSCHAFTSFORSCHUNG eV
    Poschingerstrasse 5
    Postfach 860460
    Munchen 86
    Tel: 92 24 1

Entries: 818 901 902

INSTITUTE OF PRACTITIONERS IN ADVERTISING
    44 Belgrave Square
    London SW1X 8QZ
    England
    Tel: 01 235 7020
    Telex: 918352

Entry: 753

INTERCONTINENTAL BOOK & PUBLISHING CO
    5708 Jeanne Mance
    Montreal 8
    Canada

Entry: 898

INTERNATIONAL TRADE CENTRE
    Villa le Bocage
    Palais des Nations
    Genève
    Switzerland
    Tel: 33 10 01

Entry: 828

LOGON GmbH
    2 Oskar Miller Ring 25
    München
    Tel: 28 15 01

Entry: 800

MACNENS GERMANY VERLAG GmbH
    Taunusstrasse 52
    6 Frankfurt/Main
    Tel: 23 24 38

Entry: 755

MARKET DATASEARCH LTD
Available from:
**WALLCOVERING MANUFACTURERS ASSOCIATION
OF GREAT BRITAIN**
    Prudential House
    Wellesley Road
    Croydon CR9 2ET
    England
    Tel: 01 686 3111

Entry: 868

**MARPLAN FORSCHUNGSGESELLSCHAFT FÜR
MARKT UND VERBRAUCH GmbH**
    Schloss Str 4
    D-6050 Offenbach
    Tel: 85 28 45

Entry: 795

MARPLAN LTD
    20 Eastbourne Terrace
    London W2 6LG
    England
    Tel: 01 723 7228

Entry: 853

METRA CONSULTING GROUP
    23 Lower Belgrave Street
    London SW1W 0NS
    England
    Tel: 01 730 0855

Entry: 894

MIDLAND BANK LTD
    Poultry
    London EC2P 2BX
    England
    Tel: 01 606 9911
    Telex: 8811822

Entry: 857

NATIONAL ECONOMIC DEVELOPMENT OFFICE
    1 Steel House
    11 Tothill Street
    London SW1H 9LJ
    England
    Tel: 01 222 0565

Entries: 793 794 803 867 877
802—Available from The Secretary International Freight
Movement EDEC NEDO

NEDERLANDS-DUITSE KAMER VAN KOOPHANDEL
    Freiligrathstr 27
    4000 Düsseldorf 30
    Tel: 484591
    Telex: 8584980

Entry: 780

NEUER HANDELS-VERLAG GmbH & CO KG
    Gewerbestrasse 2
    Postfach 407
    8937 Bad Wörishofen

Entry: 776

ORGANISATION FOR ECONOMIC CO-OPERATION AND DEVELOPMENT
    2 Rue André Pascal
    Paris 16e
    France
    Tel: 524 8200
    Telex: 62160

Entry: 845

POST- UND ORTSBUCHVERLAG
    Wittenerstrasse 109
    56 Wuppertal-Barmen 10
    Tel: 66 08 73

Entry: 844

PRESS & INFORMATION OFFICE OF THE GOVERNMENT OF THE FEDERAL REPUBLIC OF GERMANY
    Welckerstr 11
    Bonn
    Tel: 2 08 - 1

Entry: 796

K RADEMACHER & CO
    Adolphsbrücke 9-11
    2 Hamburg 11
    Tel: 34 23 86

Entry: 851

RSL INTERNATIONAL
Available from:
THE ENGLISH COUNTRY CHEESE COUNCIL
    5 John Princes Street
    London W1M 0AP
    England
    Tel: 01 499 7822

Entry: 872

SEIBT VERLAG DR ARTUR SEIBT
    Anzinger Strasse 1
    8 München 80
    Tel: 40 45 61

Entries: 785 856

SIRA INSTITUTE
    South Hill
    Chislehurst
    Kent
    England
    Tel: 01 467 2636
    Telex: 896649

Entry: 890

SPIEGEL VERLAG RUDOLF AUGSTEIN GmbH & CO
    Brandstwiete 19 Ost-West-Strasse
    2000 Hamburg 11

Entries: 781 822 829

STAATLICHE ZENTRALVERWALTUNG FÜR STATISTIK
    Hans-Beimier - Strasse 70/72
    102 Berlin

Entries: 859 861

STATISTISCHES BUNDESAMT
    Gustav-Stresemann-Ring 11
    Postfach 5528
    6200 Wiesbaden
    Tel: 7051
    Telex: 4186511

Entries: 754 758 760 764 765 769 799 807 811
           820 825 848 862 864 866 878 881 882
           887 888 889 899

STATISTISCHES LANDESAMT
    S. Behörden 7
    Hamburg
    Tel: 3 68 11

Entry: 860

FRANZ STEINER VERLAG
    Bahnhofstrasse 39
    62 Wiesbaden
    Tel: 37 20 11

Entry: 813

STIFTERVERBAND FUR DIE DEUTSCHE WISSENSCHAFT
    Brucker Holt 60
    43 Essen-Bredeney
    Tel: 71 10 51
    Telex: 857544

Entry: 879

UNIVERSITÄT ZU KÖLN
    Institut für Handelsforschung
    Albertus Magnus Platz
    Köln 41
    Tel: 4701
    Telex: 8882291

Entry: 842

US DEPARTMENT OF COMMERCE
   Government Printing Office
   Washington DC 20402
   Tel: 783 3238
   Telex: TWX 710 8229274

Entries: 763 833

VERBAND DER AUTOMOBILINDUSTRIE eV
   Westendstr 61
   600 Frankfurt-am-Main
   Tel: 74 02 01
   Telex: 411293

Entry: 871

VEREIN DEUTSCHER MASCHINENBAU-ANSTALTEN eV
   Lyoner Strasse
   Postfach 109
   6000 Frankfurt-am-Main
   Tel: 66031
   Telex: 411321

Entry: 863

VEREINIGUNG DEUTSCHER ELEKTRIZITÄTSWERKE
   Stresemannallee 23
   Frankfurt-am-Main 70

Entry: 792

VERLAG DER "TEXTIL-WIRTSCHAFT" DEUTSCHER FACHVERLAG GmbH

   Schumannstrasse 27
   6000 Frankfurt-am-Main
   Tel: 74 33 1

Entry: 870

VERLAG HOPPENSTEDT & CO
   Havelstrasse 9
   61 Darmstadt
   Tel: 86221
   Telex: 419258

Entries: 812 815 827 846 855 880

VERLAG J A MAYER
   Buchkremerstrasse 5-7
   51 Aachen
   Tel: 2 24 41

Entry: 884

VERLAG O HARRASOWITZ
   Taunusstrasse 6
   62 Wiesbaden
   Tel: 52 10 46

Entry: 821

VERLAG W KOHLHAMMER GmbH
   Siemensstrasse 3
   6501 Hechtsheim über Mainz
   Tel: 2 23 44

Entry: 757

WALTER DE GRUYTER & CO
   Genthiner Strasse 13
   1 Berlin 30
   Tel: 13 13 41

Entry: 824

WALTER DORN KG
   Heinrich Heine Strasse 117
   28 Bremen 1
   Tel: 44 64 33

Entry: 773

DK-DENMARK

BARCLAYS BANK
   Group Economic Intelligence Unit
   54 Lombard Street
   London EC3 3AH
   England
   Tel: 01 283 8989
   Telex: 887591

Entry: 951

BØRSEN'S FORLAG
   Vognmagergade 2
   P.O. Box 2103
   1014 København K

Entry: 980

BRITISH NATIONAL EXPORT COUNCIL
   6-14 Dean Farrar Street
   London SW1H ODX
   England
   Tel: 01 215 7877
   Telex: 27366

Entries: 954 955 956 957

BRITISH OVERSEAS TRADE BOARD
  1 Victoria Street
  London SW1H 0ET
  England
  Tel: 01 215 7877
  Telex: 27366

Entry: 981

CENTRE FRANÇAIS DU COMMERCE EXTERIEUR
  10 Av d'Iéna
  Paris 16e
  France
  Tel: 723 61 23
  Telex: 611934

Entry: 997

CONTIMART LTD
Available through:
RSGB LTD
  Crown House
  London Road
  Morden
  Surrey
  England
  Tel: 01 540 8991

Entry   959

DANISH AGRICULTURAL PRODUCERS
  2-3 Conduit St
  London W1R 0AT
  England
  Tel: 01 499 7040

Entry: 967

DANMARKS NATIONALBANK
  Holmens Kanal 17
  1093 København K
  Tel: 14 14 11
  Telex: 27051

Entries: 960 961

DANMARKS STATISTIK
  Sejrogade 11
  2100 København Ø
  Tel: 298222
  Telex: 16236

Entries: 950 953 962 963 971 978 982 983 984
          990 992 993 994 996 1004 1005 1006
          1007 1008 1013

DANSK ELVAERKERS FORENING
  Vodraffst 59
  København

Entry: 964

DANSKE IMPORTAGENTERS FORENING
Now: **DANMARKS AGENTFORENING**
  Børsen
  1217 København
  Tel: 14 49 41

Entry: 965

DEN DANSKE LANDMANDSBANK
  12 Holmens Kanal
  DK-1092 København K
  Tel: 156500
  Telex: 15880

Entries: 973 995

THE ECONOMIST
  25 St. James's Street
  London SW1A 1HG
  England
  Tel: 01 930 5155
  Telex: 24344

Entry: 1010

ECONOMIST INTELLIGENCE UNIT
  Spencer House
  27 St. James's Place
  London SW1A 1NT
  England
  Tel: 01 493 6711
  Telex: 266353

Entry: 1000

THE FINANCIAL TIMES LTD
  10 Bolt Court
  London EC4A 3HL
  England
  Tel: 01 836 5444
  Telex: 27368

Entry: 985

FISKERIMINISTERIET
  Borgergade 16
  1300 København K
  Tel: 11 03 01

Entry: 977

INVESTORS CHRONICLE
30 Finsbury Square
London EC2A 1PJ
England
Tel: 01 628 4050
Telex: 883694

Entry: 968

KØBENHAVN HANDELSBANK
2 Holmens Kanal
DK-1091 København
Tel: 12 86 00
Telex: 16784

Entries: 958 969 1001 1003

KOMPASS DENMARK A/S FORLAGET
Landskronagade 70
2100 København
Tel: 20 88 38

Entry: 987

KOGERIGET DANMARKS HANDELSKALENDER A/S
Møntergade 19
1116 København K
Tel: 12 11 95

Entry: 989

KRAK
Nytorv 17
1450 København
Tel: 12 03 08

Entries: 976 991

LLOYDS BANK LTD
Export Promotion Section
Overseas Department
6 Eastcheap
London EC3P 3AB
England
Tel: 01 283 1000
Telex: 888301

Entry: 972

**ORGANISATION FOR ECONOMIC CO-OPERATION
AND DEVELOPMENT**
Publications Office
2 Rue André Pascal
Paris 16e
France
Tel: 524 8200
Telex: 62160

Entry: 999

PER PRESS
Frederik VI's Allé 5
2000 København F

Entry: 1009

PRICE WATERHOUSE & CO
Norre Farimagsgade 64

DK-1364 København K
Tel: 11 68 46

Entry: 986

RIGSBIBLIOTEKAREMBEDET
c/o The Royal Library
Christians Brygge 8
1219 København K
Tel: 15 01 11

Entry: 1014

ROYAL DANISH MINISTRY OF FOREIGN AFFAIRS
Christiansborg
1218 København K
Tel: 15 08 25

Entry: 974

SCAN REPORT A/S
Svanemøllevej 63
2900 Hellerup

Entry: 998

SCANDINAVIAN COUNCIL FOR APPLIED RESEARCH
Box 5103
S-102 43 Stockholm 5
Sweden

Entry: 1002

A/S J H SCHULTZ
Møntergade 19
1116 København K
Tel: 14 11 95

Entry: 988

TEKNISK FORLAG A/S
Skelbaekgade 4
DK 1717 København V
Tel: 21 68 01
Telex: 16368 TEFKO DK

Entry: 1011

THE TIMES
Marketing Department
New Printing House Square
Grays Inn Road
London WC1N 2JD
Tel: 01 837 1234
Telex: 264971

Entry: 970

UDENRIGS HANDELS INFORMATIONSBUREAU
Holsteingade 19
2100 København Ø
Tel: TR 696

Entry: 1012

US BUREAU OF INTERNATIONAL COMMERCE
Government Printing Office
Washington DC 20402
USA
Tel: 783 3238
Telex: TWX 710 8229274

Entries: 952 975 979

E – SPAIN

BANCO CENTRAL
Alcalá 49 TA Centroban
Madrid 14
Tel: 2328810
Telex: 22588

Entry: 1057

BANCO DE BILBAO
Gran Via 12
Bilbao - 1
Tel: 244620
Telex: 32055

Entries: 1053 1066 1080 1081 1103
Available in UK through:
BANCO DE BILBAO
36-38 New Broad Street
London EC2M 1NU
England

BANCO DE ESPAÑA
Alcalá 50
Central Madrid 14
Tel: 2211110
Telex: 27783

Entries: 1054 1078 1091

BANCO ESPAÑOL EN LONDRES
London Fruit Exchange
Brushfield Street
London E1 6HH
England
Tel: 01 247 9888

Entry: 1087

BARCLAYS BANK
Group Economic Intelligence Unit
54 Lombard Street
London EC3 3AH
England
Tel: 01 283 8989
Telex: 887591

Entry: 1055

BRITISH OVERSEAS TRADE BOARD
1 Victoria Street
London SW1H 0ET
England
Tel: 01 215 7877
Telex: 27366

Entry: 1079

BUSINESS INTERNATIONAL SA
Chemin Rieu 12-14
1208 Genève
Switzerland
Tel: 47 83 55
Telex: 22669

Entry: 1096

DIRECTION GENERAL DE ADUANAS
Available through:
INSTITUTO NACIONAL DE ESTADISTICA
Avenida de Generalisimo 91
Madrid 16
Tel: 459 0700
Telex: 42086

Entries: 1070 1071 1072 1073 1074 1084 1085

ECONOMIST INTELLIGENCE UNIT
Spencer House
27 St James's Place
London SW1A 1NT
England
Tel: 01 493 6711
Telex: 266353

Entry: 1090

THE FINANCIAL TIMES LTD
10 Bolt Court
London EC4A 3HL
England
Tel: 01 836 5444
Telex: 27368

Entries: 1061 1095 1099

FOCUS RESEARCH LTD
31 High Holborn
London WC1V 6AX
England
Tel: 01 242 8401

Entry: 1083

INSTITUTO NACIONAL DE ESTADISTICA
Avenida de Generalisimo 91
Madrid 16
Tel: 459 0700
Telex: 42086

**Entries: 1050 1051 1052 1058 1060 1062 1063
1064 1065 1067 1069 1075 1082 1086
1088 1092 1094**

LLOYDS BANK LTD
Overseas Department
International Trade Promotion Section
6 Eastcheap
London EC3 3AB
England
Tel: 01 283 1000
Telex: 888301

Entry: 1059

MIDLAND BANK LTD
27-32 Poultry
London EC2P 2BX
England
Tel: 01 606 9911
Telex: 8811822

Entry: 1102

MINISTERIO DE COMERCIO
Available through:
INSTITUTO NACIONAL DE ESTADISTICA
Avenida de Generalisimo 91
Madrid 16
Tel: 459 0700
Telex: 42086

Entry: 1068

**ORGANISATION FOR ECONOMIC CO-OPERATION
AND DEVELOPMENT**
Publications Office
2 Rue André Pascal
Paris 16e
France
Tel: 524 82 00
Telex: 62160

Entry: 1089

SERVICIO SINDICAL DE ESTADISTICA
Paseo del Prado 18
Madrid 14

Entries: 1076 1077 1093

THE TIMES
Marketing Department
New Printing House Square
Grays Inn Road
London WC1N 2JD
England
Tel: 01 837 1234
Telex: 264971

Entries: 1097 1098 1100 1101

US BUREAU OF INTERNATIONAL COMMERCE
Government Printing Office
Washington DC 20402
USA
Tel: 783 3238
Telex: TWX 710 8229274

Entry: 1056

F – FRANCE

ASSEMBLEE PERMANENTE DES CHAMBRES D'AGRICULTURE
    9 Av George V
    Paris 8e
    Tel: 225 28 50

Entry: 1251

BANQUE DE FRANCE
    39 Rue Croix des Petits-Champs
    Paris 1e
    Tel: 261 56 72
    Telex: 220932

Entry: 1160

BANQUE NATIONALE DE PARIS
    16 Boulevard des Italiens
    Paris 9e
    Tel: 523 55 00
    Telex: 280693

Entry: 1248

BANQUE POPULAIRE
    Directeur de la Publication
    115 Rue Montmartre
    75002 Paris
    Tel: 508 61 36
    Telex: 21957

Entry: 1161

BARCLAYS BANK LTD
    Group Economic Intelligence Unit
    54 Lombard Street
    London EC3 3AH
    England
    Tel: 01 283 8989
    Telex: 887591

Entry: 1162

BRITISH EMBASSY IN PARIS / DEPT OF TRADE
    Rue du Faubourg - St - Honoré 35
    Paris 8e
    Tel: 266 91 42
or
    Export House
    50 Ludgate Hill
    London EC4M 7HU
    England
    Tel: 01 248 5757

Entry: 1249

BRITISH OVERSEAS TRADE BOARD
    1 Victoria Street
    London SW1H 0ET
    England
    Tel: 01 215 7877
    Telex: 887591

Entry: 1207

BUILDING MANAGEMENT & MARKETING CONSULTANTS LTD
Available from:
BRITISH WOODWORK MANUFACTURERS ASSOCIATION
    26 Store Street
    London WC1E 7BS
    England
    Tel: 01 636 9075

Entry: 1273

CENTRE D'ETUDES ET DE PRODUCTIVITE DES INDUSTRIES DES PAPIERS CARTONS ET CELLULOSES
    154 Boulevard Haussmann
    Paris 8e

Entry: 1238

CHAMBRE DE COMMERCE ET D'INDUSTRIE DE MARSEILLE
    Palais de la Bourse
    13001 Marseille
    Tel: 39 62 19

**Entries: 1173 1205 1208 1209 1219 1220 1243
         1280**

COMITE CENTRAL DE LA LAINE ET DE L'INDUSTRIE LAINIERE
    12 Rue d'Anjou
    Paris 8e
    Tel: 266 11 11

Entries: 1211 1212 1265

COMMERCE INTERNATIONAL
London Chamber of Commerce and Industry
    69 Cannon Street
    London EC4N 5AB
    England
    Tel: 01 236 2675

Entry: 1192

COMMISSARIAT GENERAL DU TOURISME
Service des Etudes de la Statistique
et de la Conjuncture
27 Rue Oudinot
Paris 7e

Entry: 1165

CONFREMCA
Available from:
**WALLCOVERING MANUFACTURERS ASSOCIATION
OF GREAT BRITAIN**
Prudential House
Wellesley Road
Croydon CR9 2ET
England
Tel: 01 686 3111

Entry: 1196

CREDIT COMMERCIAL DE FRANCE
103 Avenue des Champs-Elysees
75361 - Paris Cedex 08
Tel: 720 92 00
Telex: 610315

Entry: 1151

CREDIT LYONNAIS
19 Boulevard des Italiens
Paris 2e
Tel: 508 70 00
Telex: 630200

Entry: 1182

**DATAR (DELEGATION L'AMENAGEMENT DU
TERRITOIRE ET L'ACTION REGIONALE)
(FRENCH INDUSTRIAL DEVELOPMENT BOARD)**
1 Avenue Charles Floquet
75007 Paris
Tel: 783 61 20

Entries: 1186 1226

**DIRECTION GENERALE DES DOUANES ET DROITS
INDIRECTS**
Division des Etudes des Statistiques et d'Information
192 Rue St Honoré
Paris 1e
Tel: 233 66 33

Entries: 1260 1261 1262 1263 1264 1266 1278

LA DOCUMENTATION FRANÇAISE
29-31 quai Voltaire
Paris 7e
Tel: 261 50 01
Telex: 204826

Entry: 1215

THE ECONOMIST
25 St James's Street
London SW1A 1HG
England
Tel: 01 930 5155
Telex: 24344

Entries: 1185 1206

ECONOMIST INTELLIGENCE UNIT
Spencer House
27 St James's Place
London SW1A 1NT
England
Tel: 01 493 6711

Entry: 1237

**FEDERATION NATIONALE DES INDUSTRIES
ELECTRONIQUES**
11 Rue Hamelin
Paris 16e
Telex: 610296

Entry: 1213

THE FINANCIAL TIMES LTD
10 Bolt Court
London EC4A 3HL
England
Tel: 01 836 5444
Telex: 27368

Entry: 1189

FRENCH COMMERCIAL COUNSELLOR
12 Stanhope Gate
London W1
England
Tel: 01 493 5021

Entry: 1169

FRENCH EMBASSY
58 Knightsbridge
London SW1 7JT
England
Tel: 01 235 8080

Entries: 1156 1157 1158 1163 1170 1171 1178
1180 1188 1194 1195 1198 1199 1200
1201 1202 1203 1217 1221 1225 1227
1228 1229 1236 1244 1250 1252 1254
1277 1279 1281 1285

FRENCH EMBASSY PRESS & INFORMATION SERVICE
58 Knightsbridge
London SW1 7JT
Tel: 01 235 8080

Entry: 1190

FRENCH INDUSTRIAL DEVELOPMENT BOARD
See **DATAR**

Entry: 1222

GAZ DE FRANCE
Service National
Direction des Services Economiques et Commerciaux
23 Rue Philibert Delorme
Paris 17e
Tel: 766 52 62
Telex: 650483

Entry: 1204

GOWER PRESS, TEAKFIELD LTD
1 Westmead
Farnborough
Hampshire GU14 7RU
England
Tel: Farnborough (0252) 41196
Telex: 858193

Entry: 1197

INSTITUT NATIONAL DE LA STATISTIQUE ET DES ETUDES ECONOMIQUES
18 Boulevard Adolphe Pinard
75675 Paris Cedex 14
Tel: 657 11 14
Telex: 204904

Entries: 1153 1164 1172 1174 1179 1181 1183
1214 1239 1240 1241 1242 1268 1275
1276

INSTITUTE OF PRACTITIONERS IN ADVERTISING
44 Belgrave Square
London SW1X 8QZ
England
Tel: 01 235 7020
Telex: 918352

Entry: 1150

INVESTORS CHRONICLE
30 Finsbury Square
London EC2A 1PJ
England
Tel: 01 628 4050
Telex: 883694

Entry: 1191

LLOYDS BANK INTERNATIONAL
71 Lombard Street
London EC3P 3BS
England
Tel: 01 626 1500
Telex: 887053

Entry: 1168

MARPLAN LTD
Available from:
WALLCOVERING MANUFACTURERS ASSOCIATION OF GREAT BRITAIN
Prudential House
Wellesley Road
Croydon CR9 2ET
England
Tel: 01 686 3111

Entry: 1245

METRA CONSULTING GROUP LTD
23 Lower Belgrave Street
London SW1W 0NS
England
Tel: 01 730 0855

Entry: 1283

MIDLAND BANK LTD
27-32 Poultry
London EC2P 2BX
England
Tel: 01 606 9911
Telex: 8811822

Entry: 1253

MINISTERE DE L'AGRICULTURE

Directions Générales de l'Administration et du Finance
Service Central des Enquêtes et Etudes Statistiques

5 Rue Casimir - Perier
75007 Paris
Tel: 705 99 09

Entry: 1255

MINISTERE DE L'AMENAGEMENT DU TERRITOIRE DE L'EQUIPEMENT DU LOGEMENT ET DU TOURISME

244/246 Boulevard Saint-Germain
75 Paris 7e
Tel: 325 24 63
Telex: 730630

Entries: 1155 1223 1246 1259

MINISTERE DE L'ECONOMIE ET DES FINANCES

9 Rue Croix-des-Petits Champs
Paris 1e
Tel: 260 33 00

Entries: 1159 1267

MINISTERE DE L'INDUSTRIE DIRECTION DES MINES

99 Rue de Grenelle
Paris 7e
Tel: 555 9300
Telex: 270257

Entry: 1256

MINISTERE DU DEVELOPPEMENT INDUSTRIEL ET SCIENTIFIQUE

Service Central de la Statistique et des Informations
Industrielles
85 Boulevard du Montparnasse
Paris 6e
Tel: 555 93 00

Entries: 1234 1247 1257 1269 1270 1272

NATIONAL ECONOMIC DEVELOPMENT OFFICE

1 Steel House
11 Tothill Street
London SW1H 9LJ
England
Tel: 01 222 0565

Entry: 1271

ORGANISATION FOR ECONOMIC CO-OPERATION AND DEVELOPMENT

Publications Office
2Rue André Pascal
75 Paris 16e
Tel: 524 82 00
Telex: 620160

Entries: 1224 1235

OXFORD UNIVERSITY PRESS

Walton Street
Oxford
England
Tel: Oxford (0865) 56767

Entries: 1230 1231 1232 1233

PORT OF MARSEILLE AUTHORITY (PORT AUTONOME DE MARSEILLE)

23 Place de la Joliette
13217 Marseille - Cedex 1
Tel: 919066
Telex: 440746

Entry: 1184

PRODUCT & MARKETING RESEARCH LTD

319 Oxford Street
London W1R 1LA
England
Tel: 01 493 1925

Entry: 1274

SERVICE CENTRAL DE LA STATISTIQUE ET DES INFORMATIONS INDUSTRIELLES

85 Boulevard du Montparnasse
Paris 6e
Tel: 555 93 00

Entries: 1152 1166

SIRA INSTITUTE

South Hill
Chislehurst
Kent
England
Tel: 01 467 2636
Telex: 896649

Entry: 1284

SOCIETE GENERALE SERVICE CONJONCTURE
29 Boulevard Haussmann
Paris 9e
Tel: 266 54 00
Telex: 210944

Entry: 1175

SOCIETE GENERALE SIEGE SOCIAL
14 29 Boulevard Haussmann
Paris 9e
Tel: 266 54 00
Telex: 210944

Entry: 1167

SYNDICAT GENERALE DE LA CONSTRUCTION ELECTRIQUE
17 Rue Hamelin
Paris 16e
Telex: 611045

Entry: 1176

SYNDICAT GENERAL DE L'INDUSTRIE DE JUTE
33 Rue de Miromesnil
Paris 8e
Tel: 266 28 05
Telex: 660834

Entry: 1154

THE TIMES
Marketing Department
New Printing House Square
Grays Inn Road
London WC1N 2JD
England
Tel: 01 837 1234
Telex: 264971

Entries: 1187 1193 1216

UNION DES CHAMBRES SYNDICATES DE L'INDUSTRIE DU PETROLE
16 Avenue Klèber
Paris 16e
Tel: 553 42 40
Telex: 630545

Entry: 1210

UNION DES INDUSTRIES TEXTILES
10 Rue d'Anjou
Paris 8e
Telex: 640969

Entry: 1258

US DEPARTMENT OF COMMERCE
Government Printing Office
Washington DC 20402
USA
Tel: 783 3238
Telex: TWX 710 8229274

Entry: 1218

USINE PUBLICATIONS SA
17 Rue d'Uzes
Paris
Tel: 508 49 06
Telex 680876

Entry: 1282

GB – GREAT BRITAIN

ADVERTISING ASSOCIATION
Abford House
15 Wilton Road
London SW1V 1NJ
Tel: 01 828 2771

Entry: 1354

BANK OF ENGLAND
Threadneedle Street
London EC2R 8AH
Tel: 01 601 4444
Telex: 885001

Entries: 1376 1377

THE BANKER
Bracken House
10 Cannon Street
London EC4P 4BY
Tel: 01 248 8000

Entry: 1582

BENN BROS LTD
Sovereign Way
Tonbridge
Kent TN9 1RW
Tel: Tonbridge (0732) 364422
Telex: 27844

Entries: 1421 1467 1501 1624 1681 1704

BIGGAR & CO (PUBLISHERS) LTD
26 Charing Cross Road
London WC2H 0DG
Tel: 01 836 4628

Entry: **1449**

BRITISH BUREAU OF TELEVISION ADVERTISING
Knighton House
52-66 Mortimer Street
London W1N 7DG
Tel: 01 636 6866

Entries: **1385 1386**

BRITISH FOOTWEAR MANUFACTURERS ASSOCIATION
72 Dean Street
London W1V 5HB
Tel: 01 437 5573

Entries: **1494 1495**

THE BRITISH LIBRARY
Store Street
London WC1E 7DG
Tel: 01 636 0755

Entry: **1503**

BRITISH MAN-MADE FIBRES ASSOCIATION
41 Dover Street
London W1X 4DS
Tel: 01 493 7446

Entry: **1687**

BRITISH METAL CORPORATION
2 Metal Exchange Building
Leadenhall Avenue
London EC3V 1LD
Tel: 01 626 4521

Entry: **1655**

BRITISH ROAD FEDERATION
26 Manchester Square
London W1M 5RF
Tel: 01 935 0223

Entry: **1379**

BRITISH STEEL CORPORATION
Statistical Services
12 Addiscombe Road
Croydon
Surrey
CR9 3JH
Tel: 01 686 9050 Ext 294
Telex: 946372

Entry: **1551**

BRITISH TRAVEL ASSOCIATION
Now: **BRITISH TOURIST AUTHORITY**
64 St James's Street
London SW1A 1NF
Tel: 01 629 9191
Telex: 21231

Entry: **1445**

BUCKLEY PRESS LTD
The Butts
Half Acre
Brentford
Middlesex
Tel: 01 568 8441
Telex: 25657

Entry: **1545**

BUSINESS AND ECONOMIC PLANNING / SCOTTISH TOURIST BOARD
4 Golden Square
London W1R 3AE
Tel: 01 734 5919

Entry: **1496**

CAMBRIDGE INFORMATION & RESEARCH SERVICES LTD
8 Market Passage
Cambridge
CB2 3PF
Tel: Cambridge (0223) 60087

Entries: **1462 1463**

C B D RESEARCH LTD
154 High Street
Beckenham
Kent BR3 1EA
Tel: 01 650 7745

Entry: **1688**

CHEMICAL INDUSTRIES ASSOCIATION LTD
93 Albert Embankment
London SE1 7TU
Tel: 735 3001
Telex: 916672

Entry: 1720

COMART RESEARCH LTD
640 Great Cambridge Road
Enfield
Middlesex EN1 3RT
Tel: 01 366 4211

Entry: 1696

CONFEDERATION OF BRITISH INDUSTRY
21 Tothill Street
London SW1H 9LP
Tel: 01 930 6711
Telex: 21332

Entries: 1369 1426 1427 1428 1429 1437 1472
1599 1622 1651 1680 1686 1699 1712
1737 1739

CRAWFORD PUBLICATIONS LTD
The Forum
15 New Burlington Street
London W1X 1FF
Tel: 01 499 1164

Entry: 1438

DEPARTMENT OF TRADE & INDUSTRY
1 Victoria Street
London SW1H 0ET
Tel: 01 638 1717
Telex: 887358

Entry: 1435

DEVELOPMENT CORPORATION FOR WALES
15 Park Place
Cardiff CF1 3DQ
Tel: Cardiff (0222) 21208
Telex: 497190

Entry: 1526

DUN & BRADSTREET
26/32 Clifton Street
London EC2P 2LY
Tel: 01 247 4377

Entry: 1554 1555

ECONOMIST INTELLIGENCE UNIT
27 St James's Place
London SW1A 1NT
Tel: 01 493 6711
Telex: 266353

Entries: 1363 1590 1607 1613 1634 1652 1658
1708 1734

ECONOMISTS ADVISORY GROUP
Europe House
World Trade Centre
London E1 9AA
Tel: 01 481 1153
Telex: 884671

Entry: 1616

ECONTEL RESEARCH LTD
c/o World Economics Ltd
10 Charles II Street
London SW1Y 4AA
Tel: 01 839 1921

Entry: 1497

THE ELECTRICITY COUNCIL
30 Millbank
London SW1 4RD
Tel: 01 834 2333
Telex: 23385

Entry: 1507

EUROPEAN MARKETING ASSOCIATION
Available from:
INDUSTRIAL MARKETING COUNCIL
9 Aston Road
Nuneaton
Warwicks CV11 5EL
Tel: Nuneaton (0682) 67161

Entry: 1447

EXTEL STATISTICAL SERVICES
37/45 Paul Street
London EC2A 4PB
Tel: 01 253 3400
Telex: 23721

Entries: 1468 1469 1470 1471 1725

THE FEDERATION OF UNITED KINGDOM MILK MARKETING BOARDS
Thames Ditton
Surrey KT7 0EL
Tel: 01 398 4101
Telex: 928239

Entry: 1731

FERTILIZER MANUFACTURERS' ASSOCIATION
93 Albert Embankment
London SE1 7TU
Tel: 01 735 9491

Entry: 1477

THE FINANCIAL TIMES LTD
10 Bolt Court
London EC4A 3HL
Tel: 01 353 9530
Telex: 883897

Entries: 1365 1499 1524 1615 1659 1671 1701
1745

FUEL & METALLURGICAL JOURNALS LTD
Queensway House
2 Queensway
Redhill
Surrey RH1 1QS
Tel: Redhill (0737) 68611
Telex: 918669

Entry: 1691

FURNITURE INDUSTRY RESEARCH ASSOCIATION
Maxwell Road
Stevenage
Hertfordshire SG1 2EW
Tel: Stevenage (0438) 3433

Entries: 1456 1684

GOWER ECONOMIC PUBLICATIONS, TEAKFIELD LTD
1 Westmead
Farnborough
Hampshire GU14 7RU
Tel: Farnborough (0252) 41196
Telex: 858193

Entries: 1392 1431 1466 1491 1516 1525 1528
1559 1631 1654 1719

GOWER PRESS TEAKFIELD LTD
1 Westmead
Farnborough
Hampshire GU14 7RU
Tel: Farnborough (0252) 41196
Telex: 858193

Entries: 1515 1606

GRAHAM & TROTMAN LTD
Bond Street House
14 Clifford Street
London W1X 1RD
Tel: 01 493 6351

Entry: 1382

HMSO
The Government Bookshop
PO Box 569
London SE1 9NH
Tel: 01 928 6977
Telex: 266455

Entries: 1350 1356 1357 1359 1360 1366 1368
1371 1372 1380 1384 1389 1390 1393
1394 1395 1397 1398 1399 1400 1401
1402 1403 1404 1405 1406 1407 1408
1410 1411 1416 1417 1418 1430 1436
1442 1446 1457 1459 1473 1474 1475
1484 1487 1504 1505 1508 1509 1513
1514 1541 1543 1544 1563 1564 1565
1585 1586 1587 1594 1597 1598 1610
1614 1620 1621 1625 1628 1639 1641
1644 1646 1647 1648 1649 1657 1668
1678 1679 1685 1689 1698 1710 1714
1718 1738 1742

HMSO NORTHERN IRELAND
Government Bookshop
80 Chichester Street
Belfast BT1 4JY
Tel: Belfast 34488

Entries: 1361 1370 1409 1443 1444 1483 1561
1601 1642 1645 1650 1656 1677 1729

HMSO SCOTLAND
Government Bookshop
13a Castle Street
Edinburgh EH2 3AR
Tel: Edinburgh (031) 225 6333

Entries: 1358 1367 1369 1412 1413 1414 1415
1562 1643 1660 1661 1663 1664 1666
1667

INSTITUTE OF ECONOMIC AFFAIRS
    2 Lord North Street
    London SW1P 3LB
    Tel: 01 799 3745

Entry: 1722

INSTITUTE OF MARKETING
    Moor Hall
    Cookham
    Berkshire SL6 9QH
    Tel: Bourne End (06285) 24922

Entry: 1378

INSTITUTE OF PETROLEUM
    61 New Cavendish Street
    London
    W1M 8AR
    Tel: 01 636 1004
    Telex: 264380

Entries: 1556 1605 1727

INSTITUTE OF PRACTITIONERS IN ADVERTISING
    44 Belgrave Square
    London SW1X 8QZ
    Tel: 01 235 7020
    Telex: 918352

Entries: 1353 1608 1707

INTER COMPANY COMPARISONS LTD
    81 City Road
    EC1Y 1BD
    Tel: 01 253 0063

Entries: 1518 1529

INTERNATIONAL TRADE CENTRE
    Villa le Bocage
    Palais des Nations
    Genève
    Switzerland
    Tel: 33 10 01

Entry: 1576

IPC BUSINESS PRESS LTD
    Book Sales Department
    40 Bowling Green Lane
    London EC1R 0NE
    Tel: 01 837 3636
    Telex: 23839

Entries: 1492 1604 1612

IPC INDUSTRIAL PRESS LTD
    33-39 Bowling Green Lane
    London EC1
    Tel: 01 887 1277

Entry: 1451

IPC MARKETING SERVICES DEPT
    Athene House
    66 Shoe Lane
    London
    Tel: 01 353 2000

Entries: 1388 1549 1550 1578 1709

IPC TRANSPORT PRESS LTD
    Dorset House
    Stamford Street
    London SE1 9LU
    Tel: 01 261 8000

Entry: 1635

JORDAN DATAQUEST LTD
    Jordan House
    47 Brunswick Place
    London N1 6EE
    Tel: 01 253 3030

Entries: 1381 1383 1552

KELLY'S DIRECTORIES LTD
    Neville House
    Eden Street
    Kingston-upon-Thames
    Surrey
    Tel: 01 546 7722

Entries: 1352 1553

KOGAN PAGE LTD
    116a Pentonville Road
    London N1 9JN
    Tel: 01 837 7851

Entries: 1602 1726 1741

KOMPASS PUBLISHERS LTD
    RAC House
    Lansdowne Road
    Croydon CR9 2HE
    Tel: 01 686 2262

Entries: 1387 1557 1558

LLOYDS BANK LTD
71 Lombard Street
London EC3P 3BS
Tel: 01 626 1500
Telex: 887053

Entry: 1560

MANCHESTER BUSINESS SCHOOL
Booth Street West
Manchester M15 6PB
Tel: 061 273 8228

Entries: 1420 1441 1569

MEDIA EXPENDITURE ANALYSIS LTD
110 St Martin's Lane
London WC2N 4BH
Tel: 01 240 1903

Entry: 1579

MIDLAND BANK LTD
Poultry
London EC2P 2BX
Tel: 01 606 9911
Telex: 8811822

Entry: 1584

MORGAN GRAMPIAN LTD
30 Calderwood Street
Woolwich
London SE18 6QH
Tel: 01 855 7777
Telex: 896238

Entry: 1583

MUNICIPAL JOURNAL LTD
178-202 Great Portland Street
London W1N 6NH
Tel: 01 637 2400
Telex: 262568

Entries: 1592 1593

NATIONAL ECONOMIC DEVELOPMENT OFFICE
1 Steel House
11 Tothill Street
London SW1H 9LJ
Tel: 01 222 0565

Entries: 1351 1355 1364 1373 1374 1391 1425
1433 1439 1440 1454 1460 1478 1479
1480 1481 1482 1485 1486 1489 1490
1502 1511 1517 1519 1520 1530 1531
1532 1533 1534 1535 1536 1537 1538
1539 1540 1546 1548 1566 1567 1568
1570 1571 1572 1573 1577 1580 1581
1617 1619 1626 1627 1629 1630 1632
1633 1636 1637 1638 1672 1673 1675
1676 1683 1690 1694 1695 1697 1702
1703 1711 1715 1717 1721 1723 1724
1728 1730 1733 1736 1740 1744 1747
1716 (Subscriptions: Hotel and Catering EDC
Millbank Tower Millbank London SW1P 4QZ)
The following publications are available either from NEDO
— at the address above — or from HMSO
1362 1419 1422 1424 1432 1434 1452
1458 1461 1476 1488 1498 1500 1506
1510 1512 1521 1522 1523 1542 1547
1591 1611 1618 1623 1662 1674 1700
1713 1735 1746

NATIONAL INSTITUTE OF ECONOMIC & SOCIAL RESEARCH
2 Dean Trench Street
London SW1P 3HE
Tel: 01 222 7665

Entry: 1595

THE NATIONAL PORTS COUNCIL
Commonwealth House
1-19 New Oxford Street
London WC1A 1DZ
Tel: 01 242 1200

Entry: 1732

NATIONAL WESTMINSTER BANK LTD
41 Lothbury
London EC2P 2BP
Tel: 01 606 6060
Telex: 888388

Entry: 1596

NETHERLANDS-BRITISH CHAMBER OF COMMERCE
307 High Holborn
London WC1V 7LS
Tel: 01 242 1064
Telex: 23211

Entry: 1453

NEWMAN BOOKS LTD
48 Poland Street
London W1V 4PP
Tel: 01 439 3321

Entry: 1493 1653

**NORTHERN ADVERTISING AGENCY (BRADFORD)
LTD**
7 Tong Lane
Bradford BD4 0RR
Tel: Drighlington (0532) 852884

Entry: 1465

NORWEGIAN CHAMBER OF COMMERCE
Norway House
Cockspur Street
London SW1Y 5BN
Tel: 01 930 0181

Entry: 1603

PIRA RESEARCH ASSOCIATION
Randalls Road
Leatherhead
Surrey
Tel: (037 23) 76161
Telex: 929810

Entry: 1682

**REGIONAL REFERENCE PRESS, JHS MANAGEMENT
(HOLDINGS) LTD**
Regional House
Market Street
Altrincham
Cheshire WA14 1QE

Entry: 1527

ROAD TRANSPORT INDUSTRY TRAINING BOARD
Capitol House
Empire Way
Wembley
Tel: 01 902 8880

Entry: 1574

SELL'S PUBLICATIONS LTD
Sell's House
39 East Street
Epsom KT17 1BQ
Surrey
Tel: Epsom (037 27) 26376
Telex: 929912

Entries: 1665 1669 1670

THOMAS SKINNER & COMPANY (PUBLISHERS) LTD
R A C House
Lansdowne Road
Croydon
Surrey CR9 2HH
Tel: 01 686 2262

Entry: 1640

THOMAS SKINNER DIRECTORIES
Oakfield House
41/43 Perrymount Road
Haywards Heath
Sussex RH16 3BS
Tel: Haywards Heath (0444) 59188

Entries: 1375 1450 1692

**SOCIETY OF MOTOR MANUFACTURERS AND
TRADERS**
Forbes House
Halkin Street
London SW1X 7DS
Tel: 01 235 7000
Telex: 21628

Entries: 1464 1588 1589 1600

STUBBS LTD
103 Southwark Street
London SE1 0JS
Tel: 01 928 4433

Entry: 1693

TIMBER TRADE FEDERATION
Clareville House
Whitcomb Street
London WC2H 7DL
Tel: 01 839 1891

Entry: 1705

THE TIMES
Marketing Department
New Printing House Square
Grays Inn Road
London WC1N 2JD
Tel: 01 837 1234
Telex: 264971

Entry: **1706**

TRADE RESEARCH PUBLICATIONS
7 Oxfield Close
Berkhamsted
Herts HP4 3NE
Tel: Berkhamsted (04427) 3951

Entry: **1448**

TRADES UNION CONGRESS
Congress House
23-28 Great Russell Street
London WC1B 3LS
Tel: 01 636 4030

Entry: **1455**

TROPICAL PRODUCTS INSTITUTE
56/62 Gray's Inn Road
London WC1X 8LU
Tel: 01 242 5412

Entry: **1575**

WHO OWNS WHOM LTD
Mary Sumner House
24 Tufton Street
London SW2 2TP
Tel: 01 222 6823

Entry: **1743**

WOODHEAD-FAULKNER (PUBLISHERS) LTD
8 Market Passage
Cambridge
CB2 3PF
Tel: Cambridge (0223) 61633

Entry: **1423**

**WOOL RECORD BRADFORD/NATIONAL WOOL
TEXTILE EXPORT CORPORATION
WOOL RECORD**
Textile Business Press Ltd
91 Kirkgate
Bradford
West Yorkshire BD1 1SZ
Tel: Bradford (0274) 26357
N W T E C
Lloyds Bank Chambers
43 Hustlegate
Bradford
West Yorkshire BD1 1PE
Tel: Bradford (0274) 24235
Telex: 517086

Entry: **1691**

I – ITALY

**AMMINISTRAZIONE AUTONOMA DEI MONOPOLI DI
STATO**
Direzione Centrale per i Servizi delle Manufatture
Tabacchi
Ufficio Tecnico
Piazza Mastai 11
00153 Roma

Entry: **1878**

ASSOCIATION OF ITALIAN JOINT STOCK COMPANIES
11 Piazza Venezia
00187 Roma

Entry: **1841**

ASSOCIAZIONE COTONIERA ITALIANA
Via Borgonnova 11
Milano
Tel: 80 21 42
Telex: 33491

Entries: **1839 1858 1862 1877**

**ASSOCIAZIONE NAZIONALE FRA INDUSTRIE
AUTOMOBILISTICHE**
Corso Galileo Ferraris 61
10128 Torino
Tel: 57 61

Entry: **1810 1816**

BANCA D'ITALIA
Via Nazionale 91
00184 Roma
Tel: 46 48 82
Telex: 61021

Entry: 1811
Available in UK through:
BANCA D'ITALIA
108 Cannon Street
London EC4N 6HB
England
Tel: 01 623 9561
Telex: 886965

BANCA NAZIONALE DEL LAVORO
Via Vittorio Veneto 119
Roma
Tel: Centralino 46 61
Telex: 61279

Entries: 1812 1826 1834 1842 1843 1844 1861

BANCO DI ROMA
Direzione Centrale
Casella Postale 2442
00100 Roma
Tel: 6 70 01
Telex: 61005

Entries: 1831 1852 1864

BANCO DI SICILIA
Acireale
P za Leonardo Vigo 13
Roma
Tel: 60 14 00
Telex: 98091

Entry: 1824
Available in UK through:
BANCO DI SICILIA
P & O Building
Leadenhall Street
London EC3V 4PT
England
Tel: 01 626 2268
Telex: 888078

BARCLAYS BANK LTD
Group Economic Intelligence Unit
54 Lombard Street
London EC3 3AH
England
Tel: 01 283 8989
Telex: 887591

Entry: 1813

BRITISH OVERSEAS TRADE BOARD
1 Victoria Street
London SW1H 0ET
England
Tel: 01 215 7877
Telex: 27366

Entries: 1829 1835 1867

BUREAU OF AGRICULTURAL ECONOMICS
NRMA House
Northbourne Avenue
Braddon ACT
Australia 2601
Tel: 48 37 11

Entry: 1882

CENTRO PER LA STATISTICA AZIENDALE
Via A Baldesi 20
50131 Firenze
Tel: 5 07 13

Entries: 1837 1845 1855

CONFEDERAZIONE GENERALE DELL' INDUSTRIA ITALIANA
Viale dell'Astronomia 30
00144 Roma
Tel: 5 90 31
Telex: 62393

Entries: 1856 1857

CREDITO ITALIANO
Piazza Cordusio 2
20121 Milano
Tel: 80 20 41
Telex: 34434

Entry: 1881

ECONOMIST INTELLIGENCE UNIT
Spencer House
27 St James's Place
London SW1A 1NT
England
Tel: 01 493 6711
Telex: 266353

Entry: 1860

ENTE NAZIONALE ITALIANO PER IL TURISMO
Via Marghera 2
Roma
Tel: 495 27 51
Telex: 68123

Entry: 1874

THE FINANCIAL TIMES LTD
10 Bolt Court
London EC4A 3HL
England
Tel: 01 836 5444
Telex: 27368

Entry: 1833

INSTITUTE OF PRACTITIONERS IN ADVERTISING
44 Belgrave Square
London SW1X 8QZ
England
Tel: 01 235 7020
Telex: 918352

Entry: 1800

ISTITUTO CENTRALE DE STATISTICA
Via Cesare Balbo 16
Roma
Tel: Centralino 46 73
Telex: 61338

Entries: 1801 1802 1803 1804 1805 1806 1807
          1808 1815 1818 1819 1820 1821 1822
          1825 1836 1838 1847 1849 1850 1851
          1853 1869 1871 1873 1875 1876 1880

ISTITUTO MOBILIARE ITALIANO
Servizio Studi
Viale dell'Arte 25
00144 Roma
Tel: Centralino 54 50
Telex: 61256

Entries: 1840 1859

**ISTITUTO NAZIONALE PER IL COMMERCIO
ESTERO**
21 Via Liszt
Roma
Tel: 06 59 92
Telex: 61160

Entry.   1848

**ISTITUTO NAZIONALE PER LO STUDIO DELLA
CONGIUNTURA**
Via Palermo 20
00184 Roma
Tel: 48 26 51

Entry: 1823

**ISTITUTO PER LE RICERCHE E LE INFORMAZIONI
DI MERCATO E LA VALORIZZAZIONE DELLA
PRODUZIONE AGRICOLA**
43 Via Castelfidardo
Roma
Tel: 48 20 41

Entry: 1832

ITALIAN ECONOMIC CORPORATION
Now: **BANCA NAZIONALE DEL LAVORO**
33-35 Cornhill
London EC3 9DR
England
Tel: 01 623 4222
Telex: 888094

Entry: 1870

MARKET DATASEARCH LTD
Available from:
**THE WALLCOVERING MANUFACTURERS
ASSOCIATION OF GREAT BRITAIN**
Prudential House
Wellesley Road
Croydon CR9 2ET
England
Tel: 01 686 3111

Entry: 1879

MARPLAN LTD
Available from:
**WALLCOVERING MANUFACTURERS ASSOCIATION
OF GREAT BRITAIN**
Prudential House
Wellesley Road
Croydon CR9 2ET
England
Tel: 01 686 3111

Entry: 1863

MIDLAND BANK LTD
27-32 Poultry
London EC2P 2BX
England
Tel: 01 606 9911
Telex: 8811822

Entry: 1872

MINISTERO DELL INDUSTRIA E DEL COMMERCIO
Via Vittorio Veneto 33
Roma 00187
Tel: 489 081

Entries: 1817 1827 1828

OGILVY AND MATHER SpA
Piazza Santa Maria Beltrade 1
Milano
Tel: 87 91 77
Telex: 348657

Entry: 1866

**ORGANISATION FOR ECONOMIC CO-OPERATION
AND DEVELOPMENT**
Publications Office
2 Rue André Pascal
Paris 16e
France
Tel: 524 82 00
Telex: 62160

Entry: 1865

24 ORE — IL SOLE
Via Monviso 26
Milano 20154

Entry: 1854

**UNIONE NAZIONALE RAPPRESENTANTI
AUTOVEICOLI ESTERI**
Via Carducci 2
Roma
Tel: 48 07 51

Entry: 1809

US DEPARTMENT OF COMMERCE
Government Printing Office
Washington DC 20402
USA
Tel: 783 3238
Telex: TWX 710 8229274

Entries: 1814 1830 1846 1868

IRL – IRELAND

ALLIED IRISH BANKS
Lansdowne House
Ballsbridge
Dublin 4
Tel: 76 03 71
Telex: 4480

Entry: 1922

BARCLAYS BANK LTD
Group Economic Intelligence Unit
54 Lombard Street
London EC3 3AH
England
Tel: 01 283 8989
Telex: 887591

Entry: 1902

BORD FÁILTE ÉIREANN
Baggot Street
Dublin 2
Tel: 76 58 71
Telex: 5367

Entry: 1942

BRITISH OVERSEAS TRADE BOARD
1 Victoria Street
London SW1H 0ET
England
Tel: 01 215 7877
Telex: 27366

Entry: 1915

BUSINESS AND FINANCE SUPPLEMENT
Business and Finance Ltd
Botanic Road
Dublin 9
Tel: 30 35 11

Entries: 1921 1923 1932 1946

CENTRAL BANK OF IRELAND
PO Box 61
Dublin 2
Tel: 77 43 71
Telex: 4454

Entries: 1906 1914 1924

CENTRAL STATISTICS OFFICE
St. Stephen's Green House
Earlsfort Terrace
Dublin 2
Tel: 76 75 31

Entries: 1900 1901 1903 1904 1905 1907 1908
1911 1912 1913 1916 1917 1918 1930
1934 1937 1938 1940 1944 1947 1949
1950

THE CONFEDERATION OF IRISH INDUSTRY
Setanta House
Kildare Street
Dublin 2
Tel: 77 98 01
Telex: 4711

Entry: 1945

ECONOMIST INTELLIGENCE UNIT
Spencer House
27 St James's Place
London SW1A 1NT
England
Tel: 01 493 6711
Telex: 266353

Entry: 1939

ELECTRICITY SUPPLY BOARD
27 Lower Fitzwilliam Street
Dublin 2
Tel: 76 58 31
Telex: 5313

Entry: 1941

FIRST NATIONAL CITY BANK
71 St Stephen's Green
Dublin 2
Tel: 78 04 88
Telex: 5302

Entry: 1920

GENERAL PUBLICATIONS LTD
59 Merrion Square South
Dublin 2
Tel: 6 3581

Entry: 1936

GOVERNMENT PUBLICATIONS SALES OFFICE
GPO Arcade
Dublin 1
Tel: 74 25 41

Entry: 1909

INDUSTRIAL DEVELOPMENT AUTHORITY
Lansdowne House
Dublin 4
Tel: 68 66 33
Telex: 4525

Entry: 1919

INSTITUTE OF PUBLIC ADMINISTRATION
59 Lansdowne Road
Dublin 4
Tel: 68 62 33

Entry: 1925 1948

IRISH EXPORT BOARD
Merrion Hall
Strand Road
Sandymount
Dublin 4
Tel: 69 50 11
Telex: 5227

Entries: 1926 1927

IRISH EXPORTERS ASSOCIATION
Marshalsea House
Merchants qy
Dublin 8
Tel: 77 02 85

Entry: 1928

KELLY'S DIRECTORIES LTD
Neville House
Eden Street
Kingston-upon-Thames
Surrey
England
Tel: 01 546 7722

Entry: 1931

LLOYDS BANK LTD
Overseas Department
International Trade Promotion Section
6 Eastcheap
London EC3 3AB
England
Tel: 01 283 1000
Telex: 888301

Entry: 1910

McEVOY PRESS LTD
58 Middle Abbey Street
Dublin 1
Tel: 4 7697

Entry: 1929

NATIONAL BUILDING AGENCY LTD
   Hatherton
   Richmond Avenue South
   Dublin 6
   Tel: 97 96 54

Entry: 1943

**ORGANISATION FOR ECONOMIC CO-OPERATION
AND DEVELOPMENT**
   Publications Office
   2 Rue André Pascal
   Paris 16e
   France
   Tel: 524 82 00
   Telex: 62160

Entry: 1935

US DEPARTMENT OF COMMERCE
   Government Printing Office
   Washington DC 20402
   USA
   Tel: 783 3238
   Telex: TWX 710 8229274

Entry: 1933

IS — ICELAND

BARCLAYS BANK LTD
   Group Economic Intelligence Unit
   54 Lombard Street
   London EC3 3AH
   England
   Tel: 01 283 8989
   Telex: 887591

Entry: 1975

BRITISH OVERSEAS TRADE BOARD
   1 Victoria Street
   London SW1H 0ET
   England
   Tel: 01 215 7877
   Telex: 887591

Entry: 1984

CENTRAL BANK OF ICELAND
   See **SEDLABANKI ÍSLANDS**

Entry: 1978

THE FINANCIAL TIMES LTD
   10 Bolt Court
   London EC4A 3HL
   England
   Tel: 01 836 5444
   Telex: 27368

Entry: 1980

THE GOVERNMENT OF ICELAND
   (Ministry of Fisheries)
   Reykjavik

Entry: 1986

HAGSTOFA ÍSLANDS
   Hverfisgata 8-10
   Reykjavik
   Tel: 26699

Entries: 1977   1983   1985   1987   1988   1991   1992
           1993

ICELANDIC YEAR BOOK LTD
   PO Box 1396
   Reykjavik
   Tel: 11640

Entry: 1979

**ORGANISATION FOR ECONOMIC CO-OPERATION
AND DEVELOPMENT**
   Publications Office
   2 Rue André Pascal
   Paris 16e
   France
   Tel: 524 82 00
   Telex: 62160

Entry: 1990

SEDLABANKI ÍSLANDS
   Hafnarstraeti 20
   Reykjavik
   Tel: 20500
   Telex: 2020

Entry: 1981

STEINDORSPRENT HF
   Tjarnargötu 4
   PO Box 495
   Reykjavik

Entry: 1994

US DEPARTMENT OF COMMERCE
Government Printing Office
Washington DC 20402
USA
Tel: 783 3238
Telex: TWX 710 8229274

Entries: 1976 1982 1989

L – LUXEMBOURG

BARCLAYS BANK
Group Economic Intelligence Unit
54 Lombard Street
London EC3 3AH
England
Tel: 01 283 8989
Telex: 887591

Entry: 2001

BRITISH OVERSEAS TRADE BOARD
1 Victoria Street
London SW1H 0ET
England
Tel: 01 215 7877
Telex: 27366

Entry: 2011

THE FINANCIAL TIMES LTD
10 Bolt Court
London EC4A 3HL
England
Tel: 01 836 5444
Telex: 27368

Entry: 2015

INVESTORS CHRONICLE
30 Finsbury Square
London EC2A 1PJ
England
Tel: 01 628 4050
Telex: 883694

Entry: 2016

LLOYDS BANK LTD
Overseas Department
International Trade Promotion Section
6 Eastcheap
London EC3 3AB
England
Tel: 01 283 1000
Telex: 888301

Entry: 2005

LUXEMBOURG EMBASSY
27 Wilton Crescent
London SW1X 8SD
England
Tel: 01 235 6961

Entries: 2007 2008 2022 2023 2019

MIDLAND BANK LTD
27-32 Poultry
London EC2P 2BX
England
Tel: 01 606 9911
Telex: 8811822

Entry: 2021

MINISTERE D'ETAT
Service Information et Presse
3 Rue de la Congrégation
Luxembourg
Tel: 478 228
Telex: 2790

Entries: 2010 2014

SERVICE CENTRAL DE LA STATISTIQUE ET DES ETUDES ECONOMIQUES
Boîte Postale No 304
48 Rue Charles-Arendt
Luxembourg
Tel 219 21

Entries: 2000 2002 2003 2004 2006 2012 2013 2017 2018

SOCIETE DE BOURSE DE LUXEMBOURG
11 Avenue de la Porte-Neuve
Luxembourg
Tel: 2 92 17

Entry: 2020

US DEPARTMENT OF COMMERCE
Government Printing Office
Washington DC 20402
USA
Tel: 783 3238
Telex: TWX 710 8229274

Entry: 2009

N- NORWAY

ANDRESENS BANK A/S
Torvgaten 2
Oslo 1
Tel: 11 20 30
Telex: 11320

Entry: 2091

BARCLAYS BANK LTD
Group Economic Intelligence Unit
54 Lombard Street
London EC3 3AH
England
Tel: 01 283 8989
Telex: 887591

Entry: 2053

BRITISH OVERSEAS TRADE BOARD
1 Victoria Street
London SW1H 0ET
England
Tel: 01 215 7877
Telex: 27366

Entry: 2075

THE ECONOMIST
25 St James's Street
London SW1A 1HG
England
Tel: 01 930 5155
Telex: 24344

Entry: 2090

ECONOMIST INTELLIGENCE UNIT
Spencer House
27 St James's Place
London SW1A 1NT
England
Tel: 01 493 6711
Telex: 266353

Entry: 2096

THE FINANCIAL TIMES LTD
10 Bolt Court
London EC4A 3HL
England
Tel: 01 836 5444
Telex: 27368

Entries: 2065 2087

FISKERIDIREKTORATET
Møllendals V 4
5000 Bergen
Tel: Bergen 230300

Entry: 2066

INTERNATIONAL TRADE CENTRE UNCTAD/GATT
Villa le Bocage
Palais des Nations
Genève
Switzerland
Tel: 33 10 01

Entry: 2086

INVESTORS CHRONICLE
30 Finsbury Square
London EC2A 1PJ
England
Tel: 01 628 4050
Telex: 883694

Entry: 2079

LLOYDS BANK LTD
Overseas Department
Export Promotion Section
6 Eastcheap
London EC3P 3AB
England
Tel: 01 626 1500
Telex: 887053

Entry: 2061

MIDLAND BANK LTD
27-32 Poultry
London EC2P 2BX
England
Tel: 01 606 9911
Telex: 8811822

Entry: **2100**

NATIONAL BUILDING AGENCY
7 Arundel Street
London WC2R 3DZ
England
Tel: 01 836 4488
Telex: 268312

Entry: **2077**

NORGES BANK
Bankplassen 4
Oslo 1
Tel: 42 98 50
Telex: 11369

Entries: **2060 2088**

DEN NORSKE CREDITBANK
Kirkegaten 21
Oslo 1
Tel: 11 60 90
Telex: 18175

Entry: **2064**

A S ØKONOMISK LITERATUR
Ebbellsgt 3
Oslo 1
Tel: 20 90 73

Entries: **2058 2080 2092 2093 2094 2097 2103**

OPPLYSNINGSRÅDET FOR BILTRAFIKKEN (DE NORSKE VEIFRENING)
Prof Dahlsgt 1
Oslo
Tel: 60 02 68

Entry: **2055**

ORGANISATION FOR ECONOMIC CO-OPERATION AND DEVELOPMENT
Publications Office
2 Rue André Pascal
Paris 16e
France
Tel: 524 82 00
Telex: 620160

Entry: **2095**

STATISTISK SENTRALBYRÅ
Dronningensgate 16
Oslo 1
Tel: 41 3820

Entries: **2050 2051 2052 2056 2057 2059 2062
2067 2068 2069 2070 2071 2072 2074
2076 2078 2081 2082 2083 2084 2099
2101 2102 2104 2105**

THE TIMES
Marketing Department
New Printing House Square
London WC1N 2JD
England
Tel: 01 837 1234
Telex: 264971

Entry: **2089**

US DEPARTMENT OF COMMERCE
Government Printing Office
Washington DC 20402
USA
Tel: 783 3238
Telex: TWX 710 8229274

Entries: **2054 2063 2073 2085 2098**

NL – NETHERLANDS

ABC VOOR HANDEL EN INDUSTRIE CV
Fonteinlaan 3
Haarlem
Tel: 12772

Entries: **2161 2200**

ALGEMENE BANK NEDERLAND NV
  32 Vijzelstraat
  Amsterdam
  Tel: 29 91 11
  Telex: 11417

Entries: 2160 2178 2206

AMSTERDAM-ROTTERDAM BANK NV
  Herengracht 595
  Amsterdam
  Tel: 289 393
  Telex: 11006

Entries: 2152 2165 2168

BARCLAYS BANK LTD
  Group Economic Intelligence Unit
  54 Lombard Street
  London EC3 3AH
  England
  Tel: 01 282 8989
  Telex: 887591

Entry: 2156

BRITISH CHAMBER OF COMMERCE
  Raamweg 45
  Postbus 2804
  Den Haag

Entry: 2159

BRITISH OVERSEAS TRADE BOARD
  1 Victoria Street
  London SW1H 0ET
  England
  Tel: 01 215 7877
  Telex: 27366

Entry: 2176

**CENTRAAL BUREAU VAN DE KATOEN-RAYON-
EN LINNEN-INDUSTRIE**
  Arnhemsestraatweg 360
  Postbus 7
  Velp G
  Telex: 45170

Entry: 2170

CENTRAAL BUREAU VOOR DE STATISTIEK
  Oostduinlaan 2
  Den Haag
  Tel: 18 42 70
  Telex: 32692

Entries: 2151 2157 2158 2163 2167 2181 2185
          2186 2187 2188 2189 2190 2191 2192
          2193 2194 2195 2196 2197 2199 2202
          2211 2218 2221 2222 2223 2224 2226
          2227 2228 2229 2230 2231 2232 2233
          2234 2236 2237 2238 2239 2240 2241
          2242 2243 2245 2247 2249 2250

CENTRAAL PLANBUREAU
  Stolkweg 14
  Den Haag

Entry: 2162

COMMERCE CLEARING HOUSE INC
  5 Charterhouse Buildings
  London EC1
  England
  Tel: 01 253 8815

Entry: 2205

NV DRUKKERIJ H P DE SWART & ZN
  Oude Molstraat 7
  Den Haag
  Tel: 11 77 07
  Telex:

Entry: 2175

ECONOMIST INTELLIGENCE UNIT
  Spencer House
  27 St James's Place
  London SW1A 1NT
  England
  Tel: 01 493 6711
  Telex: 266353

Entry: 2213

**FEDERATIE METAAL- EN ELECTROTECHNISCHE
INDUSTRIE**
  Nassaulaan 25
  Den Haag
  Telex: 32157

Entry: 2225

FENEDEX
Bezuidenhoutseweg 76a
Den Haag
Tel: 838108

Entry: 2172

THE FINANCIAL TIMES LTD
10 Bolt Court
London EC4A 3HL
England
Tel: 01 836 5444
Telex: 27368

Entries: 2153 2154 2166 2203 2216 2217

IBN
Now: **NOM**
PO Box 19
102 Lon Corpus Den Hoorn
Groningen
Tel: 21 25 61

Entry: 2208

INSTITUTE OF PRACTITIONERS IN ADVERTISING
44 Belgrave Square
London SW1X 8QZ
England
Tel: 01 235 7020
Telex: 918352

Entry: 2150

INVESTORS CHRONICLE
30 Finsbury Square
London EC2A 1PJ
England
Tel: 01 628 4050
Telex: 883694

Entry: 2207

KOMPASS NEDERLAND NV
Van Stolkweg 6
Den Haag
Tel: 24 55 44
Telex: 31301

Entry: 2183

KON DRUKKERIJ VAN DE GARDE NV
Gamersestraat 36-44
Zaltbommel
Tel: 2312

Entry: 2212

LANDBOUW - ECONOMISCH INSTITUUT
175 Conradkade
Den Haag

Entry: 2184

LLOYDS BANK LTD
Overseas Department
International Trade Promotion Section
6 Eastcheap
London EC3 3AB
England
Tel: 01 283 1000
Telex: 888301

Entry: 2169

MIDLAND BANK LTD
27-32 Poultry
London EC2P 2BX
England
Tel: 01 606 9911
Telex: 8811822

Entry: 2219

NETHERLANDS — BRITISH CHAMBER OF COMMERCE
The Dutch House
307-8 High Holborn
London WC1V 7LS
England
Tel: 01 242 1064
Telex: 23211

Entries: 2155 2179 2215 2244

DE NEDERLANDSCHE BANK NV
Westeinde 1
Amsterdam
Tel: 6 31 33
Telex: 11355

Entry: 2214

NEDERLANDSE CENTRALE ORGANISATIE VOOR TNO
Juliana van Stolberglaan 148
Den Haag
Tel: 81 44 81

Entry: 2201

NV NEDERLANDSE SPOORWEGEN
Moreelsepark
Utrecht
Tel: Utrecht 2501

Entry: 2182

**ORGANISATION FOR ECONOMIC CO-OPERATION
AND DEVELOPMENT**
Publications Office
2 Rue André Pascal
Paris 16e
France
Tel: 524 82 00
Telex: 62160

Entry: 2209

OXFORD UNIVERSITY PRESS
Walton Street
Oxford
England
Tel: Oxford (0865) 56767

Entry: 2210

THE PETROLEUM TIMES
Dorset House
Stamford Street
London SE1
England
Tel: 01 261 8000

Entry: 2177

**ROTTERDAM CHAMBER OF COMMERCE AND
INDUSTRY
(KAMER VAN KOOPHANDEL EN FABRIEKEN VOOR
ROTTERDAM)**
Exchange Building
Coolsingel 58
Rotterdam
Tel: 14 50 22

Entry: 2235

SIRA INSTITUTE
South Hill
Chislehurst
Kent
England
Tel: 01 467 2636
Telex: 896649

Entry: 2248

STAATSDRUKKERIJ EN UITGEVERIJBEDRIJF
Christoffel Plantijnstraat
Den Haag
Tel:81 45 11
Entry: 2220

THE TIMES
Marketing Department
New Printing House Square
Grays Inn Road
London WC1N 2JD
England
Tel: 01 837 1234
Telex: 264971

Entries: 2180 2204

UITGEVERIJ J H DE BUSSY NV
Rokin 62
Amsterdam
Tel: 63511

Entries: 2174 2246

UNIVERSITY OF READING
Department of Agricultural Economics
Earley Gate
White Knights Road
Reading RG6 2AR
Tel: Reading (0734) 85123
Telex: 849489

Entry: 2164

US DEPARTMENT OF COMMERCE
Government Printing Office
Washington DC 20402
USA
Tel: 783 3238
Telex: TWX 710 8229274

Entries: 2171 2173 2198

P – PORTUGAL

BANCO DE BILBAO
Bilbao House
36 New Broad Street
London EC2M 5QQ
England
Tel: 01 638 8481
Telex: 886451

Entry: 2300

BANCO DE PORTUGAL
Rua do Comércio 148
Lisboa
Tel: 36 29 31
Telex: 16554

Entry: 2276

BANCO ESPIRITO SANTO E COMERCIAL DE LISBOA
95 Rua do Comércio 119
Lisboa
Tel: 36 03 81
Telex: 12191

Entry: 2297

BANCO PINTO E SOTTO MAYOR
Rua do Ouro 18
Lisboa
Tel: 37 02 61
Telex: 12516

Entry 2308

BANCO PORTUGUES DO ATLANTICO
Rua do Ouro
Lisboa
Tel: 36 13 21
Telex: 12692

Entries: 2295 2296 2315 2317

BARCLAYS BANK LTD
Group Economic Intelligence Unit
54 Lombard Street
London EC3 3AH
England
Tel: 01 283 8989
Telex: 887591

Entry: 2277

BRITISH NATIONAL EXPORT COUNCIL
33 Bury Street
London SW1Y 6AU
England
Tel: 01 839 1170

Entry: 2305

DEPARTMENT OF TRADE AND INDUSTRY
1 Victoria Street
London SW1H 0ET
England
Tel: 01 215 7877
Telex: 887358

Entry: 2302

THE ECONOMIST
25 St James's Street
London SW1A 1HG
England
Tel: 01 930 5155
Telex: 24344

Entry: 2279

ECONOMIST INTELLIGENCE UNIT
Spencer House
27 St James's Place
London SW1A 1NT
England
Tel: 01 493 6711
Telex: 266353

Entry: 2313

EUROPEAN FREE TRADE ASSOCIATION
9-11 Rue de Varembé
1211 Genève 20
Switzerland
Tel: 34 90 00
Telex: 22660 EFTA CH

Entry: 2316
Publications available in UK through:
Gothard House Publications Ltd
Gothard House
Henley on Thames
Oxon RG9 1AJ
England
Tel: Henley (049 12) 3602

FINANCIAL TIMES LTD
10 Bolt Court
London
EC4A 3HL
England
Tel: 01 836 5444
Telex: 27368

Entries: 2306 2309 2310 2311

INSTITUTO NACIONAL DE ESTATISTICA
Avenida Antonio José de Almeida
Lisboa 1
Tel: 80 20 80

**Entries: 2275 2280 2281 2282 2283 2284 2285
2286 2287 2288 2289 2290 2291 2292
2293 2294 2298 2299 2301 2314**

INVESTORS CHRONICLE
30 Finsbury Square
London EC2A 1PJ
England
Tel: 01 628 4050
Telex: 883694

Entry: 2307

ORGANISATION FOR ECONOMIC CO-OPERATION AND DEVELOPMENT
Publications Office
2 Rue André Pascal
Paris 16e
France
Tel: 524 82 00
Telex: 62160

Entries: 2304 2312

US DEPARTMENT OF COMMERCE
Government Printing Office
Washington DC 20402
USA
Tel: 783 3238
Telex: TWX 710 8229274

Entries: 2278 2303

S – SWEDEN

ALMQUIST AND WIKSELL FÖRLAG AB
Brunnsgränd 4
S-111 30 Stockholm
Tel: 24 52 90

Entry: 2368

BARCLAYS BANK LTD
Group Economic Intelligence Unit
54 Lombard Street
London EC3 3AH
England
Tel: 01 283 8989
Telex: 887591

Entry: 2328

BRITISH OVERSEAS TRADE BOARD
1 Victoria Street
London SW1H 0ET
England
Tel: 01 215 7877
Telex: 887591

Entry: 2338

CROOM HELM
2/10 St John's Road
London SW11 1PN
England
Tel: 01 228 9343

Entry: 2347

ECONOMIST INTELLIGENCE UNIT
Spencer House
27 St James's Place
London SW1A 1NT
Tel: 01 493 6711
Telex: 266353

Entry: 2348

EKONOMISK LITTERATUR AB
43 A Fack Sollentuna 1
Stockholm
Tel: 35 75 99

Entry: 2365

INSTITUTE OF PRACTITIONERS IN ADVERTISING
44 Belgrave Square
London SW1X 8QZ
England
Tel: 01 235 7020
Telex: 918352

Entry: 2325

INVESTORS CHRONICLE
30 Finsbury Square
London EC2A 1PJ
England
Tel: 01 628 4050
Telex: 883694

Entry: 2340

MIDLAND BANK LTD
27-32 Poultry
London EC2P 2BX
England
Tel: 01 606 9911
Telex: 8811822

Entry: 2353

MINISTRY OF FINANCE
(Finansdepartementet)
S-103 10 Stockholm 2
Tel: 763 10 00

Entry: 2364

NATIONAL BOARD OF PRIVATE FORESTRY
(Skögagarnas Riksforbund)
Box 12199
10225 Stockholm

Entry: 2350

NATIONAL SWEDISH AGRICULTURAL MARKETING BOARD
(Statens Jordbrukshamnd)
PO Box 16384
S 10327 Stockholm 16
Tel: 22 55 60

Entry: 2342

NATIONAL SWEDISH BOARD FOR CONSUMER AFFAIRS
(Konsumentverket)
Fack
16210 Vallingey
Tel: 38 04 60

Entry: 2331

PA NORSTEDT & SÖNER
Tryckerigatan 2
PO Box 2052
103 12 Stockholm 2
Tel: 22 80 40

Entries: 2352 2358

SKANDINAVISKA ENSKILDA BANKEN
Kungstradgardsgatan 8
S-106 40 Stockholm
Tel: (08) 24 65 00
Telex: 11000

Entries: 2329 2332 2351

STATE RAILWAYS BOARD (STATENS JÄRNVAGAR)
S-105 50 Stockholm C
Tel: 22 60 00
Telex: 19410

Entry: 2359

STATISTISKA CENTRALBYRÅN
Karwägen 100
Fack
S-102 50 Stockholm 27
Tel: 14 05 60

Entries: 2326 2327 2330 2335 2337 2339 2341
         2343 2344 2345 2355 2356 2366 2367

STOCKHOLM STOCK EXCHANGE
Källärgränd 2
111 29 Stockholm

Entry: 2349

SVENSKA HANDELSBANKEN
Foreign Relations Department
Arsenalsgatan
106 40 Stockholm
Tel: 22 90 20
Telex: 11090

Entries: 2354 2363

SVERIGES INDUSTRIFÖRBUND
Storgatan 19
Box 5501
114 85 Stockholm
Tel: 635020
Telex: 19990

Entry: 2357

SVERIGES KEMISKA INDUSTRIKONTOR
Storg 19
Box 5501
Stockholm
Tel: 63 50 20

Entry: 2362

SVERIGES RIKSBANK
Helgeandsholmen
Stockholm 2
Tel: 22 13 10
Telex: 19150

Entries: 2360 2361

THE SWEDISH CHAMBER OF COMMERCE IN THE UK
14 Trinity Square
London EC3
England

Entry: 2369

THE SWEDISH INSTITUTE
  (Svenska Institutet)
  Box 7072
  103 82 Stockholm
  Tel: 22 32 80

Entry: 2334

US DEPARTMENT OF COMMERCE
  Government Printing Office
  Washington DC 20402
  USA
  Tel: 783 3238
  Telex: TWX 710 8229274

Entries: 2333 2336 2346

SF — FINLAND

ALKO OY AB
  Salmisaarenranta 7
  Helsinki 18
  Tel: 60911
  Telex: 121045

Entry: 2400

**ASSOCIATION OF FINNISH METAL AND
ENGINEERING INDUSTRIES**
  Eteläranta 10
  Helsingfors 3

Entry: 2433

BANK OF FINLAND
  Institute for Economic Research
  Helsingfors 10

Entries: 2401 2402 2410

BARCLAYS BANK LTD
  Group Economic Intelligence Unit
  54 Lombard Street
  London EC3 3AH
  England
  Tel: 01 283 8989
  Telex: 887591

Entry: 2403

BRITISH OVERSEAS TRADE BOARD
  1 Victoria Street
  London SW1H 0ET
  England
  Tel: 01 215 7877
  Telex: 887591

Entry: 2427

ECONOMIST INTELLIGENCE UNIT
  Spencer House
  27 St James's Place
  London SW1A 1NT
  England
  Tel: 01 493 6711
  Telex: 266353

Entry: 2436

FEDERATION OF FINNISH INDUSTRIES
  Eteläraut 10
  Helsingfors 13

Entry: 2404

THE FINANCIAL TIMES LTD
  10 Bolt Court
  London EC4A 3HL
  England
  Tel: 01 836 5444
  Telex: 27368

Entries: 2414 2423

FINNFACTS INSTITUTE
  Union K 14
  Helsinki
  Tel: 171596

Entry: 2420

THE FINNISH FOREIGN TRADE ASSOCIATION
  E Esplanaadikatu 18
  00130 Helsingfors 13
  Tel: 12556
  Telex: 121696

Entries: 2421 2425

FINNISH FOREST INDUSTRIES
  Etelaespanadi 2
  Helsingfors 13

Entry: 2422

FINNISH TOURIST BOARD
Kluuvik 8
Helsinki 10
Telex: 122690

Entries: 2415 2417 2429

INVESTORS CHRONICLE
30 Finsbury Square
London EC2A 1PJ
England
Tel: 01 628 4050
Telex: 883694

Entry: 2444

KANSALLIS - OSAKE - PANKKI
Aleksanterinkatu 42
Helsingfors
Tel: 1631
Telex: 12412

Entries: 2408 2416

KUSTANNUS OY LIIKETIETO
Temppelikatu 6b
Helsinki

Entry: 2440

LLOYDS BANK LTD
Overseas Department
International Trade Promotion Section
6 Eastcheap
London EC3 3AB
England
Tel: 01 282 1000
Telex: 888301

Entry: 2407

MAATALOUSHALLITUKSEN TILASTOTOIMISTO
Available through:
TILASTOKESKUS
Annankatu 44
00100 Helsinki 10
Tel: 64 51 21

Entries: 2430 2431

MIDLAND BANK LTD
27-32 Poultry
London EC2P 2BX
England
Tel: 01 606 9911
Telex: 8811822

Entry. 2439

NORD-FINANZ-BANK
1 Bahnhofstrasse
8022 Zürich
Switzerland
Tel: 13 77 22
Telex: 54147

Entry: 2437

ORGANISATION FOR ECONOMIC CO-OPERATION AND DEVELOPMENT
Publications Office
2 Rue André Pascal
Paris 16e
France
Tel: 524 82 00
Telex: 62160

Entry: 2435

POHJOISMAIDEN YHDYSPANKKI
Nordiska Föreningsbanken
Helsingfors
Tel: 658611

Entry: 2451

POLITICAL & ECONOMIC PLANNING
12 Upper Belgrave Street
London SW1X 8BB
Tel: 01 235 5271

Entry: 2428

SCAN EDIT A/S
Kompagnistraede 6
DK — 1208 København K
Denmark
Tel: 01 14 19 69

Entry: 2405

SINIEN KIRJA OY
Kaisaniemenkatu 2b
Helsinki 10
Tel: 12030

Entries: 2434 2438

SUOMEN PANKKI TALOUSTIETELLINEN TUTKIMUSTAITOS
Snellmaniaukio
PO Box 160
00101 Helsinki 10
Tel: 10051
Telex: 121224

Entry: 2445

SUOMEN SELLULOOSAYHDISTYS
E Esplanadi 2
Helsinki 13
Tel: 170721
Telex: 121051

Entry: 2419

**SUOMEN TIETEELLISTEN KIRJASTOJEN
LAUTAKUNTA**
Helsinki

Entries: 2406 2441

TILASTOLLINEN PÄÄTOIMISTO
Annankatu 44
Helsingfors 10
Tel: 645121

Entries: 2442 2443 2446 2447 2448 2452

THE TIMES
Marketing Department
New Printing House Square
Grays Inn Road
London WC1N 2JD
England
Tel: 01 837 1234
Telex: 264971

Entries: 2424 2426

TULLIHALLITUKSEN TILASTOTOIMISTO
Uudenmaan Katu 1 – 5
PO Box 10 512
Helsingfors 12

Entries: 2449 2450

**UNION BANK OF FINLAND LTD
(SUOMEN YHDYSPANKKI OY)**
Aleksanterinkatu 30
00100 Helsingfors 10
Tel: 12221
Telex: 12407

Entry: 2412

US DEPARTMENT OF COMMERCE
Government Printing Office
Washington DC 20402
USA
Tel: 783 3238
Telex: TWX 710 8229274

Entry: 2432

VALTION PAINATUSKESKUS
Hakuninmaant 2
Helsingfors
Tel: 539011

Entry: 2409

WEILIN & GÖÖS OY AB
Tapiola
Ahertajant 5
Helsinki
Tel: 461322
Telex: 122597

Entry: 2418

AS YRITYSTIETO OY
PL 274
00531 Helsingfors 53
Tel: 73 57 22

Entry: 2413

INDEXES

There are two indexes giving access by title to the source entries listed in Part One. Reference is made in both indexes to each entry's unique classification number which appears immediately to the left of the title in Part One.

The running heads at the top of each page in Part One incorporate these classification numbers making it simple and quick to find the appropriate entry.

Index 1 is a complete alphabetical list of all entries.

Index 2 offers a subject analysis of the entries. The titles and their classification numbers are listed alphabetically by country of coverage, or under the International heading as the case may be, within eight principal subject groupings. These are: -

1	General Economic Handbooks and Guides
2	Population and Social, including Regional
3	National Income, Expenditure, Taxation
4	Labour Market—Wages, Prices, Conditions
5	Industrial and Services Sectors
6	Marketing, Sales and Advertising
7	Foreign Trade
8	Research

In the case of Grouping 5—The Industrial and Services Sectors a further sub classification has been adopted. There are 17 sub groupings namely:—

5 (i)	General Business Directories and Statistics
5(ii)	Agriculture, Forestry and Fishing
5 (iii)	Food, Drink and Tobacco
5 (iv)	Chemicals and Rubber
5 (v)	Ferrous and Non-ferrous Metals
5 (vi)	Engineering—Mechanical, Electrical and Electronic
5 (vii)	Textiles, Clothing, Footwear and Leather
5 (viii/Vx)	Construction and Building Materials
5 (ix)	Paper, Printing, Publishing and Media
5 (xi)	Central and Local Government
5 (xii)	Transport and Communications
5 (xiii)	Distributive Trades
5 (xiv)	Financial Services
5 (xv)	Tourism, Travel, Hotels and Leisure
5 (xvi)	Energy
5 (xvii)	Timber and Furniture

The sub groupings are presented in Index 2 in this numerical order.

INDEX 1

SOURCES LISTED ALPHABETICALLY

SOURCES LISTED ALPHABETICALLY

B

C

D

E

F

G

H

I

J

N

Q

R

S

T

U

V

W

Y

Z

INDEX 2

SOURCES BY SUBJECT AND COUNTRY

1 GENERAL ECONOMIC HANDBOOKS AND GUIDES

2 POPULATION AND SOCIAL, INCLUDING REGIONAL

3 NATIONAL INCOME, EXPENDITURE, TAXATION

4 LABOUR MARKET—WAGES, PRICES, CONDITIONS

 **INDUSTRIAL AND SERVICES SECTORS**

(i) General Business Directories and Statistics

(ii) Agriculture, Forestry and Fishing

(iii) Food, Drink and Tobacco

(iv) Chemicals and Rubber

(v) Ferrous and Non-ferrous Metals

(vi) Engineering - Mechanical, Electrical and Electronic

(vii) Textiles, Clothing, Footwear and Leather

(viii/x) Construction and Building Materials

(ix) Paper, Printing, Publishing and Media

(xi) Central and Local Government

(xii) Transport and Communications

(xiii) Distributive Trades

(xiv) Financial Services

(xv) Tourism, Travel, Hotels and Leisure

(xvi) Energy

(xvii) Timber and Furniture

6 MARKETING, SALES AND ADVERTISING

7 FOREIGN TRADE

8 RESEARCH